Han Feizi, The Art of Statecraft in Early China

Volume 1

Han Feizi
The Art of Statecraft in Early China

A Bilingual Edition

VOLUME 1

Translated by

Christoph Harbsmeier

Edited by

Jens Østergaard Petersen
Yuri Pines

BRILL

LEIDEN | BOSTON

Cover illustration: Calligraphy by Chen Qiyou, dated January 1997. Chen Qiyou (1917–2006), is the author of authoritative editions of the *Han Feizi* that this translation is based on.

Text on the cover reads: "The *Han Feizi*, a concise commentary and precise translation by He Moye (Christoph Harbsmeier)."

The Library of Congress Cataloging-in-Publication Data is available online at https://catalog.loc.gov
LC record available at https://lccn.loc.gov/2024044132

Typeface for the Latin, Greek, and Cyrillic scripts: "Brill". See and download: brill.com/brill-typeface.

ISBN 978-90-04-72344-3 (hardback, set)
ISBN 978-90-04-69907-6 (hardback, vol. 1)
ISBN 978-90-04-72343-6 (hardback, vol. 2)
ISBN 978-90-04-70033-8 (e-book, vol. 1)
ISBN 978-90-04-72353-5 (e-book, vol. 2)
DOI 10.1163/9789004700338 (vol. 1)
DOI 10.1163/9789004723535 (vol. 2)

Copyright 2025 by Christoph Harbsmeier et al. Published by Koninklijke Brill BV, Leiden, The Netherlands.
Koninklijke Brill BV incorporates the imprints Brill, Brill Nijhoff, Brill Schöningh, Brill Fink, Brill mentis, Brill Wageningen Academic, Vandenhoeck & Ruprecht, Böhlau and V&R unipress.
Koninklijke Brill BV reserves the right to protect this publication against unauthorized use. Requests for re-use and/or translations must be addressed to Koninklijke Brill BV via brill.com or copyright.com.

This book is printed on acid-free paper and produced in a sustainable manner.

Til Mudde

Contents

VOLUME 1

    Translator's Preface   XI
    Co-editor's Preface   XV
    Text Edition and Rhyme Notations   XVII
    Conventions   XVIII

Translation

1   初見秦 First Audience in Qin   3

2   存韓 Preserving Hán   19

3   難言 Problems with Speaking up   33

4   愛臣 Favoured Ministers   40

5   主道 The Way of the Ruler   45

6   有度 Having Standards   54

7   二柄 The Two Handles   69

8   揚搉 The Grand Outline   77

9   八姦 Eight Villainies   93

10   十過 Ten Faults   104

11   孤憤 Solitary Resentment   142

12   說難 Difficulties of Persuasion   155

13   和氏 Mr He   166

14 姦劫弑臣 Ministers Who Betray, Coerce or Assassinate Their Rulers   172

15 亡徵 Signs of Ruin   197

16 三守 Three Defences   214

17 備內 Guarding against the Enemy within   219

18 南面 Facing South   227

19 飭邪 Taking Measures against Deviance   235

20 解老 Explaining Laozi   255

21 喻老 Illustrating Laozi   309

22 說林上 A Forest of Persuasions, Part 1   336

23 說林下 A Forest of Persuasions, Part 2   365

24 觀行 Observing Behaviour   393

25 安危 Security and Danger   397

26 守道 Attending to the Way   406

27 用人 Employing People   413

28 功名 Achievements and Names   424

29 大體 The Cardinal Tenets   429

CONTENTS

VOLUME 2

Text Edition and Rhyme Notations   XI
Conventions   XII

30 內儲說上七術 Inner Congeries of Explanations, Part 1: The Seven Techniques   435

31 內儲說下六微 Inner Congeries of Explanations, Part 2: The Six Subtle Points   488

32 外儲說左上 Outer Congeries of Explanations, First Series, Part 1   535

33 外儲說左下 Outer Congeries of Explanations, First Series: Part 2   598

34 外儲說右上 Outer Congeries of Explanations, Second Series: Part 1   639

35 外儲說右下 Outer Congeries of Explanations, Second Series: Part 2   690

36 難一 Objections I   727

37 難二 Objections II   757

38 難三 Objections III   781

39 難四 Objections IV   810

40 難勢 Objections to "Positional Power"   829

41 問辯 Asking about Disputation   841

42 問田 Asking Tian   845

43 定法 Determining Standards   849

44 說疑 Explaining Suspicious Behaviour   857

45 詭使 Deluded Assignments   881

46 六反 Six Contrarieties   894

47 八說 Eight Explanations   912

48 八經 Eight Canonical Statements   929

49 五蠹 Five Vermin   953

50 顯學 Illustrious Teachings   989

51 忠孝第五十一 Loyal Effort and Filial Piety   1009

52 人主第五十二 Rulers of Men   1021

53 飭令第五十三 Regulating Orders   1027

54 心度第五十四 The Standard in the Heart   1032

55 制分第五十五 Controlling the Apportioning of Things   1037

Text Edition   1044

Rhyme Notations   1050

Bibliography   1053
Index of Personal Names   1063
Index of Titles   1076
Index of Keywords   1078

Translator's Preface

Together with Zhuang Zhou 莊周 (Zhuangzi 莊子), Han Fei 韓非 (d. 233 BCE) was one of the greatest writers of ancient China. The subtlety of his humour, the uncompromising consistency of his social and political analyses, the jejune candidness of his discourse, and above all his persistent analytic knack for finding the telling literary illustration of his thought through an unending stream of jokes, vignettes, anecdotes, historical snippets, popular tell-tales, tall tales, old yarn, new rumours, ancient chronicles, legends, fables old and new, naughty fabliaux, horror stories, parables, allegories, proverbs, apophthegms, maxims, adages, slogans, catchphrases, puns, *jeux d'esprit*.

The patron saint of my literary life has always remained Michel de Montaigne. Han Fei's humorous thoughtfulness, and his pervasive passion for paradox was profoundly close to that of Montaigne, but Han Fei was infinitely more than a splendidly thoughtful disgruntled recluse: arguably, he was one of the politically and socially most important literary men in Chinese history. Confucius may have had the greater impact on public professions of conventionally obligatory morality throughout the history of Chinese dynasties, but it was Han Fei who had the decisive impact on the highly civilised imperial strategic thinking that led to the foundation of Chinese imperial history: the Qin empire was founded some very few years after Han Fei's death. And the social engineering that went into the construction of dynastic Chinese power was very largely the implementation of the systematic political philosophy of one great man of letters: Han Fei.

In the introductory material for this book I do not intend to spoil the fresh fun of delving innocently and with an entirely open mind into the delights of the primary text of Han Fei. There is no end to the intellectual entertainment that the reader is entitled to look for in this book. It may be about politics, but it is at least as much about jokes and the absurdity of the human condition. And for good measure, the gentle reader may even persist long enough to run into a meticulous analytic and conceptual commentary to the book *Laozi*, followed, naturally, for good measure by another commentary written entirely in the narrative mode, illustrating the upshot of what Laozi is taken to be trying to say, really, below the surface of his text.

Reading the literature about Han Fei,[1] you might be excused for thinking that the man belonged to some Legalist school and could surely never have written

---

1 There are by now not a few systematic studies of Han Feizi in English, first and foremost the *Dao Companion to the Philosophy of Han Fei* (Goldin 2013) and the *Dao Companion to*

an approving commentary on the most important of the Daoist foundational texts. Well: that is what I mean when I say that this edition is an invitation to delve into this book with a very open mind. A mind open to the possibility that Han Fei, the most important figure in the "Legalist school" nowhere breathes a work about any such school, and was – at least for some time in his life – an aficionado of Laozi's *Daodejing* 道德經, at least devoted enough to want to compose two highly ambitious commentary-chapters on a Daoist classic.

As one peruses the *Han Feizi* over the decades the idea grows on one that Han Fei actually was very much something of an early "intellectual" in Late Warring States China. His sustained and highly systematic philosophy (and psychology!) of the social engineering needed to ensure stably controlled bureaucratic governance of the polity, was quite obviously his major practical concern. And as it happens, it was Han Fei's carefully defined strategies of structurally based and not personality based stable governance that has led to that seemingly unending recurrence of dynastic lineages of autocracy which fundamentally determine even the very Chinese character of communist rule today.

But Han Fei was indeed an intellectual. Politics was not everything to him. Being a poetically gifted great writer, his interests were broad, sometimes contradictory and apparently changing at different times of his life. As a member of a royal family, Han Fei could read widely in the kinds of documents that had nothing to do with his main focus on political philosophy and political psychology. His interests were broad, and highly literate. He was a literary man. In fact, this edition hopes to make it plain even to the modern tired and impatient eye that Han Fei was quite something of a poet, too.[2]

The *Han Feizi* is practically nowhere a prosaic text. It must be savoured, every sentence must be given the discriminating attention that the Chinese describe so well by the phrase *pin ju* 品句 "taste sentences" (as you might taste Chinese tea). My translation of this book was motivated by the fact that existing translations of the *Han Feizi* did not seem to me to show very much of such a literary ambition.[3] But there was more: I felt that the fine conceptual nuances

---

China's fa *Tradition: The Philosophy of Governance by Impartial Standards* (Pines 2024); see also Goldin 2020: 201–228 for further references.

[2] Jens Østergaard Petersen has done us all an immense favour by meticulously documenting the rhyming schemes in this book, and I am infinitely grateful to him for taking such patient care of these important matters.

[3] Burton Watson's admirable translation ([1964] 2003) comes closest to this but was only partial. Jean Lévi (1999) has been inspiring at many points. W.K. Liao's great integral pioneering translation from 1939–1959 was a very impressive achievement for its time, but I felt the time had come for a new comprehensive effort. Note that the earliest translation of *Han Feizi* into

in Han Fei's language, the nice distinctions between apparent synonyms in his vocabulary and even the subtle logical details of his grammar that had been my obsession for so many decades[4] had gone unnoticed in current English translations.

One of the toughest problems in translating a major philosophical cum literary masterpiece is deciding how to translate its keywords. Take for instance the term *fa* 法. It can refer to cosmic model or pattern as in the compound "*fa* of the Way" (*Daofa* 道法, 29.1); to legal codes, reading which makes a ruler sleepy (32.5.7); to impartial norms (*gongfa* 公法; 6.2), to objective standards (as in the compound *fadu* 法度, 6.2), and so forth. It can be established (*li* 立) by the rulers (19.7), the ministers (34.3.4), or even by Han Fei himself (42.2.1).[5] My own preference is to avoid the mechanically unified translation, but the editors pressed me to preserve a certain degree of uniformity to allow the reader to grasp the overwhelming importance of this keyword. The result was compromise: in most cases I accepted the translation of "law" (although It should be clear that in most cases such translation as "standard," "norm," "model" or "pattern" may also work). Sometimes, when "law" would be simply misleading, another translation was adopted. I acted similarly with regard to other major keywords, trying to preserve uniformity without being too rigid.

When my draft of the translation was finished and after I had discussed it at some length with Chen Qiyou 陳奇猷 (1917–2006), I looked back at what I had done, and as is inevitable with me, I lost all interest in my own work. It was not that Chen Qiyou actually had very serious objections to it: the point was that I manifestly did not feel my command of literary English was anywhere good enough to live up to the task I had set myself. My translation might usefully remain a student's crib, in an instructive clause-by-clause poetic format (*yi dou yi hang* 一讀一行) of quite some pedagogical utility, but it could never seriously aspire to do justice to the poetry and literary vigour of Han Fei's original.

The book that is now being published is the result of an initiative by Martin Kern and Paul R. Goldin who felt that this draft, awful as it was, might be revised, improved, polished and published with appropriate professional historical annotation and thus come to serve a useful purpose. Yuri Pines has undertaken to completely revise and rewrite all historical annotation. He has

---

a European language was into Russian (Ivanov 1912), but this remained scarcely known for a century, until republished electronically (http://librams.ru/book-16869.html).
4 See *Thesaurus Linguae Sericae* (https://hxwd.org) and Harbsmeier 1981.
5 For a survey of meanings of *fa* in *Han Feizi*, see Liu Sixuan 2020: 1–24. For broader discussions of various meanings of *fa* in early texts and in the recently discovered administrative and legal manuscripts, see Graziani 2024; Lau and Lüdke 2024.

also contributed a considerable number of important corrections at many points in the translation. If anything in the translation reads really smoothly, the chances are that it comes from Paul R. Goldin's enthusiastic and very generous help at an early stage, and if anything looks historically sound and well-documented, it is bound to be due to the immense care taken of these matters by Yuri Pines. And, finally, if this book has come to be published with a respectable critical text and the marking of rhymes, indeed, if this book is finally published at all, this is due to the indefatigable selfless efforts of my dear friend Jens Østergaard Petersen whose magisterial correction of the whole translation has made him the real patron of this edition of *Han Feizi*.

This book is the result of a collective effort: whatever strengths it has I beg the gentle reader to attribute to the editors who have made it all possible.

Christoph Harbsmeier,
Copenhagen, 11 October, 2023

Co-editor's Preface

Approximately twenty years ago, when I got a first glimpse of Christoph Harbsmeier's draft translation of *Han Feizi*, I was thrilled. *Han Feizi* is one of the toughest early Chinese philosophical texts to translate. Its stylistic heterogeneity is bewildering, and it demands of the translator thorough familiarity with the richness of contemporaneous philosophical, historical, and literary texts. That Christoph Harbsmeier, one of very few colleagues qualified to translate *Han Feizi*, was ready to commit years of his life to this daunting task was excellent news to all of us.

Years passed and Christoph kindly invited me to help clarify a few historical details in the first chapter, one of the toughest, historically speaking. This exercise in annotation eventually turned into years-long cooperation, which allowed me to read the translation, make a few suggestions, and add a lot of footnotes, particularly concerning historical personalities and details of *Han Feizi*'s historical narratives. Aside from being honoured to collaborate with Christoph and learn his translating patterns, I benefitted from the job because it exposed me to the full complexity of Han Fei's historical thought. I felt for a long time that multiple invocations of the past in *Han Feizi* provide an extraordinarily rich and still largely untapped source for improving our understanding of Han Fei's philosophy. Thus, whereas countless studies have been dedicated to a small number of chapters in *Han Feizi* that employ what Paul R. Goldin dubs "*Laozi* diction,"[1] few have focused on *Han Feizi*'s historical chapters, even though the latter comprise almost half of the entire text.[2] Nor did these chapters attract much interest from previous translators.[3] I hope that the present translation will help to redress this imbalance.

Han Feizi is most commonly identified with its clear turn from what Kai Vogelsang dubs "exemplary" to "sequential" history.[4] History changes, and past

---

1 Goldin 2020: 226.
2 Thirteen out of the text's fifty-five chapters are comprised of little more than historical anecdotes (chapters 10, 22–23, 30–39); two others (1–2) are based on memorials supposedly submitted by Han Fei to the king of Qin and deal with the contemporaneous interstate situation; several other chapters (e.g., 3, 7, 19, 21) are fully dominated by historical exempla, and these recur, even if with less frequency, in most other chapters as well. However, only a few studies deal with historical argumentation in the context of Han Fei's philosophy. See, in particular, Schaberg 2011 (for chapters 36–39); Queen 2013 (chapter 21); Pines 2022b (chapter 39).
3 For instance, Burton Watson included only one "historical" chapter, "Ten Faults" in his *Selected Writings of Han Feizi* ([1964] 2003).
4 Vogelsang 2024. The clearest promulgation of sequential history is in chapter 49, "Five Ver-

exempla inevitably become irrelevant (49.1–4). Worse, these exempla are based on biased and unreliable narratives; those who claim that they know what former paragons did and thought are "are either stupid or fraudulent" (50.1). But notwithstanding these observations, the text of *Han Feizi* explodes with historical narratives and anecdotes to a degree unmatched in most other philosophical texts, with the possible exception of the roughly contemporaneous *Lüshi chunqiu* 呂氏春秋. Han Fei delights in playing with stories about rulers and ministers of the past. At times he clearly invents these stories, whereas elsewhere he cites early texts, often verbatim. At times he piles up anecdotes, leaving the reader to glean their proper messages; at times he explicitly directs the reader to the desired messages, whereas at times, by contrast, he questions common wisdom and presents a counter-interpretation of an anecdote's possible lessons. Some *Han Feizi* narratives display the author's remarkable mastery of historical texts, whereas others are full of blatant anachronisms. How to reconcile this heterogeneity and how to connect Han Fei's historical narratives to his broader philosophical outlook is a topic that deserves more systematic research.

Many of *Han Feizi*'s anecdotes are based on an expectation that the reader possesses some working knowledge about hundreds of historical personalities and dozens of coups, plots, wars, and diplomatic tricks spanning millennia from the legendary past to contemporaneous events. Naturally, the twenty-two odd centuries that have passed since the text was composed make such an expectation unrealistic. It was against this backdrop that I tried to provide the reader with rudimentary information that would allow not only following the text more easily, but also hint at Han Fei's multiple ways of using and abusing history. If my notes help, however marginally, to advance interest in the immense complexity of *Han Feizi*'s historical thought, my efforts shall be rewarded many times over.*

Yuri Pines,
Beijing, November 2023

---

min," sections 1–4. For more on the "sequential" (or "evolutionary") historical outlook in *Han Feizi*, see Pines 2013b and Bai 2020.

* My contribution to this research was supported by the ISF Research Grant 568/19 and Michael W. Lipson chair in Chinese studies, the Hebrew University of Jerusalem.

Text Edition and Rhyme Notations

For a discussion of the principles used in establishing the text, see the appendix on Text Edition. This appendix explains the contents of the textual notes following each section and it contains keys to the abbreviations used there.

Rhymes are noted throughout the text, marked in subscript and enclosed in parentheses. See the appendix on Rhyme Notations for details.

Conventions

Han Fei's native state 韓 is transcribed Hán. 魏 is transcribed Wei and 衛 is transcribed Wey. The name of the state of 徐 is rendered Xú, whereas 許 is rendered Xǔ. The name of the last king of the Shang dynasty, Zhou 紂 is transcribed Zhòu to distinguish him from the Zhou 周 dynasty (when the dynasty's name appears in the same sentence as the name of the Shang tyrant, we distinguish it as Zhōu).

All dates are Before Common Era unless indicated otherwise.

In the footnotes, first person pronouns refer to the translator.

The text is divided into sections following Zhang Jue 2011. Page references are supplied for Zhang Jue 2011, referred to as "*Xilun*", and Chen Qiyou 2000, referred to as "*Xin jiaozhu*."

Translation

CHAPTER 1

初見秦 First Audience in Qin

HF 1.1 (*Xilun* 9, *Xin jiaozhu* 1)[1]

臣聞：	I, your subject, have heard:
"不知而言，	to speak about a matter that you do not understand
不智；	is unwise;
知而不言，	not to speak about a matter that you do understand
5　不忠。"	is disloyal.
為人臣不忠，	When ministers are disloyal,
當死；	they deserve death;
言而不當，	when they make proposals but are in error,
亦當死。	they likewise deserve death.
10　雖然，	Even so,
臣願悉言所聞，	I wish to speak up on what I have heard, without withholding anything –
唯大王裁其罪。	may Your Majesty determine my crime![2]

1　This chapter is based on what appears to be a memorial to an unnamed king of Qin (as marked also by the first person pronoun, *chen* 臣: I, your subject). The memorial aims to facilitate Qin's conquest of the rest of "All-under-Heaven." In *Zhanguo ce* 3.5 ("Qin 秦 1"), the same memorial is erroneously attributed to Qin's diplomat Zhang Yi 張儀 (d. 309), but this attribution is wrong: from the content of the memorial it is clear that it was submitted in the last years of King Zhaoxiang of Qin 秦昭襄王 (r. 306–251). The authorship of the memorial is the focus of intense debate, because it explicitly calls for the elimination of Han Fei's home state of Hán 韓, contradicting the memorial in chapter 2, "Preserving Hán," which aims to protect Hán by claiming its continued existence would prove valuable for Qin. Some traditional scholars, most notably Sima Guang 司馬光 (1019–1086), have suggested a cynical reading, namely that Han Fei brazenly proposed the elimination of his natal state as a way to ingratiate himself with the king of Qin (*Zizhi tongjian* 6: 222). Others have opined that the memorial was penned not by Han Fei, but by one of Qin's "guest ministers" (*ke qing* 客卿) and has been wrongly attributed to Han Fei (for the different views, see Lundahl 1992: 210–215; Zheng Liangshu 1993: 11–15; Jiang Chongyue 2000: 14–25; Song Hongbing 2010: 9–13; Dou Zhaorui 2019). A possible solution is implied by the chapter's name, "First audience in Qin": namely, that the memorial was presented during Han Fei's earlier visit to Qin during King Zhaoxiang's reign and is unrelated to his second visit (in 233), which was when "Preserving Hán" was submitted.

2　Note the mode of speech in which a proponent expresses the fear that his proposal may lead

HF 1.2 (*Xilun* 9, *Xin jiaozhu* 3)

臣聞：	I have heard:
天下陰燕、陽魏，	All the world, from Yan in the north to Wei in the south,
連荊、固齊，	have linked up with Jing (Chu), bolstered their relations with Qi,
收韓而成從，	and enlisted Hán, creating a Vertical Alliance;[3]
5　將西面以與秦強為難。	they are about to face westwards and oppose Qin resolutely.
臣竊笑之。	I take the liberty of laughing at them!
世有三亡，	In the world there are three strategies that lead to ruin,
而天下得之。	and the world has all three of them.
其此之謂乎！	This must apply to the present situation.
10　臣聞之曰：	I, your subject, have heard:
"以亂攻治者亡，	"One who attacks the orderly by means of chaos is doomed to be ruined,
以邪攻正者亡，	one who attacks the correct by means of the deviant is doomed to be ruined,
以逆攻順者亡。"	and one who attacks the compliant by means of the obstinate is doomed to be ruined."
今天下之府庫不盈，	In all the world there are now no fully stocked civil and military storehouses
15　困倉空虛，	and all granaries are gaping empty,

---

to criminal punishment (repeated in 1.5, line 39 as "speaking at the risk of my life" *mei si* 昧死). Pines (2013a: 96–97) argues that this mode of minister-ruler communication evolved on the eve of the imperial unification of 221 and dominated intercourse with the rulers thereafter.

[3] In this memorial, the term *tianxia* 天下, literally "All-under-Heaven" (translated in the text as "world," "all the world," or "the realm") excludes the state of Qin (for this exclusion, see more in Pines 2002b). Geographically speaking, the following depiction is somewhat odd: whereas Yan was indeed the northernmost state, Wei was located in the heartland of the Central Plains and not in the south, as implied by *yang* 陽 (the latter may refer to the location of Wei's capital, Daliang 大梁 to the south [*yang*] of the Yellow River). The vertical (north-south) alliance described here was directed against Qin. Notably, the state of Zhao is absent from the depiction of the "world." As explained below (note 20), in the aftermath of its disastrous defeat at Changping in 260, Zhao lost its ability to actively oppose Qin.

初見秦 FIRST AUDIENCE IN QIN

悉其士民，	but these states have mobilised all their officers and men
張軍數十百萬，	and have lined up an armed force numbering tens of millions of men:[4]
其頓首戴羽為將軍、斷死於前，	those who bow (to accept commission), wear plumes on their helmets as generals, and swear to be determined to die in the front line,
不至千人。	number more than a thousand,
20 皆以言死。	but they are all ready to die in word only –
白刃在前，	when bare blades are in front of them
斧鑕在後，	and axes and execution blocks are to the back of them,
而卻走、不能死也。	they will nonetheless run, being unable to face death.
非其士民不能死也，	This is not because these officers and men are unable to face death,
25 上不能故也。	but because their superiors are incompetent.
言賞則不與，	They promise rewards and then go on not to deliver them;
言罰則不行，	they promise punishments and then go on not to carry them out.
賞罰不信，	Rewards and punishments are not reliable,
故士民不死也。	and therefore officers and men are not willing to risk their lives.
30 今秦出號令而行賞罰，	Now, when Qin promulgates orders and ordinances and carries out rewards and punishments,
有功無功相事也。	success and failure are judged according to actual performance.
出其父母懷衽之中，	From the time its people emerge from their parents' bosom,
生未嘗見寇耳。	they have never seen a single invader,
聞戰，	but when they hear that there is war,
35 頓足徒裼，	they stamp their feet and, just half dressed,
犯白刃，	rush against bare blades,
蹈鑪炭，	ready to tread on glowing coals,

---

[4] The number is hyperbolic. It is possible that the combined military forces of the five states exceeded one or even two million soldiers and auxiliaries, but surely not "tens of millions."

斷死於前者皆是也。	determined to face death in the front line – all are like this.[5]
夫斷死與斷生者不同，	Now, being determined to face death is different from being determined to stay alive,
40　而民為之者，	but the reason why the people act in this way
是貴奮死也。	is that they value fighting to death.
夫一人奮死可以對十，	One man willing to fight to his death can oppose ten of the enemy;
十可以對百，	ten can oppose one hundred;
百可以對千，	one hundred can oppose one thousand;
45　千可以對萬，	one thousand can oppose ten thousand;
萬可以克天下矣。	and ten thousand can overpower the whole world.
今秦地折長補短，	Now, Qin's lands, roughly speaking,
方數千里，	add up to several thousand *li* square,[6]
名師數十百萬。	and its illustrious armies add up to tens of million men.[7]
50　秦之號令賞罰、地形利害，	As for its orders and ordinances and its rewards and punishments, and the relative advantages of its terrain,
天下莫若也。	Qin has no equal in the world.
以此與天下，	If Qin on the strength of this takes on all the world in battle,
天下不足兼而有也。	the whole world will not be enough for Qin to annex and control.
是故秦戰未嘗不克，	Therefore, when Qin goes to war, it never fails to win;
55　攻未嘗不取，	when it launches an attack, it never fails to conquer,

---

5　Han Fei (or other author of the memorial) exaggerates, but this does reflect the policies initiated by Shang Yang 商鞅 (d. 338) to imbue the people of Qin with martial spirit.

6　In chapter 15 ("Attracting the people") of the *Book of Lord Shang*, written at about the same time as the present chapter of *Han Feizi* (Pines 2023), the territory of Qin is estimated to be five times one thousand *li* squared, which is ca. 800,000 km² (roughly the territory of present-day Germany and France combined).

7　Han Fei continues to flatter the ruler with this plainly exaggerated number.

初見秦 FIRST AUDIENCE IN QIN

所當未嘗不破，	and whomever it faces, it never fails to destroy.
開地數千里，	It has expanded its territory by several thousand *li* square.
此其大功也。	This is its great achievement.
然而兵甲頓，	And yet, its arms and armour have lost their edge;
60　士民病，	its officers and men are worn out;
蓄積索，	its accumulated supplies have been exhausted;
田疇荒，	its fields are full of weeds;
囷倉虛，	its granaries stand empty;
四鄰諸侯不服，	all its neighbouring regional lords refuse to submit to it;
65　霸王之名不成。	and its status as a hegemonic kingdom has not been attained.
此無異故，	There is no other reason for this
其謀臣皆不盡其忠也。	but the fact that your advising ministers do not fully complete their duties of loyalty.

5 C has 強秦 with 校注 11, following 陳本; we have 秦強 with all other editions and 陳奇猷 and 張覺. 強秦 is a recurring expression in HF; probably 陳本 seeks to assimilate 秦強 to this. 13 〔以逆攻順者亡〕(校注 11, with 陳本).　19 至 is read as 止. 山仲質 emends 至 to 止.

HF 1.3 (*Xilun* 13, *Xin jiaozhu* 8)

臣敢言之：	I venture to declare:
往者齊南破荊，	In the past, Qi defeated Jing (Chu) in the south;
東破宋，	it defeated Song in the east;
西服秦，	it subjugated Qin in the west;
5　北破燕，	it defeated Yan in the north;
中使韓、魏，	and it ordered about Hán and Wei in the centre.[8]
土地廣而兵強，	Its territories were large and its armed forces strong;

8　This depicts Qi at the apex of its power during the reigns of Kings Xuan 齊宣王 (r. 319–300) and Min 齊湣王 (r. 300–284). The defeat of Chu probably refers to the victory of the Qi-Wei-Hán coalition over Chu in 301. The annexation of Song occurred in 286. Qi's "subjugation" of Qin is less historically accurate, but perhaps refers to the successful assault of the Qi-Wei-Hán coalition against Qin in 296. The defeat of Yan probably refers to Qi's brief occupation of Yan in the aftermath of domestic turmoil there in 314.

戰克攻取，	in every battle it won and in every attack it conquered;
詔令天下。	and it issued commands to all states in the world.
10　齊之清濟濁河，	Qi's clear river Ji and the murky Yellow River
足以為限；	sufficed to serve as an impediment;
長城巨防，	the great barrier of the Long Walls
足以為塞。	sufficed to serve as a barrier.[9]
齊，	Qi
15　五戰之國也，	is a state that has won five major campaigns,
一戰不克而無齊。	but when it lost a single battle, Qi was no more.[10]
由此觀之，	From this point of view,
夫戰者，	war
萬乘之存亡也。	is a matter of the survival or ruin of a large state.[11]
20　且臣聞之曰：	Moreover, I, your subject, have heard it said that
"削株無遺根[A 文/痕 kən/kən]，	"When you cut down a tree, do not leave the roots.
無與禍鄰[A 真/真 ljin/-jiən/ljěn]，	Do not court ruin,
禍乃不存[A 文/魂 dzən/dzuən]。"	and ruin will not come to you."
秦與荊人戰，	When Qin fought with Jing (Chu),
25　大破荊，	it greatly defeated it;
襲郢，	it raided the capital, Ying,
取洞庭、五湖、江南。	and took Dongting, the Five Lakes and lands to the south of the Yangzi.[12]

9　Qi was protected by the parallel flow of the Yellow River and the Ji River (the latter is, incidentally, the current course of the Yellow River) from west and northwest; whereas its Long Wall protected it from the south. For more on Qi's historical geography, see Pines 2018.

10　In 284, a grand anti-Qi coalition of Yan, Wei, Hán, Zhao, and Qin inflicted a disastrous defeat on Qi, which was, for several years, reduced to just two tiny districts. Eventually, Qi succeeded in driving out Yan's occupation forces and restored its independence, but it never again played its erstwhile role as a major power.

11　"Ten-thousand chariots" is a standard reference to a powerful state. In fact, it is doubtful whether any of the ancient states ever had this many war chariots.

12　In 278, Qin launched one of its most successful campaigns under the renowned general Bai Qi 白起 (on whom see below notes) against the state of Chu. The Chu heartland, including its centuries-old capital of Ying, was occupied, and Qin's armies temporarily occupied areas further south, in Dongting Commandery (in the north of today's Hunan Province). Their brief occupation of the areas to the south of the Yangzi in the vicinity of

初見秦 FIRST AUDIENCE IN QIN

荊王君臣亡走，	The King of Jing (Chu), the ruler as well as his ministers, fled into exile,
東服於陳。	going eastwards to find safety in Chen.
30 當此時也，	At this time,
隨荊以兵，	had Qin pursued Jing (Chu) with armed force,
則荊可舉；	Jing (Chu) could have been conquered.
荊可舉，	If Jing (Chu) had been conquered,
則其民足貪也，	its population would have been something to covet
35 地足利也，	and its territory would have been something to profit from.
東以弱齊、燕，	In the east you would have weakened Qi and Yan;
中以凌三晉。	in the centre you would have been able to sway the Three Jin.[13]
然則是一舉而霸王之名可成也，	And so, with this one stroke, your status as a hegemonic king would have been established,
四鄰諸侯可朝也，	and all neighbouring regional lords could have been made to pay their respects at your court.
40 而謀臣不為，	However, your advising ministers did nothing of the kind –
引軍而退，	they led the army into retreat
復與荊人為和。	and went on to make peace with the people of Jing (Chu).
令荊人得收亡國，	They allowed the people of Jing (Chu) to reclaim their ruined country,
聚散民，	to gather their scattered people,
45 立社稷主，	to establish the tablets of the altars of soil and grain
置宗廟，	and to establish ancestral temples,[14]
令率天下西面以與秦為難。	leading the world to face west and make trouble for Qin.

---

the Dongting Lake represented the apex of Qin's southward expansion prior to 223. For Qin's southern campaigns, see also Korolkov 2022: 65–90.

13   Han Fei's addressee is, in all likelihood, the very King Zhaoxiang of Qin under whose rule (at that time only nominal) the defeat of Chu occurred (see note 1 above). The Three Jin were the successor states of Jin 晉, namely Wei, Hán, and Zhao.

14   The master of the altars of soil and grain is the ruler of the state. In the aftermath of Qin's occupation of Ying, Chu briefly split into several competing polities. The restoration of the altars of the soil and grain (the symbolic centre of the polity) and of ancestral temples of the Chu kings marked the resurrection of Chu.

	此固以失霸王之道一矣。	This surely is case number one of losing the way of a hegemonic king.[15]
	天下又比周而軍華下，	All states in the world again banded together and camped below the Hua Mountain.
50	大王以詔破之，	Your Majesty had them ruined by issuing an order,
	兵至梁郭下。	after which your armed forces arrived below the outer walls of Liang.[16]
	圍梁數旬，	If they had surrounded Liang for several weeks,
	則梁可拔；	Liang could have been captured;
	拔梁，	once they had captured Liang,
55	則魏可舉；	Wei could have been taken;
	舉魏，	once they had taken Wei,
	則荊、趙之意絕；	Jing (Chu) and Zhao's plans would be blocked;[17]
	荊、趙之意絕，	and once Jing (Chu) and Zhao's plans are blocked,
	則趙危；	Zhao would have been in a precarious position.
60	趙危，	With Zhao in a precarious position,
	而荊狐疑；	Jing (Chu) would have been at a loss for what to do.
	東以弱齊、燕，	In the east you would have thereby weakened Qi and Yan,
	中以凌三晉。	and in the central region you would have swayed the three successor states to Jin.
	然則是一舉而霸王之名可成也，	And so, with this one stroke, your status as a hegemonic king would have been established,
65	四鄰諸侯可朝也；	and neighbouring regional lords could have been made to come to your court.

---

15 Qin did indeed have to acquiesce to the partial restoration of the battered state of Chu, which had successfully utilised the resources of the eastern part of its country to counter-attack Qin's invading forces.

16 This refers to the battle of Huayang 華陽 (to the north of Mt. Hua), which took place in 273 in the aftermath of a four-year-long campaign by Qin against Wei. Wei made use of a cease-fire with Qin to ally itself with Zhao and attack Qin's ally, Hán. The results were disastrous: Qin dispatched Bai Qi and another commander, who defeated the allied forces, inflicting on them losses totalling ca. 150,000 soldiers. The victorious Qin army then besieged the Wei capital, Daliang 大梁, but eventually had to give it up in exchange for the cession of Wei territory near Nanyang 南陽 to Qin (Yang Kuan 1998: 407–408).

17 The territory of Wei separated Chu from Zhao. With Wei routed, Chu and Zhao could no longer coordinate anti-Qin cooperation.

初見秦 FIRST AUDIENCE IN QIN

而謀臣不為，	However, your advising ministers did not do this.
引軍而退，	They led the army into retreat,
復與魏氏為和。	and went on to make peace with the ruling family of Wei.
令魏氏反收亡國，	They caused the Wei line to reclaim their ruined country,
70 聚散民，	to gather their scattered people,
立社稷主，	to establish the tablets of the altars of soil and grain,
置宗廟，	and to establish ancestral temples.
令率天下西面以與秦為難。	They caused Wei to lead the realm to face west, and make trouble for Qin.
此固以失霸王之道二矣。	This surely is case number two of losing the way a hegemonic king.
75 前者穰侯之治秦也，	Some time ago, the Marquis of Rang governed Qin.[18]
用一國之兵而欲以成兩國之功，	He deployed the armed forces of one state but tried to profit two states.[19]
是故兵終身暴露於外，	And so the soldiers spent all their lives braving the elements;
士民疲病於內，	the officers and men were worn out and sick at home;
霸王之名不成。	and your status as a hegemonic king was not attained.
80 此固以失霸王之道三矣。	This surely is case number three of losing the way of a hegemonic king.

20 〔臣〕(校注 11, with 陳本、張榜本). 張覺 notes that according to 朱筠, there was a lacuna of one graph here in 何本.　21 （迹）〔株〕(校注 11).　27 C follows 校注 11 and emends 湖 to 渚, following 顧廣圻, with 戰國策 parallel.　34 〔其〕(校注 11).　47 今〔率天下西面以與秦為難〕; 校注 11–12, following 俞樾, with 戰國策 parallel. This emendation is followed by 陳奇猷. 張覺 opposes it and holds 今 to be an official in charge of 宗廟.　57, 58 C regards 意 as a taboo replacement for 志, in order to avoid the 名 of 漢桓帝.　68 張抄 has 利 for 和; 吳本、藏本、張本、陳本 have 和.

18　The Marquis of Rang is the title of Wei Ran 魏冉, who was the single most powerful Qin official from 301 to 266.

19　The Marquis of Rang was enfeoffed in Tao, an eastern territory separated from the bulk of Qin lands by the territories of Wei and Hán. He is repeatedly accused – in his biography in *Shiji* 72 and also *Han Feizi* 43.2.3 – of using his power to benefit his own fief at Tao rather than the state of Qin. Here it is implied that Tao de facto became a separate state.

HF 1.4 (*Xilun* 18, *Xin jiaozhu* 16)

趙氏，	Zhao
中央之國也，	is a central state,
雜民所居也，	it is inhabited by a mixed population.
其民輕而難用也。	Its people are easy-going and hard to set to work.
5 號令不治，	Its orders and ordinances are not properly administered;
賞罰不信，	its rewards and punishments are not reliable;
地形不便，	its geographic conditions are not advantageous.
下不能盡其民力。	Below, it cannot make full use of the resources of the people.
彼固亡國之形也，	These are certainly the features of a state doomed to ruin,
10 而不憂民萌，	but they were still not worried about the common people,
悉其士民軍於長平之下，	and mobilised all their officers and men below the walls of Changping
以爭韓上黨。	in order to fight for Hán's city of Shangdang.[20]
大王以詔破之，	Your Majesty gave orders to destroy Zhao's army,
拔武安。	and uprooted Wu'an.[21]
15 當是時也，	At this time,
趙氏上下不相親也，	superiors and inferiors in the state of Zhao were not close to each other;
貴賤不相信也。	the noble and the base did not trust one another,
然則邯鄲不守。	and thus, Handan was left undefended.
拔邯鄲，	Had Qin taken Handan,
20 筦山東河間，	had it brought Hejian east of the Mountain under its control,
引軍而去，	had it led its army forth
西攻脩武，	to attack Xiuwu in the west,

---

[20] In 262, following Qin's attack on Hán, the latter agreed to yield the commandery of Shangdang to Qin. The governor and the leaders of the commandery preferred to yield their territory to the neighbouring state of Zhao. This resulted in a major war between Qin and Zhao: the Changping campaign, which was fought in the arid hills of southeastern Shanxi from 262 to 260. Zhao's crushing defeat at the end of that campaign marked the end of its status as a great power.

[21] Wu'an was a Zhao city. Confusingly, Wu'an jun 武安君 "Lord of Martial Tranquility" was also the title of the Qin commander Bai Qi who crushed the Zhao armies at Changping.

初見秦 FIRST AUDIENCE IN QIN

踰羊腸，	had it crossed Yangchang,
降代、上黨。	it could have subjugated Dai and Shangdang.[22]
25 代四十六縣，	Dai comprises forty-six counties;
上黨七十縣，	Shangdang comprises seventy counties –
不用一領甲，	without using a single shield
不苦一士民，	or wearing out any officers or men,
此皆秦有也。	these would both have become the possessions of Qin.
30 代、上黨不戰而畢為秦矣，	All of Dai and Shangdang would have gone to Qin without a fight,
東陽、河外不戰而畢反為齊矣，	all of Dongyang and Hewai would have reverted to Qi without a fight,[23]
中山、呼沱以北不戰而畢為燕矣。	and all of Zhongshan and the area north of Hutuo would have gone to Yan without a fight.[24]
然則是趙舉，	In this way Zhao would have been uprooted,[25]
趙舉則韓亡，	and if Zhao had been uprooted, Hán would have been ruined;
35 韓亡則荊、魏不能獨立，	and if Hán had been ruined, Jing (Chu) and Wei would be unable to stand alone.
荊、魏不能獨立，	Since Jing (Chu) and Wei would have been unable to stand alone,
則是一舉而壞韓、蠹魏、挾荊，	with this one stroke, you would have destroyed Hán, stung Wei, and pincered Jing (Chu).
東以弱齊、燕，	In the east you would have weakened Qi and Yan,

---

22   Hejian, "between the Rivers," refers to the territory between the two streams of the Yellow River (to the west of the current Hejian City 河間市, Hebei). This area, located to the east of the Taihang mountain range, was the easternmost territory of Zhao. Xiuwu, in the current Jiaozuo Municipality 焦作市 (Henan), was a major stronghold on the northern shores of the Yellow River. Yangchang is located slightly to the north of Xiuwu, closer to today's Jinyang Municipality 晉陽市 (Shanxi). Shangdang is located in central Shanxi, whereas Dai refers to the areas further to the north, closer to the northernmost reaches of the Taihang range.

23   These were Zhao's easternmost territories, to the east of the Yellow River. Hewai means "beyond the [Yellow] River."

24   The former state of Zhongshan was annexed by Zhao in 296. The Hutuo River flows from the Taihang range to the current city of Shijiazhuang and further eastward to the former course of the Yellow River.

25   The text envisions the partition of Zhao among its three neighbours, Qin, Qi, and Yan.

决白馬之口以沃魏氏，	then opened the White Horse junction to inundate Wei.[26]
40 是一舉而三晉亡，	With this one stroke, the three successor states of Jin would have been ruined,
從者敗也。	and their followers defeated.
大王垂拱以須之，	Your Majesty could have just folded your arms and waited it out,
天下編隨而服矣，	and all the world would have followed suit and submitted to you, one after the other.
霸王之名可成。	Then it would have been possible to attain the status of a hegemonic king.
45 而謀臣不為，	However, your advising ministers did not do this –
引軍而退，	they led the army into retreat,
復與趙氏為和。	and went on to make peace with Zhao.[27]
夫以大王之明，	Now, even with the brilliance of Your Majesty
秦兵之強，	and the might of the armed forces of Qin,
50 棄霸王之業，	that the mission of becoming a hegemonic king has been abandoned,
地曾不可得，	that even an addition of territory was impossible to obtain,
乃取欺於亡國，	and that you were cheated by ruined states –
是謀臣之拙也。	this was due to the incompetence of your advising ministers.
且夫趙當亡而不亡，	Now, when Zhao was due to be ruined but was not ruined,
55 秦當霸而不霸，	and when Qin was due to become the hegemon but did not become the hegemon –
天下固以量秦之謀臣一矣。	the world certainly took up for evaluation the quality of your advising ministers in Qin on this as the first point.

---

26 The White Horse junction was a narrow part of the Yellow River at which it divided into two streams: the southern, minor stream flowed more or less along the current river's course (the former Ji River), passing close to Wei's capital, Daliang. The northern course was the main stream at that time. Redirecting the Yellow River to the south would have caused a disaster on a par with the famous breach of the Huayuankou 花園口 dams in 1938 CE.

27 In fact, the peace with Zhao followed a series of defeats and defections from the Qin army between 257 and 255.

初見秦 FIRST AUDIENCE IN QIN

乃復悉士卒以攻邯鄲，	Then again, when you deployed all the officers and men in the attack on Handan,
不能拔也，	and they were unable to uproot it,[28]
棄甲兵弩，	but shed their armour, weapons, and crossbows,
60 戰竦而卻，	and retreated, shaking with fear –
天下固已量秦力二矣。	this was certainly the second point at which the world took up for evaluation the strength of Qin.
軍乃引而復，	Then the Qin army was led in retreat
并於孚下，	and gathered below the outer city wall,
大王又并軍而至，	and Your Majesty gathered all your armies to meet them there.
65 與戰不能克之也，	In battle, neither was the army able to vanquish the enemy,
又不能反，	nor was it able to make a proper retreat.
軍罷而去，	The army left the battleground, exhausted –
天下固量秦力三矣。	this was certainly the third point at which the world took up for evaluation the strength of Qin.
內者量吾謀臣，	Regarding the internal situation, they evaluated our advising ministers,
70 外者極吾兵力。	regarding the external situation they saw the limits of our military strength.
由是觀之，	From this point of view,
臣以為天下之從，	I believe that if the whole world should ally vertically,
幾不難矣。	this should hardly present any difficulty.
內者，	Yet inside our state,
75 吾甲兵頓，	our armour and weapons are run down;
士民病，	our officers and men are drained;
蓄積索，	our supplies are exhausted;
田疇荒，	our fields are full of weeds;
囷倉虛。	our granaries are empty.
80 外者，	And on the outside,
天下皆比意甚固。	the states of the world are tightly allied in intent.

---

28 The attack on Handan followed Qin's victory at Changping. However, Qin's forces were too exhausted after the three-year-long Changping campaign, and failed to overcome the state of Zhao, which was assisted by Wei. The debacle at Handan brought about execution of Qin's best general, Bai Qi, in 257 and, eventually, the dismissal (and possibly the execution) of the prime minister, Fan Sui 睢 (or Fan Ju 雎), in 255 (see more in Pines 2023).

願大王有以慮之也。 I hope Your Majesty has the proper basis for a careful deliberation on this.

20 （可聞）〔河間〕（校注 12）.   23 張抄 has 喻 for 踰.   23 （華）〔羊腸〕（校注 12）. 24 （絳）〔降代〕（校注 12）.   25 C follows 校注 12 and emends 四 to 三, with 戰國策 parallel.   26 C follows 校注 12 and emends 七十 to 十七, with 戰國策 parallel.   30 （以）代（校注 12）.   37 （拔）〔挾〕（校注 12, with 戰國策 parallel）.   38 （強）燕（校注 12）.   60 〔卻〕（校注 12）.   63 孚 is read as 郛; C has 李, with 張榜本、凌瀛初本 and 校注 12.   67 （運）〔軍〕（校注 12）.   73 （能）〔難〕（校注 12）.

HF 1.5 (*Xilun* 21, *Xin jiaozhu* 24)

且臣聞之曰： Moreover, I, your subject, have heard it said,
"戰戰栗栗[A 脂/質 ljit/ljĕt]， "If you shiver and tremble with fear,
日慎一日[A 脂/質 njit/ńźjĕt]， and are cautious every day about that day alone,
苟慎其道[B 幽/晧 dəgwx/dâu]， if you are cautious about the Way,
5 天下可有[B 之/有 gwjəgx/jŏu]。" then all the world can be possessed."
何以知其然也？ How do I know that this is so?

昔者紂為天子， In ancient times, Zhòu was the Son of Heaven,
將率天下甲兵百萬， in command of a million armoured soldiers from all the realm.[29]

左飲於淇溪， When his left flank rested for drink at the Qi Stream,
10 右飲於洹谿， and his right flank rested for drink at the Huan Brook,
淇水竭而洹水不流， the Qi went dry and the Huan ceased to flow.[30]
以與周武王為難。 He thought thereby to make trouble for King Wu of Zhou.[31]

武王將素甲三千， King Wu led three thousand men wearing armour of unadorned silk.
戰一日， Having fought for one day,

---

29 Zhòu (d. ca. 1046) is the paradigmatic bad monarch, the last tyrant of the Shang dynasty. The number of his soldiers is hugely exaggerated; it fits the Warring States period but surely not the Shang age.

30 Both Qi and Huan were small rivers if the vicinity of Shang's political stronghold, near modern Anyang.

31 King Wu of Zhou led the campaign to overthrow King Zhòu of Shang in ca. 1046. King Zhòu reportedly relied on the large size of his armies and did not make adequate preparations.

初見秦 FIRST AUDIENCE IN QIN

15	而破紂之國，	He destroyed the state under Zhòu,
	禽其身，	captured the man,
	據其地而有其民，	occupied his territory, and took possession of his people,
	天下莫傷。	but no one under Heaven suffered any harm.[32]
	知伯率三國之眾以攻趙襄主於晉陽，	Zhi Bo, leading the hosts of three states (of Jin), attacked Ruler Xiang of Zhao at Jinyang.[33]
20	決水而灌之三月，	He diverted the river and flooded the area for three months.
	城且拔矣，	When the inner city walls were about to be taken,
	襄主鑽龜筮占兆，	Ruler Xiang drilled the tortoise shell and arranged the milfoil, looking for an omen,
	以視利害，	to see the advantages and disadvantages he had
	何國可降。	and the state to which he should surrender.
25	乃使其臣張孟談，	At that point he sent out his steward Zhang Mengtan,
	於是乃潛行而出，	who then left the city in secret and on foot,
	反知伯之約，	to turn Zhi Bo's allies against him.
	得兩國之眾，	[Zhang Mengtan] gained the hosts of the other two states (Hán and Wei),
	以攻知伯，	so as to attack Zhi Bo.
30	禽其身，	He captured [Zhi Bo] in person
	以復襄主之初。	and restored Ruler Xiang to his original position.
	今秦地折長補短，	Now the lands of Qin, roughly speaking,
	方數千里，	add up to several thousand *li* square,
	名師數十百萬。	and its illustrious armies add up to tens of million men.
35	秦國之號令賞罰、地形利害，	As for the orders and ordinances and the rewards and punishments, and the relative advantages of its terrain,

---

32 Han Fei (or another author of this chapter) cautiously hints that Qin's military superiority may prove insufficient if, like in the case of King Zhòu of Shang, it arouses widespread enmity.

33 From the sixth century, political authority in the state of Jin devolved from the ruling house to powerful ministerial lineages. After a century of inter-lineage strife, only four major ministerial lineages remained: Zhi, Zhao, Hán, and Wei. In 453, Zhi Bo, the head of the Zhi lineage, allied with Hán and Wei leaders to annihilate the strongest political leader in Jin, Zhao Xiangzi 趙襄子 (d. ca. 442), but he was betrayed and overpowered by his Hán and Wei allies. In the subsequent decades, the heads of the Zhao, Wei, and Hán lineages

天下莫如也。	no state in the world is Qin's equal.
以此與天下，	If Qin sets out to conquer all the world with this,
可兼而有也。	the whole world can be annexed and possessed.
臣昧死願望見大王，	At the risk of my life, I have aspired to an audience with Your Majesty
40 言所以破天下之從、舉趙、亡韓、臣荊魏、親齊燕，	I speak of the means to destroy the Vertical Alliance that has been formed among the states of the world, to uproot Zhao, to ruin Hán,[34]
以成霸王之名，	and thereby attain your status as a hegemonic king –
朝四鄰諸侯之道。	the way to make all the neighbouring regional lords pay homage at your court.
大王誠聽其說，	If Your Majesty seriously listens to these arguments
一舉而天下之從不破，	and the Vertical Alliance of the states of world is not routed at one stroke,
45 趙不舉，	if Zhao not uprooted,
韓不亡，	if Hán not ruined,
荊、魏不臣，	if Jing (Chu) and Wei do not become your subjects,
齊、燕不親，	if Qi and Yan are not drawn near,
霸王之名不成，	if the status of a hegemonic king is not attained,
50 四鄰諸侯不朝，	and if the neighbouring regional lords do not pay homage at your court,
大王斬臣以徇國，	then your Majesty may cut me in two at the waist and display my body as a lesson to the people,
以為王謀不忠者也。	as one who did not offer loyal advice to You.

26 潛（於）行 (校注 12). **27** 〔反〕(校注 12). **37** 〔以〕(校注 12). **38**（何）〔可〕(校注 12). **38** 〔而〕(校注 12, following 陳本) which follows 張本; we follow 陳奇猷 and 張覺. **52** C adds 戒 before 也, following 校注 12

---

finalised the dissolution of Jin into three independent states (see chapter 10.5 for further details). In *Han Feizi* (as in parts of *Zhanguo ce*), Zhao Xiangzi is named by the respectful title "Ruler Xiang (or Sovereign Xiang 襄主) of Zhao." This appellation posthumously elevates Zhao Xiangzi from the position of a minister to that of a regional lord.

34　This suggestion to ruin Han Fei's home state of Hán can be contrasted with Han Fei's effort to preserve his natal state (see chapter 2 below). See more in note 1 above.

CHAPTER 2

存韓 Preserving Hán

HF 2.1.1 (*Xilun* 25, *Xin jiaozhu* 29)[1]

韓事秦三十餘年，	Hán has now served Qin for more than thirty years:
出則為扞蔽，	in foreign affairs it has acted as a defensive shield,
入則為蓆薦。	and in domestic matters it has functioned as a comfortable straw mat (for Qin to use at its pleasure).
秦特出銳師取地而韓隨之，	Qin merely had to send out crack troops to take [foreign] territory for Hán to decide to give it support.
5 怨懸於天下，	Hán became an object of resentment in all the world,
功歸於強秦。	whereas all achievement was credited to mighty Qin.
且夫韓入貢職，	Moreover, as Hán sends us tribute,
與郡縣無異也。	there is no difference between Hán and a commandery or a prefecture.
今臣竊聞貴臣之計，	Now, your servant has heard the plans of your distinguished minister,
10 舉兵將伐韓。	that Qin should mobilise and prepare to attack Hán.
夫趙氏聚士卒，	In fact, Zhao[2] has assembled a military force
養從徒，	and is encouraging the adherents of the Vertical Alliance,[3]

---

1 Like chapter 1, this chapter is based on Han Fei's memorial to the king of Qin, but the difference could not be greater. If Sima Qian's narration is correct, this memorial was presented during Han Fei's fateful visit to Qin in 233, when he tried in vain to dissuade King Zheng (the would-be First Emperor of Qin, r. 246–210, emp. 221–210) from annexing Han Fei's home state. The memorial ends with a counter-argument by Han Fei's nemesis (and alleged classmate), Li Si 李斯 (d. 208). According to Sima Qian's version of events, following his futile attempt to save the Hán, Li Si orchestrated Han Fei's imprisonment; Han Fei died in Qin custody.
2 Han Fei speaks here of "the Zhao line," because the state was a patrimony of its ruling lineage.
3 The Vertical (North-South) Alliance was directed against Qin (see also chapter 1.1 and note 3 there).

欲贅天下之兵，	intending to swell its ranks with the troops of the states of all the world:
明秦不弱，	it announces that if Qin is not weakened,
15 則諸侯必滅宗廟，	the regional lords will be sure to have their ancestral temples destroyed,
欲西面行其意，	and it intends to turn westward (against Qin) to achieve its aims.
非一日之計也。	This sort of plan is not composed in a single day.
今釋趙之患，	If you now ignore Zhao, which is a threat,
而攘內臣之韓，	but reject Hán, which is your domestic servant,
20 則天下明趙氏之計矣。	then everybody will understand the strategy of Zhao.

4 取（韓）地而〔韓〕隨之 (校注 22, following 王先慎)。 7 張抄 has 暗 for 職; all other editions have 職。 9 今（日）臣 (校注 22)。 12 〔徒〕 (校注 22; 藏本、張本、陳本、趙本 have 徒; 吳本、張抄、錢抄無 do not.) 20 陳奇猷 adds 得 after 計, following old commentary by 謝希深 (994–1039)。

HF 2.1.2 (*Xilun* 26, *Xin jiaozhu* 29)

夫韓，	Now, Hán
小國也，	is a small state,
而以應天下四擊，	and in order to respond to strikes from all directions,
主辱臣苦，	its rulers have borne humiliation and its ministers have suffered hardships,
5 上下相與同憂久矣。	and so for a long time now, those above and those below have shared anxieties.
脩守備，	They built defensive structures,
戒強敵，	took guard against strong enemies,
有蓄積，	piled up supplies,
築城池以守固。	and constructed walls and moats to ensure a solid defence.
10 今伐韓，	If you attack Hán now,
未可一年而滅，	you cannot destroy it within a year,
拔一城而退，	but if you take out one city and then withdraw,
則權輕於天下，	you will be regarded as a lightweight by all,
天下摧我兵矣。	and the states of world will crush our forces.[4]

---

4 It is remarkable that Han Fei would use the first person like this, referring to the armies of Qin as "our forces."

存韓 PRESERVING HÁN   21

15	韓叛，	If Hán rebels,
	則魏應之，	Wei will respond,
	趙據齊以為援，	and Zhao will be assisted by Qi.
	如此，	Under such conditions,
	則以韓、魏資趙假齊，	Hán and Wei will help Zhao obtain support from Qi,
20	以固其從，	so as to strengthen its Vertical Alliance,
	而以與爭強，	and on this basis they will compete [with Qin] for supremacy.
	趙之福而秦之禍也。	This would be good fortune for Zhao, but disaster for Qin.
	夫進而擊趙不能取，	Now, if you advance to strike Zhao, but are unable to take it,
	退而攻韓弗能拔，	and if, when you withdraw to attack Hán, you are unable to overcome it,
25	則陷銳之卒勩於野戰，	then your crack soldiers will become burnt out in open field battles
	負任之旅罷於內攻，	and your transport troops will exhaust themselves providing supplies,
	則合群苦弱以敵而共二萬乘，	and this means that you will gather an army which is embittered and weakened, in order to face an enemy totalling twenty thousand war chariots.[5]
	非所以亡韓之心也。	This is not an approach that will ensure the demise of Hán.
	均如貴臣之計，	If you follow the plans of the distinguished minister,
30	則秦必為天下兵質矣。	Qin will surely become the target of all troops in the world,
	陛下雖以金石相弊，	and then, even though Your Majesty is as long-lived as metal and stone,
	則兼天下之日未也。	the day when you can unify All-under-Heaven will never come.

17 Reading 援 as 原 with 吳汝綸; 陳奇猷 and 校注 regard this reading as plausible; 張覺 suggests that 原 may mean 'to rely on' and 陳奇猷 suggests that 原 may be a mistake for 厚.　28 （趙）〔韓〕(校注 23).　28 （人）〔臣〕(校注 23).

---

5 The combined forces of Hán and Zhao, two powerful "ten-thousand chariot" states.

HF 2.1.3 (*Xilun* 28, *Xin jiaozhu* 34)

今賤臣之愚計：
使人使荊，
重幣用事之臣，
明趙之所以欺秦者；
與魏質以安其心，

從韓而伐趙，
趙雖與齊為一，
不足患也。
二國事畢，
則韓可以移書定也。

是我一舉，
二國有亡形，

則荊、魏又必自服矣。

故曰：
"兵者，
凶器也。"
不可不審用也。
以秦與趙敵，
衡加以齊，
今又背韓，
而未有以堅荊、魏之心。

夫一戰而不勝，

則禍構矣。

計者，
所以定事也，

Now, your lowly servant's inept plan is as follows:
Send an envoy to Jing (Chu)
to offer lavish gifts to the ministers in charge,
and explain how Zhao has crossed Qin,
and exchange hostages with Wei in order to put their minds at ease.

If you cause Hán to follow you and attack Zhao,
then, even if Zhao and Qi unite,
this will be no cause for concern.
When the business concerning those two states has been concluded,
the matter of Hán can be settled by the dispatch of a missive.

So, when through one action on our part,
these two states (Zhao and Qi) are pushed to the brink of ruin,
then Jing (Chu) and Wei are bound to submit to us on their own accord.

So it is said:
"Arms
are inauspicious implements."[6]
You must deploy them judiciously.
If Qin opposed Zhao,
and Qi were added lengthwise (as a shield for Zhao),
and if now moreover you turn back on Hán,
without having any plans to strengthen ties with Jing (Chu) and Wei,
then, if in a single battle (against Hán) you are not victorious,
disaster will ensue.

Plans
are the means by which affairs are settled;

---

6   Compare *Laozi* 31.

存韓 PRESERVING HÁN

不可不察也。	they must be investigated.
趙、秦強弱，	Who is stronger, Zhao or Qin,
在今年耳。	will be decided within this year.
且趙與諸侯陰謀久矣。	Moreover, Zhao has long made secret plans (against Qin) with the regional lords.
30 夫一動而弱於諸侯，	if now, in one move, you appear weak to the regional lords,
危事也；	this is a dangerous matter;
為計而使諸侯有意我之心，	if you make plans that cause the regional lords to have schemes against us,[7]
至殆也。	this is absolutely lethal.
見二疏，	To exhibit these two instances of neglect
35 非所以強於諸侯也。	is not how to appear strong to the regional lords.
臣竊願陛下之幸熟圖之！	It is my humble hope that Your Majesty will grant this matter your careful attention.
夫攻伐而使從者間焉，	For if you launch an attack (on Hán) and cause the Vertical Alliance to avail themselves of this opportunity,
不可悔也。	it will be too late for regret.

1 之（遇）愚(校注 23). 3 張抄 has 弊 for 幣; all other editions have 幣. 10（轉）〔韓〕(校注 23, following 顧廣圻). 19 衡 is read as 橫, with 尹桐陽. 27（韓）〔趙〕(校注 23, following 蒲坂圓). 32（伐）〔我〕(校注 23). 37 We have 夫, with 藏本、張本、陳本 and 王先謙、陳奇猷、張覺; C lacks 夫, with 吳本、張抄、錢抄、趙本 and 校注 16. 37（聞）〔間〕(校注 23).

Memorial by Li Si to the King of Qin

HF 2.2.1 (*Xilun* 29, *Xin jiaozhu* 37)

詔以韓客之所上書，	By decree, the memorial submitted by the guest from Hán
書言韓子之未可舉，	(a memorial proposing that the Hán cannot yet be successfully attacked)
下臣斯。	has been remanded to your servant [Li] Si.

---

7 They will think that Qin is weak and can be opposed.

	臣斯甚以為不然。	Your servant [Li] Si strongly disagrees.
5	秦之有韓，	Qin's relation to Hán
	若人之有腹心之病也，	is like a man's relation to an illness in his stomach.
	虛處則恟然，	If he lives quietly, it just feels painful,
	若居濕地，	but if he stays in a damp place,
	著而不去，	it becomes virulent and will not go away,
10	以極走，	and if he runs fast,
	則發矣。	the disease will break out openly.
	夫韓雖臣於秦，	Although Hán behaves as a servant to Qin,
	未嘗不為秦病，	it will never cease to be a plague for Qin.
	今若有卒報之事，	If at the present moment there should come an urgent report about some affair,
15	韓不可信也。	Hán is not to be trusted.
	秦與趙為難，	Between Qin and Zhao there is trouble;
	荊蘇使齊，	Jing Su is on a mission to Qi,
	未知何如。	but we still do not know the outcome.[8]
	以臣觀之，	In my view,
20	則齊、趙之交未必以荊蘇絕也；	the relations between Qi and Zhao will not necessarily be disrupted through the efforts of Jing Su,
	若不絕，	and if they are not,
	是悉秦而應二萬乘也。	then it will take all the resources of Qin to resist two states each mustering ten thousand chariots.
	夫韓不服秦之義而服於強也，	Now, Hán will not submit to Qin's rightful demands, but it will submit to its strength.
	今專於齊、趙，	If we now concentrate solely on Qi and Zhao,
25	則韓必為腹心之病而發矣。	Hán will surely become an illness in the stomach which will break out openly.
	韓與荊有謀，	If there is a conspiracy between Hán and Jing (Chu)
	諸侯應之，	and the regional lords follow suit,
	則秦必復見崤塞之患。	then Qin will surely encounter again a disaster like that at the Yao Pass.[9]

4 〔臣斯〕(校注 23, with 陳本).　22 （趙）〔秦〕(校注 23, following 王渭, quoted by 顧廣圻).

8　Nothing is known about Jing Su. He appears to have been Qin's envoy to Qi.
9　The phrase "Disaster of Yao Pass" possibly conflates two events. One is Qin's disastrous defeat by Jin at Yao (or Xiao, 殽 or 崤), the location between the eponymous mountain ridge and the

存韓 PRESERVING HÁN

HF 2.2.2 (*Xilun* 31, *Xin jiaozhu* 39)

非之來也，	[Han] Fei's arrival
未必不以其能存韓也、為重於韓也。	is perhaps connected with his ability to work for the survival of Hán and to make Hán gain in importance.
辯說屬辭，	Advancing persuasions and weaving words,
飾非詐謀，	he decorates falsehoods and plans deceitfully.
5 以釣利於秦，	He angles for advantage from Qin
而以韓利闚陛下。	and scrutinises Your Majesty with Hán's advantage in mind.
夫秦、韓之交親，	If the relations between Qin and Hán grow closer,
則非重矣，	Han Fei will gain in influence.
此自便之計也。	These are plans of personal advantage.[10]

HF 2.2.3 (*Xilun* 32, *Xin jiaozhu* 40)

臣視非之言，	I, your subject, have examined Han Fei's proposals.
文其淫說靡辯，	He expresses well his seductive explanations and elegant arguments
才甚，	and is very talented.
臣恐陛下淫非之辯而聽其盜心，	I fear that Your Majesty may be seduced by Han Fei's arguments, and that you may follow his thievish designs,
5 因不詳察事情。	if you do not examine closely the actual conditions.
今以臣愚議：	Now, I have an inept suggestion:
秦發兵而未名所伐，	If Qin sends out its troops without declaring who is to be attacked,

---

Yellow River, either in today's Sanmenxia Municiplity 三門峽市 or Luoning County 洛寧縣, in 627 (*Zuozhuan* Xi 33.3). The second is a lesser-known assault on Qin by members of the vertical alliance in 296, in which the Hán troops allegedly fought at the forefront (*Zhanguo ce* 18.11 ["Zhao 趙 1"]). This latter event is later referred to by Li Si in his memorial to the King of Hán.

10 This is precisely the accusation launched in *Han Feizi* (e.g. chapter 49.14) against the travelling persuaders: they seek primarily personal gain, manipulating inter-state relations to their own advantage.

則韓之用事者以事秦為計矣。	then the superiors of Hán will make serving Qin its strategy.
臣斯請往見韓王，	I, your servant Si, ask to go see the King of Hán
10　使來入見，	to cause him to come to Qin for an audience.
大王見，	When Your Majesty receives him,
因內其身而勿遣，	you should detain him and not send him off again.
稍召其社稷之臣，	Then one by one summon the leading ministers of [Hán's] altars of soil and grain,[11]
以與韓人為市，	and negotiate a deal with them (to release their king) –
15　則韓可深割也。	and then you can carve deep into Hán territory.
因令蒙武發東郡之卒，	Subsequently you should order Meng Wu to send forth soldiers from the Eastern Commandery,
闚兵於境上而未名所之，	and let [your enemies] get a glimpse of the troops on the border, but without declaring where they are headed.
則齊人懼而從蘇之計。	Then the people of Qi will become scared and follow [Jing] Su's plan (of severing relations between Qi and Zhao).
是我兵未出而勁韓以威擒，	In this way, without our troops leaving the country, Hán, tough as it is, will be captured by sheer intimidation,
20　強齊以義從矣。	and mighty Qi will follow us on account of our just cause.
聞於諸侯也，	Once this comes to the attention of the other regional lords,
趙氏破膽，	Zhao will find its fighting spirit crushed,
荊人狐疑，	and the people of Jing (Chu) will be assailed by doubts –
必有忠計。	they will then surely make plans that are loyal (to us).
25　荊人不動，	If the people of Jing (Chu) do not move against us,
魏不足患也，	Wei will be no cause for worry,

---

[11] The "ministers of the altars" are the chief ministers who are responsible for the state's very survival. The preservation of the altars of soil and grain symbolised the state's continued existence.

則諸侯可蠶食而盡，	and so the regional lords can be nibbled up in the fashion of a silkworm,
趙氏可得與敵矣。	and we can rival Zhao.
願陛下幸察愚臣之計，	I hope Your Majesty will grace this inept servant's plan with your attention,
30　無忽。	and not ignore it.

16 We emend 象武 to 蒙武, with 史記 mention, following 王渭, quoted by 顧廣圻; 校注 18–19 also suggests this emendation. C has 象武, with all editions, 陳奇猷 and 張覺.

HF 2.2.4 (*Xilun* 33, *Xin jiaozhu* 41)

秦遂遣斯使韓也。¹²　　Qin subsequently sent [Li] Si as an envoy to Hán.

Letter conveyed by Li Si to the King of Hán

HF 2.3.0 (*Xilun* 33, *Xin jiaozhu* 42)

李斯往詔韓王，	Li Si went to deliver a message to the King of Hán.
未得見，	Having not yet obtained an audience,
因上書曰：	he submitted a memorial which read,

HF 2.3.1 (*Xilun* 34, *Xin jiaozhu* 42)

昔秦、韓勠力一意，	In former times, Qin and Hán joined forces in common purpose,
以不相侵，	and since they did not encroach upon one another,
天下莫敢犯，	no one in the realm dared to oppose them.
如此者數世矣。	The situation has been like this for several generations.
5　前時五諸侯嘗相與共伐韓，	Not long ago, five regional lords launched a combined attack on Hán,

---

12　This is an editorial remark by the ancient editors of the *Han Feizi*; ditto for the next sentences in 2.3.0.

秦發兵以救之。	and Qin sent forces to come to its rescue.[13]
韓居中國，	Hán is situated among the central states;
地不能滿千里，	its territory does not quite reach one thousand *li* square.
而所以得與諸侯班位於天下、君臣相保者，	The reason why Hán can be ranked among the regional lords in the realm and that its rulers and ministers are able to stay alive,
10 以世世相教事秦之力也，	is that for generations they have taught each other to serve the superior power of Qin.
先時五諸侯共伐秦，	In the past, when the five regional lords launched a combined attack on Qin,[14]
韓反與諸侯先為鴈行以嚮秦軍於關下矣。	Hán on the contrary led the formation of the regional lords, facing the forces of Qin below the [Hangu] Pass.
諸侯兵困力極，	The army of the regional lords was hard-pressed and its strength exhausted,
無奈何，	and it had no way out,
15 諸侯兵罷。	and so it retreated.
杜倉相秦，	When Du Cang was prime minister in Qin,[15]
起兵發將以報天下之怨而先攻荊。	he raised an army and sent out generals to avenge the resentment caused by all states of the realm, and he first launched an attack against Jing (Chu).
荊令尹患之，	The prime minister of Jing (Chu) was worried
曰：	and said:
20 '夫韓以秦為不義，	"Hán considers Qin unjust,
而與秦兄弟共苦天下。	yet maintains brotherly relations with Qin, together causing bitter suffering to the realm.
已又背秦，	Not long afterwards, Hán has turned its back on Qin
先為鴈行以攻關，	and leads the formation of troops to attack the [Hangu] Pass.
韓則居中國，	Hán has its place among the central states,

---

13 In all likelihood this refers to Qin's intervention to save its ally, Hán, from the combined attack of Wei and Zhao in 273 (the Huayang campaign, for more on which see chapters 1.3 note 16, and 50.5 note 17). However, Li Si surely exaggerates: there was never a five-state coalition against Hán.

14 There were two attacks of Qin by Hán, Wei, and Qi, namely in 298 and 296. In the latter, other states may have joined (probably Zhao and either Song or Zhongshan), but there is some confusion in the sources.

15 Nothing is known about Du Cang.

存韓 PRESERVING HÁN

25 展轉不可知。' — but it is so inconstant that no one knows what it will do next."
天下共割韓上地十城以謝秦, — Then all states in the realm together cut off ten cities from Hán's Shang territory,[16]
解其兵。 — so that it withdrew its troops.[17]
夫韓嘗一背秦而國迫地侵, — Once Hán had turned against Qin, its state was pressured and its territory encroached upon,
兵弱至今, — and its troops have since been weak.
30 所以然者, — The reason for this is that
聽姦臣之浮說, — you listened to the groundless persuasions of treacherous ministers
不權事實, — and did not weigh the facts.
故雖殺戮姦臣, — In this way, even if you were to execute your treacherous ministers,
不能使韓復強。 — you would not be able to restore Hán to its former strength.

12 (關)〔關〕(校注 23).   17 (失)〔先〕(校注 23).   31 (人)〔臣〕(校注 23).

HF 2.3.2 (*Xilun* 36, *Xin jiaozhu* 44)

今趙欲聚兵士, — Now Zhao plans to amass its officers and men,
卒以秦為事, — and all of a sudden makes trouble for Qin.
使人來借道, — They have sent someone here to ask for passage,
言欲伐秦, — stating that they intend to attack Qin,
5 其勢必先韓而後秦。 — but, given the circumstances, they will surely take Hán first and then Qin.
且臣聞之: — Moreover, I have heard that
'脣亡, — "When the lips are gone,
則齒寒。' — the teeth become cold."[18]
夫秦、韓不得無同憂, — Qin and Hán are stuck sharing the same troubles:

---

16 Shangdi 上地 stands for Shangdang 上黨 Commandery, to the west of Taihang Mountains, Shanxi. This territory was long coveted by Qin (chapter 1, note 20).

17 The sources are too confused to determine whether or not Li Si's version of these events is reliable.

18 This famous saying is first attested in *Zuozhuan* (Xi 5.8), and repeated in many Warring States-period texts (see also *Han Feizi* 10.5). The background was Jin's attack on the state of Guo 虢/郭. Jin asked for passage through the territory of Guo's northern neighbour, the state of Yu 虞, and the ruler of Yu did not heed a warning that this would endanger

10	其形可見。	how things stand with them is clear to anyone.
	魏欲發兵以攻韓，	When Wei intended to send forth its troops and attack Hán,
	秦使人將使者於韓。	Qin dispatched someone to turn the Wei envoy over to Hán.
	今秦王使臣斯來而不得見，	Now the King of Qin has ordered me, your servant [Li] Si, to come here, but I have been unable to obtain an audience.
	恐左右襲曩姦臣之計，	I fear that your advisers carry on the plots of your treacherous ministers of the past
15	使韓復有亡地之患。	and again make Hán suffer a loss of territory.
	臣斯不得見，	If I do not obtain an audience,
	請歸報，	I request to return and report on my mission –
	秦、韓之交必絕矣。	then the relations between Qin and Hán will surely be severed.
	斯之來使，	I, Si, have come on this mission
20	以奉秦王之歡心，	in order to offer the good will of the King of Qin,
	願效便計，	hoping to propose a strategy that is advantageous [to Hán].
	豈陛下所以逆賤臣者邪？	Can it really be that Your Majesty rejects a humble servant in this way?
	臣斯願得一見，	I, your servant [Li] Si, hope to obtain a single audience,
	前進道愚計，	to step forward and present my inept plan;
25	退就葅戮，	after I have stepped back, you may punish me by making mincemeat of me.
	願陛下有意焉。	It is my hope that Your Majesty will give this matter your full attention.
	今殺臣於韓，	If you now kill me, your servant, here in Hán,
	則大王不足以強，	that will not suffice to strengthen Your Majesty,
	若不聽臣之計，	but if you do not listen to my plans,
30	則禍必搆矣。	that will spell certain disaster for you.
	秦發兵不留行，	Once Qin has sent out troops, they will not stop marching,
	而韓之社稷憂矣。	and Hán's altars of soil and grain will be a cause for worry.

---

his own country. He allowed the Jin army to cross through Yu's territory and Yu was duly conquered by Jin. Li Si warns that Zhao plans to eliminate Hán rather than fight with Qin.

存韓 PRESERVING HÁN

臣斯暴身於韓之市，	Once my body is exposed in the Hán market,
則雖欲察賤臣愚忠之計，	although you might want to look into this lowly servant's inept but loyal plan,
35　不可得已。	you will not be able to do so.
邊鄙殘，	When your border regions are being decimated
國固守，	and the capital has to be resolutely defended,
鼓鐸之聲於耳，	when the sound of drums and gongs resound in your ears,
而乃用臣斯之計，	then using your humble servant's plans
40　晚矣。	will be too late.
且夫韓之兵於天下可知也，	Moreover, the condition of the Hán troops is known throughout the realm,
今又背強秦。	but in spite of this you turn your back on mighty Qin.
夫棄城而敗軍，	Once you have abandoned your city walls and lost your army,
則反掖之寇必襲城矣。	thieves in your immediate entourage will scale down the city walls.
45　城盡則聚散，	If the city walls are all gone, settlements will be dispersed,
聚散則無軍矣，	and if settlements are dispersed, there will be no army any more.
城固守，	If the cities (on the other hand) are firmly defended,
則秦必興兵而圍王一都，	Qin is bound to raise troops to besiege Your Majesty's capital.
道不通，	When the roads are blocked,
50　則難必，	trouble is sure to arrive,
謀，	and even if you lay plans,
其勢不救，	the situation will be beyond repair,
左右計之者不用，	and any plots of your advisers will be useless.
願陛下熟圖之。	I hope Your Majesty will consider this matter carefully.
55　若臣斯之所言有不應事實者，	If my proposal does not agree with the realities of the situation,
願大王幸使得畢辭於前，	I hope that your Your Majesty, will graciously allow me to finish my presentation in front of you.
乃就吏誅不晚也。	Then afterwards it will not be too late to go to the law officials and be punished.

秦王飲食不甘，	The King of Qin does not find his food and drink palatable
遊觀不樂，	and does not enjoy himself on his sightseeing tours.
60　意專在圖趙，	His mind is fixed on making plans against Zhao.
使臣斯來言，	He ordered me to come and make these proposals,
願得身見，	hoping that I could obtain a personal audience,
因急與陛下有計也。	since I urgently wish to deliberate together with Your Majesty.
今使臣不通，	Now, if you prevent me from communicating this message,
65　則韓之信未可知也，	it would mean that there would be uncertainty concerning Hán's good faith;
夫秦必釋趙之患而移兵於韓，	Qin would surely disregard the threat from Zhao and move its forces against Hán.
願陛下幸復察圖之，	I hope Your Majesty will grace this matter with your attention
而賜臣報決。	and honour me, your servant, by informing me of your verdict.

16 〔得〕(校注 23).　46 〔聚散〕(校注 23).　62 〔見〕(校注 23).

CHAPTER 3

難言 Problems with Speaking up

HF 3.1 (*Xilun* 39, *Xin jiaozhu* 48)

臣非非難言也，	It is not as if I, your subject Fei,[1] is someone who has trouble speaking –
所以難言者：	but the reasons why someone might have trouble speaking up are these:
言順比滑澤，	If your proposals are agreeable and mellifluous,
洋洋纚纚然，	voluminous and effuse,
5　則見以為華而不實；	then they will be considered pretentious and lacking in substance.
敦厚恭祗，	If you are sincere and respectful,
鯁固慎完，	firm and cautious,
則見以為拙而不倫；	then you will be considered inept and wishy-washy.
多言繁稱，	If you speak too much and make frequent quotations,
10　連類比物，	lining up comparable categories and contrasting the nuances of things,
則見以為虛而無用；	then you will be considered superficial and useless.
總微說約，	If you come up with subtle summaries and concise explanations,
徑省而不飾，	all relevant and unadorned,
則見以為劌而不辯；	then you will be considered rough-hewn and dull.
15　激急親近，	If you are brisk and go right to the point,
探知人情，	and pry deeply into the motivations of others,
則見以為譖而不讓；	then you will be considered slanderous and unrelenting.
閎大廣博，	If you are comprehensive and wide-ranging,
妙遠不測，	far-reaching and unfathomable,
20　則見以為夸而無用；	then you will be considered grandiloquent and irrelevant.

1　This is one of very few chapters in *Han Feizi* (aside from 2 and 42) in which Han Fei is identified.

家計小談，	If your talk is about petty family matters,
以具數言，	and you speak of them giving their exact number,
則見以為陋；	then you will be considered simple-minded.
言而近世，	If your speeches keep to what is trendy,
25 辭不悖逆，	and your formulations are uncontroversial,
則見以為貪生而諛上；	then you will be held to fawn to your superiors for fear of your life.
言而遠俗，	If your speeches diverge from the accepted,
詭躁人間[A 元/山 krian/kǎn]，	and artfully upset common sense,
則見以為誕[A 元/旱 danx/dân]；	then you will be considered bizarre.
30 捷敏辯給，	If you are quick-witted, with a ready supply of arguments,
繁於文采[B 之/海 tshəgx/tshậi]，	full of rhetorical flourishes,
則見以為史[B 之/止 sljəgx/ṣï]；	then you will be considered a pettifogger.[2]
殊釋文學，	If you pointedly reject literary studies,
以質信言，	and lend credibility to your speech through straight talk,
35 則見以為鄙；	then you will be considered crude.[3]
時稱詩書[C 魚/魚 sthjag/śjwo]，	If you often quote the *Poems* and the *Documents*[4]
道法往古[C 魚/姥 kagx/kuo]，	and talk of taking antiquity as your model,
則見以為誦。	then you will be regarded as one who just reels off what he has memorised.
此臣非之所以難言而重患也。	These are reasons why I, your subject [Han] Fei, find it hard to speak, and they make me seriously worried.

5 張抄 has 光 for 見; 吳本、張木、陳本、趙本 have 見.　**6** C emends 敦祗恭厚 of all editions to 敦厚恭祗.　**34** C corrects 信 to 性, regarding 信 as mistaken. We have 信, with 吳本、張抄、錢抄、趙本 and with 校注, 陳奇猷, 張覺. 藏本、張本、陳本 have 性.

2　*Shi* 史, often translated as "historian," was the designation for an archivist and a scribe (with other concomitant duties) from Shang times onwards. In late Warring States times the word could occasionally have a pejorative meaning, "[mere] scribe." Recall that scribes, essential as they were for bureaucracy's functioning (Yates 2014), occupied mostly low positions in the governing apparatus (see also Selbitschka 2018).

3　Throughout his texts, Han Fei tends to use every opportunity to denigrate literary pursuits. In this context, however, he does stress the importance of literary excellence. Zheng Liangshu (1993: 20) takes this as evidence that the present chapter belongs to the early period of Han Fei's career.

4　*Poems* and *Documents* were two major canonical works cited as repository of the ancients' wisdom. These texts are currently associated primarily with the Confucians, but in the Warring States period they were a common point of reference for literati of any persuasion.

難言 PROBLEMS WITH SPEAKING UP

HF 3.2 (*Xilun* 41, *Xin jiaozhu* 52)

故度量雖正，	Thus, even though your assessments might be correct,
未必聽也；	you will not necessarily be heard,
義理雖全，	and even though you may be in full command of all the principles of righteousness,
未必用也。	you will not necessarily be employed.
5　大王若以此不信，	And if Your Majesty considers what is said unreliable
則小者以為毀訾誹謗，	then, at the very least, you shall be maligned and slandered,
大者患禍災害死亡及其身。	and, at worst, troubles, misfortune, disaster, harm, will be your lot.
故子胥善謀而吳戮之，	Thus Zixu was good at making plans, but the state of Wu had him executed;[5]
仲尼善說而匡圍之，	Confucius was good at persuading, but the people of Kuang laid siege to him.[6]
10　管夷吾實賢而魯囚之。	Guan Yiwu (Guan Zhong) was truly worthy, but Lu incarcerated him.[7]
故此三大夫豈不賢哉？	Does it mean that these three grandees were unworthy?
而三君不明也。	No, but their three rulers were not clear-sighted.[8]
上古有湯，	In highest antiquity there was Tang,
至聖也；	the pinnacle of sagehood.
15　伊尹，	(Tang's minister) Yi Yin,

---

[5] Wu Zixu, the architect of the state of Wu's rise to eminence, became increasingly critical of the policy choices of his employer, King Fuchai 吳王夫差 (r. 495–473). Angered by Zixu's criticism, Fuchai ordered him to commit suicide in 484. In the Warring States period Wu Zixu became the paragon of loyalty.

[6] See *Lunyu* 9.15. Confucius's trouble in Kuang had nothing to do with any ungrateful employer.

[7] At the beginning of his illustrious career, Guan Zhong, the would-be architect of Lord Huan of Qi's 齊桓公 (r. 685–643) hegemony, supported Lord Huan's rival, Prince Jiu 公子糾, who was backed by the state of Lu (see also chapter 23, note 24). Having overpowered Prince Jiu, Lord Huan demanded that Lu hand Guan Zhong over. Upon his arrival in Qi, however, Guan Zhong was released and appointed to an important position.

[8] Note the weakness of Han Fei's examples. Only Wu Zixu was the victim of his ruler. Confucius' misfortunes at Kuang and Guan Zhong's imprisonment in Lu have nothing to do with their rulers' inability to heed their advice.

至智也。	the pinnacle of intelligence.⁹
夫至智說至聖，	Now, the pinnacle of intelligence was advising the pinnacle of sagehood,
然且七十說而不受，	but even after seventy attempts, Yi Yin's advice was not accepted.
身執鼎俎為庖宰，	He had to hold the cauldrons and the cutting boards himself while serving as a cook,
20 昵近習親，	in order to draw near to Tang's inner circle and gain confidence –
而湯乃僅知其賢而用之。	only then did Tang appreciate his worth and employ him.¹⁰
故曰：	So it is said:
以至智說至聖，	even when the pinnacle of intelligence gives advice to the pinnacle of sagehood,
未必至而見受，	he will not necessarily be accepted as soon as he shows up –
25 伊尹說湯是也；	Yi Yin's attempt to advise Tang proves the point.
以智說愚必不聽，	When an intelligent person gives advice to a stupid person, he will certainly not be heeded –
文王說紂是也。	King Wen's advice to Zhòu proves the point.
故文王說紂而紂囚之；	So King Wen tried to advise Zhòu, but Zhòu incarcerated him.
翼侯炙；	The Marquis of Yi was roasted;
30 鬼侯臘；	the Marquis of Gui was made into dried meat;
比干剖心；	Bigan had his heart carved out;
梅伯醢；	the Earl of Mei was pickled;¹¹
夷吾束縛；	Yiwu [Guan Zhong] was thrown in fetters;¹²

---

9   Tang the Successful 成湯 was the founder of the Shang dynasty, while Yi Yin was his most famous aide.

10 The story of Yi Yin's beginnings as a humble cook and getting close to Tang is widespread in Warring States texts. No text, though, mentions the attempted "seventy persuasions" presented to Tang by Yi Yin.

11 The four men were victims of Shang's tyrant, Zhòu. The Marquis of Yi 翼侯 is probably the same person identified in *Shiji* 3 as Marquis of E 鄂侯, and Marquis of Gui is probably the same as Marquis of Jiu 九侯. Once two of the "three eminences" at the Shang court (the third being the would-be King Wen of Zhou), they were executed by Zhòu. Bigan was Zhòu's uncle, who remonstrated vehemently and was killed by the tyrant. Less is known of the Earl of Mei.

12 See note 7 above.

難言 PROBLEMS WITH SPEAKING UP

而曹覊奔陳； Ji of Cao had to flee to Chen;[13]
35 伯里子道乞； Master Baili begged in the streets;[14]
傅說轉鬻； Fu Yue was sold from one man to the next;[15]
孫子臏腳於魏； Sunzi [Sun Bin] had his kneecaps sliced off in Wei;[16]

吳起抆泣於岸門， Wu Qi wiped away his tears at Anmen,
痛西河之為秦， distressed that the Xihe region would belong to Qin,
40 卒枝解於楚； and was finally dismembered in Chu.[17]
公叔痤言國器反為悖， Gongshu Cuo spoke of "a talent fit to rule a state," but was considered insane,
公孫鞅奔秦； and Gongsun Yang had to flee to Qin;[18]
關龍逄斬； Guanlong Pang was beheaded;[19]
萇弘分胣； Chang Hong was disembowelled;[20]

---

13 Ji was apparently the Crown Prince of Cao. According to the *Gongyang zhuan*, he fled to Chen in 670 because his multiple remonstrances were ignored.

14 Baili Xi 百里奚, an advisor to Lord Mu of Qin 秦穆公 (r. 659–621) allegedly sold himself as a bondservant and tended oxen so as to get in contact with Lord Mu. For doubts over the historicity of Baili Xi, see Thatcher 1988. It is not clear when he was active, if at all, as a beggar.

15 Though Fu Yue is mentioned throughout the literature as a worthy advisor to King Wuding of Shang 商王武丁 (late 13th century), this is the only place that says he was sold from one person to another as a slave.

16 Sun Bin 孫臏 (fourth century), the famous strategist, had his kneecaps amputated in Wei. This mutilation did not prevent him from avenging himself by defeating the Wei army in 341.

17 When Wu Qi, a famous statesmen and military strategist, served in Wei, he was deployed to guard the Xihe region, to the west of the Yellow River. According to *Lüshi chunqiu* 11.5 ("Chang jian" 長見), when he was slandered and replaced, he wept at the site of Anmen, predicting that soon after his replacement the area would be seized by Qin. He then left to Chu, where his reforms aroused resentment among the leading nobles, who had him killed in 381.

18 According to *Lüshi chunqiu* 11.5 ("Chang jian"), repeated in *Shiji* 68: 2228, the Wei prime minister Gongshu Cuo recommended on his deathbed that Gongsun Yang (the future Shang Yang – a "talent fit to rule a state") be either employed as chief minister or executed, so as to prevent him from harming Wei in the future. Lord (later King) Hui of Wei 魏惠公/王 (r. 369–319) considered this advice the nonsense of a dying man and ignored it. Shang Yang made great career in Qin, strengthening it at the expense of Wei.

19 Guanlong Pang was a righteous remonstrator at the court of Xia's tyrant Jie 桀, who had him executed. He is typically presented as a parallel figure to Bigan of the Shang court (note 11 above).

20 Chang Hong, a prescient statesman at the Zhou court in the late sixth century, acquired in the Warring States-period texts the attributes of a superhuman sage. *Zuozhuan* narrates

45	尹子穽於棘；	Yinzi was thrown into a bramble pit;
	司馬子期死而浮於江；	Sima Ziqi floated dead down the Yangzi River;[21]
	田明辜射；	Tian Ming was drawn and quartered;[22]
	宓子賤、西門豹不鬥而死人手；	Fu Zijian and Ximen Bao never quarrelled with anyone, but died at the hands of others;[23]
	董安于死而陳於市；	Dong Anyu died and had his body exposed in the marketplace;[24]
50	宰予不免於田常；	Zai Yu could not escape from Tian Chang;[25]
	范雎折脅於魏。	and Fan Sui had his ribs broken in Wei.[26]
	此十數人者，	These more than a dozen of people
	皆世之仁賢忠良有道術之士也，	were each the most humane, worthy, loyal, and skilled gentlemen of their times, and they were all in possession of techniques of the Way,
	不幸而遇悖亂闇惑之主而死。	and yet they encountered perverse and benighted rulers and so unfortunately suffered death.
55	然則雖賢聖不能逃死亡避戮辱者，	That even the worthy and sagacious cannot escape death, execution, and defilement,
	何也？	why is that?
	則愚者難說也，	It is because stupid rulers are difficult to advise.
	故君子難言也。	That is why the noble man finds it hard to offer proposals.
	且至言忤於耳而倒於心，	Moreover, the best words grate upon the ear and go against the heart:

---

only that he was killed as part of internecine struggle in the state of Jin (to whose nobles he was connected by marriage). It is not clear to which version of Chang's death Han Fei refers here.

21 Ziqi or Prince Jie 公子結 (d. 479) was the Minister of War of Chu. He was murdered by the rebellious Sheng, Duke of Bai, whom Ziqi initially patronised (chapter 21, note 45). Ziqi is said to have been murdered at the court of Chu and not thrown into the Yangzi (*Zuozhuan*, Ai 16.5).

22 Nothing is known about this person.

23 Fu (or Mi) Zijian was one of Confucius' disciples; Ximen Bao (fl. 400) was one of the model administrators in the service of Wei. Nothing is known of how they died.

24 Dong Anyu (d. 496) was a household servant of the Zhao lineage in Jin. He volunteered to become a scapegoat in order to help his master overpower his enemies amid the domestic turmoil in Jin. See *Zuozhuan*, Ding 13.2 and 14.2.

25 Zai Yu, whose appellative was Ziwo 子我, was a disciple of Confucius who served the Tian lineage in Qi. In all likelihood, the story of his martyrdom is a result of a misunderstanding: Tian Chang, the notorious usurper (of whom more in chapter 7, note 3), killed another person with the appellative Ziwo (that person was Kan Zhi 闞止; *Zuozhuan*, Ai 14.3).

26 At the beginning of his career in Wei, Fan Sui (d. 255) was slandered by his rival and severely beaten. In due course, he became head of the Qin government.

難言 PROBLEMS WITH SPEAKING UP　　　　　　　　　　　　　39

60　非賢聖莫能聽，　　　　　　　no one but a worthy or sagely ruler can heed them.
　　願大王熟察之也。　　　　　　I hope Your Majesty may consider this carefully.

28〔而紂〕(校注 29).　　38（收）〔扠〕(校注 29, following 盧文弨).　　41 張抄 has 座 for 座; all editions except 吳鼎本 have 座.　　47 射 is read as 磔, with 俞樾.　　58（不少）〔難言〕(校注 29).

CHAPTER 4

愛臣 Favoured Ministers

HF 4.1 (*Xilun* 48, *Xin jiaozhu* 59)

愛臣太親[A 真/真 tshjin/tshjěn]，
必危其身[A 真/真 sthjin/śjěn]；
人臣太貴[B 微/未 kwjədh/kjwěi]，
必易主位[B 微/至 gwjədh/jwi]；
5 主妾無等[C 之/海 təgx/tậi]，

必危嫡子[C 之/止 tsjəgx/tsï]；
兄弟不服[D 之/屋 bjək/bjuk]，
必危社稷[D 之/職 tsjək/tsjək]。

臣聞：
10 千乘之君無備[E 之/至 bjiəgh/bji]，

必有百乘之臣在其側[E 之/職 tsrjək/tsjək]，

以徙其民而傾其國[E 之/德 kwək/kwək]；

萬乘之君無備[E 之/至 bjiəgh/bji]，

必有千乘之家在其側[E 之/職 tsrjək/tsjək]，

15 以徙其威而傾其國[E 之/德 kwək/kwək]。

	When your favoured ministers are too close, they will assuredly endanger your person.
	When a minister is too highly honoured, he will assuredly take the ruler's place.
	When there is no distinction in rank among the ruler's wife and his consorts, this will necessarily endanger his heir.
	When a ruler's brothers are not submissive, this will necessarily endanger the altars of soil and grain.
	I, your subject, have heard[1] that when the ruler of a thousand chariot state fails to take precautions, there is bound to come, by his side, a minister with a hundred chariots who will shift the allegiance of [the ruler's] people and overturn his state.[2] When the ruler with ten thousand chariots fails to take precautions, there is bound to be, by his side, a grandee with a thousand chariots who will dislodge [the ruler's] authority and overturn his state.[3]

---

1 Han Fei's self-reference as *chen* 臣 "I, your subject," suggests that the present chapter was designed as a memorial to a king, probably the king of Hán. Ditto for chapters 3, 6, 19, and 51.

2 A "thousand-chariot" state is a medium-sized state. Counting the power of ministerial houses by their number of chariots goes back to the aristocratic Springs-and-Autumns period (770–453), when ministers possessed autonomous allotments that functioned as mini-states. By Han Fei's time, this situation was long gone, just as the number of a state's chariots had long ceased to be an indicator of its military power.

3 The similarity to *Mengzi* 1.1 is so striking that one is tempted to read "I, your subject, have heard" as a reference to that text.

愛臣 FAVOURED MINISTERS   41

是以姦臣蕃息[E 之/職 sjək/sjək]，
主道衰亡。

Thus, when wicked ministers proliferate, the way of the ruler declines.

是故諸侯之博大[F 祭/泰 dadh/dâi]，

For this reason, that the territories of regional lords are extensive

天子之害[F 祭/泰 gadh/γâi]也；
群臣之富太[*F 祭/祭 thadh/thâi]，

harms the Son of Heaven; that the ministers are extravagant and wealthy

君主之敗[F 祭/夬 pradh/pai]也。
將相之管主而隆家，
此君人者所外[F 祭/泰 ŋwadh/ŋwâi]也。

ruins the ruler. Generals and chancellors who control the ruler and exalt their own families – these are the sort that a ruler should get rid of.

萬物莫如身之至貴也，

Among the myriad things, nothing is more precious than [the ruler's] person,

位之至尊也，

nothing more dignified than [the ruler's] rank,

主威之重[G 東/用 drjuŋh/djwoŋ]，

nothing more weighty than the ruler's authority,

主勢之隆[G 中/東 gljəŋw/ljuŋ]也。

nothing more exalted than the ruler's position of power.

此四美者，
不求諸外，
不請於人，
議之而得之矣。

These four points of excellence are not to be sought from outside, nor can they be begged of others – they are obtained by going about things in the right way.

故曰：
人主不能用其富，

So it is said: a ruler who is unable to make use of these items of wealth

則終於外也。
此君人者之所識也。

will end up being ostracised. These are things that a ruler of men should bear in mind.

17 江有誥 suggests moving 主道衰亡 one line up; 邵增樺 follows this and has 是以主道衰亡，姦臣蕃息. The rhyme on 息 then terminates the passage. 龍宇純 regards 亡 as a residue (壞字) of 匿[之/職 nrjək/njək], which would make this line rhyme with lines 10–16.   20 Following 邵增樺, 太富 is emended to 富太, i.e. 富泰, which makes this line rhyme.   22 隆（國）家 (校注 33).   23 C suggests emending 所外 to 所以外 to parallel with 終於外 below.   25〔位之至尊也〕(校注 33).   26〔主威之重〕(校注 33).   27〔主勢之隆也〕(校注 33).   31 議 is read as 義.

HF 4.2 (*Xilun* 50, *Xin jiaozhu* 62)

昔者紂之亡、	In ancient times, the ruin of King Zhòu
周之卑，	and the humbling of the House of Zhōu
皆從諸侯之博大也。	were both the result of the extensive territories of the regional lords.[4]
晉之分也、	That Jin was divided
齊之奪也，	and that power was seized in Qi
皆以群臣之太富也。	both happened because their ministers were extravagant and wealthy.[5]
夫燕、宋之所以弒其君者，	As for how the rulers in Yan and Song could be assassinated –
皆以類也。	they were both of this kind.[6]
故上比之殷、周，	Thus, comparing the early cases of Yin (Shang) and Zhōu,
中比之燕、宋，	and comparing the later cases of Yan and Song,
莫不從此術也。	we see that all [the usurpers] followed these techniques.
是故明君之蓄其臣也，	Therefore, when a clear-sighted ruler nourishes his ministers,
盡之以法，	he makes them do their best by means of laws
質之以備。	and tests them by means of ancillary measures.

---

4 This is an odd claim. It is true that the house of Zhōu declined because of the excessive power of regional lords; but the same cannot be said of the demise of the last Shang (Yin) king, Zhòu. Nor does this topic recur in Han Fei's other discussions of Zhòu's end.

5 Over the course of the sixth century the ruling houses in Jin and Qi (two of the most powerful states of the Springs-and-Autumns period) were completely eclipsed by powerful ministerial houses. In the state of Jin, three victors of the inter-lineage feuds – the Zhao, Hán, and Wei houses – had divided their state among themselves (see chapter 1, note 33). In Qi, the single victor in the internecine conflicts was the Tian (Chen) lineage, the heads of which usurped power in 481 (chapter 7, note 3) but continued to rule for another century through the puppet lords of the legitimate Jiang 姜 house before assuming the throne themselves.

6 Both Yan and Song are discussed in chapter 7 below. In Song, the government was usurped at some point in the fourth century by the Supervisor of Fortifications, Zihan 子罕, the head of one of the collateral branches of the ruling lineage. In Yan, King Kuai's 燕王噲 attempt to yield the throne to his meritorious minister, Zizhi 子之 in 314, caused domestic conflict, foreign occupation, and the king's own death.

愛臣 FAVOURED MINISTERS

故不赦死，	Therefore, he does not pardon those condemned to death
不宥刑；	and does not show clemency in punishments.
赦死、宥刑，	To pardon the condemned and to show clemency in punishments –
是謂威淫。	this is called to slacken authority:
社稷將危，	the altars of soil and grain will be imperilled
國家偏威。	and the state and the [ministerial] houses will have a skewed distribution of authority.
是故大臣之祿雖大，	Therefore, although the great ministers have high emoluments,
不得藉威城市；	they should not be allowed to derive authority from their cities;
黨與雖眾，	although they have many adherents and partisans,
不得臣士卒。	they should not be allowed to treat their officers and soldiers as subjects.
故人臣處國無私朝[A 宵/宵 trjagw/tjäu]，	Thus when ministers live in the capital, they should not hold court in private,
居軍無私交[A 宵/肴 kragw/kau]；	and when they stay with the army, they should not conduct foreign relations in private.[7]
其府庫不得私貸於家[B 魚/麻 krag/ka]。	They should not make private loans to members of their lineage from their treasuries and armouries –
此明君之所以禁其邪[B 魚/麻 sgjiag/zja]。	this is how a clear-sighted ruler puts a stop to their wickedness.
是故不得四從[C 東/用 dzjuŋh > -uaŋh ?/dzjwoŋ]， 不載奇兵[C 陽/庚 pjiaŋ/pjeŋ]。	Thus ministers do not get a four-horse escort or carry unregulated weapons onboard their carriages.

---

7 The latter clause reflects a frequently encountered situation during the prolonged campaigns of the Warring States period, whereby a general (often a high minister who had assumed command) had to negotiate with leaders of other states without first seeking the approval of his own king. Such *ad hoc* diplomatic efforts were the result of military necessity, but they could be utilised to pursue the general's (or the minister's) personal interests.

非傳非遽[D 魚/御 gjagh/gjwo]，

載奇兵革，

罪死不赦[D 魚/禡 hrjiagh/śja]。

此明君之所以備不虞[D 魚/虞 ŋwjag/ŋju]者也。

When someone who is not an official courier or an express courier
carries an unregulated weapon or shield onboard their carriage,
he should be sentenced to death without pardon.
This is how the clear-sighted ruler guards against the unforeseen.

8 C follows 張本 and has 此 for 以, with 校注 33. We read 以 as 此.

CHAPTER 5

主道 The Way of the Ruler

HF 5.1 (*Xilun* 55, *Xin jiaozhu* 66)

道者，	The Way
萬物之始[A 之/止 sthjəgx/šï]，	is the origin of the myriad things
是非之紀[A 之/止 kjəgx/kï]也。	and the guideline of right and wrong.
是以明君守始[A 之/止 sthjəgx/šï]，	Therefore, the clear-sighted ruler holds unto the beginning
以知萬物之源[B 元/元 ŋwjan/ŋjwɐn]，	in order to know the source of the myriad things,
治紀[A 之/止 kjəgx/kï]，	and he examines the guideline
以知善敗之端[B 元/桓 tuan/tuân]。	in order to know the beginnings of success and failure.
故虛靜以待，	Thus, empty and inactive, he waits [for things to happen],
令名自命[C 耕/映 mjiŋh/mjɐŋ]也，	making titles name themselves,
令事自定[C 耕/徑 diŋh/dieŋ]也。	and making assignments determine themselves.
虛則知實之情[C 耕/清 dzjiŋ/dzjän]，	Being empty, he knows the true condition of that which is full;
靜則知動者正[C 耕/勁 tjiŋh/tśjäŋ]。	being inactive, he knows the standard by which to act.
有言者自為名[C 耕/清 mjiŋ/mjän]，	Those who have proposals produce their own titles,
有事者自為形[C 耕/青 giŋ/yieŋ]；	and those who have assignments produce their own performance.
形名參同，	When performance and title match each other,
君乃無事焉，	the ruler does not need to be involved –
歸之其情[C 耕/清 dzjiŋ/dzjän]。	he lets them revert to what they really are.
故曰：	So it is said:
君無見其所欲[D 侯/燭 grjuk/jiwok]，	A ruler should not show what he desires.

20 君見其所欲[D 侯/燭 grjuk/jiwok]，
    臣自將離琢[D 侯/覺 truk/ṭåk]；

    君無見其意[E 之/志 ʔjəgh/ʔi]，
    君見其意[E 之/志 ʔjəgh/ʔi]，
    臣將自表異[E 之/志 rəgh/jiɨ]。

25 故曰：
    去好去惡[F 魚/暮 ʔagh/ʔuo]，
    臣乃見素[F 魚/暮 sagh/suo]；

    去智去舊[*G 之/宥 gwjəgh/gjǒu]，
    臣乃自備[G 之/至 bjiəgh/bji]。

30 故有智而不以慮[H 魚/御 ljagh/ljwo]，
    使萬物知其處[H 魚/御 khrjagh/tśhjwo]；
    有行而不以賢[I 真/先 gin/γien]，
    觀臣下之所因[I 真/真 ʔjin/ʔjiĕn]；
    有勇而不以怒[J 魚/姥 nagx/nuo]，
35 使群臣盡其武[J 魚/麌 mjagx/mju]。

    是故去智而有明[K 陽/庚 mjiaŋ/mjɐŋ]，
    去賢而有功[K 東/東 kuŋ > kuaŋ ʔ/kuŋ]，
    去勇而有強[K 陽/陽 gjaŋ/gjaŋ]。
    群臣守職，
40 百官有常[K 陽/陽 djaŋ/źjaŋ]，

---

1 *Su* 素, or "raw, undyed silk," is a metaphor for the state of things as they really are, without deception or embellishment, hence "true colours."

When a ruler shows what he desires,
his ministers will carve and polish themselves;

A ruler should not show what he intends.
When a ruler shows what he intends,
his ministers will claim that they have exceptional talents.

So it is said:
Discard likes, discard dislikes,
and your ministers will show their true colours;[1]

discard wisdom, discard precedents,
and your ministers will be on guard all by themselves.

So the ruler has wisdom, but does not use it to deliberate;
instead, he makes the myriad things know their [proper] place.
He has abilities, but does not use them to act,
instead, he observes what causes his ministers [to act];
he has courage, but does not use it to become enraged;
instead, he makes the ministers exert their martial spirit.

Therefore, he discards wisdom, yet obtains clarity of vision;
he discards abilities, yet obtains achievements;
he discards courage, yet obtains strength.
All ministers attend to their duties,
and all the many officials follow their constant patterns;

主道 THE WAY OF THE RULER

因能而使之，
是謂習常[K 陽/陽 djaŋ/źjaŋ]。
故曰：
寂[L 幽/錫 sdiəkw/dziek]乎其無位而處[M 魚/語 khrjagx/tśhjwo]，
漻[L 幽/蕭 gliəgw/lieu]乎莫得其所[M 魚/語 skrjagx/ṣjwo]。
明君無為於上，
群臣竦懼乎下[M 魚/馬 gragx/ɣa]。
明君之道，
使智者盡其慮[N 魚/御 ljagh/-jəï, -jəï ?/ljwo]，
而君因以斷事[N 之/志 dzrjəgh/-jəï/dẓï]，
故君不窮於智[N 佳/寘 trjigh/-jiei/tjĕ]；
賢者敕其材[N 之/咍 dzəg/-əï/dzậi]，
君因而任之[N 之/之 tjəg/-jəï/tśï]，
故君不窮於能[N 之/咍 nəg/-əï/nậi]；
有功則君有其賢[O 真/先 gin/ɣien]，
有過則臣任其罪[N 微/賄 dzədx/-əi/dzuậi]，
故君不窮於名[O 耕/清 mjiŋ/mjäŋ]。

是故不賢而為賢者師[N 脂/脂 srjid/-jiəi/ṣji]，
不智而為智者正[O 耕/清 tjiŋ/tśjäŋ]。
臣有其勞，
君有其成[*O 耕/清 djiŋ/źjäŋ]，
此之謂賢主之經[O 耕/青 kiŋ/kieŋ]也。

He gives them tasks on the basis of their abilities –
this is called "to follow constant patterns."
So it is said:
All quiet, he does not occupy any position,

all calm, no one knows where he is.

Above, a clear-sighted ruler does not act assertively,
yet all his ministers shiver in fear below.
The Way of a clear-sighted ruler
is to make the wise fully utilise their cognitive powers,
with the ruler deciding matters on the basis of these,
and therefore he never runs out of wisdom.
As for the worthy, he makes them improve their talents,
the ruler employing them on the basis of these,
and therefore he never runs out of abilities.
When there are achievements, the ruler claims the ability as his own;
when there are failures, the ministers are made responsible for the crimes,
and therefore the ruler never runs out of good reputation.

In this way, the ruler is the mentor of the able, although he lacks abilities himself;
he is the standard for the intelligent, although he is not intelligent himself.
The ministers toil away,
while the ruler claims their achievements;
this is called "the enduring guideline for being an able ruler."[2]

---

2   Since one has just been told that the ruler is not *xian* 賢 "worthy/talented," this use the phrase 賢主 "worthy/talented ruler" is puzzling.

8 C has 故虛靜以待令 with all editions; we follow 山仲質 (quoted by 松皐圓 and 津田鳳卿, followed by 張覺) and emend to 故虛靜以待.　　28 All editions have 去舊去智; we follow 王念孫 and emend to 去智去舊 in order to have rhyme 舊 with 備; 王念孫 is followed by C and 張覺. 陳奇猷 suggests emending 舊 to 奮; this would break the rhyme.　　32 C emends 有行而不以賢 to 有賢而不以行, with 校注 following 王先慎. 張覺 holds this to be unnecessary, positing that in order to make this line rhyme with the following line ending in 因, Han Fei has changed the position of the words 賢 and 行. The sentence should be understood as 有賢而不以行, but not emended.　　57 君（子）不 (校注 39–40).　　59 為（上）智 (校注 40).　　61 C has 君有其成功 with all editions and 校注; we follow 王先謙 and emend to 君有其成 in order for 成 to rhyme; followed by 張覺.

HF 5.2 (*Xilun* 60, *Xin jiaozhu* 74)

道在不可見，
用在不可知[A 佳/支 trig/tjě]；

虛靜無事，
以闇見疵[A 佳/支 dzjig/dzjě]。

5　見而不見，
聞而不聞，
知而不知[A 佳/支 trig/tjě]；

知其言以往[B 陽/養 gwjaŋx/jwaŋ]，
勿變勿更[B 陽/庚 kraŋ/keŋ]，
10　以參合閱焉[B 元/仙 gwjan/jän]。

官有一人[C 真/真 njin/ńźjěn]，
勿令通言[B 元/元 ŋjan/ŋjen]，
則萬物皆盡[C 真/軫 dzjinx/dzjěn]。

函掩其跡[D 佳/昔 tsjik/tsjäk]，
15　匿其端[E 元/桓 tuan/tuân]，
下不能原[E 元/元 ŋwjan/ŋjwen]；

去其智[D 佳/寘 trjigh/tjě]，

The Way consists in being invisible;
the utilisation (of the Way) consists in being unknowable.

Empty and still, unoccupied by any affairs,
[the ruler] observes the faults of others from the shadows.

He sees but is not seen;
he hears but is not heard;
he knows but is not known.

After understanding a proposal,
do not allow any changes or alterations,
but check words against deeds and observe the performance.

For each office there is one person –
do not allow officials to communicate with each other,
so that all the myriad things[3] are carried through to the end.

[The ruler] hides his tracks,
conceals his motivations,
and those below him are unable to trace them to their source.

Discard your intellect,

3　Note that "things" here include human undertakings.

主道 THE WAY OF THE RULER

絕其能[F 之/咍 nəg/nâi]，
下不能意[F 之/志 ʔjəgh/ʔï]。

eliminate your abilities,
and those below you are unable to guess your intentions.

保吾所以往而稽同[G 東/東 duŋ/duŋ]之，

You must hold on to [the proposals] you have previously [heard] and check whether they conform to [the performance demonstrated];[4]

謹執其柄而固握[G 侯/覺 ʔruk/ʔâk]之；

you must take care to hold on to the handle [of power] and grasp it firmly.

絕其能[F 之/咍 nəg/nâi]，
破其意[F 之/志 ʔjəgh/ʔï]，

Eliminate your abilities,
ruin the chances of others guessing your intentions,

毋使人欲[G 侯/燭 grjuk/jiwok]之。

and do not allow them to desire [your handle of power].

不謹其閉[H 脂/霽 pidh/-iei/piei]，
不固其門[I 文/魂 mən/muən]，
虎乃將存[I 文/魂 dzən/dzuən]。
不慎其事[H 之/志 tsrjəgh/-jəï/tṣï]，
不掩其情[J 耕/清 dzjiŋ/dzjäŋ]，

When you are not careful about closing your doors,
when you do not make sturdy your gates,
then tigers will come into being.[5]
When you are not cautious in your business,
when you do not cover up the realities of your situation,

賊乃將生[J 耕/庚 sriŋ/ṣeŋ]。
弒其主，
代其所[K 魚/語 skrjagx/sjwo]，
人莫不與[K 魚/語 ragx/jiwo]，

then villains will emerge.
They will assassinate their ruler,
take his place,
and there will be no one who does not side with them:

故謂之虎[K 魚/姥 hagx/xuo]。
處其主之側[L 之/職 tsrjək/tṣjək]，
為姦匿[L 慝之/德 hnək/thək]，
閒其主之忒[L 之/德 thək/thək]，

hence they are called tigers.
Residing in the entourage of their ruler as treacherous ministers,
they are on the watch for the ruler to make a mistake,

故謂之賊[L 之/德 dzək/dzək]。
散其黨，
收其餘[M 魚/魚 rag/jiwo]，

so they are called villains.
Scatter their factions,
deal with what remains of them,

---

4 以往 here resumes 知其言以往 some lines above.
5 Note the highly unusual comparison of ministers to the tigers ready to devour the ruler. See also chapter 8.7.

閉其門，
奪其輔[M 魚/虞 bjagx/bju]，
國乃無虎[M 魚/姥 hagx/xuo]。

大不可量，
45 深不可測[N 之/職 tshrjək/tṣhjək]，
同合刑名，
審驗法式[N 之/職 sthjək/śjək]，

擅為者誅，
國乃無賊[N 之/德 dzək/dzək]。

50 是故人主有五壅[O 廱 東/鍾 ʔjuŋ/ʔjwoŋ]：
臣閉其主曰壅[O 廱 東/鍾 ʔjuŋ/ʔjwoŋ]，
臣制財利曰壅[O 廱 東/鍾 ʔjuŋ/ʔjwoŋ]，
臣擅行令曰壅[O 廱 東/鍾 ʔjuŋ/ʔjwoŋ]，
臣得行義曰壅[O 廱 東/鍾 ʔjuŋ/ʔjwoŋ]，
55 臣得樹人曰壅[O 廱 東/鍾 ʔjuŋ/ʔjwoŋ]。

臣閉其主，
則主失位；
臣制財利，

則主失德；
60 臣擅行令，

則主失制；
臣得行義，

則主失明[P 萌 陽/耕 mraŋ/mɛŋ]；
臣得樹人，

65 則主失黨[P 陽/蕩 taŋx/tâŋ]。

bar their gates,
and snatch away their support,
then there will be no tigers in the state.

Be so encompassing as to be immeasurable,
so deep as to be unfathomable;
compare performance and title,
and examine and test the laws and administrative rules.

Punish those who act without authorisation,
and the state will have no villains.

Thus, a ruler may face five types of obstruction.
A minister who blocks in the ruler is one type of obstruction;
A minister who controls [the state's] assets and benefits is one type of obstruction;
A minister who issues orders on his own authority is one type of obstruction;
A minister who is allowed to practise his own justice is one type of obstruction.
A minister who is allowed to establish people [in office] is one type of obstruction.

When a minister blocks in the ruler,
the ruler will lose his position;
when a minister controls [the state's] assets and benefits,
the ruler will lose his means of munificence;
when a minister issues orders on his own authority,
the ruler will lose his command;
when a minister is allowed to practice his own justice,
the ruler will lose his people;
when a minister is allowed to plant people in office,
the ruler will lose his adherents.

主道 THE WAY OF THE RULER

此人主之所以獨擅[Q 元/線 djanh/ʑjän]也， These are the ways that a ruler uses to maintain exclusive control;
非人臣之所以得操[Q 宵/豪 tshagw/tshâu]也。 they are what a minister should not be allowed to take charge of.

22 吳本、張抄、錢抄、藏本、張本 have 絕其能望; C deletes 能 from 絕其能望, with 陳本, following 校注 40; 陳本 has 絕其望; 趙本 has 絕其能. 絕其望 is not implausible; 絕其能 is chosen here because of the rhyme.　36 C emends 臣 to 匿, following 王念孫. 匿 is read as 慝[之/德 hnək/thək].　37 We emend 聞 to 閒, read as 伺, with 王念孫; followed by 張覺.　63 明 is here, as often in HF, used for 萌, i.e. 氓.

HF 5.3 (*Xilun* 60, *Xin jiaozhu* 81)

人主之道[A 幽/晧 dəgwx/dâu]， The Way of the ruler
靜退以為寶[A 幽/晧 pəgwx/pâu]。 is to take calmness and withdrawal as his treasures.
不自操事而知拙與巧[A 幽/巧 khrəgwx/khau]， The ruler does not personally handle tasks, but understands what is inept and what is astute;
不自計慮而知福與咎[A 幽/有 gjəgwx/gjəu]。 he does not personally make plans, but understands what brings good and bad fortune.
是以不言而善應[B 蒸/證 ʔjəŋh/ʔjəŋ]， Thus, the ruler does not speak, and yet excels at responding;
不約而善增[B 蒸/登 tsəŋ/tsəŋ]。 he does not restrict himself, and yet excels at adding [tasks].
言已應[B 蒸/證 ʔjəŋh/ʔjəŋ]， When the ruler has responded to a proposal,
則執其契； he maintains it as a contract;
事已增[B 蒸/登 tsəŋ/tsəŋ]， when a task has been added,
則操其符； he holds on to it as a tally.
符契之所合， It is in the matching of tallies and contracts
賞罰之所生[B 耕/庚 sriŋ > sriəŋ ʔ/ʂeŋ]也。 that rewards and punishments are born.

故群臣陳其言， Thus, when the ministers make proposals,
君以其言授其事， the ruler uses the proposals to assign tasks to them,
事以責其功。 and uses their tasks to hold them responsible for their achievement.
功當其事， When the achievement fits the task,
事當其言則賞； and the task fits the proposal, he rewards;

功不當其事，	when the achievement does not fit the task,
事不當其言則誅。	or the task does not fit the proposal, he punishes.
20 明君之道，	It is the Way of a clear-sighted ruler
臣不得陳言而不當。	that ministers are not allowed to present proposals that they fail to live up to.
是故明君之行賞也，	Thus the distribution of rewards by the clear-sighted ruler
曖乎如時雨{C 魚/爂 gwjagx/ju}，	is mild like timely rain,
百姓利其澤{C 魚/陌 drak/ḍek}；	and the hundred clans crave his largesse;[6]
25 其行罰也，	his meting out of punishments,
畏乎如雷霆，	awes like a thunderbolt,
神聖不能解也。	and even a sage cannot absolve himself of them.
故明君無偷賞，	So, for the clear-sighted ruler, there are no careless rewards
無赦罰。	and there are no pardoned punishments.
30 賞偷，	When rewards are careless,
則功臣墮其業，	meritorious ministers will be lax in the performance of their duties;
赦罰，	when punishments are pardoned,
則姦臣易為非。	treacherous ministers will think nothing of doing wrong.
是故誠有功，	Therefore, when there really is merit,
35 則雖疏賤必賞；	then even though the person may be remotely related [to the ruler] and lowly, he will inevitably be rewarded;
誠有過，	when there really is a transgression,
則雖近愛必誅。	then even though the person may be closely related [to the ruler] and favoured [by him], he will inevitably be punished.
疏賤必賞，	When the remotely related and lowly are inevitably rewarded,

---

6 By Han Fei's time, "the hundred clans" had become a standard reference for "the people."

主道 THE WAY OF THE RULER

近愛必誅， and the closely related and favoured are inevitably punished,

則疏賤者不怠， then the remotely related and lowly will not become remiss,

而近愛者不驕也。 and the closely related and favoured will not become arrogant.

5 〔而〕(校注 40).　21 〔得〕(校注 40).　31 C has 墮 for 惰 with 錢抄、藏本、張本、陳本 and 校注 39. 吳本、張抄、趙本 have 惰.　38 〔疏賤必賞〕(校注 40), with commentary by 張子象 in 鹽鐵論.

CHAPTER 6

有度 Having Standards

HF 6.1 (*Xilun* 68, *Xin jiaozhu* 94)

國無常強，	No state is forever strong
無常弱。	or forever weak.
奉法者強，	When he who upholds the law is strong,
則國強；	the state is strong;
5　奉法者弱，	when he who upholds the law is weak,
則國弱。	the state is weak.
荊莊王并國二十六，	King Zhuang of Jing (Chu) annexed twenty-six states
開地三千里；	and opened up lands measuring three thousand *li* square,
莊王之氓社稷也，	but when he passed away and left the altars of the soil and grain,[1]
10　而荊以亡。	Jing (Chu) collapsed.[2]
齊桓公并國三十，	Lord Huan of Qi annexed thirty states
啟地三千里；	and opened up lands measuring three thousand *li* square,
桓公之氓社稷也，	but when he passed away and left the altars of the soil and grain,
而齊以亡。	Qi collapsed.[3]
15　燕襄王以河為境，	King [Zhao]Xiang of Yan[4] had the Yellow River as his border

---

1　The altars were the ritual symbols of statehood.
2　Historically speaking, this is an imprecise statement. Whereas King Zhuang of Chu (r. 613–591) was indeed the most powerful ruler of this state, he did not annex 26 states, nor did his death mark the collapse of Chu. The historical context of this passage is opaque.
3　This is again inaccurate. First, Lord Huan of Qi (r. 685–643) was actually very hesitant with regard to annexations; in the latter half of his reign he refrained from them altogether. Second, whereas Qi did enter a prolonged crisis following Lord Huan's death, it did not "collapse" as a result.
4　The name of King Zhaoxiang of Yan 燕昭襄王 (r. 313–279) is usually abbreviated as King Zhao rather than King Xiang. Having ascended the throne after dynastic turmoil and foreign occupation, King Zhaoxiang restored Yan's position as one of the major powers in the northeastern part of the Chinese world.

有度 HAVING STANDARDS

以薊為國,	and Ji as his capital,
襲涿、方城,	[Ji being] girdled by Zhuo and Fangcheng.
殘齊,	He laid waste to Qi,
平中山。	and levelled Zhongshan with the ground.[5]
20 有燕者重,	Those who had Yan's support were reckoned to be powerful;
無燕者輕;	those who lacked Yan's support were reckoned to be weak,
襄王之氓社稷也,	but when he passed away,
而燕以亡。	Yan was ruined.[6]
魏安釐王攻燕救趙,	King Anxi of Wei attacked Yan, rescued Zhao,
25 取地河東;	and took territory in Hedong.[7]
攻盡陶、衛之地;	He attacked and completely occupied the lands of Tao and Wey,[8]
加兵於齊,	applied military force to Qi,
私平陸之都;	and appropriated its stronghold, Pinglu.[9]

---

5   Not all of these statements are accurate. First, it is not at all clear why King Zhaoxiang of Yan would attack Zhuo and Fangcheng, which were locations within his own state (although it is possible that this hints at his campaigns against the occupying Qi forces in Yan ca. 313). Second, he certainly did not occupy Zhongshan; this state was occupied by one of Yan's rivals, Zhao, in 296. By contrast, "laying waste to Qi" refers to King Zhaoxiang's real major achievement: the victorious campaign of general Yue Yi 樂毅 in 284, which resulted in the occupation of almost all of Qi. From a historical point of view this passage remains puzzling.

6   Once again, this is an imprecise statement. While the death of King Zhaoxiang did bring about the reversal of Yan's fortunes (in particular, the loss of control of Qi), the state was in no way ruined.

7   King Anxi of Wei (r. 276–243) intervened in 257 to save the beleaguered state of Zhao from Qin's attack in the aftermath of the Changping campaign (on which see chapter 1, note 20). Yan was indeed Qin's ally, but only at a slightly later point during its ongoing clashes with Zhao; hence Han Fei's statement is probably confused. The meaning of "took territory in Hedong" is uncertain; possibly, as Chen Qiyou suggests, it refers to Wei's partial occupation of the areas east of the lower reaches of the Yellow River in the wake of the defection of Qin's local governor, Wang Ji 王稽, to Wei in 255.

8   Tao was Qin's easternmost stronghold in today's Dingtao, the westernmost part of Shandong province. The state of Wey 衛 was located slightly to the northwest. Its occupation by Wei 魏 is not clearly attested in the extant sources, but chapter 49.15 of *Han Feizi* (see note 41 there) hints that Wey probably allied with Qin and was attacked by Wei; Wey was then relocated to a new capital, Yewang 野王. Yang Kuan (1998: 420) dates these events to 254.

9   Pinglu was one of Qi's westernmost strongholds, to the north of today's Jining 濟寧市 (Shandong). It is not clear when it was occupied by Wei's forces.

攻韓拔管，	He attacked Hán, seized Guan,[10]
30　勝於淇下；	and was victorious at the Qi River.[11]
睢陽之事，	In the Suiyang campaign
荊軍老而走；	the Jing (Chu) forces were worn down and ran away;
蔡、召陵之事，	at the battles of Cai and Shaoling,
荊軍破；	the Jing (Chu) army was routed;[12]
35　兵四布於天下，	His armies spread across the realm;
威行於冠帶之國；	and his dominance was recognised in all the states where ceremonial headgear and belts were worn,[13]
安釐王死而魏以亡。	but when he died, Wei collapsed.[14]
故有荊莊、齊桓，	Thus, as long as [King] Zhuang of Jing (Chu) and [Lord] Huan of Qi were alive,
則荊、齊可以霸；	Jing (Chu) and Qi were able to be hegemons;
40　有燕襄、魏安釐，	as long as [King Zhao]Xiang of Yan and [King] Anxi of Wei were alive,
則燕、魏可以強，	Yan and Wei were able to be strong.
今皆亡國者，	Now, the reason why all these have been ruined
其群臣官吏皆務所以亂而不務所以治也。	is that their ministers and officials were all striving for what leads to turmoil, and not for what leads to good order.
其國亂弱矣，	When a state is already weakened by turmoil,
45　又皆釋國法而私其外，	and everyone moreover sets aside the laws of the state and acts in a private capacity outside the laws,

---

10　Guan was located to the northeast of the Hán capital, near the banks of the Yellow River.

11　It is not clear which victory is referred to here. The Qi River is a tributary of the Wey River 衛河, in northeastern Henan.

12　These statements are perplexing. In the currently available sources there are no signs of these campaigns by Wei. During King Anxi's reign Wei was primarily pressed by Qin, and occasionally organised anti-Qin coalitions (with Chu in 257 and 247). The notion that Wei would inflict major defeats on Chu of which we know nothing from other sources is very odd. On the other hand, these events would have occurred in Han Fei's lifetime and he is not likely to have invented them. So, either our main source for the late Warring States history – *Shiji* – is more flawed than is usually assumed, or chapter 6 of *Han Feizi* was produced long after his death, or these are just cases of textual corruption.

13　That is, in all civilised parts of the world.

14　Once again, "collapsed" is an exaggeration. Wei was annexed by Qin in 225, eighteen years after King Anxi's death and eight years after Han Fei's own death.

有度 HAVING STANDARDS

則是負薪而救火也，	this is just like hauling firewood to put out a fire:
亂弱甚矣！	the result is even more turmoil and weakness.

24 （政趙救燕）〔攻燕救趙〕（校注 51, following 顧廣圻, with 史記). 26 C has 魏 with 校注 43, but notes that 魏 refers to 衛, being subservient to or conquered by 魏; we emend to 衛, following 顧廣圻, with 飾邪 chapter. 37 〔王〕（校注 51). 28 荊莊、齊桓（公）（校注 51). 38 故有荊莊、齊桓（公）（校注 51).

HF 6.2 (*Xilun* 72, *Xin jiaozhu* 91)

故當今之時，	So, to turn to the present times,
能去私曲、就公法者，	if you are able to remove selfish tricks and keep to the impartial law,
民安而國治；	the people will be tranquil and the state well-ordered;
能去私行、行公法者，	if you are able to remove selfish actions and enact impartial law,
5　則兵強而敵弱。	your armies will grow strong and your enemies will become weak.
故審得失、有法度之制者，	Thus, if the ruler examines gain and loss and maintains a system of laws and standards,
加以群臣之上，	imposing it on all his ministers,
則主不可欺以詐偽；	then he cannot be cheated through fraud or fabrication.
審得失、有權衡之稱者，	If the ruler examines gain and loss and maintains a scale for weighing matters
10　以聽遠事，	in dealing with far-away affairs,
則主不可欺以天下之輕重。	then he cannot be cheated as to the true weight of matters in all the realm.
今若以譽進能，	Now, if you promote the able on the basis of praise,
則臣離上而下比周；	ministers will turn their backs on their superiors and band together below;
若以黨舉官，	if promotions are based on factional ties,
15　則民務交而不求用於法。	the people will strive to establish connections and no longer seek employment based on the law.[15]

15　This is a recurring topic in *Han Feizi*: appointments based on the self-serving discourse of

故官之失能者其國亂，	Thus, when the offices forego capable men, the state will be in turmoil;
以譽為賞，	if rewards are offered on the basis of praise
以毀為罰也，	and punishments imposed on the basis of slander,
則好賞惡罰之人，	then the people, liking rewards and disliking punishments,
20 釋公行，	will discard impartial actions
行私術，	and follow selfish techniques,
比周以相為也。	banding together and acting on each other's behalf.
忘主外交，	They will disregard the ruler and make external connections,
以進其與，	in order to advance their associates,
25 則其下所以為上者薄矣。	so subordinates will have little reason to serve their superiors.
交眾、與多，	When their acquaintances are numerous and their associates many,
外內朋黨，	when they have factions both outside and inside,
雖有大過，	then, although they might have committed serious transgressions,
其蔽多矣。	most of them will be covered up.
30 故忠臣危死於非罪，	In this way, loyal ministers will be in danger of death, though not for any crime,
姦邪之臣安利於無功。	whereas villainous ministers will take pleasure in the benefits they have obtained, though they do not have any achievements.
忠臣之所以危死而不以其罪，	When loyal ministers are in danger of death, but not for any crime of their own,
則良臣伏矣；	good ministers will lie low;
姦邪之臣安利不以功，	when wicked ministers take pleasure in the benefits they have obtained, but they do not have any achievements,
35 則姦臣進矣；	treacherous ministers will advance.
此亡之本也。	These are the roots of ruin.

"elevating the worthy" empower the creators of "public opinion" below, the talkative intellectuals, who mislead rulers and promote their own partisans, praising them as worthies. For an earlier discussion of this topic, see the *Book of Lord Shang*, chapter 25.1–2.

有度 HAVING STANDARDS

若是，	If the situation is like this,
則群臣廢法而行私重，	ministers will spurn the law, acting to promote their own influence,
輕公法矣。	while making light of impartial law.
40 數至能人之門，	They will come again and again to the gates of men with political clout,
不壹至主之廷；	but not once will they turn up at the ruler's court.
百慮私家之便，	They will come up with hundreds of deliberations for the private advantage of their families,
不壹圖主之國。	but not present a single plan for the benefit of their ruler's state.
屬數雖多，	Though his subordinates might be many,
45 非所以尊君也；	this will not make the ruler venerated;
百官雖具，	though he might have many officials on hand,
非所以任國也；	they will not be of the kind to whom he can entrust the state's affairs.
然則主有人主之名，	Under such conditions, while the ruler has the name of a ruler of men,
而實託於群臣之家也。	in reality he has entrusted himself to the ministerial houses.
50 故臣曰：	Therefore I, your subject, say[16]
亡國之廷無人焉。	"In a state doomed to ruin there is nobody at court."
廷無人者，	Saying that there is nobody at court
非朝廷之衰也。	is not to say that the court is laid waste –
家務相益，	rather, ministerial houses attend to each other's profit,
55 不務厚國；	and do not attend to enriching the state;
大臣務相尊，	great ministers devote themselves to venerating each other,
而不務尊君；	but not to venerating the ruler;
小臣奉祿養交，	and minor ministers take their salaries and cultivate political connections,
不以官為事。	but do not make official duties any concern of theirs.
60 此其所以然者，	Things like these come about

---

16 On Han Fei's self-reference as *chen* 臣 "I, your subject," which suggests that the present chapter was designed as Han Fei's memorial to a king, see chapter 4, note 1.

60   CHAPTER 6

由主之不上斷於法，	when a ruler does not settle things from above using laws,
而信下為之也。	but instead trusts his subordinates to do it.
故明主使法擇人，	Therefore, a clear-sighted ruler uses the law to select personnel,
不自舉也；	but does not advance them himself;
65 使法量功，	he uses the law to assess their achievements,
不自度也。	but does not gauge their achievements himself.[17]
能者不可弊，	When people with abilities cannot be hidden away,
敗者不可飾，	when the incompetent cannot be dressed up,
譽者不能進，	when those who are praised are not advanced [based on praise alone],
70 非者弗能退，	and when those who are criticised are not demoted [based on criticism alone],
則君臣之間明辯而易治，	then there will be a clear distinction between ruler and minister, and it will be easy to govern,
故主讎法則可也。	and therefore if the ruler complies with law, then [the administration] will be acceptable.

25 C suggests the reading 也 for 矣.　33 〔臣〕(校注 51).　45 〔以〕(校注 51).　55 張抄、錢抄 have 圖; 吳本、藏本、張本、陳本、趙本 have 國.

HF 6.3 (*Xilun* 76, *Xin jiaozhu* 99)

賢者之為人臣，	When a man of worth becomes a minister,
北面委質，	he faces north[18] and does fealty;
無有二心。	he does not have divided loyalties.
朝廷不敢辭賤，	When at court, he does not presume to decline humble assignments;
5 軍旅不敢辭難；	when in the army, he does not presume to decline perilous tasks.
順上之為，	He obeys the initiatives of the throne,
從主之法，	and follows the laws laid down by the ruler;

17　Cf. *Guanzi* 46: 917 ("Ming fa" 明法). Here Han Fei raises the role of the law (or standards) to a new pitch: even the choice of qualified personnel at the top level must be governed by law.

18　The ruler's proper position is facing south, so all others face north when in attendance.

有度 HAVING STANDARDS

虛心以待令，	he awaits orders with a receptive mind,
而無是非也。	and does not himself argue what is right and what is wrong.
10 故有口不以私言，	Thus he has a mouth, but does not use it for self-interested proposals;
有目不以私視，	he has eyes, but he does not use them for self-interested analysis,
而上盡制之。	and the ruler completely controls them.[19]
為人臣者，	A minister
譬之若手，	may be likened to your hands:
15 上以脩頭，	above, they groom the head,
下以脩足；	below, they groom the feet;
清暖寒熱，	chills and heat, hot and cold,
不得不救入；	they must keep from intruding;
鎮鋣傅體，	even when the (formidable) Moye sword threatens your body,
20 不敢弗搏。	they would not dare not to fight it.
無私賢哲之臣，	[A ruler] must not show personal favour to worthy and knowledgeable ministers,
無私事能之士。	or towards gentlemen employed because of their talents.
故民不越鄉而交，	As a result, the people will not make connections beyond their district,[20]
無百里之慼。	nor establish relations a hundred *li* away.
25 貴賤不相踰，	The noble and the base will not overstep their bounds
愚智提衡而立，	and the foolish and wise will each stand in their place, in balance.
治之至也。	Such is the perfection of good order.

---

19 The mouth and eyes. Note here that Han Fei's ideal minister is completely reduced to the ruler's obedient tool. This is not the constant position of the text: in chapter 14, for instance, far-sighted ministers who are able to change their country's destiny are praised precisely for the independence of their stance.

20 *Xiang* 鄉 is a sub-county unit, the tiniest administrative unit during the Warring States period. Han Fei implies that in an ordered state, "gentlemen" or "men of service" (*shi* 士) will have only vertical responsibilities to the ruler and will not cultivate horizontal ties with like-minded individuals.

今夫輕爵祿，	Now as for those who would make light of ranks and emoluments
易去亡，	and who would readily leave
30　以擇其主，	in order to choose their own ruler –
臣不謂廉。	these I would not call honest and upright.[21]
詐說逆法，	Those who persuade deceitfully and contravene the law,
倍主強諫，	who turn against the ruler and remonstrate pungently –
臣不謂忠。	these I would not call loyal.[22]
35　行惠施利，	Those who practice generosity and dole out benefits,
收下為名，	who gather followers to make a name for themselves –
臣不謂仁。	these I would not call benevolent.
離俗隱居，	Those who leave the vulgar world to live in seclusion,
而以詐非上，	who criticise the superiors with deceptive words –
40　臣不謂義。	these I would not call righteous.
外使諸侯，	Those who serve regional lords abroad,
內耗其國，	while wasting the resources of their states at home,
伺其危嶮之陂，	who wait for times of crisis to arrive,
以恐其主曰：	so that they can frighten their rulers and say:
45　"交非我不親，	"Were it not for me, ties with foreign powers would not be close;
怨非我不解"，	were it not for me, your enmities would not be resolved,"
而主乃信之，	who nonetheless are trusted by the ruler
以國聽之。	who follows their advice along with his state.

21　Here Han Fei attacks high-minded gentlemen who were ready to decline employment under a corrupt ruler to seek appointment elsewhere. Note that the more radical type of these purists, those who rejected service altogether, are criticised separately below.

22　Steadfast remonstrance was a hallmark of model ministers praised by Confucians, most notably by Han Fei's purported teacher, Xunzi (see his "The Way of the Minister" 臣道 chapter). For Han Fei these remonstrators are undermining the ruler's authority and are hence not loyal.

有度 HAVING STANDARDS   63

	卑主之名以顯其身，	They debase the ruler's name to make themselves illustrious;
50	毀國之厚以利其家，	they wreck the wealth of the state in order to profit their own households –
	臣不謂智。	these I would not consider wise.[23]
	此數物者，	These several things[24]
	險世之說也，	are propositions that are advanced in hazardous times,
	而先王之法所簡也。	disparaged by the laws of the former kings.[25]
55	先王之法曰：	The laws of the former kings said:
	"臣毋或作威[A 微/微 ʔwjəd/ʔjwěi]，	"Ministers should not become the source of authority;
	毋或作利[A 脂/至 ljidh/-jiəi/lji]，	they should not become the source of benefits,
	從王之指[A 脂/旨 krjidx/-jiəi/tśji]；	but should follow the king's directives;
	無或作惡[B 魚/暮 ʔagh/ʔuo]，	they should never be the source of evil,
60	從王之路[B 魚/暮 glagh/luo]。"	but should follow the king's path."[26]
	古者世治之民，	In ancient times, the people who lived in well-governed times
	奉公法，	upheld the impartial law,
	廢私術，	and rejected selfish techniques;
	專意一行，	they concentrated their thoughts and unified their actions
65	具以待任。	and attended to their assignments with all they had.

18 C deletes 入 from 張抄, with 張榜本 (校注 51); we follow all other editions and 張覺.   19 傅 is read as 附.   39 (作)〔詐〕(校注 51, following 王煥鑣).   65 具 is read as 俱.

---

23 Han Fei is regularly critical of powerful ministers who connived with foreign polities to enhance their prestige at home. See in particular chapter 31.
24 Incorruptibility, loyalty, benevolence, righteousness, and wisdom.
25 This appeal to the laws of the former kings is an odd rhetorical strategy in *Han Feizi*, as the text insists that the authority of the past can be easily manipulated (see especially chapters 49–50). For other positive invocations of the former kings, see 19.2, 19.8, and 25.2.
26 The last two lines of this rhymed law of the former kings are found in the "Hongfan" 洪範 chapter of *Shangshu* 尚書. See also *Lüshi chunqiu* 1.4 ("Gui gong" 貴公).

HF 6.4 (*Xilun* 80, *Xin jiaozhu* 107)

夫為人主而身察百官，	If, as a ruler, you want to supervise all officials personally,
則日不足，	your days will be insufficient,
力不給。	and your strength will not be enough.
且上用目，	Moreover, when superiors go by what meets the eye,
5　則下飾觀；	inferiors will make themselves attractive to behold;
上用耳，	when superiors go by what meets the ear,
則下飾聲；	inferiors will make themselves attractive to listen to;
上用慮，	and when superiors rely on deliberations,
則下繁辭。	inferiors will come up with elaborate disquisitions.
10　先王以三者為不足，	The former kings regarded these three as insufficient,
故舍己能而因法數，	so they dismissed their own abilities and relied on laws and methods,
審賞罰。	and paid careful attention to administering rewards and punishments.
先王之所守要，	These were what former kings paid heed to as essential,
故法省而不侵。	and so their laws were few but not infringed upon.
15　獨制四海之內，	They controlled all within the Four Seas all alone,
聰智不得用其詐，	and so the clever and wise could not use deception,
險躁不得關其佞，	jabberers could not apply flattery;
姦邪無所依。	and the treacherous and wicked had no one on which to rely.
遠在千里外，	Even as far away as one thousand *li*,
20　不敢易其辭；	people did not dare to change the words [of the royal edicts].[27]
勢在郎中，	Power was within the ruler's secretariat;

---

[27]　In an ideal centralised state, the king's pronouncements and edicts are disseminated accurately throughout the realm and not twisted by crooked officials en route. Cf. chapter 26 of

有度 HAVING STANDARDS

不敢蔽善飾非；	nobody dared to hide goodness or embellish wrongdoings.
朝廷群下，	All the subordinates at court
直湊單微，	simply pooled their individually weak capabilities[28]
25 不敢相踰越。	and never ventured to infringe upon each other's duties.
故治不足而日有餘，	Thus, in ordering the government, there was not enough to do and yet plenty of time to do it:[29]
上之任勢使然也。	the ruler's reliance on his position of power brought this about.

1 為（之）人主 (校注 51, with 張榜本).

HF 6.5 (*Xilun* 81, *Xin jiaozhu* 111)

夫人臣之侵其主也，	The way in which ministers infringe upon their ruler
如地形焉，	is just like [moving in confusing] terrain:
即漸以往，	they continuously move along,
使人主失端，	causing the ruler to lose his bearings,
5 東西易面而不自知。	so that east and west change directions without his being aware of it.
故先王立司南以端朝夕。	Thus, the former kings established the compass in order to align themselves to the east and west.
故明主使其群臣不遊意於法之外，	Therefore, the clear-sighted ruler ensures that his ministers do not think of anything beyond the law,
不為惠於法之內，	that they do not distribute favours (even) within the bounds of the law,
動無非法。	and that in whatever they do they never break the law.

the *Book of Lord Shang*, which prescribes the death penalty for local officials who modify a single character in the legal text without authorisation.
28   That is, they would combine their forces only in service of their ruler.
29   This expression occurs in the "Monarch and Hegemon" 王霸 chapter of the *Xunzi* (*Xunzi* 11: 223).

10	法，	Laws
	所以凌過遊外私也；	are that by which you attack transgressions and keep selfish interests away;
	嚴刑，	strict punishments
	所以遂令懲下也。	are that by which you execute orders and chastise inferiors.
	威不貳錯，	Authority must not be imposed from two sources,
15	制不共門。	and control must not come from a shared gate.
	威、制共，	When authority and control are shared,
	則眾邪彰矣；	all manner of wickedness will manifest itself;
	法不信，	when the law is capricious,
	則君行危矣；	the ruler will be in peril;
20	刑不斷，	when punishments are not resolute
	則邪不勝矣。	wickedness will not be defeated.
	故曰：	So it is said:
	巧匠目意中繩，	An expert carpenter could conform to the ink-line by visual inspection,
	然必先以規矩為度；	yet he must first take the compass and the T-square as his standard;
25	上智捷舉中事，	a superbly wise man will act adroitly and get everything right,
	必以先王之法為比。	yet he must first align matters in relation to the laws of the former kings.
	故繩直而枉木斲，	Thus, when the ink-line is straight, warped wood will be cut straight;
	準夷而高科削，	when the level is horizontal, protrusions will be pared off;
	權衡縣而重益輕，	when the scales are hung, excess from the heavy side will be added to the lighter side;
30	斗石設而多益少。	when bushels and piculs are calibrated, excess from the abundant side will be added to the lacking side.
	故以法治國，	Thus, ruling a state by use of the law
	舉措而已矣。	is simply a matter of enacting it.
	法不阿貴，	The law does not pander to the noble persons,
	繩不撓曲。	the ink-line does not bend to the crooked wood.
35	法之所加，	When the law is applied,
	智者弗能辭，	the wise cannot make excuses for not following it,

有度 HAVING STANDARDS

勇者弗敢爭。	and the courageous will not dare to contend with it.
刑過不避大臣，	Punishments for transgressions should not spare great ministers,[30]
賞善不遺匹夫。	and rewards for good deeds should not bypass ordinary people.
40 故矯上之失，	For correcting the oversights of superiors,
詰下之邪，	for prosecuting the wickedness of subordinates,
治亂決繆，	for bringing order to chaos and sorting out tangles,
絀羨齊非，	for removing the superfluous and evening out the incorrect,
一民之軌，	and for uniting the path of the people,
45 莫如法。	nothing is as good as the law.
屬官、威民，	For being strict with officials and establishing your authority over the people,
退淫殆，	for removing wantonness and sloth,
止詐偽，	for stopping all manner of deception,
莫如刑。	nothing is as good as punishments.
50 刑重，	When punishments are heavy,
則不敢以貴易賤；	the noble will not dare to look down upon the lowly;
法審，	when the laws are clear,
則上尊而不侵，	those above are honoured and their prerogatives inviolate.
上尊而不侵，	That the ruler is honoured and his prerogatives inviolate,
55 則主強而守要，	is because he is strong and adheres to the essential.
故先王貴之而傳之。	That is why the former kings valued [laws and punishments] and transmitted them.

---

30   This appears to be a direct assault on a vestige of legal practices from the aristocratic age, famously cited in the "Qu li" 曲禮 chapter of the *Records of the Rites* 禮記: "[mutilating] punishments do not reach the grandees above" 刑不上大夫. For a similar insistence on the uniform application of punishments to everybody without taking into account their former merits and positions, see also *Book of Lord Shang* 17.3.

人主釋法用私，

則上下不別矣。

However, when the ruler dismisses the law and follows his private inclinations,

there will be no distinction between superior and inferior.

4, 6 The C editors note: 「端」原當作「正」，避秦始皇諱改作「端」。　**10** C adds 峻 before 法 with 校注 51–52, following 王先慎, with 管子 parallel.　**11** C emends to 所以禁過外私也 with 校注 51–52, following 王先慎, with 管子 parallel.　**14**（貸）〔貳〕(校注 52, following 劉師培).　**14** 錯 is read as 措.　**27** 張抄、錢抄 have 柱 for 枉.　**29** 縣 is read as 懸.　**42** 繆 is read as 謬　**43** 絀 is read as 黜.　**46** All editions have 屬; we emend to 厲 following 王念孫.

CHAPTER 7

二柄 The Two Handles

HF 7.1 (*Xilun* 88, *Xin jiaozhu* 120)

明主之所導制其臣者，	A clear-sighted ruler directs and controls his ministers
二柄而已矣。	with just two handles.
二柄者，	These two handles
刑、德也。	are punishment and munificence (*de*).[1]
5 何謂刑、德？	What is meant by punishment and munificence?
曰：	I say:
殺戮之謂刑，	executing is called punishment;[2]
慶賞之謂德。	praising and rewarding is called munificence.
為人臣者畏誅罰而利慶賞，	Ministers are afraid of punishments and fines, and covet praise and rewards.
10 故人主自用其刑德，	Therefore, when a ruler employs the punishments and munificence that belong to him,
則群臣畏其威而歸其利矣。	his ministers will be in awe of his authority and seek his benefits.
故世之姦臣則不然：	However, the treacherous ministers of our age are not like that:
所惡，	Whomever *they* hate,
則能得之其主而罪之；	they can get their ruler to condemn;
15 所愛，	whomever *they* favour,
則能得之其主而賞之。	they can get their ruler to reward.

---

1 "Munificence" here stands for *de*, which is often translated as "moral virtue" or "charismatic power." The reader should bear in mind that all the three meanings are implicit in the term as used throughout the chapter. To preserve his charismatic power, the ruler should be morally upright and also able to benefit his subjects through his munificence.

2 There existed corporal punishments other than the death penalty. Han Fei gives an extreme example as a clarification of the term.

今人主非使賞罰之威利出於己也，	Now, if a ruler fails to ensure that the benefits of rewards and the authority of punishments stem from him alone,
聽其臣而行其賞罰，	and if he heeds his ministers in administering rewards and punishments,
則一國之人皆畏其臣而易其君，	then all people in the whole state will stand in awe of the ministers and slight the ruler,
20　歸其臣而去其君矣。	turning to the ministers and abandoning the ruler.
此人主失刑德之患也。	This is the calamity of a ruler's losing control over punishment and munificence.
夫虎之所以能服狗者， 爪牙也。	Now the reason why a tiger can subdue a dog is its claws and fangs.
使虎釋其爪牙而使狗用之，	Suppose the tiger were to relinquish its claws and fangs and let the dog use them:
25　則虎反服於狗矣。	the tiger would instead submit to the dog.
人主者， 以刑德制臣者也，	As for the ruler, he controls ministers through punishments and munificence.
今君人者釋其刑德而使臣用之，	Now, if the ruler gives up punishments and munificence, and allows his ministers to use them,
則君反制於臣矣。	the ruler will instead be controlled by his ministers.
30　故田常上請爵祿而行之群臣，	Thus Tian Chang requested ranks and emoluments from above, and distributed them to the ministers;
下大斗斛而施於百姓，	he increased the sizes of the picul and the five-picul measures below and dispensed grain to the hundred clans.[3]

---

3 Tian Chang is the most notorious figure in *Han Feizi*, the epitome of the malicious usurper. His seizure of power in the state of Qi in 481 became a watershed event in the history of the Springs-and-Autumns period. Thenceforth, Tian Chang's descendants were the de facto rulers of Qi, although it took another century before they assumed power de jure. Not much is known about Tian Chang's maintenance of rewards (this may well be Han Fei's invention). The story of manipulating measures is recorded in *Zuozhuan* (Zhao 3.3b) but is attributed to

二柄 THE TWO HANDLES

此簡公失德而田常用之也， Through this, Lord Jian lost his munificence,[4] whereas Tian Chang made use of it,

故簡公見弒。 and, consequently, Lord Jian was assassinated.

子罕謂宋君曰： Zihan said to the ruler of Song:[5]

35 "夫慶賞、賜予者， "Handing out rewards and granting boons
民之所喜也， are what the people like,
君自行[A 陽/庚 graŋ/ɣɐŋ]之； so the ruler should do these things himself;
殺戮、刑罰者， executions, punishments, and fines
民之所惡也， are what the people hate,
40 臣請當[A 陽/唐 taŋ/tâŋ]之。" so I beg to take charge of them."

於是宋君失刑而子罕用之。 Hence, the ruler of Song lost control of punishments, whereas Zihan made use of them,

故宋君見劫。 and, consequently, the ruler of Song was coerced.

田常徒用德而簡公弒， Tian Chang merely used munificence, yet Lord Jian was assassinated.

子罕徒用刑而宋君劫。 Zihan merely used punishments, yet the ruler of Song was coerced.

45 故今世為人臣者兼刑德而用之， Since the ministers of our age combine the employment of punishments and munificence,

則是世主之危甚於簡公、宋君也。 the peril of the rulers of our age is even greater than that of Lord Jian and the ruler of Song.

Tian Chang's predecessors. The Tian lineage leaders (either a father or grandfather of Tian Chang) employed two sets of measures: a larger one for lending out grain to their subjects, and a smaller one for collecting revenues. In this way they benefited the people below and amassed support for their future usurpation.

4 Normally "losing *de*" 失德 refers to the loss of charismatic power, or morality, or both, but not here. Lord Jian of Qi ruled for just three years (484–481) before being overthrown by Tian Chang, and his enthronement itself had been manufactured by Tian Chang in the first place.

5 Zihan's usurpation in the state of Song occurred in the fourth century, but the details are not narrated in *Records of Historian* and can only be tentatively restored from scattered references in *Han Feizi* and an entry in the *Bamboo Annals* (cited in the *Suoyin* gloss to *Shiji* 38: 1632). Zihan was a Song minister from the Huang 皇 branch of the Dai 戴 lineage, one of the leading aristocratic lineages in this state. His personal name was Xi 喜. For details, see Yang Kuan 2016: 310–313. Note that even Han Fei is not aware exactly who the object of Zihan's usurpation was, referring to the victim neutrally as "the ruler of Song."

72   CHAPTER 7

故劫殺擁蔽之，	They coerce, assassinate, block in, and keep the ruler in ignorance.
主兼失刑德而使臣用之，	For a ruler to lose control of punishments and munificence and let his ministers exercise these powers
而不危亡者，	and not be imperilled or brought to ruin –
50 則未嘗有也。	this is something that has never happened.

12 故 is read as 顧.   25 〔於〕(校注 58, with 意林 quotation).   43 張抄 has 常罕 for 田常. 47 擁 is read as 壅.   48 （非）〔兼〕(校注 58, following 陶鴻慶 and 津田鳳卿); 并 is also a possible emendation. C punctuates after 主.

HF 7.2 (*Xilun* 91, *Xin jiaozhu* 126)

人主將欲禁姦，	If a ruler wishes to prohibit treachery,
則審合刑名；	he must examine and compare performance and title.
刑名者，	"Performance and title,"
言異事也。	refers to whether one's proposals differ from one's tasks.
5 為人臣者陳而言，	When a minister has laid out a proposal,
君以其言授之事，	the ruler, on the basis of this proposal, assigns him a task,
專以其事責其功。	and solely on the basis of this task, demands achievements of him.
功當其事，	When the achievements match the task,
事當其言，	and the task matches the proposal,
10 則賞；	he is rewarded;
功不當其事，	when the achievements do not match the task,
事不當其言，	or the task does not match the proposal,
則罰。	he is punished.
故群臣其言大而功小者則罰，	Thus, if a minister makes a big proposal but achieves little, he will be punished.
15 非罰小功也，	It is not that [the ruler] punishes minor achievements,
罰功不當名也；	but he punishes achievements that do not match their titles.

二柄 THE TWO HANDLES

群臣其言小而功大者亦罰，	If a minister makes a minor proposal and achieves major achievements, he will also be punished.
非不說於大功也，	It is not that the ruler is not delighted by major achievements,
以為不當名也害甚於有大功，	but he considers that the harm of an achievement failing to match its title outweighs a major achievement,
20 故罰。	and that is why he is punished.
昔者韓昭侯醉而寢，	In ancient times, Marquis Zhao of Hán[6] was drunk and fell asleep.
典冠者見君之寒也，	The Supervisor of the Crown noticed that the ruler was cold
故加衣於君之上，	and put a jacket over him.
覺寢而說，	The ruler awoke from his slumber, pleased,
25 問左右曰：	and asked his entourage:
"誰加衣者？"	"Who put this jacket over me."
左右對曰：	His entourage replied:
"典冠。"	The Supervisor of the Crown."
君因兼罪典衣與典冠。	The ruler then punished both the Supervisor of the Jacket and the Supervisor of the Crown.
30 其罪典衣，	He punished the Supervisor of the Jacket,
以為失其事也；	because he considered him to have failed at his task;
其罪典冠，	he punished the Supervisor of the Crown,
以為越其職也。	because he considered him to have exceeded his office.
非不惡寒也，	It is not that he did not dislike the cold,
35 以為侵官之害甚於寒。	but he considered the harm of infringing upon another office to outweigh that of the cold.
故明主之畜臣，	Thus, the clear-sighted ruler rears his ministers,
臣不得越官而有功[A 東/東 kuŋ > kuaŋ ?/kuŋ]，	so that they cannot overstep their official duties in order to make achievements,
不得陳言而不當[A 陽/宕 taŋh/tâŋ]。	and cannot make proposals that do not match their tasks.

---

6 Marquis Zhao of Hán (r. 362–333) was the employer of Shen Buhai 申不害 (d. 337), one of the thinkers whom Han Fei respected. Marquis Zhao appears several times in *Han Feizi* as a positive example of a ruler who implements governing techniques adequately.

越官則死[B 脂/旨 sjidx/-jiəi/sji]，	When they exceed their official duties, they must die;
40　不當則罪[B 微/賄 dzədx/-əi/dzuậi]。	when they do not match their proposals, they must be punished.
守業其官，	If they attend to their tasks in their office,
所言者貞也，	and if what they propose is held to a strict standard,
則群臣不得朋黨相為矣。	then ministers will not be able to form factions and work for one another.

2–3 All editions have 審合刑名者; we emend to 審合刑名；刑名者, following 陶鴻慶 (校注 58).　4 C emends 異 to 與, following 校注 58, following 顧廣圻. 吳本、張抄、錢抄、藏本、張本 have 言異事也; 陳本、趙本 have 不異事也. We see no reason to emend, following 張覺.　19 C emends 也 to 之, following 王先慎; we see no reason to emend, following 張覺.

HF 7.3 (*Xilun* 95, *Xin jiaozhu* 130)

人主有二患：	For the ruler there are two perils:
任賢，	if he appoints the worthy,
則臣將乘於賢以劫其君；	ministers will rely on worthiness and coerce the ruler;
妄舉，	if he promotes people arbitrarily,
5　則事沮不勝。	tasks will stall and not succeed.
故人主好賢，	So, when a ruler favours the worthy,
則群臣飾行以要君欲，	all the ministers will adorn their conduct so as to pursue what the ruler desires.[7]
則是群臣之情不效；	As a result, the true disposition of the ministers will not show up clearly.
群臣之情不效，	And when the true disposition of the ministers does not show up clearly,
10　則人主無以異其臣矣。	a ruler has no means of discriminating among his ministers.
故越王好勇而民多輕死；	Thus, the King of Yue was fond of valour and many people made light of death;[8]

7　This statement is strongly reminiscient of one of the ideas in *Mozi* (e.g., "Elevating the worthy" 尚賢 chapters), according to which once a ruler decided on the criteria for promotion, all aspiring employees would align their behaviour accordingly. Several examples below also occur in *Mozi*.

8　This is a reference to King Goujian of Yue 越王勾踐 (r. 496–464) (see chapter 17, note 4). For his fondness of reckless bravery, see, e.g., *Mozi*, "Impartial care" or "Universal love"

二柄 THE TWO HANDLES	
楚靈王好細腰而國中多餓人；	King Ling of Chu liked slim waists, and many people starved themselves in his state;⁹
齊桓公妒外而好內，	Lord Huan of Qi was jealous of his ministers and fond of his harem,
故豎刁自宮以治內；	so Young Servant Diao castrated himself in order to take charge of the harem;¹⁰
15 桓公好味，	Lord Huan loved exquisite food,
易牙蒸其子首而進之；	so Yiya steamed his own son's head and presented it;¹¹
燕子噲好賢，	Zikuai of Yan favoured the worthy,
故子之明不受國。	so Zizhi made a show of not accepting the state.¹²
故君見惡，	If a ruler reveals his dislikes,
20 則群臣匿端；	the ministers will hide their inclinations;
君見好，	if a ruler shows his likes,
則群臣誣能。	the ministers will feign abilities.
人主欲見，	If the ruler's desires are visible,
則群臣之情態得其資矣。	the ministers will have the wherewithal to [adjust] their demeanor.

("*Jian'ai* 兼愛") 2 and 3; see also *Han Feizi* 30.3.2 and chapter 30, note 52. This topic is discussed also in the *Yue gong qi shi* 越公其事 manuscript from the Tsinghua University collection and in the parallel *Wu wang Fuchai qishi fa Yue* 吳王夫差起師伐越 manuscript discovered in 2020 in Tomb 46 at Zaolinpu Paper Mill 棗林鋪造紙廠, in Jingzhou (Hubei). See Pines 2022a: 398.

9 King Ling of Chu's 楚靈王 (r. 540–529) fondness of slim waists is again mentioned in *Mozi*, "Impartial care 2"; the phrase itself appears verbatim in *Yanzi chunqiu* 7.11 and in *Xunzi* ("The way of the ruler" ["Jun dao" 君道]); in the latter the fondness of slim waists is attributed to King Ling's grandfather, King Zhuang of Chu.

10 It is possible that the negative image of Lord Huan of Qi is confounded here with that of his infamous father, Lord Xiang (齊襄公, r. 698–686), who fornicated with his sister (see details in Schilling and Ptak 1998). Young Servant Diao's self-castration in order to be granted entry into the lord's harem is narrated, aside from *Han Feizi*, in *Guanzi* 32, "Minor appraisals" ("Xiao cheng" 小稱).

11 The story of Yiya boiling his son's head was created during the Warring States period; it is paralleled in *Guanzi* 32 "Minor appraisals" and later texts. Grotesque details aside, it is true that after Lord Huan's death, the machinations of Yiya and Eunuch Diao led to domestic turmoil in Qi and the collapse of its hegemony (*Zuozhuan*, Xi 17.5).

12 This refers to the infamous abdication of King Kuai (or Zikuai) of Yan to his minister, Zizhi, in 314. The details differ from one text to another, but there is no doubt that a real abdication did take place, bringing about civil war in Yan and its occupation by forces from the neighbouring states of Qi and Zhongshan. See more in Pines 2005: 268–271.

故子之託於賢以奪其君者也，

豎刁、易牙因君之欲以侵其君者也。
其卒子噲以亂死，
桓公蟲流出戶而不葬。

此其故何也？
人君以情借臣之患也。

人臣之情非必能愛其君也，

為重利之故也。

今人主不掩其情，
不匿其端，
而使人臣有緣以侵其主，

則群臣為子之、田常不難矣。

故曰：
"去好去惡[A 魚/暮 ʔagh/ʔuo]，
群臣見素[A 魚/暮 sagh/suo]。"
群臣見素[A 魚/暮 sagh/suo]，
則大君不蔽[A 祭/祭 pji-adh/pjiäi]矣。

In this way, Zizhi relied on worthiness in order to seize power from his ruler;
and Young Servant Diao and Yiya conformed to the ruler's desires in order to encroach upon him.
In the end, Zikuai died because of turmoil;
as for Lord Huan, the maggots from his corpse came streaming out through the door before he was buried.[13]
What were the reasons for this?
This is the disaster that comes when a rulers lets his ministers make use of his real feelings.
A minister's basic disposition is such that it is not necessary that he loves his ruler –
he acts to maximise his personal benefits.

Now, if the ruler does not conceal his feelings or hide his motivations,
but lets ministers have grounds upon which to infringe upon their ruler,
then for ministers to become like Zizhi or Tian Chang is not difficult.

So it is said:
"Discard likes, discard dislikes
and ministers will show their true colours."[14]
When ministers show their true colours,
the great ruler will not be hoodwinked by them.

13 C deletes 外, following 校注 58; 吳本、張抄、錢抄、趙本 have 外; 藏本、張本、陳 do not. We follow 陳奇猷 and 張覺.　**14** 張抄 has 官 for 宮.　**19** 君（子）見 (校注 58–59).　**28**（尸）〔戶〕(校注 59).　**38** 好〔去〕惡 (校注 59).

13　See *Shiji* 32: 1494 and chapter 10, note 56.
14　Compare to chapter 5.1, which may be the source of this self-referential citation.

CHAPTER 8

揚搉 The Grand Outline

C has 權 instead of 搉. 吳本、藏本、張本、趙本 have 揚權; 張抄、鏡抄 have 揚榷. 陳本 has 楊權. 揚搉 is a compound; it attested in *Erya* 爾雅 with the meaning 都凡; 搉 has been corrupted into 權, see 校注 59, 張覺 98, 陳奇猷 37–38.

HF 8.1 (*Xilun* 100, *Xin jiaozhu* 137)

天有大命[A 耕/映 mjiŋh/mjeŋ]，
人有大命[A 耕/映 mjiŋh/mjeŋ]。

夫香美[B 脂/旨 mjidx/-jiəi/mji]、脆味[B 微/未 mjədh/-jəi/mjwĕi]，
厚酒[C 幽/有 tsjəgwx/tsjŏu]、肥肉[C 幽/屋 ŋrjəkw/ńźjuk]，
甘口而疾形[E 耕/青 giŋ/ɣieŋ]；
曼理[F 之/止 ljəgx/lĭ]、皓齒[F 之/止 thjəgx/tśhĭ]，
說情[E 耕/清 dzjiŋ/dzjän]而捐精[E 耕/清 tsjiŋ/tsjän]。
故去甚去泰[G 祭泰 thadh/thâi]，
身乃無害[G 祭/泰 gadh/ɣâi]。
權不欲見，
素無為[G 歌/支 gwjar/jwĕ]也。

事在四方[H 陽/陽 pjaŋ/pjaŋ]，
要在中央[H 陽/陽 ʔjaŋ/ʔjaŋ]。

Heaven has its great mandate,
humans have their great mandate.

Aromatic and tender delicacies,[1]
rich ale and fatty meats

are sweet to the palate yet harmful to the body.
A delicate complexion and sparkling white teeth
will satisfy your libido but deplete your subtle essence.
So, if you shun indulgence and excess,[2]
your body will suffer no harm.
Your political leverage should never be on display,
and you should always practise non-assertive action.

Undertakings should be performed by [the ministers in charge of] the four quarters,
but the essential power should always remain at the centre.

---

1 Zhang Jue (2011: 100) argues that *cui* 脆 acquired its sense of "crispy, brittle" only later and in Han Fei's time meant "soft," being the antonym of *jian* 堅.
2 Cf. *Laozi* 39.

聖人執要[I 宵/笑 ʔjiagwh/ʔjiäu]，
15 四方來效[I 宵/效 gragwh/ɣau]。

虛而待[J 之/海 dəgx/dậi]之，
彼自以[J 之/止 rəgx/jï]之。
四海既藏[K 陽/唐 dzaŋ/dzâŋ]，
道陰見陽[K 陽/陽 raŋ/jiaŋ]。
20 左右既立[L 緝/緝 gljəp/ljəp]，
開門而當[K 陽/宕 taŋh/tâŋ]。

勿變勿易[L 佳/昔 rik/-jiek/jiäk]，
與二俱行[K 陽/庚 graŋ/ɣɐŋ]，
行之不已[M 之/止 rəgx/jï]，
25 是謂履理[M 之/止 ljəgx/lï]也。

The sage holds on to the essential
and [the ministers of] the four quarters come to offer their contributions.
Unassertive and empty, he awaits them,
and all by themselves they follow his lead.
As he encompasses all within the Four Seas,
he observes the overt through the hidden.
When his entourage has been established,
then, when the gates [of speech] are opened, [each proposal] will be fitting.

Avoiding change, avoiding deviation,
he marches along with the Two.[3]
Travelling on this path incessantly,
this is called treading the path of principle.[4]

8 去（泰）甚(校注 71)。

HF 8.2 (*Xilun* 103, *Xin jiaozhu* 141)

夫物者有所宜[A 歌/支 ŋjar/ŋjě]，

材者有所施[A 歌/支 sthjiar/śjě]，

各處其宜[A 歌/支 ŋjar/ŋjě]，
故上無為[A 歌/支 gwjar/jwě]。
5 使雞[B 佳/齊 kig/-iei/kiei]司夜[C 魚/禡 riagh/jia]，
令狸[B 之/止 ljəgx/-jəï/lï]執鼠[C 魚/語 hrjagx/śjwo]，
皆用其能[D 之/咍 nəg/nậi]，
上乃無事[D 之/志 dzrjəgh/dẓï]。

Just as things have that which they are suited for,
so human capacities have their fitting applications.
If each finds his proper place,
the ruler has no cause for assertive action.
He makes the cock take charge of the night
and orders the weasel to catch rats.

When all exercise their appropriate skills,
the ruler can be without matters to take care of.

---

3 That is, with name and performance, the core principles for governing the realm on the basis of proposals and service.

4 Chapter 20 elaborates on the notion of *li* 理 "principle," a central concept in several later trends in Chinese thought. See D.C. Lau 1989. For a broader perspective on *li*, see Deng Guoguang 2011.

揚搉 THE GRAND OUTLINE

上有所長[E 陽/陽 drjaŋ/djaŋ]，	When the ruler has something he excels at,
事乃不方[E 陽/陽 pjaŋ/pjaŋ]。	then his undertakings will be without direction.[5]
矜而好能[F 之/咍 nəg/nậi]，	If he is boastful and delights in his own abilities,
下之所欺[F 之/之 khjəg/khï]；	he will be cheated by inferiors;
辯惠好生，	if he is eloquent, knowledgeable, or fond of raising [discussions],
下因其材[F 之/咍 dzəg/dzậi]。	his subordinates will adapt to his talents.
上下易用，	When superiors and subordinates swap functions,
國故不治[F 之/之 drjəg/ḍï]。	the state will be in disorder.

4 All editions have 上下; we emend to 上 following 梁啟雄, cf. also 上乃無事 below.   13 惠 is read as 慧.

HF 8.3 (*Xilun* 104, *Xin jiaozhu* 145)

用一之道[A 幽/晧 dəgwx/dâu]，	Use the Way of unified control
以名為首[A 幽/有 hrjəgwx/śjǒu]，	by taking titles as the principal point.
名正[B 耕/勁 tjiŋh/tśjäŋ]物定[B 耕/徑 diŋh/dieŋ]，	When titles are correctly aligned, things will settle;
名倚[C 歌/紙 ʔjarx/-jei/ʔjě]物徙[C 佳/紙 sjigx/-jei/sjě]。	whereas when titles are slanted, things will shift.
故聖人執一以靜[D 耕/靜 dzjiŋx/dzjäŋ]，	And so the sage maintains a single-minded concentration with stillness,
使名[D 耕/清 mjiŋ/mjäŋ]自命[D 耕/映 mjiŋh/mjeŋ]，	as he makes titles impose themselves,
令事自定[D 耕/徑 diŋh/dieŋ]。	and makes tasks settle themselves.
不見其采，	He does not show his colours,
下故素正[D 耕/勁 tjiŋh/tśjäŋ]。	and so his subordinates become plain and straight.
因而任[*E 之/止 dzrjəgx/dẓï]之，	He employs them in response to circumstances,

---

5 The use of *fang* 方 here is puzzling – rhyming words often are.

	使自事[E 之/志 dzrjəgh/dẓï]之；	and makes them take charge of their business themselves.
	因而予[F 魚/語 ragx/jiwo]之，	He confers responsibilities on them according to circumstances,
	彼將自舉[F 魚/語 kjagx/kjwo]之；	and they themselves get things done;
	正與處[F 魚/語 khrjagx/tśhjwo]之，	he deals with people according to [which names] are correct,
15	使皆自定之，	and makes everybody decide [their responsibilities] for themselves.
	上以名舉[F 魚/語 kjagx/kjwo]之。	The ruler promotes people according to their titles;
	不知其名[G 耕/清 mjiŋ/mjän]，	when he does not know [the appropriateness of] their title,
	復脩其形[G 耕/青 giŋ/γieŋ]。	he oversees their performance.
	形名參同，	He holds up performance and title against each other,
20	用其所生[G 耕/庚 sriŋ/ṣeŋ]。	and implements the outcome of this.
	二者誠信[G 真/震 sjinh/sjĕn]，	When these two things are managed in good faith,
	下乃貢情[G 耕/清 dzjiŋ/dzjäŋ]。	Then those below will offer up their true thoughts.

1 〔之〕(校注 71). 10 因而仕之: all editions have 任; we emend to 仕 to rhyme with 事, following conjecture by 江有誥. The meaning is not changed.

HF 8.4 (*Xilun* 106, *Xin jiaozhu* 145)

	謹脩所事，	Work diligently at your tasks,
	待命於天[A 真/先 thin/thien]；	and await the commands of Heaven;
	毋失其要，	do not lose the essential,
	乃為聖人[A 真/真 njin/ńźjĕn]。	and you will become a sage.
5	聖人之道[B 幽/晧 dəgwx/dâu]，	The Way of the sage
	去智與巧[B 幽/巧 khrəgwx/khau]；	is to discard cleverness and craftiness.
	智巧不去，	If cleverness and craftiness are not discarded,
	難以為常[C 陽/陽 djaŋ/źjaŋ]；	[the Way of the sage] will be difficult to hold constant.

揚搉 THE GRAND OUTLINE

民人用之，
其身多殃[C 陽/陽 ʔjaŋ/ʔjaŋ]；
主上用之，
其國危亡[C 陽/陽 mjaŋ/mjaŋ]。

If an ordinary person should use [cleverness and craftiness],
his body will suffer much misfortune;
if the ruler should use them,
his state will be in danger of ruination.

因天之道[D 幽/晧 dəgwx/dâu]，
反形之理[E 之/止 ljəgx/lĭ]，
督參鞫[D 幽/屋 kjəkw/kjuk]之，
終則有始[E 之/止 sthjəgx/śĭ]；
虛以靜後，
未嘗用己[E 之/止 kjəgx/kĭ]。

Adapt to the Way of Heaven,
return to the principles of manifest reality;
survey, check, and investigate them,
and when you have reached the end, begin anew.
Be empty-minded and stay calmly in the rear,
never making use of your own self.

凡上之患[F 元/諫 gwranh/ɣwan]，
必同其端[F 元/桓 tuan/tuân]；
信而勿同[G 東/東 duŋ/duŋ]，
萬民一從[G 東/鍾 dzjuŋ/dzjwoŋ]。

In general, the ruler's disasters
are inevitably due to agreeing with the points [made by his ministers].
If [the ruler] entrusts matters to [his ministers], but does not express his agreement [with them],
the myriad people will follow him as one.

2, 4 According to 龍宇純, 天人 continues HF 8.3 rhyme as a 真/耕 hedge-rhyme; 夫 however marks a new section and begins a new rhyme.　15 鞠 is read as 鞫.　16 有 is read as 又.

HF 8.5 (*Xilun* 107, *Xin jiaozhu* 152)

夫道者，
弘大而無形；
德者，
覈理而普至；
至於群生[A 耕/庚 sriŋ/ʂeŋ]，
斟酌用之；
萬物皆盛[A 耕/勁 djiŋh/ʑjäŋ]，
而不與其寧[A 耕/青 niŋ/nieŋ]。

The "Way",
is vast in extent, yet has no definite shape;
"natural endowment (*de*)"
realises the patterns of things, reaching everywhere.
When it comes to living creatures,
if you use [the Way and natural endowment] in proper measure,
all the myriad things will flourish,
yet [the Way and natural endowment] do not participate in the well-being of these individual things.

道者，
10 下周於事，
因稽而命[A 耕/映 mjiŋh/mjɐŋ]，

與時死生[*A 耕/庚 sriŋ/ṣɐŋ]；
參名異事，

通一同情[A 耕/清 dziŋ/dzjäŋ]。

15 故曰：
道不同於萬物，

德不同於陰陽[B 陽/陽 raŋ/jiaŋ]，

衡不同於輕重[B 東/用 drjuŋh > drjuaŋh ʔ/djwoŋ]，
繩不同於出入[C 緝/緝 njəp/ńźjəp]，

20 和不同於燥濕[C 緝/緝 hrjəp/śjəp]，

君不同於群臣。

凡此六者，
道之出[D 微/術 thjət/-jət?/tśhjuĕt]也。
道無雙，
25 故曰一[D 脂/質 ʔjit/-jiət/ʔjiĕt]。
是故明君貴獨道之容。

君臣不同道[E 幽/晧 dəgwx/dâu]，

下以名禱[E 幽/晧 təgwx/tâu]。
君操其名[F 耕/清 mjiŋ/mjäŋ]，
30 臣效其形[F 耕/青 giŋ/yieŋ]，
形名參同，

上下和調也。

The "Way",
is present in all things in the world below,
and thus it penetrates all things and endows them with life,
causing them to be born and die in season.
Sort out names and distinguish among different undertakings,
connecting with Oneness and aligning with the essence of things.
So it is said:
The Way is not identical with the myriad things;
Natural endowment (*de*) is not identical with Yin and Yang;
scales are not identical with lightness and heaviness;
an ink-line is not identical with the degree of deviation being measured;
a tuning instrument is not identical with the dry or a wet state [of the strings to be tuned];
and the ruler is not identical with his ministers.

Altogether, these six
are products of the Way.
The Way has no counterpart,
so it is said to be One.
And so the clear-sighted ruler reveres the demeanor of the Solitary Way.
The ruler and the ministers do not follow the same Way;
subordinates plead according to their titles,
and the ruler manages their titles,
The ministers provide their performance,
and when performance and title are identical,
superiors and subordinates become well attuned.

揚搉 THE GRAND OUTLINE

12 All editions have 生死; we emend to 死生 for 生 to rhyme with 命 and 情, following conjecture by 顧廣圻; 江有誥 silently emends. The emendation has support in parallel in 舊注, as pointed out by 龍宇純. 17 〔於〕(校注 71–72). 21 (群於)〔於群〕(校注 72). 32 江有誥 conjectures that 調 is a (graphical) mistake for 同, and that this 同 rhymes with the 同 in the line above. 龍宇純 sees a rhyme between 調 and 同.

HF 8.6 (*Xilun* 110, *Xin jiaozhu* 156)

凡聽之道，	In general, the Way of listening [to proposals]
以其所出[A 微/術 thjət/tśhjuĕt]，	is that what is sent out
反以為之入[A 緝/緝 njəp/ńźjəp]。	should be turned around and made to be what comes back in.[6]
故審名以定位[A 緝/至 gwjəph/jwi]，	In this way, [the ruler] checks the titles [of officials] in order to determine their positions
明分以辯類[A 微/至 ljədh/ljwi]。	and distinguishes clearly between [positions] in order to differentiate the different categories [of duties].
聽言之道，	The Way of listening to proposals is such
溶若甚醉[B 微/至 tsjədh/-jiəi/tsjwi]。	that one should be casual and give the impression of being dead drunk.
脣乎齒[B 之/止 thjəgx/-jəĭ/tśhĭ]乎，	The lips! The teeth!
吾不為始[B 之/止 sthjəgx/-jəĭ/śĭ]乎。	I will not be the one to commence!
齒乎脣[C 文/諄 djən/dźjuĕn]乎，	The teeth! The lips![7]
愈惛惛[C 文/魂 hmən/xuən]乎。	I get more and more muddled!
彼自離[D 歌/支 ljiar/-jiar/-jiei/ljĕ]之，	Let them take apart [their proposals] themselves;
吾因以知[D 佳/支 trig/-jiəi/tjĕ]之；	I will then understand them.
是非輻湊[E 侯/候 tshugh/tshə̆u]，	Right and wrong [proposals] all come together like the spokes of a wheel,
上不與構[E 侯/候 kugh/kə̆u]。	but the ruler does not meddle with them.
虛靜無為，	That the ruler should be empty, still, and non-acting

---

6 If someone claims a certain competence (referred to as a "title" in the following), this claim should be used by the ruler to check this person's performance.

7 This refers to those of the ministers.

道之情[F 耕/清 dzjiŋ/dzjäŋ]也； is based upon the nature of the Way;
参伍比物， that he should classify and compare things,
事之形[F 耕/青 giŋ/ɣieŋ]也。 is based upon the disposition of [assigned] tasks.

20 参之以比物， Juxtapose things in order to check [performance],

伍之以合虛； arrange things in order to align yourself with emptiness.[8]

根幹不革， When the root and the trunk are maintained intact,

則動泄不失矣。 nothing will go wrong, whether it is moving or resting.[9]

動[G 東/董 duŋx/duŋ]之溶[G 東/鍾 grjuŋ/jiwoŋ]之， Whether matters move or rest,
25 無為而攻[*G 東/東 kuŋ/kuŋ]之。 reform them through non-assertive action.
喜[H 之/止 hjəgx/xï]之， If you like something,
則多事[H 之/志 dzrjəgh/dẓï]； undertakings will multiply;
惡[I 魚/暮 ʔagh/ʔuo]之， if you dislike something,
則生怨[I 元/願 ʔwjanh/ʔjwɐn]。 resentment will be created.
30 故去喜去惡[J 魚/暮 ʔagh/ʔuo]， Therefore, discard likes and dislikes
虛心以為道舍[J 魚/禡 sthjiagh/śja]。 and empty your mind and make it an abode for the Way.

上不與共[K 東/用 gjuŋh/gjwoŋ]之， When the ruler does not share [his power] with [his ministers],

民乃寵[K 東/腫 hljuŋx/ṭhjwoŋ]之； the people will be fond of him;
上不與義[L 歌/寘 njarh/ŋjě]之， When the ruler does not engage in debates with [his ministers],
35 使獨為[L 歌/支 gwjar/jwĕ]之。 he makes each act by himself.

上固閉內局[M 耕/青 kwiŋ/kiweŋ]， The ruler keeps the door to his inner chambers firmly shut,

從室視庭[M 耕/青 diŋ/dieŋ]， and from this room he surveys the court.
咫尺已具[N 侯/遇 gjugh > gjuagh ʔ/gju]， Once the measuring rod has been set,
皆之其處[N 魚/御 khrjagh/tśhjwo]。 everything will fall into place.

---

8 Wu 伍 "to subsume under categories for study" is a technical term which recurs in the binome can wu 參伍 "cross-check and classify."

9 The sentence is not easily decipherable. "Roots and trunk" seems to refer to basic legal and administrative procedure.

揚搉 THE GRAND OUTLINE

以賞者賞，	Those who should be rewarded will be rewarded,
以刑者刑[O 耕/青 giŋ/γieŋ]，	whereas those who should be punished will be punished,
因其所為，	all on the basis of what they have done,
各以自成[O 耕/清 djiŋ/źjäŋ]。	and each taking place by itself.
善惡必及，	When good or bad [performance] is bound to catch up with you,
孰敢不信[O 真/震 sjinh/sjěn]？	who would dare to be untrustworthy?
規矩既設[P 祭/薛 sthjat/śjät]，	Once the circle and T-square have been set,
三隅乃列[P 祭/薛 ljat/ljät]。	the [remaining] three corners will be aligned.[10]

5 辯 is read as 辨. 23 泄 is read as 歇. 25（改）〔攻〕(校注 72, following 陶鴻慶, to rhyme with 溶). 34 義 is read as 議. 37 庭（參）(校注 72).

HF 8.7 (*Xilun* 114, *Xin jiaozhu* 163)

主上不神[A 真/真 djin/dźjěn]，	When the ruler above fails to be secretive,
下將有因[A 真/真 ʔjin/ʔjiěn]；	those below him will have a basis [for scheming against him];
其事不當[B 陽/宕 taŋh/tâŋ]，	when he does not get things right,
下考其常[B 陽/陽 djaŋ/źjaŋ]。	his inferiors will investigate their general practicability.
若天若地[C 歌/至 diarh/-jei/dji]，	Be like Heaven, be like Earth –
是謂累解[C 佳/蟹 krigx/-riei/kaï]；	that is called 'being harmonious'.
若地若天[D 真/先 thin/thien]，	Be like Earth, be like Heaven –
孰疏孰親[D 真/真 tshjin/tshjěn]？	who is distant, who is close?[11]
能象天地，	He who takes Heaven and Earth as models
是謂聖人[D 真/真 njin/ńźjěn]。	is called a sage.
欲治其內，	If he wants his internal affairs to be well-governed,
置而勿親[D 真/真 tshjin/tshjěn]；	he places people in offices and avoids being familiar with them;

10 Cf. *Lunyu* 7.8.
11 The ruler should be detached from and out of reach of all of his subjects.

欲治其外，
官置一人[D 真/真 njin/ńźjĕn]；
15 不使自恣，
安得移并[D 耕/勁 pjiŋh/pjän]？

大臣之門，
唯恐多人[D 真/真 njin/ńźjĕn]。

凡治之極[E 之/職 gjək/gjək]，
20 下不能得[E 之/德 tək/tək]。

周合刑名，

民乃守職[E 之/職 tjək/tśjək]；

去此更求，
是謂大惑[E 之/德 gwək/ɣwək]。
25 猾民愈眾，

姦邪滿側[E 之/職 tsrjək/tṣjək]。

故曰：
毋富人而貸[E 之/代 thəgh/thậi]焉，

毋貴人而逼[E 之/職 pjiək/pjək]焉，

30 毋專信一人而失其都國[E 之/德 kwək/kwək]焉。

腓大於股，

難以趣走[F 侯/厚 tsugx/tsŏu]；

12　If the high ministers are able to dispense largesse or issue punishments (as discussed in chapter 7), then cliques will form around them, endangering the ruler.

if he wants his external affairs to be well-governed,
he establishes one person for each office
and does not let them do as they please –
for how would they then be able to shift around and encroach on the offices of others?

As for the gates of the senior ministers,
he only fears that too many people gather there.[12]

In general, at the height of good governance,
those below are unable to gain control [of the reins of government].

If you comprehensively compare performance and title,

the people will keep to their duties.

If you discard this and seek something else,
it is called "great confusion."
Glib deceivers will grow more and more numerous,

and treacherous and deviant people will crowd around you.

So it is said:
do not enrich others and then borrow from them;

do not ennoble others and then be coerced by them;

do not exclusively trust one person, lest you lose [both] your administrative centres and your state.

If the calf of the leg were larger than the thigh,
it would be hard to run fast.

揚搉 THE GRAND OUTLINE

主失其神，	If the ruler loses his secretiveness,
虎隨其後[F 侯/厚 gugx/ɣǒu]；	tigers[13] will follow in his rear;
主上不知，	if the ruler does not realise this,
虎將為狗[F 侯/厚 kugx/kǒu]。	the tigers will become like dogs.[14]
主不蚤止[G 之/止 tjəgx/tśǐ]，	If the ruler does not nip this in the bud,
狗益無已[G 之/止 rəgx/jiǐ]	dogs will proliferate endlessly.
虎成其群，	When the tigers form their packs,
以弒其母[G 之/厚 məgx/mǒu]；	they will assassinate even their own mother.
為主而無臣，	If you are the ruler but do not have [reliable] ministers,
奚國之有[G 之/有 gwjəgx/jǒu]？	then what state is there for you to possess?
主施其法[H 葉/乏 pjap/pjwep]，	When the ruler enacts laws,
大虎將怯[H 葉/業 khjap/khjep]；	the great tigers will become faint-hearted;
主施其刑[I 耕/青 giŋ/ɣieŋ]，	when the ruler enacts punishments,
大虎自寧[I 耕/青 niŋ/nieŋ]。	the great tigers will acquiesce of themselves;
法刑苟信[J 真/震 sjinh/sjěn]，	when the application of laws and punishments is reliable,
虎化為人[J 真/真 njin/ńźjěn]，	the tigers will be transformed into men,
復反其真[J 真/真 tjin/tśjěn]。	reverting to their true state.

6 累解 should possibly be reversed to read 蟹埣[歌/果 kwarx/kuâ], with the meaning 平正.　30 張抄 has 郡 for 都.　32 趣 is read as 趨.　47 王先慎 reads 信 as 申.　47（狗）〔苟〕校注 72; all editions have 狗; we emend to 苟 following 盧文弨 and 太田方.

HF 8.8 (Xilun 117, Xin jiaozhu 170)

欲為其邦[*A 東/江 pruŋ/påŋ]，	If you wish to run a state,
必伐其聚[A 蒸 東/東 dzuŋ/dzuŋ]；	you must attack the accumulation [of supporters by your ministers];
不伐其聚[A 蒸 東/東 dzuŋ/dzuŋ]，	if you do not attack this,
彼將聚眾[A 中/送 tjəŋwh/tśjuŋ]。	[the ministers] will gather hordes [of supporters].
欲為其地[B 歌/至 diarh/-jei/dji]，	If you wish to administer your territory,

---

13　Tigers are those ministers who represent mortal threats to their ruler (see also chapter 5.2).
14　Dogs are ostensibly submissive, but beneath this apparent subservience they are ruler-devouring tigers.

必適其賜[B 佳/賔 stjigh/-jiei/sjě] ；

不適其賜[B 佳/賔 stjigh/-jiei/sjě] ，
亂人求益[B 佳/昔 ʔjik/-jiek/ʔjäk] 。
彼求[C 幽/尤 gjəgw/gjŏu]我予[D 魚/語 ragx/-jo/jiwo] ，
假仇[C 幽/尤 gjəgw/gjŏu]人斧[D 魚/麌 pjagx/-juo/pju] ；
假之不可[E 歌/哿 kharx/khâ] ，
彼將用之以伐我[E 歌/哿 ŋarx/ŋâ] 。

黃帝有言曰：
"上下一日百戰。"

下匿其私，
用試其上[F 陽/漾 djaŋh/ʑjaŋ] ；
上操度量[F 陽/漾 ljaŋh/ljaŋ] ，
以割其下。
故度量之立，

主之寶[G 幽/晧 pəgwx/pâu]也；
黨與之具[H 侯/遇 gjugh/gju] ，
臣之寶[G 幽/晧 pəgwx/pâu]也。
臣之所不弒其君者，

黨與不具[H 侯/遇 gjugh/gju]也。

故上失扶寸[I 文/慁 tshənh/-uən/tshuən] ，

下得尋常[J 陽/陽 djaŋ/ʑjaŋ] 。
有國之君[I 文/文 kwjən/-jən/kjuən] ，
不大其都[J 魚/模 tag/tuo] ；

you must properly adjust your bestowals [of land];
if you do not properly adjust your bestowals,
riotous people will want more and more.
If you give whatever they demand,

that amounts to lending an axe to your enemies.
To lend them an axe will not do:
they will go on to use it to attack yourself.

The Yellow Thearch had a saying:[15]
"Superiors and inferiors fight a hundred battles each single day."
Inferiors hide their private ambitions
in order to sound out their superiors;
superiors wield standards and measures
in order to curb their subordinates.
And so, the establishment of standards and measures
is the ruler's treasure;
the formation of factions and cliques
is the minister's treasure.
The only reason why ministers do not assassinate their rulers,
is that their factions and cliques are not established yet.
So, when the superior misses by a few inches,
his inferiors gain by yards.
The ruler, in charge of the capital,
does not enlarge the secondary cities [of his ministers];[16]

---

15   The Yellow Thearch is the mythical progenitor of Chinese civilisation, whose figure gained particular prominence in the texts associated with the so-called Huang-Lao 黃老 school represented by the "Yellow Thearch's Manuscripts" (*Huangdi shu* 黃帝書), unearthed in 1973 from Tomb 3, Mawangdui. The historian Sima Qian identified Han Fei himself as adherent of Huang-Lao (*Shiji* 63: 2146), yet the Yellow Thearch is only rarely invoked as an authority in *Han Feizi*; hence the above statement is somewhat exceptional.
16   That a secondary city (*du* 都, a regional administrative centre) should be kept small in

揚摧 THE GRAND OUTLINE

有道之臣[I 真/真 grjin/-jiən/źjĕn]，   ministers who follow the Way
不貴其家[J 魚/麻 krag/ka]。   do not ennoble members of their families.
有道之君[J 文/文 kwjən/-jən/kjuən]，   A ruler who follows the Way
不貴其臣[I 真/真 grjin/-jiən/źjĕn]；   does not ennoble his ministers.
貴之富[K 之/宥 pjəgh/pjŏu]之，   If the ruler ennobles and enriches them,
彼將代[K 之/代 dəgh/dậi]之。   they will eventually replace him.
備危恐殆[K 之/海 dəgx/dậi]，   If you are prepared for danger and apprehensive of life-threatening situations,
急置太子[K 之/止 tsjəgx/tsǐ]，   and if you establish a crown prince with expediency,[17]
禍乃無從起[K 之/止 khjəgx/khǐ]。   there will be nowhere for misfortune to arise.

1 All editions have 國; we follow 顧廣圻 and 洪頤煊 in regarding 國 as a taboo character for 邦[東/江 pruŋ/påŋ], rhyming with 聚.   2 聚 is read as 冣 with 顧廣圻 and 洪頤煊. The 冣[侯/遇 dzjugh/dzju] reading could also be regarded as rhyming.   17 （下）〔上〕（校注 72）.   26 下得尋常: 意林 continues with 君不可不慎, 慎[真/震 djinh/źjĕn] rhymes with 寸; 龍宇純 suggests emending on the basis of 意林.   26 陶鴻慶 holds that the passage from 內索 to 其罰 should be moved here for reasons of rhyme.   27 陶鴻慶 holds that the passage from 有國之君 to 無從起 should be moved close to 勿弛而弓一栖兩雄 for reasons of rhyme.   34 （備）〔彼〕（校注 72, following 顧廣圻）.

HF 8.9 (Xilun 119, Xin jiaozhu 170)

內索出圄[A 魚/語 njagx/njwo]，   When it comes to putting people in fetters or releasing them from prison,
必身自執其量度[*A 魚/暮 dagh/duo]。   you must personally hold onto the standards of assessment.
厚者虧[B 歌/支 khwjar/khjwĕ]之，   If people are affluent, reduce their wealth,
薄者靡[B 歌/紙 mjiarx/mjĕ]之。   If people are in want, increase their wealth.
虧靡有量[C 陽/漾 ljaŋh/ljaŋ]，   When reducing or increasing, you must have standards,
毋使民比周，   lest the people band together
同欺其上[C 陽/漾 djaŋh/źjaŋ]。   and collude in cheating their ruler.

comparison to the capital, is noted already in *Zuozhuan* (e.g., Yin 1.4a; Huan 18.3; Zhao 11.10).

17   *Han Feizi* 15 places an emphasis on the dangers associated with appointing a crown prince.

虧之若月[D 祭/月 ŋwjat/ŋjwet]，
靡之若熱[D 祭/薛 njat/ńźjät]。
10 簡令謹誅，
必盡其罰[D 祭/月 bjat/bjwet]。

When reducing, you should be [gradual] like the [waxing and waning] moon,
when increasing, you should be [gradual] like the onset of heat in summer.
Simplify statutes, be meticulous in executions,
and be sure to see your punitive actions through to the end.

2 All editions have 度量; we follow 江有誥 in emending to 量度 to rhyme with 囿. 量 could also be excrescent.

HF 8.10 (*Xilun* 121, *Xin jiaozhu* 170)

毋弛而弓[A 蒸/東 kwjəŋ/kjuŋ]，
一棲兩雄[A 蒸/東 gwjəŋ/juŋ]。
一棲兩雄，
其鬥嚷嚷[B 顏 元/刪 ŋran/ŋan]；
5 豺狼在牢，
其羊不繁[B 元/元 bjan/bjwen]。
一家二貴，
事乃無功[C 東/東 kuŋ/kuŋ]；
夫妻持政，
10 子無適從[C 東/鍾 dzjuŋ/dzjwoŋ]。

Do not slacken your bow,
lest there be two roosters on one perch.
When there are two roosters on one perch,
there will be noisy struggles.
When there are jackals and wolves in the fold,
the sheep will not procreate.
If one household has two persons who are venerated,
its undertakings will be unsuccessful.
When the husband and wife both manage a household,
their children will not know whom to follow and obey.[18]

HF 8.11 (*Xilun* 122, *Xin jiaozhu* 170)

為人君者，
數披其木[A 侯/屋 muk > muak ?/muk]，

A ruler of men
often prunes his trees,

---

18   This abhorrence of the dispersal of power above is a persistent topic in Warring States literature. See, e.g., *Xunzi* 11: 223–224 ("Wang ba" 王霸); *Guanzi* 23: 472 ("Ba yan" 霸言) and 52: 998–999 ("Qi chen qi zhu" 七臣七主); *Shenzi*, fragments 58–60 ("De li" 德立); *Huang Di shu*, 1: 30–31 ("Da fen" 大分); *Lüshi chunqiu* 17.8: 1132 ("Zhi yi" 執一).

揚攉 THE GRAND OUTLINE

毋使木枝扶疏[A 魚/魚 srjag/sjwo]； lest their branches grow all over;
木枝扶疏[A 魚/魚 srjag/sjwo]， for if their branches grow all over,
將塞公閭[A 魚/魚 ljag/ljwo]， they will block the gates of the lord,
私門將實， and if the private gates [of ministerial houses] fill up,

公庭將虛[A 魚/魚 hjag/xjwo]， the lord's halls[19] will be empty
主將壅圉[*A 魚/語 ŋjagx/ŋjwo]。 and the ruler will be penned in.
數披其木[A 侯/屋 muk > muak ʔ/muk]， [The ruler] often prunes his trees,
無使木枝外拒[A 魚/語 gjagx/gjwo]； lest their branches grow long;
木枝外拒[A 魚/語 gjagx/gjwo]， for if their branches grow long,
將逼主處[A 魚/御 khrjagh/tśhjwo]。 they will encroach on his abode.
數披其木[A 侯/屋 muk > muak ʔ/muk]， He often prunes his trees,
毋使枝大本小[A 宵/小 sjagwx/sjäu]； lest the branches become large and the trunks small;

枝大本小[A 宵/小 sjagwx/sjäu]， for if the branches become large and the trunks small,

將不勝春風[B 侵/東 pjəm/pjuŋ]； they will not stand up to the storms of spring;

不勝春風[B 侵/東 pjəm/pjuŋ]， and if they do not stand up to the storms of spring,

枝將害心[B 侵/侵 sjəm/sjəm]， the branches will harm the heartwood.
公子既眾[B 中/送 tjəŋwh/tśjuŋ]， When the junior lines are many,
宗室憂唫[B 侵/侵 ŋjəm/ŋjəm]。 the main family should worry and groan.

止之之道[C 幽/晧 dəgwx/dâu]： The way to stop this
數披其木[C 侯/屋 muk > muak ʔ/muk]， is to prune the trees often,
毋使枝茂[C 幽/候 məgwh/mə̆u]； lest their branches grow too abundant.
木數披[D 歌/支 phjiar/phjĕ]， If he often prunes his trees,
黨與乃離[D 歌/支 ljiar/ljĕ]。 the factions will be dispersed.

掘其根本[E 文/混 pənx/-uən/puən]， Dig out their roots,
木乃不神[E 真/真 djin/-jiən/dźjĕn]； and the trees will lose their vitality;
填其洶淵[E 真/先 ʔwin/ʔiwen]， fill up the swirling pool,
毋使水清[E 耕/清 tshjiŋ/-jieŋ/tshjäŋ]。 lest its waters become agitated.
探其懷[F 微/皆 gwrəd/ɣwăi]， Probe their inner thoughts
奪之威[F 微/微 ʔwjəd/ʔjwĕi]； and divest them of any authority.

---

19 The ruler is here uncharacteristically defined by the archaic term duke/lord (*gong* 公) to emphasise the affinity between the ruler and the principle of impartiality or common interest (*gong* 公).

主上用之，
若電若雷[F 微/灰 ləd/luâi]。

The ruler uses this [technique]
like lightning, like thunder.

2–22 木 appears to have an aberrant pronunciation throughout this section.　8 We emend 圍 to 圉, following 顧廣圻 and 龍宇純 in order to rhyme with 拒 and 處.　26 顧廣圻, 俞樾 and 陳啟天 regard 本 as excrescent, making 神 rhyme with 根[文/痕 kən/kən]. 盧文弨 reverses order of 根本. 陳奇猷 regards this as unnecessary, since 本 and 神 can be held to rhyme.

CHAPTER 9

八姦 Eight Villainies

HF 9.1.0 (*Xilun* 125, *Xin jiaozhu* 181)

凡人臣之所道成姦者有八術。	Altogether, there are eight techniques that ministers follow when they perpetrate treachery.¹

HF 9.1.1 (*Xilun* 126, *Xin jiaozhu* 181)

一曰"同床[A 陽/陽 dzrjaŋ/dzjaŋ]"。	The first is called "bedfellows."
何謂"同床"?	What is meant by "bedfellows"?
曰:	It is as follows:
貴夫人,	A wife who is honoured,
5 愛孺子,	young concubines that one dotes upon,
便僻好色,	fawning maidens and comely lads;
此人主之所惑也。	these are what lead a ruler astray.
託於燕處之虞,	They use the pleasures of leisure as pretext
乘醉飽之時,	and avail themselves of times when you are drunk and satiated,
10 而求其所欲,	to seek what they desire –
此必聽之術也。	this is the technique that ensures that they are heard.
為人臣者內事之以金玉,	When ministers bribe (their cronies) in the inner court with presents of gold and jade
使惑其主,	to make them confound their ruler;
此之謂"同床[A 陽/陽 dzrjaŋ/dzjaŋ]"。	this is what is meant by "bedfellows."

1 All editions have 在 following 曰; this has been deleted as excrescent, as an echo of the following 在旁, following 陶鴻慶. 6 僻 is read as 嬖. 8 虞 is read as 娛.

---

1 Note the special use of *shu* 術 in this chapter as referring to ministerial trickery, which is quite different from the use of this term in the rest of the book.

HF 9.1.2 (*Xilun* 127, *Xin jiaozhu* 181)

二曰"在旁[A 陽/唐 baŋ/bâŋ]"。	The second is called "those at your side."
何謂"在旁"？	What is meant by "those at your side"?
曰：	It is as follows:
優笑侏儒，	Jesters and dwarves,
5　左右近習，	aides and cronies,
此人主未命而唯唯，	these people say, 'Yes! Yes!' before a ruler has given an order,
未使而諾諾，	and before he has given an assignment, they say 'Will do! Will do!'
先意承旨，	They anticipate [the ruler's] intentions, they make up to his will
觀貌察色以先主心者也。	and are the kind of people who observe appearances and examine facial expressions, so as to anticipate what is on the ruler's mind.
10　此皆俱進俱退，	They all come forward as a group and withdraw as a group;
皆應皆對，	they all respond and all reply (in unison)
一辭同軌以移主心者也。	and are the kind of people who are unison in their phrasing and follow the same path, so as to influence the ruler's thinking.
為人臣者內事之以金玉玩好，	Inside the court, ministers cultivate their cronies with gold, jade, playthings, and beautiful objects,
外為之行不法，	and on the outside they skew laws in behalf of them,
15　使之化其主，	all in order to let these people mould their ruler.
此之謂"在旁[A 陽/唐 baŋ/bâŋ]"。	This is what is meant by "those at your side."

13 （比）〔之〕（校注 79）.

HF 9.1.3 (*Xilun* 127, *Xin jiaozhu* 181)

三曰"父兄[A 陽/庚 hwjiaŋ/xjweŋ]"。	The third is called "uncles and brothers."
何謂"父兄"？	What is meant by "uncles and brothers"?
曰：	It is as follows:
側室公子，	Princes of his own generation and sons not in the line of inheritance
5　人主之所親愛也；	are people for whom the ruler cares and feels affection.

八姦 EIGHT VILLAINIES

大臣廷吏，	Senior ministers and court officials
人主之所與度計也。	are people with whom the ruler makes plans.
此皆盡力畢議，	They all do their best to deliberate thoroughly,
人主之所必聽也。	and the ruler is bound to listen to them.
10　為人臣者事公子側室以音聲子女，	When ministers ingratiate themselves with secondary princes, using music and young maidens,
收大臣廷吏以辭言，	when they win over senior ministers and officials with polished speeches;
處約言事，	when they enter into pacts and speak on official matters.
事成則進爵益祿，	and when they advance them in rank and increase their emoluments when matters succeed,
以勸其心，	spurring them on
15　使犯其主，	and leading them to oppose their ruler.
此之謂"父兄[A 陽/庚 hwjiaŋ/xjweŋ]"。	This is what is meant by "uncles and brothers."

10 事（畢）公 (校注 79).

HF 9.1.4 (*Xilun* 128, *Xin jiaozhu* 182)

四曰"養殃[A 陽/陽 ʔjaŋ/ʔjaŋ]"。	The fourth is called "breeding disaster."
何謂"養殃"？	What is meant by "breeding disaster"?
曰：	It is as follows:
人主樂美宮室臺池，	A ruler enjoys fine palaces, chambers, terraces, and ponds;
5　好飾子女狗馬以娛其心，	he is fond of adorning maidens and dressing up hounds and horses to keep himself entertained,
此人主之殃也。	but this spells disaster for a ruler.
為人臣者盡民力以美宮室臺池，	When ministers exhaust the people's strength to beautify palaces, chambers, terraces, and ponds,
重賦斂以飾子女狗馬，	when they increase taxes and levies in order to be able to adorn maidens and dress up hounds and horses,
以娛其主而亂其心，	all in order to entertain the ruler and confuse his mind,
10　從其所欲，	when they go along with his desires
而樹私利其間，	and secure private gains from this –
此謂"養殃[A 陽/陽 ʔjaŋ/ʔjaŋ]"。	this is what is meant by "breeding disaster."

HF 9.1.5 (*Xilun* 129, *Xin jiaozhu* 182)

五曰"民萌[A 陽/耕 mraŋ/mɛŋ]"。	The fifth is called "common people."
何謂"民萌"？	What is meant by "common people"?
曰：	It is as follows:
為人臣者散公財以說民人，	When ministers distribute public assets[2] in order to please the people,
行小惠以取百姓，	and carry out trifling acts of generosity in order to win over the hundred clans,
使朝廷市井皆勸譽己，	making everyone praise them, from the palace halls to the market places,
以塞其主而成其所欲，	so as to block off the ruler and achieve what they desire.
此之謂"民萌[A 陽/耕 mraŋ/mɛŋ]"。	This is what is meant by "common people."

HF 9.1.6 (*Xilun* 130, *Xin jiaozhu* 182)

六曰"流行[A 陽/庚 graŋ/ɣeŋ]"。	The sixth is called "rampant eloquence."
何謂"流行"？	What is meant by "rampant eloquence?"
曰：	It is as follows:
人主者，	As for the ruler,
固壅其言談，	if he is blocked off from proposals and debates,
希於聽論議，	and rarely hears discussions and deliberations,
易移以辯說。	he will easily be swayed by sophistry.
為人臣者求諸侯之辯士，	The ministers will search for the most eloquent gentlemen among the employees of the regional lords;
養國中之能說者，	they will cultivate the state's most persuasive persons,
使之以語其私；	and have them talk in favour of their private interests.
為巧文之言，	They will make up proposals with clever rhetoric
流行之辭，	and fashionable phrases;
示之以利勢[B 祭/祭 sthjadh/śjäi]，	they will suggest to the ruler where his profitable situation lies,

---

2 "Public assets" 公財 could in principle be translated also as "the duke's (ruler's) assets," but in this context the duke's personal property is not at issue.

八姦 EIGHT VILLAINIES

懼之以患害[B 祭/泰 gadh/γâi]，	and scare him with impending trouble and harm,
15 施屬虛辭以壞其主，	deploying empty slogans in order to wreck him.
此之謂"流行[A 陽/庚 graŋ/γeŋ]"。	This is what is meant by "rampant eloquence."

15 壞 is attested in 吳本、張抄、錢抄、藏本、張本、趙本, 懷 by 陳本、嚴本. 壞 is possibly a corruption of 環, cognate to 營、瑩 'to confuse'; cf. 釋評 358 and 陳奇猷.

HF 9.1.7 (*Xilun* 130, *Xin jiaozhu* 182)

七曰"威強[A 陽/陽 gjaŋ/gjaŋ]"。	The seventh is called "strength of authority."
何謂"威強"？	What is meant by "strength of authority"?
曰：	It is as follows:
君人者，	The ruler
5 以群臣百姓為威強者也。	is one who gains strength of authority through his ministers and all the hundred clans.
群臣百姓之所善，	Whatever the ministers and the hundred clans consider good,
則君善之；	the ruler will consider good,
非群臣百姓之所善，	and whatever the ministers and the hundred clans do not consider good,
則君不善之。	the ruler will not consider good.
10 為人臣者，	Ministers
聚帶劍之客，	will gather retainers wielding swords;
養必死之士，	they will raise soldiers who have no fear of death
以彰其威；	in order to flaunt their authority.
明為己者必利[C 脂/至 ljidh/lji]，	They will point out that those who work for them are sure to profit
15 不為己者必死[C 脂/旨 sjidx/sji]，	and those who do not are sure to die,
以恐其群臣百姓而行其私[C 脂/脂 sjid/sji]，	so as to terrorise both (the rest of) the ministers and the hundred clans, in pursuit of their private ends.
此之謂"威強[A 陽/陽 gjaŋ/gjaŋ]"。	This is what is meant by "strength of authority."

4 (臣)〔人〕(校注 79).

HF 9.1.8 (*Xilun* 131, *Xin jiaozhu* 182)

八曰"四方[A 陽/陽 pjaŋ/pjaŋ]"。	The eighth is called "the four directions."
何謂"四方"？	What is meant by "the four directions"?
曰：	It is as follows:
君人者，	When the ruler's
5　國小，	state is small,
則事大國；	he will serve a bigger state;
兵弱，	when his military force is weak,
則畏強兵。	he will stand in dread of powerful military forces.
大國之所索，	When a big state demands something,
10　小國必聽；	a small state is bound to listen;
強兵之所加，	when a strong military force is deployed,
弱兵必服。	a weak military force is bound to submit.
為人臣者，	The ministers
重賦斂，	will then increase taxes and levies,
15　盡府庫，	exhaust the storehouses and armouries;
虛其國以事大國，	deplete the state in order to serve the greater state
而用其威求誘其君；	and use its authority in an attempt to cajole their ruler.
甚者舉兵以聚邊境而制斂於內，	In the worst case, they will raise an army [in the big state] and assemble it on the borders in order to constrain their central regions;
薄者數內大使以震其君，	in the best case, they will regularly invite large delegations [from the big state] in order to throw their ruler off balance
20　使之恐懼，	and fill him with fear.
此之謂"四方[A 陽/陽 pjaŋ/pjaŋ]"。	This is what is meant by "the four directions."

HF 9.1.9 (*Xilun* 132, *Xin jiaozhu* 182)

凡此八者，	In general, these eight things,
人臣之所以道成姦，²	are the paths which ministers follow in order to achieve their wicked aims
世主所以壅劫，	and the means by which the ruler is blocked in and coerced,
失其所有也，	losing everything he has.
5　不可不察焉。	You should not fail to investigate them.

2 The C editors note: 此句有誤，疑本作「人臣所道以成姦」。(cf. HF 9.1.0).

八姦 EIGHT VILLAINIES

HF 9.2.1 (*Xilun* 132, *Xin jiaozhu* 190)

明君之於內也，	The clear-sighted ruler treats his inner quarters
娛其色而不行其謁，	in a way that he enjoys their beauty but does not act on their petitions
不使私請。	or allow their personal requests.

HF 9.2.2 (*Xilun* 133, *Xin jiaozhu* 190)

其於左右也，	He treats his entourage
使其身必責其言，	in a way that when he employs them, he makes them accountable for their proposals,
不使益辭。	and he does not allow them to make inflated reports.

HF 9.2.3 (*Xilun* 133, *Xin jiaozhu* 190)

其於父兄大臣也，	He treats uncles and brothers and senior ministers
聽其言也必使以罰任於後，	in a way that, when he listens to their proposals, he makes sure to use the threat of punishment to hold them responsible for the outcome,
不令妄舉。	and so does not allow them to make reckless suggestions.

HF 9.2.4 (*Xilun* 134, *Xin jiaozhu* 190)

其於觀樂玩好也，	In watching musical performances and fiddling with playthings,
必令之有所出，	he ensures that they have a proper provenance
不使擅進、擅退，	and does not allow them to be proffered or withdrawn without authorisation;
不使群臣虞其意。	and so he does not allow ministers to figure out his intentions.

3 擅進〔擅退〕(校注 79, following 陳奇猷).   4 不使（擅退）群臣 (校注 79, following 陳奇猷).

HF 9.2.5 (*Xilun* 135, *Xin jiaozhu* 190)

其於德施也，	As for dispensing munificence,
縱禁財、發墳倉、利於民者，	releasing restricted goods, opening the brimming granaries, and other measures that benefit the people,
必出於君，	these must always originate from the ruler,
不使人臣私其德。	and it should never be allowed for ministers to draw private advantage from such dispensations of munificence.

HF 9.2.6 (*Xilun* 135, *Xin jiaozhu* 190)

其於說議也，	In arguments and debates,
稱譽者所善、毀疵者所惡，	regarding those who are acclaimed by people who praise them and those who are vilified by people who malign them,
必實其能、察其過，	he is sure to verify their abilities and investigate their faults,
不使群臣相為語。	not allowing ministers to argue in support of one another.

HF 9.2.7 (*Xilun* 135, *Xin jiaozhu* 190)

其於勇力之士也，	Regarding soldiers of courage and strength,
軍旅之功無踰賞，	he does not exceed the standard rewards for those with military achievements;
邑鬥之勇無赦罪，	he does not grant any amnesty to bravoes in local feuds,
不使群臣行私財。	and does not allow ministers to make use of their assets for private (military) ends.

1 〔於〕(校注 79).　2 張抄 has 喻 for 踰.

八姦 EIGHT VILLAINIES

HF 9.2.8 (*Xilun* 136, *Xin jiaozhu* 190)

其於諸侯之求索也，	Regarding entreaties from regional lords,
法則聽之，	when they conform to the standards, he heeds them;
不法則距之。	when they do not, he rejects them.

3 距 is read as 拒.

HF 9.3 (*Xilun* 136, *Xin jiaozhu* 194)

所謂亡君者，	When someone is called "a doomed ruler,"
非莫有其國也，	it not a ruler who has no state of his own,
而有之者皆非己有也。	but one who has a state which he does not have by himself.
令臣以外為制於內，	He allows his ministers to take control of internal affairs on the basis of external connections;
則是君人者亡也。	this spells ruin for a ruler.
聽大國為救亡也，	If he acquiesces to a great state in order to avoid his ruin,
而亡亟於不聽，	ruin will come sooner than if he had not done so.
故不聽。	That is why he should not acquiesce.
群臣知不聽，	When his ministers know that he does not acquiesce,
則不外諸侯；	they will not make external connections with the regional lords;
諸侯之不聽，	when the regional lords are not acquiesced in,
則不受臣之誣其君矣。	they will not bid the ministers calumniate against their ruler.

11 C emends 之 to 知 following 顧廣圻 and 校注 79; we find this unnecessary, following 張覺.
12 （之臣）〔臣之〕（校注 79）.

HF 9.4 (*Xilun* 137, *Xin jiaozhu* 196)

明主之為官職爵祿也，	A clear-sighted ruler establishes offices and duties, ranks and stipends,
所以進賢材、勸有功也。	in order to promote the talented and encourage those with achievements.

故曰：	So it is said,
賢材者處厚祿、任大官；	the worthy and talented enjoy sizeable stipends and occupy high positions,
5　功大者有尊爵、受重賞。	and those who have great achievements receive honoured ranks and heavy rewards.
官賢者量其能，	When appointing the worthy, a ruler measures their talents;
賦祿者稱其功。	when bequeathing emoluments, he weighs their achievements.
是以賢者不誣能以事其主，	Therefore, the worthy will not falsely claim abilities in order to serve their ruler,
有功者樂進其業，	and men of achievement will joyfully offer their skills,
10　故事成功立。	and so tasks will be completed and achievements will be established.
今則不然，	Nowadays this is not so.
不課賢不肖、論有功勞，	[Rulers] do not examine worth versus unworthiness and do not assess whether there is merit or achievement.
用諸侯之重，	They employ those who have the support of the regional lords
聽左右之謁，	and heed requests from their own entourage.
15　父兄大臣上請爵祿於上，	Uncles, brothers and senior ministers request rank and emolument from their ruler,
而下賣之以收財利及以樹私黨。	then sell them down for properties and goods and use these to establish private factions.
故財利多者買官以為貴，	Thus, those with many properties and goods purchase office in order to raise their social standing;
有左右之交者請謁以成重。	those with connections in the ruler's entourage ask for special audiences in order to bolster their importance.
功勞之臣不論，	Ministers with merit and achievements are not assessed;
20　官職之遷失謬。	reallocations of offices and duties become misguided.
是以吏偷官而外交，	And so minor officials perform their duties perfunctorily but establish external connections,
棄事而財親。	neglect their duties and only concern themselves with wealth.

八姦 EIGHT VILLAINIES

是以賢者懈怠而不勸，	And so it is that the worthies become lazy and indifferent
有功者墮而簡其業，	and those who have merit become remiss and shirk their duties –
25 此亡國之風也。	these are the practices of a state that is doomed to ruin.

12 C adds 不 before 論 with 校注 79, following 王先慎; we find this unnecessary, with 張覺.
22 C reverses order of 財 and 親; we find this unnecessary, with 張覺.

CHAPTER 10

十過 Ten Faults

HF 10.0 (*Xilun* 142, *Xin jiaozhu* 199)

十過：	The Ten Faults are as follows:
一曰行小忠，	One: the practice of petty loyalty –
則大忠之賊也。	this is the foe of great loyalty.
二曰顧小利，	Two: the concern for petty gains –
則大利之殘也。	this is to the detriment of great gains.
三曰行僻自用，	Three: to act in a deviant manner, being wilful,
無禮諸侯，	and being impolite to the regional lords –
則亡身之至也。	this ends in personal ruin.
四曰不務聽治而好五音，	Four: to fail to attend to political matters, enjoying the five tones of music –
則窮身之事也。	this is something that leads a person into trouble.
五曰貪愎喜利，	Five: to be greedy and stubborn, and to delight in profit –
則滅國殺身之本也。	this is what leads to the destruction of your state and to getting yourself killed.
六曰耽於女樂，	Six: to indulge in female musicians
不顧國政，	and ignore the administration of the state –
則亡國之禍也。	this is a misfortune that will ruin your state.
七曰離內遠遊而忽於諫士，	Seven: to leave the court on distant trips, ignoring remonstrating officials –
則危身之道也。	this is a way to endanger your life.
八曰過而不聽於忠臣，	Eight: To have made a mistake, yet not to heed loyal ministers,
而獨行其意，	and only go your own way –

十過 TEN FAULTS

20 則滅高名為人笑之始也。	this is the beginning of the destruction of your good name and of becoming a laughingstock for all.
九曰內不量力， 外恃諸侯， 則削國之患也。	Nine: not to assess domestic strength, and to rely on the regional lords abroad – this will lead to the disaster of having your state decimated.
十曰國小無禮， 25 不用諫臣， 則絕世之勢也。	Ten: when your state is small and you show no ritual politeness, and you do not employ ministers to remonstrate with you –[1] these are the circumstances by which your line of inheritance will be severed.

HF 10.1 (*Xilun* 143, *Xin jiaozhu* 200)

奚謂小忠？	What is meant by 'petty loyalty'?
昔者楚共王與晉厲公戰於鄢陵，	In ancient times, King Gong of Chu and Lord Li of Jin fought a battle at Yanling,[2]
楚師敗，	where the Chu army was defeated
而共王傷其目。	and King Gong was injured in his eye.
5 酣戰之時，	In the heat of the battle[3]
司馬子反渴而求飲，	Marshal Zifan felt thirsty and looked for something to drink.
豎穀陽操觴酒而進之。	Young Servant Guyang held up a cup of ale and offered it.
子反曰：	Zifan said:
"嘻！	"Ha!
10 退，	Out of my sight!

---

[1] This clause contradicts Han Fei's assault on remonstrating ministers in chapter 6.3.
[2] This battle took place in 575; Jin's victory put an end to Chu's attempts to retain interstate hegemony for the next thirty years. For an earlier version of the story, see *Zuozhuan*, Cheng 16.5k.
[3] The use of *han* 酣 "be tipsy" in the transferred sense of being in the heat of battle is somewhat odd. The *Zuozhuan* relates that Zifan was drunk *after* the battle, which is a more reliable version.

酒也。"	That is ale."
穀陽曰：	Guyang said:
"非酒也。"	"This is not ale."
子反受而飲之。	Zifan accepted it and drank it.
15　子反之為人也，	Zifan was the sort of person
嗜酒，	who loved ale,
而甘之，	and he found it so sweet
弗能絕於口，	that he was unable to put it down
而醉。	and became drunk.
20　戰既罷，	When the fighting was over,
共王欲復戰，	King Gong wanted to renew the battle
令人召司馬子反，	and sent someone to summon Marshal Zifan,
司馬子反辭以心疾。	but he declined on the grounds of a heart ailment.
共王駕而自往，	King Gong yoked his carriage, went over in person,
25　入其幄中，	entered the tent,
聞酒臭而還，	noticed the stench of ale, and turned around,
曰：	saying:
"今日之戰，	"In today's fighting,
不穀親傷，	I myself was injured.
30　所恃者，	The person I was relying upon
司馬也，	was the marshal,
而司馬又醉如此，	but the marshal has gone on to get drunk like this:
是亡楚國之社稷而不恤吾眾也。	this is to ruin the altars of soil and grain of Chu and to fail to empathise with my troops.
不穀無復戰矣。"	I shall not renew battle."
35　於是還師而去。	With that, he turned his army around and departed.
斬司馬子反以為大戮，	He had Marshal Zifan cut in two in a great public execution.[4]
故豎穀陽之進酒，	So, when Young Servant Guyang offered up the ale,
不以讎子反也，	it was not an act of enmity against Zifan.
其心忠愛之而適足以殺之。	In his heart, he was loyal and cared for him, but it turned out to be enough to get him killed.

4　*Zuozhuan* (Cheng 16.5l) relates that Marshal Zifan committed suicide, while King Gong actually wanted to spare him.

十過 TEN FAULTS

40 故曰：
　行小忠，
　則大忠之賊也。

So it is said:
The practice of petty loyalty
is the foe of great loyalty.

2 張抄 has 王共 for 共王.　12 〔穀陽曰〕(校注 100).　33 （言）〔恤〕(校注 100).

HF 10.2 (*Xilun* 145, *Xin jiaozhu* 202)

奚謂顧小利？
昔者晉獻公欲假道於虞以伐虢。

荀息曰：
"君其以垂棘之璧與屈產之乘
5 賂虞公，
　求假道焉，
　必假我道。"
君曰：
"垂棘之璧，
10 吾先君之寶也，
　屈產之乘，
　寡人之駿馬也。
　若受吾幣不假之道，
　將奈何？"

What is meant by 'concern for petty gains'?
In ancient times, Lord Xian of Jin wanted to obtain right of passage from Yu in order to attack Guo.[5]

Xun Xi[6] said,
"If you take the jade disks from Chuiji and the team-horses bred in Qu
to bribe the Lord of Yu
and request right of passage,
he is bound to grant it to us."[7]
The ruler said:
"The jade disks from Chuiji
are treasures from my ancestors;
the team-horses bred in Qu
are the most outstanding horses I have.
If he accepts my gifts but does not grant us right of passage,
what are we to do?"

5　Lord Xian of Jin 晉獻公 (r. 676–651) is the ruler under whom Jin started expanding robustly, regaining its position as the major regional power. The elimination of Guo was a major milestone en route to Jin's ascendancy to supremacy in the Yellow River basin. Guo was one of the major polities early in the Springs-and-Autumns period. Its capital, Shangyang 上陽 was located near today's Sanmenxia, to the south of the Yellow River, but it possessed an important stronghold (secondary capital) of Xiayang (下陽 or 夏陽) to the north of the River. Yu was located further to the north of Xiayang. Jin's capital was much further to the north. As Yu was in between Jin and Guo on the Dianling 顛軨 road, the only route through the Zhongtiao Mountains 中條山 into the Sanmenxia Basin, the Jin army had to pass through it in order to reach Guo (Jin Shenhe and Xie Hongxi 2007).

6　Xun Xi (d. 651) was Jin's chief minister under Lord Xian.

7　See *Zuozhuan*, Xi 2.2.

15	荀息曰：	Xun Xi said:
	"彼不假我道，	"If he does not grant us right of passage,
	必不敢受我幣。	he will surely not dare to accept our gifts.
	若受我幣而假我道，	If he accepts our gifts and grants us right of passage,
	則是寶猶取之內府而藏之外府也，	this amounts to taking the treasures from the inner storehouse and keeping them in the outer storehouse;
20	馬猶取之內廄而著之外廄也。	with the horses, it is like taking them from the inner stables and keeping them in the outer stables.
	君勿憂。"	You should not worry about this, my lord."
	君曰：	The ruler said,
	"諾。"	"All right."
	乃使荀息以垂棘之璧與屈產之乘賂虞公而求假道焉。	He then ordered Xun Xi to take the jade disks from Chuiji and the team-horses bred in Qu and bribe the Duke of Yu and request right of passage from him.
25	虞公貪利其璧與馬而欲許之。	The Duke of Yu was greedy for the jade disk and the horses, and he wanted to accede to the request.
	宮之奇諫曰：	Gong Zhi Qi[8] remonstrated, saying,
	"不可許。	"This request should not be granted.
	夫虞之有虢也，	Yu is to Guo
	如車之有輔。	like a carriage having staffs bracing the wheels.[9]
30	輔依車，	The staffs are attached to the carriage,
	車亦依輔，	but the carriage is also attached to the staffs.
	虞虢之勢正是也。	The situation of Yu and Guo is exactly like this.
	若假之道，	If you grant them right of passage,
	則虢朝亡而虞夕從之矣。	the morning Guo is ruined, Yu will follow suit in the evening.
35	不可，	This will not do.
	願勿許。"	I hope you will not grant the request."
	虞公弗聽，	The Lord of Yu did not heed this advice,
	遂假之道。	and accordingly granted Jin right of passage.

---

8 Gong Zhi Qi was a wise minister at the court of Yu. In *Zuozhuan* Xi 2.2, Xun Xi predicts that Gong Zhi Qi's remonstrance would not be heeded.

9 *Fu* 輔 refers to a pair of staffs used to strengthen the wheel when the load was heavy; cf. Dewall 1964: 40, Duan Di 2016: 182, Yang Zhishui 2000: 442–444.

十過 TEN FAULTS

荀息伐虢克之，	Xun Xi attacked Guo and vanquished it;
40 還反處三年，	three years after his return,
興兵伐虞，	he raised an army to attack Yu,
又克之。	vanquishing it as well.[10]
荀息牽馬操璧而報獻公，	Xun Xi, leading the horses and carrying the jade disks, reported the event to Lord Xian of Jin.
獻公說曰：	He was pleased and said:
45 "璧則猶是也。	"The jade disk is as before;
雖然，	However,
馬齒亦益長矣。"	the horses have grown longer in the tooth."
故虞公之兵殆而地削者，	So, the forces of the Duke of Yu became imperilled and his territory was pared away –
何也？	why is this?
50 愛小利而不慮其害。	He craved petty gains and did not take precautions against the ensuing harm.
故曰：	So it is said:
顧小利，	Concern for petty gains
則大利之殘也。	is what impairs large gains.

10 張抄 has 芃 for 先。 20 著 is read as 貯。 39 〔剋〕 (校注 100–101); we normalise to 克。

HF 10.3 (*Xilun* 148, *Xin jiaozhu* 204)

奚謂行僻？	What is meant by 'acting extravagantly'?
昔者楚靈王為申之會，	In ancient times King Ling of Chu conducted a meeting at Shen.[11]
宋太子後至，	The Crown Prince of Song was late to arrive.
執而囚之；	and the King detained him and had him put in prison,[12]

---

10 According to *Zuozhuan* (Xi 2.2 and 5.8), there were two attacks by Jin against Guo: a joint attack with Yu in 658 in which Guo's northern stronghold Xiayang (note 5 above) was conquered and a second in 655 which saw Guo annexed by Jin and Yu subsequently attacked and also annexed by the same Jin army that eliminated Guo.

11 This meeting occurred in 538 (*Zuozhuan*, Zhao 4.3). It marked the apex of King Ling's power. King Ling 楚靈王 (r. 540–529) was the most powerful (and ruthless) Chu ruler, during whose lifetime Chu briefly rose to dominate much of the Zhou world.

12 The Crown Prince was the future Lord Yuan of Song 宋元公 (r. 531–517). He arrived at Shen after the ceremonies were over, and was not granted an audience with King Ling.

5	狎徐君；	where he was impertinent with the ruler of Xú,[13]
	拘齊慶封。	and he arrested Qing Feng of Qi.[14]
	中射士諫曰：	A palace guard[15] remonstrated, saying,
	"合諸侯不可無禮，	"When calling together the regional lords, one must follow decorum.
	此存亡之機也。	This is the key to survival or ruin.
10	昔者桀為有戎之會，	In ancient times Jie conducted a meeting with the Rong,
	而有緡叛之；	and the people of Min rebelled;[16]
	紂為黎丘之蒐，	Zhòu went on a royal hunt at Liqiu,
	而戎、狄叛之；	and the Rong and Di rebelled.[17]
	由無禮也。	All this was because of a lack of decorum.
15	君其圖之。"	Milord, you should reconsider."
	君不聽，	The ruler did not listen,
	遂行其意。	and went on to act as he had intended.
	居未期年，	Not even a year had passed,
	靈王南遊，	when King Ling was on an expedition to the south
20	群臣從而劫之。	and his ministers accordingly seized his throne.
	靈王餓而死乾溪之上。	King Ling of Chu starved to death on the Ganxi River.[18]

However, he was not put in prison. Han Fei perhaps confuses the destinies of the Prince of Song and of the ruler of Xú 徐 (see *Zuozhuan*, Zhao 4.3b).

13 Xú was a small state in present-day Anhui province. Its ruler, Yichu 義楚, was detained during the meeting because King Ling suspected him of clandestinely supporting Chu's rival, Wu (Yichu's mother's state).

14 Qing Feng 慶封 (d. 538), the former dictator of Qi, had to flee his home state after his rule was overthrown. He was received by the King of Wu, who granted him an allotment in Zhufang. Following the meeting at Shen, King Ling and his allies captured Zhufang and had Qing Feng executed. For details, see *Zuozhuan* (Zhao 4.4).

15 In *Zuozhuan* (Zhao 4.3c), this remonstrance is made by a high official, Wu Ju 伍舉, the grandfather of the famous Wu Zixu 伍子胥.

16 In *Zuozhuan* (Zhao 4.3c), Jie holds the meeting at a place called Reng 仍. The Rong and Min are apparently non-Sinitic ethnic groups, just like the Di in the following sentence.

17 In *Zuozhuan* (Zhao 4.3c) the rebellion was carried out by the Eastern Yi.

18 This is a somewhat inaccurate narrative. King Ling's expedition to Ganxi (or Qianxi), during which his brothers seized power, took place in 529, a full eight years after the Shen meeting. Ganxi was located to the east, and not to the south, of the Chu capital. And King Ling did not starve to death, but rather committed suicide after the capital was captured by his rebel brothers, and his sons were killed. For the drama of his downfall, see *Zuozhuan*, Zhao 13.2.

十過 TEN FAULTS

故曰：	So it is said:
行僻自用，	To act in a deviant manner, being wilful
無禮諸侯，	and rude to the regional lords –
25 則亡身之至也。	this ends in personal ruin.

2 （命）〔會〕(校注 101). 18 張抄 has 末 for 未.

HF 10.4 (*Xilun* 149, *Xin jiaozhu* 205)

奚謂好音？	What is meant by 'loving music'?
昔者衛靈公將之晉，	In ancient times, Lord Ling of Wey was about to go to Jin.[19]
至濮水之上，	Arriving at the banks of the Pu River,
稅車而放馬，	he unhitched the carriages and set the horses loose
5 設舍以宿。	and made camp for the night.
夜分，	At midnight,
而聞鼓新聲者而說之。	he heard someone strumming an unusual tune and delighted in it.
使人問左右，	He sent some people to ask his entourage about this,
盡報弗聞。	but all of them reported that they did not hear it.
10 乃召師涓而告之，	Then the lord summoned Music Master Juan and told him,
曰：	saying:
"有鼓新聲者，	"There is someone who is strumming an unusual tune.
使人問左右，	I have sent some people to ask my entourage,
盡報弗聞。	but all of them have reported that they did not hear it.
15 其狀似鬼神，	It seemed like it was coming from a ghost or spirit –
子為我聽而寫之。"	you listen to this for me and imitate it."
師涓曰：	Master Juan said:
"諾。"	"I shall do as commanded."
因靜坐撫琴而寫之。	And so he sat down quietly and played his zither to imitate the tune.

---

19   Lord Ling of Wey reigned from 534 to 493.

20 師涓明日報曰：	Master Juan reported the next day:
"臣得之矣，	"I have got the tune,
而未習也，	but I have still not practised it properly.
請復一宿習之。"	I ask leave to practise it for another night."
靈公曰：	Lord Ling said:
25 "諾。"	"Agreed."
因復留宿。	And so he stayed for another night.
明日，	By the next day,
已習之，	the Music Master had learned it.
遂去之晉。	Later, the lord left and proceeded to Jin.
30 晉平公觴之於施夷之臺。	Lord Ping of Jin toasted him on the Shiyi terrace.
酒酣，	When they were tipsy with ale,
靈公起。	Lord Ling rose from his seat
公曰：	and said,
"有新聲，	"There is a new tune.
35 願請以示。"	I would like to ask them to perform it for you."
平公曰：	Lord Ping said:
"善。"	"Good."
乃召師涓，	Then Lord Ling summoned Master Juan,
令坐師曠之旁，	ordered him to sit next to Master Kuang,[20]
40 援琴鼓之。	to take up his zither and to play the tune on it.
未終，	Before he had finished
師曠撫止之，	Master Kuang touched his arm and stopped him,
曰：	saying:
"此亡國之聲，	"This is a tune of a state doomed to ruin.
45 不可遂也。"	You should not continue."
平公曰：	Lord Ping asked:
"此道奚出？"	"Where is this tune from?"
師曠曰：	Music Master Kuang said:
"此師延之所作[A 魚/暮 tsagh/tsuo]，	"It is the creation of Master Yan:
50 與紂為靡靡之樂[A 宵/覺 ŋrakw/ŋâk]也，	he was making extravagant music for [the tyrant] Zhòu.
及武王伐紂[B 幽/有 drjəgwx/-jou/djə̂u]，	When King Wu attacked Zhòu,
師延東走[B 侯/厚 tsugx/-ou/tsə̂u]，	Music Master Yan fled towards the east;
至於濮水而自投[B 侯/侯 dug/-ou/də̂u]。	when he got as far as the River Pu, he threw himself in.

---

20   Master Kuang is renowned not merely as a master musician, but also as an eloquent and wise advisor. His admonitions are frequently cited in *Zuozhuan*.

十過 TEN FAULTS

故聞此聲者，	So, whoever heard this tune
55 必於濮水之上。	must have been at the Pu River.
先聞此聲者，	He who first hears this tune
其國必削，	is bound to have his territory reduced.
不可遂。"	You should not continue."
平公曰：	Lord Ping said:
60 "寡人所好者，	"What I appreciate above all
音也，	is music.
子其使遂之。"	You should let him continue."
師涓鼓究之。	Master Juan strummed the tune to the end.
平公問師曠曰：	Lord Ping asked Master Kuang:
65 "此所謂何聲也？"	"What is this tune called."
師曠曰：	Master Kuang replied:
"此所謂清商也。"	"It is called 'pure *shang*'."
公曰：	The lord said:
"清商固最悲乎？"	"Is pure *shang* really the saddest tone."
70 師曠曰：	Music Master Kuang said:
"不如清徵。"	"It is not as sad as 'pure *zhi*'."
公曰：	The lord asked:
"清徵可得而聞乎？"	"May I hear pure *zhi*."
師曠曰：	Master Kuang said:
75 "不可。	"That is not advisable.
古之聽清徵者，	Those who, in ancient times, listened to pure *zhi*
皆有德義之君也。	were all virtuous and righteous rulers.
今吾君德薄，	Now our ruler's virtue is slight;
不足以聽。"	you are not qualified to listen to it."
80 平公曰：	Lord Ping said:
"寡人之所好者，	"What I appreciate above all
音也，	is music.
願試聽之。"	I very much desire to listen to it."
師曠不得已，	Master Kuang had no alternative.
85 援琴而鼓。	He took the zither and began to play.
一奏之，	When he played it for the first time,
有玄鶴二八，	two groups of eight reddish-black cranes
道南方來，	came from the south
集於郎門之垝。	and settled on the circular wall atop the palace entrance.
90 再奏之，	When he played it for the second time,
而列。	they formed rows.
三奏之，	When he played it for the third time,

延頸而鳴，	they craned their necks and sang;
舒翼而舞，	they spread their wings and danced.
95 音中宮商之聲，	When he struck the *gong* and *shang* notes,
聲聞于天。	the sound resonated in the heavens.
平公大說，	Lord Ping was greatly delighted,
坐者皆喜。	and those who were sitting with him were all pleased.
平公提觴而起為師曠壽，	Lord Ping raised a goblet and rose to drink to the long life of Master Kuang.
100 反坐而問曰：	When he had returned to his seat he asked:
"音莫悲於清徵乎？"	"Is there no music sadder than pure *zhi*."
師曠曰：	Master Kuang said:
"不如清角。"	"It is not as sad as pure *jue*."
平公曰：	Lord Ping said:
105 "清角可得而聞乎？"	"May I hear pure *jue*."
師曠曰：	Master Kuang said:
"不可。	"That is not advisable.
昔者黃帝合鬼神於泰山之上，	In ancient times, when the Yellow Thearch assembled the ghosts and spirits on Mount Tai,
駕象車而六蛟龍，	they rode on ivory carriages pulled by six hornless dragons.
110 畢方並鎋，	Bifang kept pace with the axle-caps;
蚩尤居前，	Chiyou was in front;[21]
風伯進掃，	the Lord of Wind proceeded, sweeping away as he went;
雨師灑道，	the Master of Rain sprinkled the way;
虎狼在前，	tigers and wolves were the front guard;
115 鬼神在後，	ghosts and spirits were the rear guard;
騰蛇伏地，	flying snakes crouched on the ground;
鳳皇覆上，	phoenixes hovered above.
大合鬼神，	On the occasion of this grandiose reunion of ghosts and spirits,
作為清角。	he made pure *jue*.
120 今吾君德薄，	Now our ruler's virtue is slight;
不足聽之。	you are not qualified to listen to it.

---

21   For the Yellow Thearch, see chapter 8, note 15. Bifang is glossed as a "magical bird with gorgeous plumage, said to be responsible for forest fires" (*Huainanzi*, cited from Major et al. 2010: 522n93). Chiyou, by contrast, is the most infamous personality from the Yellow Thearch's era, a notorious rebel who was eventually killed off by the Yellow Thearch.

十過 TEN FAULTS

聽之，	If you listen to it,
將恐有敗。"	I'm afraid there will be defeat ahead."
平公曰：	Lord Ping said:
125 "寡人老矣，	"I am already an old man,[22]
所好者音也，	and what I appreciate above all is music,
願遂聽之。"	so I would like to hear it anyway."
師曠不得已而鼓之。	Master Kuang, having no alternative, played it.
一奏之，	He played it once,
130 有玄雲從西北方起；	and reddish-black clouds formed in the northwest.
再奏之，	He played it twice,
大風至，	and there was a great wind;
大雨隨之，	heavy rains followed,
裂帷幕，	which destroyed the curtains,
135 破俎豆，	broke the ritual foot-stands,
墮廊瓦。	and smashed the tiles in the corridors.
坐者散走，	Those who were in attendance scattered and fled.
平公恐懼，	Lord Ping was frightened,
伏于廊室之間。	and lay prostrate between the porch and the building.
140 晉國大旱，	In the state of Jin, there was a great drought,
赤地三年。	which scorched the earth for three years.
平公之身遂癃病。	And Lord Ping's own body became decrepit and ill.
故曰：	So it is said:
不務聽治[C 之 / 志 drjəgh/ḍï]，	To fail to attend to political matters
145 而好五音不已[C 之 / 止 rəgx/jɨï]，	while enjoying the five tones of music without end –
則窮身之事[C 之 / 志 dzrjəgh/dẓï]也。	this is something that leads a person into trouble.

4 稅 is read as 脫.   16 〔我〕(校注 101, with 論衡 parallel).   28（而）〔已〕(校注 101, with 論衡 parallel).   47 C emends 道奚 to 奚道, following 王念孫; we find this unnecessary.   64（涓）〔曠〕(校注 101).   100〔坐〕(校注 101).   120（主）〔吾〕(校注 101, following 顧廣圻).   129（而）〔之〕(校注 101).   142（瘖）〔癃〕(校注 101, with 藝文類聚 quotation).

---

22   Lord Ping assumed power in 557, some 25 years before his guest, Lord Ling of Wey. Hence it is probable that he was rather old by the time of Lord Ling's visit.

HF 10.5 (*Xilun* 154, *Xin jiaozhu* 212)

奚謂貪愎？	What is meant by 'being greedy and stubborn'?
昔者智伯瑤率趙、韓、魏而伐范、中行，	In ancient times, Zhi Bo Yao, leading Zhao, Hán, and Wei, attacked Fan and Zhonghang
滅之。	and destroyed them.[23]
反歸，	After he had returned,
休兵數年，	and had rested his armed forces for several years,
因令人請地於韓。	he ordered someone to ask for land from Hán.
韓康子欲勿與，	Han Kangzi did not want to give it up,[24]
段規諫曰：	but Duan Gui remonstrated, saying,
"不可不與也。	"It is inadvisable not to give it up.
夫知伯之為人也，	Zhi Bo is the sort of person
好利而驚愎。	who is eager for gain and arrogant and stubborn.
彼來請地而弗與，	If such a person comes asking for territory and you refuse to give it to him,
則移兵於韓必矣。	it is inevitable that he will move his armies against Hán:
君其與之。	you must give it to him.
與之彼狃，	If you do, that man will become overconfident,
又將請地他國。	and will request land from other states.
他國且有不聽，	Among these other states, there will be one that will not cooperate.
不聽，	When they do not cooperate,
則知伯必加之兵。	Zhi Bo is bound to apply military force.
如是，	Like this,
韓可以免於患而待其事之變。"	Hán can avoid disaster and wait for things to change.
康子曰：	Kangzi said:
"諾。"	"Approved."
因令使者致萬家之縣一於知伯。	He had an envoy hand over a county with ten thousand households to Zhi Bo.[25]

---

23 For the ministerial lineages of Jin, see chapter 1, note 33. But in the current passage Han Fei's narrative is inaccurate, as in elmost every text from the late Warring States period onwards. Zhi Bo (Zhi the Elder), who fought the Fan and Zhonghang lineages in the civil war of 497–490, was Zhi Li 知躒, or, possibly, Li's son Zhi Jia 知甲. As for Zhi Bo, who was killed in 453 after an epic struggle with the Zhao lineage, he was named Yao 瑤, and was Zhi Jia's son. He played no role in the downfall of the Fan and Zhonghang lineages.

24 Han Kangzi was head of the Hán lineage.

25 Here and throughout the story, Han Fei superimposes contemporaneous realities upon

十過 TEN FAULTS

25 知伯說，	Zhi Bo was delighted,
又令人請地於魏。	and went on to send someone to request land from Wei.
宣子欲勿與，	[Wei] Xuanzi[26] did not want to give it up,
趙葭諫曰：	but Zhao Jia remonstrated, saying,
"彼請地於韓，	"That man asked for land from Hán,
30 韓與之。	and Hán gave it to him.
今請地於魏，	Now he is asking for land from Wei.
魏弗與，	If Wei refuses to give it to him,
則是魏內自強，	this would be attending to the internal strength of Wei,
而外怒知伯也。	but, on the outside, this would arouse Zhi Bo's anger.
35 如弗予，	If you refuse to grant it to him,
其措兵於魏必矣。	it is inevitable that he will use armed force against Wei:
不如予之。"	it is better to grant it to him."
宣子曰：	Xuanzi said,
"諾。"	"Approved."
40 因令人致萬家之縣一於知伯。	He had someone hand over a county with ten thousand households to Zhi Bo.
知伯又令人之趙請蔡、皋狼之地，	Zhi Bo went on to send someone to Zhao, requesting the lands of Cai and Gaolang.[27]
趙襄子弗與。	Zhao Xiangzi refused to give it to him,[28]
知伯因陰約韓、魏將以伐趙。	and Zhi Bo therefore entered into a secret agreement with Hán and Wei to attack Zhao.
襄子召張孟談而告之曰：	Zhao Xiangzi summoned Zhang Mengtan and told him,
45 "夫知伯之為人也，	"Zhi Bo is the sort of person
陽親而陰疏。	who is overtly friendly but secretly hostile.

---

those of the time of Zhi Bo's downfall (ca. 453). Back then, Hán had yet to become a full-fledged polity and was unlikely to have possessed sizeable counties that could be traded with Zhi Bo.

26 Wei Xuanzi (d. 446) headed the Wei lineage at that time.
27 Neither Cai (which was then located in near today's Fengtai, Anhui, on the Huai River, and was on the verge of being annexed by Chu) nor Gaolang (located near today's Lüliang, western Shanxi) belonged to Zhao back then.
28 Zhao Xiangzi (d. ca. 442) was Zhi Bo's most powerful rival at the time.

	三使韓、魏而寡人不與焉，	Three times, he has sent embassies, [first] to Hán and Wei, [and now to us], but I have not given him what he wanted.
	其措兵於寡人必矣。	It is inevitable that he will use military force against me.
	今吾安居而可？"	Now, what can we do in this situation?"
50	張孟談曰：	Zhang Mengtan said,
	"夫董閼于，	"As for Dong Yanyu,
	簡主之才臣也，	he was a gifted minister under Ruler Jian.[29]
	其治晉陽，	He governed Jinyang,[30]
	而尹鐸循之，	and Yin Duo inherited his position.
55	其餘教猶存，	The abundant influence of Dong's teachings still lingers.
	君其定居晉陽而已矣。"	You could just take shelter in Jinyang."
	君曰：	The ruler said;
	"諾。"	"All right."
	乃召延陵生，	He summoned Master Yanling[31]
60	令將車騎先至晉陽，	and ordered him to lead chariots and horsemen[32] and be the first to reach Jinyang.
	君因從之。	The ruler followed behind them.
	君至，	When the ruler arrived,
	而行其城郭及五官之藏。	he toured the inner and outer walls and the storehouses of the five offices.
	城郭不治，	The inner and outer walls had not been maintained;
65	倉無積粟，	the granaries had no stockpiles of grain;
	府無儲錢，	the treasury had no cash;
	庫無甲兵，	the armouries had no armour or weapons;
	邑無守具。	and the settlement was defenceless.
	襄子懼，	Xiangzi was frightened.
70	乃召張孟談曰：	He summoned Zhang Mengtan, saying,
	"寡人行城郭及五官之藏，	"I have toured the inner and outer walls and the storehouses of the five offices,

---

29   Zhao Jianzi (d. 476) was Zhao Xiangzi's father and the de facto founder of the autonomous Zhao polity. In chapter 3, Dong Yanyu (d. 496) is called Dong Anyu 董安于 (for his noble self-sacrifice, see note 24 there).

30   Jinyang was the capital of Zhao.

31   The identity of this person is not clear.

32   The deployment of cavalry is yet another late Warring States-period anachronism.

	皆不備具，	and none are well supplied.
	吾將何以應敵？"	How am I going to respond to the enemy."
	張孟談曰：	Zhang Mengtan said:
75	"臣聞聖人之治，	"I have heard that the governance of a sage
	藏於民，	is stored in the people,
	不藏於府庫，	not in treasuries and armouries;
	務脩其教不治城郭。	a sage strives to perfect their training, not to maintain their walls.[33]
	君其出令，	You should issue an order
80	令民自遺三年之食，	to have the people set aside enough food for three years,
	有餘粟者入之倉；	and if there is surplus grain, to put it in the granaries;
	遺三年之用，	have them set aside enough money for three years,
	有餘錢者入之府；	and where there is surplus cash, put it in the treasury.
	遺有奇人者使治城郭之繕。"	Anyone with energy to spare should be made to repair the inner and outer walls."
85	君夕出令，	In the evening the ruler issued the order.
	明日，	By the next day,
	倉不容粟，	the granaries had no room for more grain,
	府無積錢，	the treasuries had no place to pile more cash,
	庫不受甲兵。	the armouries could not accept more armour or weapons.
90	居五日而城郭已治，	After five days had passed, the inner and outer walls had been repaired,
	守備已具。	and the defences were complete.
	君召張孟談而問之曰：	The ruler summoned Zhang Mengtan and asked him,
	"吾城郭已治，	"My inner and outer walls are well built;
	守備已具，	my defensive arrangements are complete;
95	錢粟已足，	there is enough cash and grain,
	甲兵有餘。	and an abundance of weapons and armour,
	吾奈無箭何？"	but what can I do without arrows?"

---

33 Note how radically these recommendations diverge from what is generally associated with Han Fei's views.

張孟談曰：
　"臣聞董子之治晉陽也，

公宮之垣皆以荻蒿楛楚牆之，

　有楛高至于丈，
　君發而用之。"
　於是發而試之，

　其堅則雖菌簬之勁弗能過也。

君曰：
　"吾箭已足矣，
　奈無金何？"
　張孟談曰：
　"臣聞董子之治晉陽也，

公宮令舍之堂，

　皆以鍊銅為柱、質。

　君發而用之。"
　於是發而用之，

　有餘金矣。
號令已定，
　守備已具。
　三國之兵果至。

至則乘晉陽之城，

　遂戰。
三月弗能拔。
　因舒軍而圍之，
　決晉陽之水以灌之。

Zhang Mengtan said:
"I have heard that when Master Dong (Dong Yanyu) governed Jinyang,
all around the official residence, he planted a wall of *di* and *gao* reeds and *ku* bushes and *chu* trees.
Some *ku* trees are more than three poles high.
You should pull them up and use them."
With that, [Zhao Jianzi] pulled up some *ku* trees and tried them out.
They were so strong that even the hardest bamboo could not surpass them.
The ruler said:
"We have enough arrows,
but how about metal?"
Zhang Mengtan said:
"I have heard that when Master Dong governed Jinyang,
in all the official residences as well as housing for officials,
the columns and column bases were made of bronze.
You should take these down and use them."
Thereupon [Zhao Jianzi] took them down and used them,
and there was more than enough metal.
The public commands were fixed;
the defensive arrangements were complete;
and the armies of the three states arrived as expected.[34]
When they arrived, they rode up to the walls of Jinyang,
and a battle ensued.
For three months, they were unable to capture it,
so they spread out the army and encircled it.
They breached [the dikes of] the river at Jinyang to flood the place,

---

34　The armies of the Zhi, Wei, and Hán lineages are referred to here as the armies of the "three states," although none of the heads of these lineages was at that time recognised as a regional lord.

十過 TEN FAULTS

圍晉陽三年。	and in this way they besieged Jinyang for three years.[35]
城中巢居而處，	In the city, the people took shelter in birds' nests.[36]
懸釜而炊，	They had to hang their pots to cook their food;
財食將盡，	their supplies and food were about to be depleted;
士大夫羸病。	the gentlemen and the grandees were growing weak and sick.
襄子謂張孟談曰：	Xiangzi said to Zhang Mengtan,
"糧食匱，	"Our food is in short supply;
財力盡，	our resources and forces are exhausted;
士大夫羸病，	and our gentlemen and grandees are weakened and sick.
吾恐不能守矣！	I fear we cannot hold out.
欲以城下，	I wish to surrender the city,
何國之可下？"	but to which state should we surrender?"
張孟談曰：	Zhang Mengtan said:
"臣聞之，	"I have heard,
亡弗能存，	when faced with ruin, if you cannot survive,
危弗能安，	and when faced with danger, if you cannot remain calm,
則無為貴智矣。	you can never be counted as noble and wise.
君釋此計者。	You should discard that plan.
臣請試潛行而出，	I request to be allowed to try to sneak out
見韓、魏之君。"	and meet with the rulers of Hán and Wei."
張孟談見韓、魏之君曰：	Zhang Mengtan met with the rulers of Hán and Wei, and said,
"臣聞脣亡齒寒。	"I have heard, when the lips are removed, the teeth become cold.[37]
今知伯率二君而伐趙，	Now, Zhi Bo is leading you two in attacking Zhao,
趙將亡矣。	and Zhao is about to be lost.
趙亡，	If Zhao is lost,
則二君為之次。"	then you two will be next."

---

35   Different versions of the story report different lengths for the siege of Jinyang. This chapter, as well as *Zhanguo ce* 18.2 ("Zhao 1"), give the period of three years; *Han Feizi* 1.5 reports three months, which seems more likely.

36   Due to flooding.

37   For this phrase, see chapter 2, note 18. Its earliest usage is in *Zuozhuan*, Xi 5.8.

二君曰：	The two rulers said,
150 "我知其然也。	"We know this.
雖然，	However,
知伯之為人也麤中而少親。	Zhi Bo is of the sort of man who is crude in heart and has few close friends.
我謀而覺，	If we organise a plot and are discovered,
則其禍必至矣。	disaster is bound to arrive.
155 為之奈何？"	What can we do?"
張孟談曰：	Zhang Mengtan said:
"謀出二君之口而入臣之耳，	"The plot will leave your mouths and enter my ears;
人莫之知也。"	no one else will know about it."
二君因與張孟談約三軍之反，	And so the two rulers, with Zhang Mengtan, agreed that the three armies would revolt,[38]
160 與之期日。	and set a date with him.
夜遣孟談入晉陽，	At night, they sent Mengtan back into Jinyang,
以報二君之反。	to report on the revolt of the two rulers.
襄子迎孟談而再拜之，	Xiangzi welcomed Mengtan, bowing twice.
且恐且喜。	He was both terrified and delighted.
165 二君以約遣張孟談，	The two rulers, having sent Zhang Mengtan back with the agreement,
因朝知伯而出，	then had an audience with Zhi Bo and went out,
遇智過於轅門之外。	encountering Zhi Guo outside the gate of the commander's camp.
智過怪其色，	Zhi Guo found their expressions suspicious,
因入見知伯曰：	and went in to see Zhi Bo, saying,
170 "二君貌將有變。"	"The two rulers' countenances suggest that something foul is afoot."
君曰：	The ruler (Zhi Bo) said:
"何如？"	"How do they appear?"
曰：	He replied:
"其行矜而意高，	"They walk with an air of pride and high ideals;
175 非他時之節也，	they are not comporting themselves as they used to.
君不如先之。"	It would be better if you struck them first."

38　The revolt consisted of two armies only (those of Hán and Wei), but if Zhao is included it may count as three.

十過 TEN FAULTS

	君曰：	The ruler said:
	"吾與二主約謹矣，	"I made a careful agreement with those two rulers.
	破趙而三分其地，	We will break Zhao and divide its territory into three.
180	寡人所以親之，	The reason why I cultivate a close relationship with them
	必不侵欺。	is that they will never trespass against me.
	兵之著於晉陽三年，	The troops have been deployed at Jinyang for three years.
	今旦暮將拔之而嚮其利，	Any time now, we will capture the city and enjoy our spoils.
	何乃將有他心？	Why should they have other thoughts?
185	必不然。	It is surely not as you said.
	子釋勿憂，	You should forget this and stop worrying.
	勿出於口。"	And don't breathe another word about this."
	明旦，	The next morning,
	二主又朝而出，	the two rulers again had an audience and went out,
190	復見智過於轅門。	and again saw Zhi Guo at the gate of the commander's camp.
	智過入見曰：	Zhi Guo went in to see Zhi Bo and said:
	"君以臣之言告二主乎？"	"Did you inform the two rulers of what I said."
	君曰：	The ruler said:
	"何以知之？"	"How did you know."
195	曰：	He said:
	"今日二主朝而出，	"Today, when the two rulers had an audience and then went out,
	見臣而其色動，	they saw me and their expression changed,
	而視屬臣。	and they stared at me.
	此必有變，	This certainly indicates that something foul is afoot.
200	君不如殺之。"	You had better kill them."
	君曰：	The ruler said:
	"子置勿復言。"	"You should set this aside, and don't speak of it again."
	智過曰：	Zhi Guo said:
	"不可，	"That is unacceptable.
205	必殺之。	You certainly must kill them.
	若不能殺，	If you cannot bring yourself to kill them,

遂親之。"	you should cultivate a closer relationship with them."
君曰：	The ruler said:
"親之奈何？"	"Why cultivate a closer relationship with them."
210 智過曰：	Zhi Guo said:
"魏宣子之謀臣曰趙葭，	"Wei Xuanzi has an adviser named Zhao Jia,
韓康子之謀臣曰段規，	and Han Kangzi has an adviser named Duan Gui.
此皆能移其君之計。	These two are able to change their rulers' plans.
君其與二君約，	You should agree with these two men,
215 破趙國，	that once you break the state of Zhao,
因封二子者各萬家之縣一。	you will proceed to enfeoff them each with a county of ten thousand households.
如是，	If you do that,
則二主之心可以無變矣。"	the attitudes of the two rulers may not be bent on something foul."
知伯曰：	Zhi Bo said:
220 "破趙而三分其地，	"Having broken Zhao and divided the territory into three,
又封二子者各萬家之縣一，	if I then enfeoff those two men each with a county of ten thousand households,
則吾所得者少。	then what I get will be too little.
不可。"	That is not acceptable."
智過見其言之不聽也，	Zhi Guo, seeing that his words were not being heeded,
225 出，	left,
因更其族為輔氏。	and then changed his lineage-name to Fu.
至於期日之夜，	When night fell on the appointed day,
趙氏殺其守堤之吏而決其水灌知伯軍。	Zhao killed the dyke guard, and dredged the waters to inundate Zhi Bo's army.
知伯軍救水而亂，	Zhi Bo's army was in disarray fighting the flood.
230 韓、魏翼而擊之，	Hán and Wei attacked him from the wings,
襄子將卒犯其前，	and Xiangzi led his solders in a sudden attack in the front.
大敗知伯之軍而擒知伯。	They completely routed Zhi Bo's army and captured Zhi Bo.
知伯身死軍破。	Zhi Bo himself died and his armies were broken.
國分為三，	His state was divided into three,
235 為天下笑。	and he became the laughing stock of all the realm.

十過 TEN FAULTS

故曰：	So it is said,
貪愎好利，	to be greedy, stubborn, and fond of profit –
則滅國殺身之本也。	this is the basis for the destruction of your state and for getting yourself killed.

37 〔不如予之〕（校注 101）.   38 〔曰〕（校注 101, with 戰國策 parallel）.   46 （規）〔親〕（校注 101, with 戰國策 parallel）.   51 張抄 has 子 for 于.   56 The C editors note: 以下「已矣君曰諾乃召延陵生」至「而國之不服者三十三夏后氏」，四部叢刊本錯葉顛倒，現據乾道本移正，見《韓非子校注》，頁 83–93。   60 將（軍）車（校注 101, with 戰國策 parallel）.   76 （臣）〔民〕（校注 101, following 顧廣圻）.   104 菌 is read as 箘.   104 （餘）〔籞〕（校注 101）.   109 〔之〕（校注 101, with 戰國策 parallel）.   121 〔舒〕（校注 101）.   122 All editions have 決; C emends 決 to 治; we find this unnecessary. C ostensibly follows 校注 101; 校注 90 however has 決.   140 （失）〔釋〕（校注 101, with 戰國策 parallel）.   173 〔曰〕（校注 101, following 王先慎）.   183 嚮 is read as 饗.   198 屬 is read as 矚.   214 （與其）〔其與〕（校注 101, with 戰國策 parallel）.

HF 10.6 (*Xilun* 162, *Xin jiaozhu* 221)

奚謂耽於女樂？	What is meant by 'indulging in female musicians'?
昔者戎王使由余聘於秦，	In ancient times, the King of the Rong sent Youyu to pay a formal visit to Qin,
穆公問之曰：	and Lord Mu of Qin asked him:[39]
"寡人嘗聞道而未得目見之也，	"I have on occasion heard about the Way, but I have never seen it with my own eyes.
願聞古之明主得國失國常何以？"	I hope to learn about the clear-sighted rulers of ancient times, by what regular principles they won or lost their states."
由余對曰：	Youyu replied:
"臣嘗得聞之矣，	"I once had the opportunity to hear about this.
常以儉得之，	They consistently won their states with frugality,
以奢失之。"	and lost them through extravagance."
穆公曰：	Lord Mu said,
"寡人不辱而問道於子，	"I have inquired about the Way with no concern for my humiliation,
子以儉對寡人何也？"	so why have you replied to me in terms of thrift."

---

39 The Rong occupied territories to the west and northwest of Qin. Lord Mu (r. 659–621) was the most illustrious and powerful leader of Qin prior to the fourth century. This is the earliest and most detailed narration of the anecdote about the sagacious Youyu and Lord Mu of Qin in the entire corpus of pre-imperial texts.

由余對曰：	Youyu replied:
"臣聞昔者堯有天下，	"I have heard, in ancient times, when Yao was in possession of All-under-Heaven,
15 飯於土簋，	he ate from earthenware vessels
飲於土鉶。	and drank from earthenware pots.
其地南至交趾，	His territory extended south to Jiaozhi
北至幽都，	and north to Youdu;[40]
東西至日月之所出入者，	in the east and west, it extended to the places where the sun and moon rise and set.
20 莫不賓服。	Everyone submitted to him.
堯禪天下，	Yao abdicated rule over the realm;
虞舜受之，	Shun received it
作為食器，	and invented food vessels.
斬山木而財之，	He cut down mountain trees and made use of them;
25 削鋸脩其迹，	he hewed and sawed them and polished the traces;
流漆墨其上，	he coated them with lacquer and ink,
輸之於宮以為食器。	transported them to the palace, and used them as food vessels.
諸侯以為益侈，	The regional lords considered this extravagant,
國之不服者十三。	and the states that refused to submit to him numbered thirteen.[41]
30 舜禪天下而傳之於禹，	Shun abdicated rule of the realm and passed it on to Yu.
禹作為祭器，	Yu created sacrificial vessels,
墨染其外，	dyed the outsides with dark ink,
而朱畫其內，	and painted the insides with vermillion.[42]
縵帛為茵，	He used plain silk for his mattresses,

40　Jiaozhi is normally identified with the areas of northern Vietnam. Youdu was supposedly the capital of the northernmost of the so-called Nine Provinces, Youzhou 幽州 (near today's Beijing). The extent of territory under Yao's rule narrated here is paralleled almost verbatim in the "Moderation in Expenditures B" (節用中) chapter of *Mozi*, which also hails Yao's frugality.

41　This is a rare instance of the reigns of the two paragons Yao and Shun being strongly contrasted.

42　This is indeed the shape of some examples of Neolithic ceramicware from China. It could be that occasional discoveries of such early burial sites gave rise to the association of this style with Yu.

	十過 TEN FAULTS	
35	蔣席頗緣，	he had mats made of wild rice straw with decorated borders.
	觴酌有采，	His goblets and ladles were brightly coloured,
	而樽俎有飾。	his chalices and bowls decorated.
	此彌侈矣。	This was even more extravagant,
	而國之不服者三十三。	and the states that did not submit to him numbered thirty-three.
40	夏后氏沒，	When the Xiahou[43] line disappeared,
	殷人受之。	the people of Yin (Shang) took over.
	作為大路，	They made large carriages
	而建九旒，	and established the system of banners with nine pendants.
	食器雕琢，	Food vessels were sculpted and carved;
45	觴酌刻鏤，	goblets and ladles were engraved and inlaid with metal;[44]
	白壁堊墀，	the walls were chalked and the stairways plastered;
	茵席雕文。	mattresses and mats were decorated with patterns.
	此彌侈矣，	This was even more extravagant,
	而國之不服者五十三。	and the states that refused to submit numbered fifty-three.
50	君子皆知文章矣，	[Now,] all the noble men have become connoisseurs of literary refinements
	而欲服者彌少。	and those who want to submit have become fewer still.
	臣故曰：	So it is said:
	儉其道也。"	frugality is the way."
	由余出，	When Youyu had left,
55	公乃召內史廖而告之，	Lord [Mu] summoned the Court Scribe Liao,
	曰：	and said,
	"寡人聞鄰國有聖人，	"I have heard, when a neighbouring state has a sage,
	敵國之憂也。	this is a worry for its rivals.
	今由余，	Now, Youyu
60	聖人也，	is a sage,

---

43 The (legendary) Xia dynasty, Yu's descendants.
44 It is interesting to note that the use of metal (bronze) did indeed begin during the Shang dynasty.

	寡人患之，	and I consider him a problem.
	吾將奈何？"	What should we do?"
	內史廖曰：	the Court Scribe Liao said:
	"臣聞戎王之居，	"I have heard that the dwelling of the King of the Rong
65	僻陋而道遠，	is secluded and distant;
	未聞中國之聲。	he has never heard the songs of the central states.[45]
	君其遺之女樂，	You should present him with female musicians
	以亂其政，	in order to throw his administration into disarray,
	而後為由余請期，	and, after that, request more meetings with Youyu,
70	以疏其諫，	to keep him from remonstrating.
	彼君臣有間而後可圖也。"	Once there is a rift between ruler and minister [among your opponents], you will be able to make plans [to subdue them]."
	君曰：	The ruler said:
	"諾。"	"Approved."
	乃使內史廖以女樂二八遺戎王，	Thereupon he sent the Court Scribe Liao to give two rows of eight female musicians to the King of the Rong,
75	因為由余請期。	and then to request more meetings with You Yu.
	戎王許諾，	The King of the Rong acquiesced.
	見其女樂而說之，	He saw the female musicians and was delighted with them.
	設酒張飲，	He set out ale and threw a drinking party,
	日以聽樂，	and he spent day after day listening to the music.
80	終歲不遷，	For the rest of the year, he did not move [to new pastures],
	牛馬半死。	and half of his oxen and horses died.[46]
	由余歸，	Youyu returned,
	因諫戎王，	and then remonstrated with the King of the Rong,
	戎王弗聽。	but the King of the Rong would not heed him.
85	由余遂去之秦。	Youyu then left the Rong and went to Qin.[47]

---

45 Here Qin is unequivocally identified as a representative of the Central States, whereas many other late Warring States-period texts refer to it conversely as a cultural outsider.

46 This interesting observation demonstrates some understanding of the needs of a pastoral economy.

47 Note this hint at the damaging impact of Central Plains culture on the frugal and simple

十過 TEN FAULTS

秦穆公迎而拜之上卿，	Lord Mu of Qin welcomed him, appointing him superior minister,
問其兵勢與其地形。	and consulted him on the military situation of the Rong and topography of their lands.
既以得之，	Once he got this information,
舉兵而伐之，	he raised an army and attacked the Rong,
90 兼國十二，	annexing twelve states,
開地千里。	and opening up a territory of a thousand *li*.
故曰：	So it is said:
耽於女樂，	To indulge in female musicians
不顧國政，	and ignore the administration of the state,
95 則亡國之禍也。	is a misfortune that will ruin your state.

5（何常）〔常何〕(校注 101, following 松皋圓). 25（之）〔其〕(校注 101). 32 王念孫 emends 染 to 漆 (讀書雜志·餘編上 1031–1032); C follows 王念孫; we follow 陳奇猷 and 張覺. 40 The C editors note: 由「已矣君曰諾乃召延陵生」至此，四部叢刊本錯葉顛倒，現據乾道本移正，見《韓非子校注》，頁 83–93。 42 路 is read as 輅. 45 酌 is read as 勻. 46（四）〔白〕(校注 101, following 顧廣圻). 69（其）〔期〕(校注 101). 74〔內〕(校注 101, following 顧廣圻). 95〔則〕(校注 102, following 王先慎).

HF 10.7 (*Xilun* 166, *Xin jiaozhu* 226)

奚謂離內遠遊？	What is meant by 'leaving the court and going on distant journeys'?
昔者齊景公遊於海而樂之。	In ancient times, Lord Jing of Qi travelled to the sea and enjoyed it.[48]
號令諸大夫曰：	He issued an order to the various dignitaries, saying,

---

Rong pastoralists, and compare to the historical attempt to "spoil" the Xiongnu through luxurious gifts under the Han dynasty (see *Shiji* 110: 2899).

48　Lord Jing of Qi ruled from 547 to 490. He was the last ruler of Qi from the Jiang 姜 clan to retain a semblance of authority, despite having already been eclipsed by powerful ministerial lineages, one of which – the Chen/Tian lineage – usurped power soon after Lord Jing's death. Lord Jing is well known as the primary interlocutor of his famous remonstrator, Yan Ying 晏嬰 (Yanzi, d. ca. 500; chapter 30, note 11). In this version of the anecdote, the chief protagonist is Tian Chengzi 田成子 (or Tian Chang), the infamous usurper (see chapter 7, note 3). The commentators replace him with Lord Jing of Qi based on the parallel story in Liu Xiang's *Garden of Persuasions* (*Shuo yuan* 説苑). Their primary aim is to avoid the improbable situation that loyal advice is given to the morally corrupt leader Tian Chengzi. However, judging by the context, Tian may be a more fitting candidate, since it is difficult to believe that those who dwelt in the capital would plot against Lord Jing.

"言歸者死。"	"Whoever speaks of turning back must die."
5　顏涿聚曰：	Yan Zhuoju said,[49]
"君遊海而樂之，	"You are on a journey to the sea and enjoying it,
奈臣有圖國者何？	but what if one of the ministers is plotting against the state?
君雖樂之，	Though you are enjoying yourself now,
將安得？"	what will the future hold?"
10　齊景公曰：	Lord Jing of Qi said:
"寡人布令曰：	"I have sent out an order that said,
'言歸者死',	'Whoever speaks of turning back must die,'
今子犯寡人之令。"	and now you have violated my order."
援戈將擊之。	He took a battle axe and was about to strike him.
15　顏涿聚曰：	Yan Zhuoju said,
"昔桀殺關龍逢而紂殺王子比干，	"In ancient times, Jie killed Guanlong Pang and Zhòu killed Prince Bigan.[50]
今君雖殺臣之身以三之可也。	Now, even if you were to kill me, making a third [example], it would be acceptable.
臣言為國，	I speak for the sake of the state,
非為身也。"	not for my own sake."
20　延頸而前曰：	He stretched out his neck, stepped forward and said:
"君擊之矣！"	"Milord, go ahead and strike me."
君乃釋戈趣駕而歸。	The ruler dropped his battle axe, hastened to have his carriages yoked and returned home.
至三日，	After three days,
而聞國人有謀不內齊景公者矣。	he heard that some of the denizens of the capital had conspired not to allow him back.
25　齊景公所以遂有齊國者，	The reason why Lord Jing of Qi did indeed maintain control over the state of Qi
顏涿聚之力也。	was the power of Yan Zhuoju.
故曰：	So it is said:
離內遠遊[A 游 幽/尤 rəgw/jiǒu]，	Leaving the court on distant journeys
則危身之道[A 幽/晧 dəgwx/dâu]也。	is a way to endanger your life.

2, 10（田成子）〔齊景公〕(校注 102, with 說苑 parallel).　15 C has 逢 for 逢.　24（田成子）〔齊景公〕(校注 102, with 說苑 parallel).　24 內 is read as 納.　25（田成子）〔齊景公〕(校注 102, with 說苑 parallel).

49　Yan Zhuoju is mentioned in *Lüshi chunqiu* 呂氏春秋 4.3 ("Zun shi" 尊師) and later texts as a former robber who studied with Confucius and became a loyal servant of the Lord of Qi.

50　Guanlong Pang and Bigan are both paradigmatic remonstrators (chapter 3, notes 19 and 11).

十過 TEN FAULTS 131

HF 10.8 (*Xilun* 167, *Xin jiaozhu* 228)

奚謂過而不聽於忠臣？	What is meant by 'having made a mistake yet not heeding loyal ministers'?
昔者齊桓公九合諸侯，	In ancient times, Lord Huan of Qi assembled the regional lords nine times,
一匡天下，	ordered the world under one leader,
為五伯長，	and was supreme among the Five Hegemons.
5　管仲佐之。	Guan Zhong assisted him,[51]
管仲老，	but when Guan Zhong grew old
不能用事，	and was unable to conduct public business,
休居於家。	he retired to his home.
桓公從而問之曰：	Then Lord Huan of Qi asked him,
10　"仲父家居有病，	"Uncle Zhong, you are home-bound with an illness;
即不幸而不起此病，	if, unhappily, you do not recover from this illness,
政安遷之？"	to whom should I transfer political responsibility?"
管仲曰：	Guan Zhong said:
"臣老矣，	"I, your subject, am old,
15　不可問也。	and am not someone to consult.
雖然，	Nonetheless,
臣聞之，	I have heard that
知臣莫若君，	when it comes to understanding a minister, no one surpasses the ruler,
知子莫若父。	and when it comes to understanding a son, no one surpasses the father.
20　君其試以心決之。"	You must try to decide the matter on the basis of your own heart."
君曰：	The ruler said:
"鮑叔牙何如？"	"How about Bao Shuya."[52]
管仲曰：	Guan Zhong said:
"不可。	"He is unacceptable.

51　Lord Huan of Qi is the first and most famous of the Springs-and-Autumns period hegemons. Together with his chief minister, Guan Zhong (d. 645), they form the paradigmatic pair of a clear-sighted ruler and his worthy aide.

52　Bao Shuya was Guan Zhong's long-time acquaintance. In the aftermath of the fratricidal struggle in the state of Qi in which the future Lord Huan defeated his brother, Prince Jiu (see chapter 3, note 7), Bao Shuya sided with Lord Huan, and Guan Zhong with Prince Jiu. It was due to Bao Shuya that Guan Zhong was pardoned and appointed to the top

25	鮑叔牙為人， 剛愎而上悍。	Bao Shuya is the sort of person who is inflexible and stubborn, and he values ferociousness.
	剛則犯民以暴，	Being inflexible, he will offend the people with his cruelty;
	愎則不得民心，	being stubborn, he will not gain the people's allegiance;
	悍則下不為用。	and being ferocious, his inferiors will not make themselves employable.
30	其心不懼， 非霸者之佐也。" 公曰： "然則豎刁何如？" 管仲曰：	In his mind there is no fear: he is not the aide for the hegemon." The lord said: "Well then, how about Young Servant Diao." Guan Zhong said:
35	"不可。 夫人之情莫不愛其身。	"He is unacceptable. It is human instinct that everyone cares for his own body.
	公妒而好內， 豎刁自獖以為治內。	You are jealous and fond of your women, so Young Servant Diao castrated himself in order to administer the harem.[53]
	其身不愛，	He does not even care for his own body,
40	又安能愛君？" 公曰： "然則衞公子開方何如？" 管仲曰： "不可。	how could he care for his ruler." The lord said: "If so, how about Prince Kaifang of Wey."[54] Guan Zhong said: "He is unacceptable.
45	齊、衞之間不過十日之行，	From Qi to Wey is no more than a ten-day's journey,
	開方為事君， 欲適君之故， 十五年不歸見其父母，	but Kaifang, in order to serve you, desiring to please you, has not once gone back to see his parents in fifteen years.

---

    position in the administration of his erstwhile enemy. However, now at the end of his life, Guan Zhong places the ruler's interests above his private friendship.

53 See chapter 7, note 10.

54 Prince Kaifang (or Qifang 啟方) of Wey is, in all likelihood, Lord Wen of Wey 衞文公, who sojourned briefly as a fugitive in Qi (for the most unequivocal identification, see the recently unearthed *Xinian* manuscript, chapter 4 [Škrabal 2014: 26]). In late Warring States texts, such as *Guanzi*, *Han Feizi*, and *Lüshi chunqiu*, he becomes a stock conspiratorial figure at the court of Lord Huan of Qi.

	此非人情也。	This is contrary to human instinct.
50	其父母之不親也，	He is not even close with his parents,
	又能親君乎？"	how could he be close with his ruler."
	公曰：	The lord said:
	"然則易牙何如？"	"If so, how about Yiya."
	管仲曰：	Guan Zhong said:
55	"不可。	"He is unacceptable.
	夫易牙為君主味。	When Yiya was in charge of the cooking for you,
	君之所未嘗食唯人肉耳，	the only thing you had never eaten was human flesh.
	易牙蒸其子首而進之，	So Yiya steamed his son's head and offered it to you;[55]
	君所知也。	this is something you already know.
60	人之情莫不愛其子，	It is human instinct that no one does not care for his children,
	今蒸其子以為膳於君，	but he steamed his son's head in order to make a delicacy for his ruler:
	其子弗愛，	If he did not care for his own son,
	又安能愛君乎？"	how could he care for his ruler."
	公曰：	The lord said:
65	"然則孰可？"	"Very well! But who, then, is acceptable."
	管仲曰：	Guan Zhong said:
	"隰朋可。	"Xi Peng is acceptable.
	其為人也，	He is of the sort
	堅中而廉外，	who is inwardly firm and incorruptible in his relations with others;
70	少欲而多信。	he has few desires and plenty of good faith.
	夫堅中，	Now, when someone is inwardly firm,
	則足以為表；	he is qualified to serve as a model for others;
	廉外，	when someone is incorruptible,
	則可以大任；	he can be given great responsibilities;
75	少欲，	when someone has few desires,
	則能臨其眾；	he will be able to deal with the masses;
	多信，	when someone has plenty of good faith,
	則能親鄰國。	he can cultivate close relations with neighbouring states.
	此霸者之佐也，	This man could be an aide to the hegemon.
80	君其用之。"	You should use him."

---

55 See chapter 7, note 11.

君曰：	The ruler said:
"諾。"	"Approved."
居一年餘，	More than a year passed,
管仲死，	and Guan Zhong died.
85 君遂不用隰朋而與豎刁。	The ruler in the end did not employ Xi Peng, but sided with Young Servant Diao.
刁涖事三年，	When Young Servant Diao had run the government for three years,
桓公南遊堂阜，	Lord Huan travelled to Tangfu,
豎刁率易牙、衛公子開方及大臣為亂。	and Young Servant Diao led Yiya, Prince Kaifang of Wey, and the senior ministers in revolt.
桓公渴餒而死南門之寢、公守之室，	Lord Huan died of thirst and hunger in the bedroom by the southern gate, in his secured building.
90 身死三月不收，	Three months after he had died, his body had still not been collected;
蟲出于戶。	maggots were crawling out from under the door [to his bedchamber].[56]
故桓公之兵橫行天下，	So, the armies of Lord Huan crisscrossed the world,
為五伯長，	and he was supreme among the Five Hegemons,
卒見弒於其臣，	but in the end, he was assassinated by his own ministers,

---

56 This interpretation of Lord Huan's death is patently wrong. Lord Huan was not assassinated, but died of old age after 43 years on the throne. What happened after his death, however, confirms the insight placed in Guan Zhong's mouth in the above anecdote: the cook Yiya and Young Servant (eunuch) Diao orchestrated a coup that replaced the designated heir with another one of Lord Huan's many sons, and the ensuing turmoil delayed Lord Huan's encoffining by 67 days ("three months" meaning that third month since his death had started) (*Zuozhuan*, Xi 17.5). The story of the maggots crawling out of Lord Huan's bedchamber appears in a variety of Warring States-period texts besides *Han Feizi*: e.g., *Yanzi chunqiu* 1.16: 43; *Lüshi chunqiu* 1.3 ("Gui gong" 貴公); *Guanzi* 32: 609 ("Xiao cheng" 小稱), and later *Records of the Historian* (*Shiji* 32: 1494). Noma Fumichika (1994) is probably right that the crawling maggots were added the original story of his delayed encoffining as a grotesque embellishment. Yet his speculation that the origin of the maggot story was *Han Feizi* 36.3.1 is not convincing, nor is his proposal that the 67-day delay was an error in *Zuozhuan*. (Noma claims that Lord Huan's death was narrated twice in *Zuozhuan*: once, according to the Xia calendar, allegedly used in Qi, which lagged two months behind the Zhou calendar, and once again according to the Lu/Zhou calendar. This assertion is problematic because in all likelihood, the Yin rather than the Xia calendar was used in Qi; see also Yoshimoto 1991).

95 而滅高名，	had his lofty name destroyed,
為天下笑者，	and became a laughingstock for all the world.
何也？	Why was this?
不用管仲之過也。	It was the mistake of not acting in accordance with Guan Zhong's advice.
故曰：	So it is said:
100 過而不聽於忠臣，	When you have made a mistake yet do not heed loyal ministers,
獨行其意，	but act independently on the basis of your own ideas,
則滅其高名為人笑之始也。	this is the beginning of destroying your lofty name and becoming a laughingstock for all.

26 上 is read as 尚.   41〔公〕(校注 102).   42〔衛〕(校注 102).   43（曰）管仲曰(校注 102).

HF 10.9 (*Xilun* 172, *Xin jiaozhu* 232)

奚謂內不量力？	What is meant by 'not assessing your domestic strength'?
昔者秦之攻宜陽，	In the past, when Qin attacked Yiyang,
韓氏急。	the House of Hán was desperate.[57]
公仲朋謂韓君曰：	Gongzhong Peng told the ruler of Hán:[58]
5 "與國不可恃也，	"Our allies cannot be relied upon.
豈如因張儀為和於秦哉！	We had better use Zhang Yi and sue for peace with Qin![59]
因賂以名都而南與伐楚，	At the same time, we should present them with a famous city and join them in the south to attack Chu;
是患解於秦而害交於楚也。"	by this means, our trouble with Qin will be resolved, and the damage imposed on Chu."

[57] Qin's assault on Yiyang happened in 308. Gongzhong Peng's plan to divert Qin's aggression from Hán to Chu is reported also in *Zhanguo ce* 26.17 ("Hán 韓 1"), and in the "Hereditary House of Hán" chapter of the *Records of the Historian*; both date this plan to 315, when Qin attacked another location in Hán, Zhuoze 濁澤. Yiyang was Hán's stronghold on the middle reaches of Luo 洛 River, to the west of the modern city of Yiyang.

[58] Gongzhong Peng was Hán's prime minister. He was a member of a minor branch of the Hán royal lineage. Hence below he is referred to as Han Peng.

[59] Zhang Yi (d. 309) was a singularly powerful Qin minister and diplomat, usually associated with the formation of pro-Qin "horizontal alliance."

公曰： The lord said:[60]
"善。" "Excellent!"
乃警公仲之行， Then he signalled that Gongzhong would go on his journey,
將西和秦。 and would make peace with Qin in the west.
楚王聞之， When the King of Chu learned about this
懼， he became frightened.
召陳軫而告之曰： He summoned Chen Zhen[61] and announced to him:
"韓朋將西和秦， "Hán Peng (Gongzhong Peng) is going to make peace with Qin in the west.
今將奈何？" What should we do."
陳軫曰： Chen Zhen said:
"秦得韓之都一， "Qin has obtained one city from Hán.
驅其練甲， They will send out their crack troops,
秦、韓為一以南鄉楚， and Qin and Hán will unite to face Chu in the south.
此秦王之所以廟祠而求也， This is what the King of Qin has prayed for in his ancestral temple.
其為楚害必矣。 There is no doubt that this will inflict damage on Chu.
王其趣發信臣， Your Majesty must quickly dispatch your most trusted minister,
多其車， with many carriages
重其幣， and large amounts of gifts
以奉韓曰： to present to Hán, saying:
'不穀之國雖小， 'My state may be small,
卒已悉起， but we have mobilised all our soldiers.
願大國之信意於秦也。 I hope your great state will be true to your intentions against Qin.
因願大國令使者入境視楚之起卒也。'" And so I hope that your great state will send an envoy into our territory who will observe the mobilisation of soldiers in Chu.'"

60　By this time, the ruler of Hán had already assumed a royal title. Referring to him as a "duke" is possibly a scribal error (the neutral designation of "ruler" 君 is used for the Hán ruler throughout the rest of the anecdote).

61　Chen Zhen is one of the famous travelling persuaders of the late fourth century; for a while he served Qin (where he was Zhang Yi's rival). At the time of the anecdote, he was employed by Chu. The king of Chu should be King Huai 楚懷王 (r. 328–299).

十過 TEN FAULTS

韓使人之楚，	Hán sent someone to Chu,
楚王因發車騎，	and so the King of Chu then dispatched carriages and horsemen.
陳之下路，	He lined them up at the downward road,
35 謂韓使者曰：	and told the envoy from Hán:
"報韓君，	"Report to the ruler of Hán
言弊邑之兵今將入境矣。"	that our poor settlements' troops will presently enter his realm [to assist against Qin]."
使者還報韓君，	The envoy returned and reported to the ruler of Hán,
韓君大悅，	who felt greatly relieved
40 止公仲。	and stopped Gongzhong.
公仲曰：	Gongzhong said:
"不可。	"That is not advisable.
夫以實害我者，	The one who really harms us
秦也；	is Qin;
45 以名救我者，	the one who ostensibly rescues us
楚也。	is Chu.
聽楚之虛言而輕強秦之實禍，	To listen to Chu's empty words and make light of the real disaster impending from powerful Qin,
則危國之本也。"	endangers the very foundations of the state."
韓君弗聽。	The ruler of Hán did not accept this.
50 公仲怒而歸，	Gongzhong was enraged and returned home,
十日不朝。	and for ten days did not attend court.
宜陽益急，	Yiyang grew more desperate;
韓君令使者趣卒於楚，	the ruler of Hán sent envoys to hurry the forces from Chu.
冠蓋相望而卒無至者。	Their caps and canopies were within sight of each other, but no troops arrived.
55 宜陽果拔，	Yiyang was taken in the end,
為諸侯笑。	and Hán became the laughingstock of the regional lords.
故曰：	So it is said:
內不量力，	Not to assess domestic strength
外恃諸侯者，	and to rely on the regional lords abroad –
60 則國削之患也。	this will lead to the disaster of a decimated state.

43（告）〔害〕(校注 102, following 吳闓生).　47 輕（誣）強, following 王念孫.

HF 10.10 (*Xilun* 174, *Xin jiaozhu* 234)

奚謂國小無禮？	What is meant by 'your state is small and you show no ritual politeness'?
昔者晉公子重耳出亡，	In ancient times, Prince Chong'er of Jin went into exile;
過於曹，	when he passed through Cao,
曹君袒裼而觀之。	the ruler of Cao observed him when he was naked.[62]
5 釐負羈與叔瞻侍於前。	Xi Fuji and Shuzhan[63] were in attendance before him.
叔瞻謂曹君曰：	Shuzhan said to the ruler of Cao:
"臣觀晉公子，	"I have observed the prince from Jin,
非常人也。	and he is not an ordinary person.
君遇之無禮，	You have treated him without proper politeness;
10 彼若有時反國而起兵，	if he one day returns to his state and raises an army,
即恐為曹傷。	I fear this would harmful for Cao.
君不如殺之。"	You had better kill him."
曹君弗聽。	The ruler of Cao did not take the advice.
釐負羈歸而不樂，	Xi Fuji returned home and was in a bad mood.
15 其妻問之曰：	His wife asked him:
"公從外來而有不樂之色，	"You have come in from outside and have an unhappy look –
何也？"	why is that?"
負羈曰：	Fuji said:
"吾聞之，	"I have heard,
20 有福不及，	'If good fortune is in the offing, it will not reach you,
禍來連我。	but if disasters come, they are sure to entangle you.'
今日吾君召晉公子，	Today our ruler summoned the prince from Jin,
其遇之無禮。	treating him without ritual politeness.

---

62 The story of Chong'er's 19 years of wandering before he seized power in Jin in 636 is told in *Zuozhuan* (Xi 23.6 and 24.1), *Discourses of the States* (*Guoyu* 10 [Jin 4]), and the bamboo manuscript *Xinian* from the Tsinghua University collection (section 6); it is also retold in numerous other texts. The *Han Feizi* account differs from these in many details.

63 Shuzhan was in fact a minister from Zheng and not from Cao. In *Zuozhuan* (Xi 23.6d) and *Discourses of the States* (*Guoyu* 10.1), he is cited as an opponent of the Lord of Zheng's maltreatment of Chong'er. Xi Fuji's role in *Han Feizi* resembles that of *Zuozhuan* story (Xi 23.6c).

十過 TEN FAULTS

	我與在前，	I was right there,
25	吾是以不樂。"	and that is why I am unhappy."
	其妻曰：	His wife said:
	"吾觀晉公子，	"I have observed the prince from Jin,
	萬乘之主也；	and he is indeed a ruler of a ten-thousand chariot state;[64]
	其左右從者，	his entourage and followers
30	萬乘之相也。	are indeed ministers of a ten-thousand chariot state.
	今窮而出亡過於曹，	Now he is in difficulty, exiled, and passing through Cao,
	曹遇之無禮。	but Cao has treated him rudely.
	此若反國，	If this man regains his state,
	必誅無禮，	he is bound to punish those who were impolite to him,
35	則曹其首也。	and Cao will be at the head of the list.
	子奚不先自貳焉。"	Why don't you preempt this by betraying [Cao's ruler]."
	負羈曰：	Fuji said:
	"諾。"	"Excellent."
	盛黃金於壺，	He put gold into a pot,
40	充之以餐，	filled the rest of it with foodstuffs,
	加璧其上，	added a *bi*-jade on top,
	夜令人遺公子。	and during the night sent someone to present these things to the prince.
	公子見使者，	When the prince saw the emissary,
	再拜，	he bowed twice,
45	受其餐而辭其璧。	and received the food but refused the jade.
	公子自曹入楚，	The prince proceeded from Cao to Chu,
	自楚入秦。	and from Chu to Qin.[65]
	入秦三年，	After he had been in Qin for three years,
	秦穆公召群臣而謀曰：	Lord Mu of Qin convened his ministers and consulted with them, saying:
50	"昔者晉獻公與寡人交，	"In ancient times, my relations with Lord Xian of Jin were good;
	諸侯莫弗聞。	the regional lords all knew about it.

---

64   This is a statement of the prince's capabilities, presenting him as a great leader and implying that he will reclaim power in his state.

65   This corresponds, notwithstanding certain inaccuracies, to Chong'er's route back home.

獻公不幸離群臣，	Unfortunately, Lord Xian has left his ministers;
出入十年矣。	this happened about ten years ago.[66]
嗣子不善，	His heir is not of the good sort.
55 吾恐此將令其宗廟不祓除而社稷不血食也。	I am afraid that this man will cause his ancestral temples not to be kept clean, and there will be no blood offerings at the altars of soil and grain.[67]
如是弗定，	When things are in such a state and we refuse to put them right,
則非與人交之道。	that is not a way of maintaining good relations with others.
吾欲輔重耳而入之晉，	I want to help Chong'er re-enter Jin.
何如？"	What do you think."
60 群臣皆曰：	All the ministers said,
"善。"	"Good."
公因起卒。	The lord thereupon raised soldiers.
革車五百乘，	He mobilised five hundred armoured chariots,
疇騎二千，	gathered two thousand horsemen
65 步卒五萬，	and fifty thousand foot soldiers;[68]
輔重耳入之于晉，	he helped Chong'er re-enter Jin,
立為晉君。	and established him as the ruler of Jin.
重耳即位三年，	After Chong'er had been on the throne for three years
舉兵而伐曹矣。	he raised an army and attacked Cao.[69]
70 因令人告曹君曰：	At the same time, he sent someone to tell the ruler of Cao, saying:
"懸叔瞻而出之，	"Tie up Shuzhan and bring him out of the city,
我且殺而以為大戮。"	I will presently have him killed and stage a large-scale public execution."

---

66   After Lord Xian's death in 651, his designated heirs were murdered by officials who sought to establish one of the elder scions as the new ruler. Qin supported Prince Yiwu, who ascended the Jin throne as Lord Hui (r. 650–637). Soon after his ascendancy, Lord Hui turned his back on Qin, which in due course offered its support to Lord Hui's half-brother and rival, Chong'er.

67   That is, the destruction of the state.

68   This is another anachronism: the composition of Qin's army in Han Fei's narration reflects the realities of the Warring States period when the bulk of the army consisted of infantrymen and the cavalry were deployed, in addition to war chariots. In the Springs-and-Autumns period, the army's strength was calculated in terms of its chariots only.

69   Chong'er ascended the throne of Jin in 636 (he is posthumously known as Lord Wen). He attacked Cao in 632 (i.e. after four years, not three). This was part of his complex strategy to challenge the state of Chu, the major power of that age and Cao's patron.

十過 TEN FAULTS

又令人告釐負羈曰：	He also sent someone to tell Xi Fuji:
"軍旅薄城，	"The army is pressing close to the city wall.
75　吾知子不違也。	I remember well that you did not offend me.
其表子之閭，	You should put a mark on your gates.
寡人將以為令，	I shall issue an order,
令軍勿敢犯。"	ordering the army not to dare to violate these areas."
曹人聞之，	When the people of Cao heard about this,
80　率其親戚而保釐負羈之閭者七百餘家。	there were more than seven hundred families who led their relatives and found refuge in Xi Fuji's neighbourhood.[70]
此禮之所用也。	This was the effect of ritual politeness.
故曹，	Cao
小國也，	was a small state,
而迫於晉、楚之間，	pressed in between Jin and Chu,
85　其君之危猶累卵也，	and its ruler's position was as precarious as a stack of eggs,
而以無禮涖之，	but he approached the Prince of Jin rudely.
此所以絕世也。	That is why his hereditary line was severed.[71]
故曰：	So it is said:
國小無禮，	If your state is small and you show no ritual politeness,
90　不用諫臣，	and if you do not make use of remonstrating ministers,
則絕世之勢也。	that is a situation in which your hereditary line will be severed.

41 張抄 has 壁 for 璧.

70　According to *Zuozhuan*, after conquering Cao, Lord Wen did indeed issue an order stating that no one ought dare to enter Xi Fuji's residence. However, two of Jin's commanders violated this order and set it on fire. One of the assailants was executed on Lord Wen's orders (see *Zuozhuan*, Xi 28.3). For an analysis of the similarities and differences between *Zuozhuan* and other versions of Xi Fuji's story, see Li Wai-yee 2023: 136–141.

71　Another inaccuracy. Lord Wen of Jin did destroy Cao early in 632, but decided to restore its ruler later in the same year. Cao perished when it was conquered by the state of Song in 487.

CHAPTER 11

孤憤 Solitary Resentment

HF 11.1 (*Xilun* 180, *Xin jiaozhu* 239)

智術之士，	A gentleman who understands the techniques of governance
必遠見而明察，	must be far-sighted and investigate with clear sight,
不明察，	for one who does not investigate with clear sight
不能燭私；	cannot expose private interests.
5 能法之士，	A gentleman who is competent in law
必強毅而勁直，	must be strong and firm, tough and straight.
不勁直，	If he is not tough and straight,
不能矯姦。	he cannot correct treachery.
人臣循令而從事，	Ministers who comply with orders in conducting affairs
10 案法而治官，	and stick to law when they administer their official duties,[1]
非謂重人也。	these are not the ones we call "political heavyweights."
重人也者，	As for political heavyweights,
無令而擅為，	without orders, they act on their own authority,
虧法以利私，	abusing law to further their private interests.
15 耗國以便家，	They squander what belongs to the state in order to benefit their lineage,
力能得其君，	and, through their power, they are able to gain the support of the ruler.
此所為重人也。	These are the ones we call political heavyweights.
智術之士明察，	A gentleman who understands the techniques of governance investigates with clear sight.

---

1 Here, *shi* 事, "tasks," are initiated by order and do not necessarily form a regular part of one's official duties; they are distinct from *guan* 官, "official duties," which are determined by law.

孤憤 SOLITARY RESENTMENT   143

	聽用，	If he is heeded and employed,
20	且燭重人之陰情；	this will immediately expose the hidden disposition of political heavyweights.
	能法之士勁直，	A gentleman who is capable of implementing law who is tough and straight,
	聽用，	if he is heeded and employed,
	且矯重人之姦行。	will immediately correct the seditious practices of political heavyweights.
	故智術能法之士用，	So, when gentlemen are employed who understand the techniques of governance and are capable of implementing law,
25	則貴重之臣必在繩之外矣。	noble and heavyweight ministers are sure to remain outsiders.[2]
	是智法之士與當塗之人，	Thus, gentlemen who understand law and people in control
	不可兩存之仇也。	are enemies who cannot coexist.

1 智 is read as 知.   17 The C editors note: 準上文「非謂重人也」, 此「為」字當作「謂」。. We read 為 as 謂.   18, 24, 26 智 is read as 知.

HF 11.2 (*Xilun* 182, *Xin jiaozhu* 240)

	當塗之人擅事要，	When the people in control arrogate to themselves the essential aspects of undertakings,
	則外內為之用矣。	those within the country and outside will be utilised by them.
	是以諸侯不因，	Thus, if the regional lords do not fall in line with them,
	則事不應，	their undertakings will get no response,
5	故敵國為之訟；	and so the [regional lords in] rival states will sing their praises;
	百官不因，	if officials do not fall in line with them,
	則業不進，	their undertakings will not be advanced,

2 Literally, "beyond the ink-line." Very often, the ink-line is a metaphor for the law. The ink-line was a tool for demarcating boundaries, and serves as a metaphor relating to standards, as though to say that the type of official in question is at once an outsider and a deviant, substandard.

144   CHAPTER 11

故群臣為之用；	and so the various ministers all work for them;
郎中不因，	if [the ruler's] retinue does not fall in line with them,
10　則不得近主，	they will not get to be close to the ruler,
故左右為之匿；	and so his entourage covers up [the heavyweights' misconduct];
學士不因，	if gentlemen of learning do not fall in line with them,
則養祿薄禮卑，	their emoluments will be slight and they will be treated with contempt,
故學士為之談也。	and so the gentlemen of learning speak on their behalf.
15　此四助者，	These four accomplices[3]
邪臣之所以自飾也。	are the means by which evil ministers make themselves look good.
重人不能忠主而進其仇，	The political heavyweights will never be loyal to the ruler, if it means promoting their enemies;[4]
人主不能越四助而燭察其臣，	the ruler of men will never get past the four accomplices, if it means exposing and investigating the ministers,[5]
故人主愈弊而大臣愈重。	and so the ruler becomes ever more ignorant and the senior ministers ever more powerful.

4 訟 is read as 頌.　19 弊 is read as 蔽.

HF 11.3 (*Xilun* 183, *Xin jiaozhu* 240)

凡當塗者之於人主也，	In general, those in control treat their ruler
希不信愛也，	so [cleverly] that it is rare that they are not trusted and loved
又且習故。	and they moreover become the ruler's confidants.

3　The regional lords, the officials, the retinue, and the men of learning who assist the political heavyweights in charge.
4　"Enemies" are the clear-sighted officials praised by Han Fei earlier.
5　That is, those good itinerant gentlemen "who understand the techniques" will never be promoted, first because they are blocked by their natural enemies, the heavyweights, and second because the ruler, duped by his entourage, would never learn of their existence.

孤憤 SOLITARY RESENTMENT

5	若夫即主心，	As for becoming closer to the ruler's heart,
	同乎好惡，	they share his likes and dislikes
	固其所自進也。	and solidify their means of self-promotion.
	官爵貴重[A 東/用 drjuŋh/djwoŋ]，	When offices and ranks go to the noble and the heavyweights,
	朋黨又眾[A 中/送 tjəŋwh/tśjuŋ]，	their factions swell even larger,
	而一國為之訟[A 東/用 sgjuŋh/zjwoŋ]。	and the whole state will sing their praise.
10	則法術之士欲干上者，	On the other hand, gentlemen skilled in laws and techniques of rule[6] wish to shield their sovereign,[7]
	非有所信愛之親、習故之澤也，	not because they have the intimacy of the trusted and beloved, nor because they enjoy the favours of the confidants,
	又將以法術之言矯人主阿辟之心，	but in order to use proposals based on laws and techniques of rule to straighten the ruler's biased heart.
	是與人主相反也。	This places them in opposition to the ruler.
	處勢卑賤，	The position they occupy is lowly,
15	無黨孤特。	without a faction, and isolated.
	夫以疏遠與近愛信爭，	Now, if someone who is distant from the ruler competes with those who are close, beloved, and trusted,
	其數不勝也；	the odds are that he will not win.
	以新旅與習故爭，	If a newcomer and outsider competes with old confidants,
	其數不勝也；	the odds are that he will not win.
20	以反主意與同好惡爭，	If someone who opposes the ruler's intent competes with those who share the ruler's likes and dislikes,
	其數不勝也；	the odds are that he will not win.

---

6 This is the first occurrence in *Han Feizi* of the important technical term *fashu* 法術 "laws and techniques" (an alternative translation could be "statecraft based on law"). This technical term is particularly common in chapters 11, 13, and 14; it also appears with high frequency in chapter 52.

7 The word *shang* 上 often refers specifically to the ruler.

以輕賤與貴重爭，	If someone who is lightweight and base competes with the noble heavyweights,
其數不勝也；	the odds are that he will not win.
以一口與一國爭，	If a single mouth competes with the whole state,
25　其數不勝也。	the odds are that he will not win.
法術之士操五不勝之勢，	The gentlemen skilled in laws and techniques of rule hold five non-winning strategic positions;
以歲數而又不得見；	they can count the years but still do not obtain an audience.
當塗之人乘五勝之資，	The men in control avail themselves of the five winning resources,
而旦暮獨說於前。	and persuade the ruler without competition, from dawn to dusk.
30　故法術之士奚道得進，	So, in what way could the gentlemen skilled in laws and techniques of rule obtain advancement?
而人主奚時得悟乎？	And when would the ruler come to appreciate them?
故資必不勝而勢不兩存，	Their resources are such that they will not win and their strategic position such that they cannot coexist [with the heavyweights],
法術之士焉得不危？	so how could the gentlemen skilled in laws and techniques of rule fail to be endangered?
其可以罪過誣者，	If [the heavyweights] can slander [the gentlemen skilled in laws] as criminals and transgressors,
35　以公法而誅之；	they punish them according to the impartial law;
其不可被以罪過者，	and if they cannot slander them as criminals and transgressors,
以私劍而窮之。	they end them by the private use of swords.
是明法術而逆主上者，	Thus, those who are clear about laws and techniques of rule and oppose their ruler above,
不僇於吏誅，	if they do not die from punishment at the hands of officials,
40　必死於私劍矣。	they are bound to die by hired swords.
朋黨比周以弊主，	Those who form factions and cliques to keep the ruler ignorant,
言曲以便私者，	and give crooked proposals in service of private interests,

孤憤 SOLITARY RESENTMENT

必信於重人矣。	are bound to be trusted by the political heavyweights.
故其可以功伐借者，	So, the latter can use the pretence of some achievement
45　以官爵貴之；	and seek honour through office and rank;
其不可借以美名者，	and if they cannot make a pretence [of achievement] to attain a fine reputation,
以外權重之。	they will gain importance through foreign powers.[8]
是以弊主上而趨於私門者，	Therefore, those who keep the ruler ignorant and rush to private gates,[9]
不顯於官爵，	if they do not become illustrious in office or rank,
50　必重於外權矣。	they are bound to gain importance through foreign powers.
今人主不合參驗而行誅，	Now rulers carry out punishments without checking the evidence,
不待見功而爵祿，	and confer rank and emoluments having seen no achievements,
故法術之士安能蒙死亡而進其說？	so how could the gentlemen skilled in laws and techniques of rule risk death and ruin to advance their persuasions?
姦邪之臣安肯棄利而退其身？	And why would wicked ministers reject profit and put themselves last?
55　故主上愈卑，	For these reasons the ruler becomes ever more debased
私門益尊。	and private gates ever more respected.

---

12 辟 is read as 僻。　14（世）〔勢〕(校注 III)。　20〔惡〕(校注 III, following 顧廣圻)。　35〔以〕(校注 III, with 張榜本)。　39 僇 is read as 戮。C emends 僇 to 戮 (校注 III)。　41 弊 is read as 蔽。　46（明）〔名〕(校注 III)。　48 弊 is read as 蔽。　54 乘 of all editions is emended to 棄, following 劉師培 and 津田鳳卿。

8　This refers to a common situation in the Warring States period whereby foreign powers meddled in appointments made at the court of their allies (in some exceptional cases, a single person could be simultaneously appointed at several courts). Needless to say, Han Fei bitterly criticises this kind of situation.

9　"Private gates" are the gates of those heavyweight ministers who control promotions and ranks in the state of the benighted monarch.

HF 11.4 (*Xilun* 186, *Xin jiaozhu* 246)

夫越雖國富兵強，	As for Yue, though the state is wealthy and its army strong,
中國之主皆知無益於己也，	the rulers of the central states all know that it is of no advantage to them,
曰：	and say:
"非吾所得制也。"	"This is not something that we would be able to control."[10]
今有國者雖地廣人眾，	Now, as for a state, though its territory might be vast and its population numerous,
然而人主壅蔽，	if the ruler is blocked off and kept ignorant
大臣專權，	and his senior ministers monopolise power,
是國為越也。	such a state is a 'state of Yue' (which cannot be controlled).
智不類越，	If you understand that [your state] is not like Yue,
而不智不類其國，	but do not understand how to prevent it from becoming of that category (i.e. uncontrollable),[11]
不察其類者也。	then you do not investigate the different types of things.
人之所以謂齊亡者，	People say that the reason why Qi was ruined
非地與城亡也，	is not that its territory and walls were ruined,
呂氏弗制而田氏用之；	but that the Lü lineage was unable to control it, whereas the Tian lineage gained control.[12]
所以謂晉亡者，	The reason why Jin was ruined

---

10   Yue can refer either to the state of Yue (which reached the apex of its power in the fifth century but disintegrated in the fourth century), or to the vast territory in China's southeast, comprising roughly the present-day provinces of Zhejiang, Fujian, Guangdong, and Guangxi (in addition to northern Vietnam), or to various polities that existed in the latter territory. Here the second or the third meaning is implied. It is a fascinating testimony to the fact that just a few years before the Qin unification, many, if not most, rulers of the Warring States considered Yue too difficult to control and abandoned attempts to incorporate it. Note that immediately after the annexation of the Warring States, the First Emperor of Qin subjugated the Yue territories.

11   Because the political heavyweights have taken over effective control.

12   This refers to Han Fei's favourite topic: the usurpation in Qi by the Tian/Chen lineage (see chapter 7, especially note 3). The Lü lineage were descendants of the founder of the state of Qi, Grand Duke Wang 太公望.

孤憤 SOLITARY RESENTMENT

亦非地與城亡也，	is likewise not that its territory and walls were ruined,
姬氏不制而六卿專之也。	but that the Ji lineage was not in control and the six senior ministers[13] monopolised control over it.
今大臣執柄獨斷，	Now, when the senior ministers hold the levers and make independent decisions,
而上弗知收，	whereas the ruler does not know how to regain these levers:
20 是人主不明也。	this is because the ruler lacks clarity of insight.
與死人同病者，	People who have the same illness as a dead person
不可生也；	cannot be made to live;
與亡國同事者，	states that have the same undertakings as a ruined state
不可存也。	cannot be preserved.
25 今襲跡於齊、晉，	Now, following in the footsteps of Qi and Jin
欲國安存，	and wanting the state to survive in peace –
不可得也。	this is impossible to achieve.

1 〔國〕(校注 111).　9, 10 The C editors note: 「類」字疑為「制」字之誤。. We do not emend.　9, 10 智 is read as 知.　12 (主)〔之〕(校注 111, following 松皋圓).

HF 11.5 (*Xilun* 188, *Xin jiaozhu* 248)

凡法術之難行也，	In general, the difficulty of implementing laws and techniques of rule
不獨萬乘，	does not apply only to a state of ten thousand chariots:
千乘亦然。	it is the same for a state of a thousand chariots.[14]

13　From the sixth century, the ruling house of Jin, which belonged to the Zhou royal clan (the Ji 姬), was sidelined by powerful ministerial lineages (chapter 1, note 33). Normally the term "six senior ministers" refers to the Fan 范, Zhonghang 中行, Zhi 知, Hán 韓, Zhao 趙, and Wei 魏 lineages. The first two were eliminated by their rivals in the civil war of 497–490; the Zhi fell in 453 (see chapter 10.5 above); and the last three (Han Fei himself belonged to one of them) divided the state of Jin amongst themselves in 403.

14　On the calculation of a state's power according to its number of chariots, see chapter 4, note 2. It is not clear why Han Fei bothers to bring up the minor states here, since by

	人主之左右不必智也，	Those in the entourage of a ruler are not necessarily intelligent,
5	人主於人有所智而聽之，	and if the ruler considers somebody intelligent and listens to him,
	因與左右論其言，	and then discusses this man's proposals with his entourage,
	是與愚人論智也；	this is to discuss matters of intellect with the stupid.
	人主之左右不必賢也，	Those in the ruler's entourage are not necessarily worthy;
	人主於人有所賢而禮之，	if the ruler considers somebody worthy and treats him with decorum,
10	因與左右論其行，	and then discusses this man's behaviour with his entourage,
	是與不肖論賢也。	this is to discuss worth with the unworthy.
	智者決策於愚人，	If the intelligent have their stratagems decided by the stupid,
	賢士程行於不肖，	and if worthy gentlemen have their actions assessed by the unworthy,
	則賢智之士羞而人主之論悖矣。	then the worthy and intelligent gentlemen will be humiliated, and the ruler's deliberations will be confused.
15	人臣之欲得官者，	As for ministers who wish to obtain office,
	其脩士且以精絜固身，	the cultivated gentlemen make their persons firm through refined purity
	其智士且以治辯進業。	and the intelligent gentlemen advance in their trade by perfecting rhetoric.
	其脩士不能以貨賂事人，	The cultivated gentlemen cannot dispense bribes so as to serve others,
	恃其精潔；	but rely on their refined purity,
20	而更不能以枉法為治，	and [the intelligent gentlemen] are even less able to conduct their official business by perverting laws,

---

his lifetime most of these had already been annexed by powerful, "ten-thousand chariot" polities. Maybe this is a hint at the declining power of his home state of Hán?

孤憤 SOLITARY RESENTMENT

則脩智之士不事左右， and so, if cultivated and intelligent gentlemen will not serve the ruler's entourage,

不聽請謁矣。 and will not listen to requests for an interview,

人主之左右， then those in the entourage of the ruler

行非伯夷[A 脂/脂 rid/ji]也， will not behave like Boyi.[15]

25 求索不得[B 之/德 tək/tək]， When they do not obtain what they request [of the cultivated gentlemen],

貨賂不至[A 脂/至 tjidh/tśji]， and bribes do not reach them,

則精辯之功息[B 之/職 sjək/sjək]， their "merits" based on refined rhetoric cease,

而毀誣之言起[B 之/止 khjəgx/khï]矣。 whereas slanderous and fraudulent words arise.[16]

治辯之功制於近習， When merits based on refined rhetoric are controlled by cronies,

30 精潔之行決於毀譽， whereas purity of conduct is judged by slanderers and flatterers,

則脩智之吏廢， then cultivated and intelligent officials[17] will be dismissed,

則人主之明塞矣。 and the clear perspective of the ruler will be blocked.

不以功伐決智行， When you do not judge intellect and conduct on the basis of achievement,

不以參伍審罪過， or examine crimes on the basis of verification,

35 而聽左右近習之言， but listen to the words of your entourage and cronies,

則無能之士在廷， then incompetent gentlemen will be at the court,

而愚汙之吏處官矣。 and stupid and foul officials will occupy the offices.

19 張覺 inserts 其智士 before 更.　27 （亂）〔辯〕（校注 111, following 張榜本）.

15　Boyi was a symbol of moral purity (see chapter 14, note 24).

16　The cultivated gentlemen (men of service) would not turn to members of the ruler's entourage for promotion. The entourage would be deprived of bribes (through which interviews with the ruler and promotions were obtained). Moreover, the ability of entourage members to employ rhetoric so as to invent fictitious merit would vanish as well, having been thwarted by cultivated specialists in laws and techniques of rule. Thus, resentful, the entourage would join forces to slander the cultivated men of service.

17　The term *li* 吏 often refers to low-ranking clerks, but in some cases can refer to high officials and clerks alike. See Liu Min 2014.

HF 11.6 (*Xilun* 191, *Xin jiaozhu* 251)

萬乘之患，	Disaster in a state of ten thousand chariots
大臣太重；	is when the senior ministers are too powerful;
千乘之患，	disaster in a state of a thousand chariots
左右太信；	is when the entourage are trusted too much.
5 此人主之所公患也。	This is the common disaster for rulers.
且人臣有大罪，	Moreover, as for ministers committing great crimes
人主有大失，	and rulers suffering great losses,
臣主之利相與異者也。	the reason is to be found in the differences in the interests of the ministers and the rulers.
何以明之哉？	How can I make that clear?
10 曰：	It is as follows:
主利在有能而任官，	The ruler's interest is in having people of ability employed in the offices,
臣利在無能而得事；	the ministers' interest is in not having ability, yet being allowed to serve.
主利在有勞而爵祿，	The ruler's interest is that rank and emolument go to those who have made an effort;
臣利在無功而富貴；	the ministers' interest is in being without achievement, yet enjoying wealth and nobility.
15 主利在豪傑使能，	The ruler's interest is to use the powerful and eminent according to their abilities;
臣利在朋黨用私。	the ministers' interest lies in factions and in serving their private ends.
是以國地削而私家富，	This is why the state's lands are pared away while private families become wealthy
主上卑而大臣重。	and why the ruler is debased, whereas the senior ministers become heavyweights,
故主失勢而臣得國，	and so the ruler loses his strategic position and the ministers gain control of the state,
20 主更稱蕃臣，	and the ruler is renamed an 'enfeoffed minister,'

孤憤 SOLITARY RESENTMENT

而相室剖符。	whereas the chancellor's family breaks the official tallies.[18]
此人臣之所以譎主便私也。	This is how ministers cheat their rulers and serve their private purposes.
故當世之重臣，	So, as for the powerful ministers of the present age,
主變勢而得固寵者，	if there were a change in the strategic position of the ruler, only two or three out of ten
25 十無二三。	would retain stable favour.
是其故何也？	Why is this?
人臣之罪大也。	It is because of the great crimes of the ministers.
臣有大罪者，	Now ministers who commit great crimes
其行欺主也，	engage in deception against the ruler,
30 其罪當死亡也。	and their crimes are deserving of death.
智士者遠見而畏於死亡，	The intelligent gentlemen are far-sighted and afraid of death or ruin;
必不從重人矣；	surely they will not follow the political heavyweights.
賢士者脩廉而羞與姦臣欺其主，	As for the worthy gentlemen, they will cultivate moral purity, and will be ashamed to join the treacherous ministers to cheat the ruler,
必不從重臣矣。	and are sure not to join the heavyweight ministers.
35 是當塗者之徒屬，	Under such circumstances, the followers of men in power
非愚而不知患者，	either stupidly do not understand the impending disaster,
必汙而不避姦者也。	or, in their filth, fail to avoid treachery.
大臣挾愚汙之人，	When the senior ministers have stupid and foul people under their wings –
上與之欺主，	above, they collude to cheat the ruler;
40 下與之收利侵漁，	and below, they reap profit and trespass against others.

18　Breaking the tallies in two (or more precisely, granting one half of a tally to underlings) was the prerogative of the ruler. Here it is usurped by the chancellor and his progeny.

朋黨比周，They form factions and cliques
相與一口，and coordinate their talk,
惑主敗法，confusing the ruler and ruining the rule of law,
以亂士民，so that they wreak havoc among the gentlemen and the common people
45 使國家危削，and cause the state to be endangered and truncated

主上勞辱，and the ruler to be exhausted and humiliated.
此大罪也。This is the greatest of crimes.

臣有大罪而主弗禁，When a minister commits a great crime and the ruler does not put a stop to it,
此大失也。this is the greatest of mistakes.

50 使其主有大失於上，If someone brings it about that the ruler makes great mistakes above
臣有大罪於下，and ministers commit great crimes below,
索國之不亡者，then avoiding the ruin of the state,
不可得也。will be an impossibility.

5 公 is read as 共. 8 C reverses order of 相與, following 顧廣圻, reading 與 as 舉, and notes:「與」讀為「舉」。下文列數人主人臣之利害相反，不一而足，故曰「舉相異」。 We do not follow this reading. 20 蕃 is read as 藩.

CHAPTER 12

說難 Difficulties of Persuasion

HF 12.1 (*Xilun* 195, *Xin jiaozhu* 254)

凡說之難：	In general, the difficulties of persuasion [are as follows]:
非吾知之有以說之之難也，	It is not that you know something, but have difficulty persuading others with it,
又非吾辯之能明吾意之難也，	nor that you argue about something, but have difficulty clarifying your meaning;
又非吾敢橫失而能盡之難也。	nor that you dare to speak unbridledly, but have difficulty expressing yourself completely.
5 凡說之難：	In general, the problem of persuasion
在知所說之心，	consists in knowing the mind of the person to be persuaded
可以吾說當之。	and in being able to make your persuasion fit.

4 失 is read as 佚.

HF 12.2 (*Xilun* 197, *Xin jiaozhu* 254)

所說出於為名高者也，	If the person to be persuaded is one of those who are concerned with a lofty name,
而說之以厚利，	and you persuade him with considerations of substantial profit,
則見下節而遇卑賤，	you will be seen as morally inferior, treated as lowly,
必棄遠矣。	and bound to be discarded and estranged.
5 所說出於厚利者也，	If the person to be persuaded is one of those who are concerned to maximise gain,
而說之以名高，	and you persuade him by saying that his name will be elevated,
則見無心而遠事情，	you will be seen as mindless, kept away from the conduct of affairs,
必不收矣。	and surely not admitted [to his vicinity].

所說陰為厚利而顯為名高者也，	If the person you are persuading is one who is secretly concerned to maximise gain, but makes a show of being concerned with a lofty name,
10　而說之以名高，	and you persuade him by saying that his name will be elevated,
則陽收其身而實疏之；	then on the surface he will admit your person to his vicinity, but in reality he will keep you at a distance;
說之以厚利，	if you persuade him by referring to maximising gain,
則陰用其言顯棄其身矣。	he will secretly use your proposals, but make a show of rejecting you as a person.
此不可不察也。	This absolutely must be investigated.

HF 12.3 (*Xilun* 198, *Xin jiaozhu* 256)

夫事以密成，	Affairs succeed when they are kept secret;
語以洩敗。	talks fail when there are leaks.
未必其身洩之也，	You might not necessarily leak it yourself,
而語及所匿之事，	but if, in conversation, you touch upon a matter that has been held secret,
5　如此者身危。	your person will be in danger.
彼顯有所出事，	If the other person makes a show that something motivates his undertakings,
而乃以成他故，	but he actually wishes to accomplish some other result,
說者不徒知所出而已矣，	and if the persuader knows not only the ostensible motivation,
又知其所以為，	but also the ulterior motives,
10　如此者身危。	the persuader will be in danger.
規異事而當，	If you plan an extraordinary undertaking and do it appropriately,
知者揣之外而得之，	but some clever [intermediary] figures it out from the outside,
事洩於外，	and the matter leaks out,
必以為己也，	the ruler will think it was you,
15　如此者身危。	and your person will be in danger.

說難 DIFFICULTIES OF PERSUASION

周澤未渥也，	When the ruler's favour for you is not yet deep,
而語極知，	but your speech is extremely intelligent,
說行而有功，	then if your persuasion is implemented and there is success,
則德忘；	your virtuous contribution will be forgotten;
說不行而有敗，	if your persuasion is not implemented and there is defeat,
則見疑，	you will be held in suspicion.
如此者身危。	Either way, you will be in danger.
貴人有過端，	If a nobleman has transgressing intentions,
而說者明言禮義以挑其惡，	and the persuader speaks openly of ritual and propriety, poking at that person's vices,
如此者身危。	he will be in danger.
貴人或得計而欲自以為功，	If a nobleman gets a plan from someone, but wishes to count the success as his own,
說者與知焉，	and the persuader knows this situation,
如此者身危。	he will be in danger.
強以其所不能為，	If you force the ruler to do what he cannot do
止以其所不能已，	and insist on stopping him from doing what he cannot stop doing,
如此者身危。	you will be in danger.
故與之論大人，	So, if you discuss great people with him,
則以為間己矣；	he will think you are interposing yourself;
與之論細人，	if you discuss humble people with him
則以為賣重。	the ruler will think you are peddling influence.
論其所愛，	When you pass judgment on someone he likes,
則以為藉資；	he will think you are relying on that man's support;
論其所憎，	if you pass judgment on someone he dislikes,
則以為嘗己也。	he will think you are testing him.
徑省其說，	When you present your persuasions concisely,
則以為不智而拙之；	he will think you are unintelligent and inept;
米鹽博辯，	when you are trivially detailed and wide-ranging in your rhetoric,
則以為多而交之。	he will think it wordy and convoluted.

略事陳意，	When you put your ideas concisely,
45 則曰怯懦而不盡；	he will say you are timid and not thorough;
慮事廣肆，	when you consider matters in broad and expansive detail,
則曰草野而倨侮。	he will say you are arrogant and rude.
此說之難，	These are the difficulties of persuasion,
不可不知也。	and they must be understood.

5〔者〕(校注 119).　12, 17 知 is read as 智.　36（增）〔憎〕(校注 119).　43（交）〔久〕(校注 119, with 張榜本). We interpret 交 as 交雜, following 蒲阪圓; 于鬯 reads 交 as 較, interpreting it as 駁.

HF 12.4 (*Xilun* 200, *Xin jiaozhu* 261)

凡說之務，	In general, the concern in persuasion
在知飾所說之所矜而滅其所恥。	is in understanding how to embellish[1] whatever the person to be persuaded is proud of and to gloss over whatever he is ashamed of.
彼有私急也，	If the other party has private exigencies,
必以公義示而強之。	you must present the matter in terms of impartial righteousness and back up his intentions.
5 其意有下也，	When his intentions are low,
然而不能已，	but he cannot be stopped from going through with them,
說者因為之飾其美而少其不為也。	the persuader should dress this up for him as being admirable and argue that few people are not doing such things.
其心有高也，	When his mind is set on some high purpose
而實不能及，	but he is not able to live up to it,
10 說者為之舉其過而見其惡而多其不行也。	the persuader should focus on transgressions [of moral actions], show their ugly points, and argue that not many people act in accordance with such high principles.

1　Mie 滅 "destroy" is here used in an unusual abstract causal sense: "cause to disappear; gloss over."

說難 DIFFICULTIES OF PERSUASION 159

有欲矜以智能，	If he is given to bragging about his intellect and abilities,
則為之舉異事之同類者，	then bring up different cases of the same sort
多為之地，	and provide him with more evidence[2] in his favour;
使之資說於我，	make him cherish your explanations,
15 而佯不知也以資其智。	but at the same time pretend that you are not clever in order to buttress his [supposed] wisdom.
欲內相存之言，	If you want to submit proposals so that he keeps you in his inner circle,
則必以美名明之，	then overtly appeal to his fine reputation
而微見其合於私利也。	but show subtly that [the proposal] fits his private interest.
欲陳危害之事，	If you want to account for a dangerous and harmful undertaking,
20 則顯其毀誹而微見其合於私患也。	then illustrate how it will defame him, but subtly show that [refraining from doing it] fits his private worries.
譽異人與同行者，	You should praise other people who act in the same way as he;
規異事與同計者。	make plans which have the same strategy as he, though the goals may be different.
有與同汙者，	If there are those who have the same blemishes as he,
則必以大飾其無傷也；	then you should be sure to make them look beautiful and harmless;
25 有與同敗者，	if there are those who have suffered the same defeats,
則必以明飾其無失也。	then you should be sure to clarify that they were not at fault.
彼自多其力，	If he overestimates his own power,

---

2 The use of *di* 地 "earth, ground" to mean "evidence" is striking, but it does find corroborative support in the *Heguanzi* 鶡冠子, as pointed out by Liang Qixiong.

則毋以其難概之也；	you should not cut him down to size[3] by pointing out the difficulty of a task;
自勇其斷，	if he regards his decisions as courageous,
30 則無以其謫怒之；	you should not anger him through your censure;
自智其計，	if he considers his own plans intelligent,
則毋以其敗窮之。	you should not tax him by referring to their failures.
大意無所拂悟，	In the general ideas you proffer, do not in any way oppose him;
辭言無所繫縻，	in speaking do not in any way cause any friction –
35 然後極騁智辯焉。	only then can you fully deploy your intelligence and rhetoric.
此道所得，	If you achieve this way [of persuasion],
親近不疑而得盡辭也。	you will get close [to the ruler] without arousing suspicion and all your proposals will reach their full potential.

29（之）〔其〕(校注 120).　32 拂悟 is read as 咈忤.

HF 12.5 (*Xilun* 203, *Xin jiaozhu* 261)

伊尹為宰，	Yi Yin acted as a cook
百里奚為虜，	and Baili Xi had himself taken prisoner:[4]
皆所以干其上也。	these were the means by which they achieved their rise to power.
此二人者，	These two men
5 皆聖人也；	were both sages,
然猶不能無役身以進，	but they still had no way to avoid being reduced to servitude in order to advance in rank.
如此其汙也！	This is the kind of humiliation to which they exposed themselves.

3　*Gai* 概 "levelling stick" was an instrument used to level the amount of grain in a bushel-measure to ensure the exact amount. The word is apparently used here in a derived generalised sense.

4　Yi Yin was aide to the future founder of the Shang dynasty, Tang the Successful. Reportedly, in order to gain Tang's trust, he sought employment as a cook (see chapter 3, note 10). For Baili Xi, see chapter 3, note 14.

說難 DIFFICULTIES OF PERSUASION 161

今以吾言為宰虜，	Now, to make oneself a cook or a slave
而可以聽用而振世，	so as to be heard and employed, and then to shake the world –
10 此非能仕之所恥也。	this is not something that a competent office-holder would be ashamed of.
夫曠日離久，	Now, if, after having spent a great deal of time
而周澤既渥，	you receive the ruler's abundant favour:
深計而不疑，	if you raise no suspicions when you make far-reaching plans,
引爭而不罪，	if you are not condemned when you disagree with the ruler,
15 則明割利害以致其功，	then you will clearly distinguish between advantage and disadvantage in order to bring meritorious achievements to fruition,
直指是非以飾其身，	and directly point out right and wrong in order to improve the ruler's person.
以此相持，	When persuader and ruler support each other in this way,
此說之成也。	this is the consummation of persuasion.

6 進（加）(校注 120)。　8 高亨 considers 言 as a redundant echo of 吾, followed by 陳奇猷。
12 （未）〔既〕(校注 120)。　16 飾 is read as 飭。

HF 12.6 (*Xilun* 204, *Xin jiaozhu* 266)

昔者鄭武公欲伐胡，	In ancient times, Lord Wu of Zheng wished to attack the state of Hu[5]
故先以其女妻胡君以娛其意。	so he first married his daughter to the ruler of Hu in order to mollify the ruler's thinking.
因問於群臣：	Thereupon he asked his ministers:
"吾欲用兵，	"I intend to deploy my military forces,
5 誰可伐者？"	Who should be attacked."
大夫關其思對曰：	The senior officer Guan Qisi replied:
"胡可伐。"	"The Hu ought to be attacked."

---

5 Lord Wu of Zheng, one of the most powerful leaders at the beginning of Eastern Zhou, reigned from 770 to 744. Nothing is known of his attack against Hu. *Zuozhuan* records a Hu

武公怒而戮之，	Lord Wu flew into a rage and executed him,
曰：	saying,
"胡，	"Hu
兄弟之國也。	is a state with which we have brotherly relations.
子言伐之，	Now you propose to attack them.
何也？"	How can this be?"
胡君聞之，	When the ruler of the Hu heard about this,
以鄭為親己，	he considered that Zheng was in close alliance with him,
遂不備鄭。	so he made no defensive preparations against Zheng.
鄭人襲胡，	Then the men of Zheng invaded Hu
取之。	and took it.
宋有富人，	In Song there was a wealthy man.[6]
天雨牆壞。	It rained and a wall collapsed.
其子曰：	The son said:
"不築，	"If we do not rebuild it,
必將有盜。"	there are bound to be thieves."
其鄰人之父亦云。	An old man from the neighbourhood said the same thing.
暮而果大亡其財。	During the night, he did indeed lose property on a large scale.
其家甚智其子，	The family considered the son very intelligent
而疑鄰人之父。	and were suspicious of the old neighbour.
此二人說者皆當矣，	The suggestions of these two[7] were both to the point,
厚者為戮，	[but], if, in the more serious case, the persuader was executed,
薄者見疑，	and, in the slighter case, he became the object of suspicion,

---

statelet near modern Fuyang, Anhui, which was eliminated by Chu in 495. It is possible that another statelet with the same name existed during Lord Wu of Zheng's time; alternatively, it may be Han Fei's own mix-up or outright invention. The "current" version of *Bamboo Annals* mention that in 763 "Zheng put to death its grandee Guan Qisi," echoing the story in *Han Feizi*, but this may be a forged account borrowed from *Han Feizi* itself or, more likely, from Han Fei's biography in *Shiji*, which includes chapter 12 in full.

6 For another version of this episode, see chapter 23.37.
7 Guan Qisi and the old neighbour.

說難 DIFFICULTIES OF PERSUASION 163

則非知之難也，	then it is not a problem of understanding –
處知則難也。	it is situating your understanding that is the problem.
故繞朝之言當矣，	Thus Rao Zhao's words were to the point,
其為聖人於晉，	and he was considered a sage in Jin,
35 而為戮於秦也，	but he was executed in Qin.[8]
此不可不察。	This must be investigated.

HF 12.7 (*Xilun* 207, *Xin jiaozhu* 267)

昔者彌子瑕有寵於衛君。	In ancient times, Mi Zixia was in the favour of the ruler of Wey.[9]
衛國之法，	It was the law in Wey
竊駕君車者罪刖。	that whoever rode the ruler's carriage without authorisation was to have his feet amputated.[10]
彌子瑕母病，	Once Mi Zixia's mother fell ill.
5 人間往夜告彌子，	Someone went out secretly and told Master Mi at night.
彌子矯駕君車以出。	Master Mi, using a fake order, rode in one of the ruler's carriages.
君聞而賢之，	The ruler heard about this and considered him worthy,
曰：	saying:
"孝哉！	"How filial!
10 為母之故，	For the sake of his mother
忘其刖罪。"	he thought nothing of a crime punishable by mutilation of the feet."

---

8 In 614, the Jin people deployed a complex ruse to get a fugitive minister, Shi Hui 士會, back to Jin from Qin. A Qin grandee, Rao Zhao, realised that Shi Hui's mission to Jin was merely a pretense to allow his permanent return to the home state, but he failed to convince the Lord of Qin of this (*Zuozhuan* Wen 13.2). The subsequent execution of Rao Zhao is not narrated in *Zuozhuan*, but it could have been known to Han Fei from another source. *Chunqiu shiyu* 春秋事語, a silk manuscript from Tomb 3, Mawangdui 馬王堆 (Hunan), contains an anecdote about Rao Zhao's attempt to prevent Shi Hui's departure, and tells of Rao's ultimate execution in Qin.

9 Mi Zixia was a lover of Lord Ling of Wey 衛靈公 (r. 534–493). On his power in Wey, see *Han Feizi* 30.1.1 and 39.4.

10 Amputation of a foot was a common corporal punishment in China.

異日，	Another day,
與君遊於果園，	Master Mi was on a tour with the ruler in an orchard.
食桃而甘，	He was eating a peach and found it very sweet.
15 不盡，	Before finishing,
以其半啗君。	he gave the remaining half to the ruler to taste.
君曰：	The ruler said:
"愛我哉！	"How you love me!
忘其口味以啗寡人。"	You disregard how good it is and give me a taste."
20 及彌子色衰愛弛，	When Master Mi's looks had faded and their love had slackened,
得罪於君，	he fell afoul of the ruler.
君曰：	The ruler said:
"是固嘗矯駕吾車，	"This fellow once faked an order and rode in my carriage;
又嘗啗我以餘桃。"	moreover, he once gave me a half-eaten peach to eat."
25 故彌子之行未變於初也，	So, Master Mi's behaviour had not changed from the start,
而以前之所以見賢而後獲罪者，	but the reasons why he was seen as worthy before, later got him condemned –
愛憎之變也。	that is because the ruler's likes and dislikes had changed in the meantime.
故有愛於主，	Thus if you have a loving relationship with the ruler,
則智當而加親；	your knowledge will count as correct and you will become even closer [to him];
30 有憎於主，	if you have an acrimonious relationship with the ruler,
則智不當見罪而加疏。	your knowledge will not count as correct and you will be condemned and estranged.
故諫說談論之士，	Thus gentlemen who engage in remonstrating, advising and passing judgments
不可不察愛憎之主而後說焉。	must investigate whether the ruler feels love or acrimony before giving advice.

3 張抄 has 則 for 刖. 28–31 The C editors note: 此文有誤。《史記·老子韓非列傳》作「故有愛於主，則知當而加親；見憎於主，則罪當而加疏」。疑《韓非子》本作「故有愛於主，則智不當而加親；有憎於主，則智當而加疏」。

說難 DIFFICULTIES OF PERSUASION

HF 12.8 (*Xilun* 209, *Xin jiaozhu* 269)

夫龍之為虫也，	Now, a dragon is a thing that crawls.
柔可狎而騎也；	You can get close to it and ride it when it is in a soft mood;
然其喉下有逆鱗徑尺，	but under its throat it has inverted scales about one foot long.
若人有嬰之者，	If someone disturbs that area,
5 則必殺人。	the dragon is bound to kill him.
人主亦有逆鱗，	The ruler also has inverted scales;
說者能無嬰人主之逆鱗，	if a persuader can avoid disturbing the ruler's inverted scales,
則幾矣。	he has almost achieved [his purpose].

4, 7 嬰 is read as 攖.

CHAPTER 13

和氏 Mr He

HF 13.1 (*Xilun* 210, *Xin jiaozhu* 271)

楚人和氏得玉璞楚山中，	Mr He from Chu found an unworked piece of jade in the Chu mountains.
奉而獻之厲王。	He offered it with both hands to King Li.[1]
厲王使玉人相之。	King Li ordered a jade specialist to assess the piece.
玉人曰：	The jade specialist said:
5　"石也。"	"This is just a stone!"
王以和為誑，	The King thought Mr He was a fraud,
而刖其左足。	and cut off his left foot.
及厲王薨，	When King Li died,
武王即位，	King Wu ascended the throne.
10　和又奉其璞而獻之武王。	Mr He took his unworked jade once again, and presented it to King Wu.
武王使玉人相之。	King Wu ordered a jade specialist to assess it,
又曰：	and the man said once again:
"石也。"	"This is just a stone."
王又以和為誑，	The King again thought Mr He was a fraud,
15　而刖其右足。	and cut off his right foot.
武王薨，	When King Wu died,
文王即位。	King Wen ascended the throne.
和乃抱其璞而哭於楚山之下，	Then Mr He took the jade in his arms and wailed at the foot of the Chu mountain
三日三夜，	for three days and three nights.
20　淚盡而繼之以血。	Once his tears were exhausted, he continued by weeping blood.
王聞之，	When the King heard about this,
使人問其故，	he sent someone to ask why,

1　There was no King Li of Chu. Perhaps the reference is to King Li of Zhou 周厲王 (r. 877–841), but later the jade is presented to Kings Wu and Wen of Chu (r. 740–690 and 689–675, respectively). Some later versions of the story resolve the confusion: there the three kings are Kings Wu, Wen, and Cheng of Chu (r. 671–626).

和氏 MR HE

曰：	saying:
"天下之刖者多矣，	"Lots of people in this world have had their feet amputated –
25 子奚哭之悲也？"	why are you wailing so pathetically?"
和曰：	He said:
"吾非悲刖也，	"I am by no means sad about the amputation of my feet;
悲夫寶玉而題之以石，	I am sad that this precious jade was deemed a stone,
貞士而名之以誑，	and an honest gentleman has been labelled a fraud.
30 此吾所以悲也。"	That is why I am so sad."
王乃使玉人理其璞而得寶焉，	The king thereupon ordered a jade specialist to cut the unworked jade, and a precious jade came of it.
遂命曰"和氏之璧。"	Then they named it Mr He's jade disk.

18 The C editors note: 「楚」字疑應作「荊」，後人回改誤作「楚」字，《淮南子·脩務》正作「荊」。   25 The C editors note: 「奚」下疑應有「獨」字。. We see no reason to add 獨.

HF 13.2 (*Xilun* 212, *Xin jiaozhu* 273)

夫珠玉，	Pearls and jade
人主之所急也。	are what rulers of men urgently seek.
和雖獻璞而未美，	Mr He may have proffered an unworked piece of jade which was not yet beautiful,
未為主之害也，	but this does not count as harming the ruler.
5 然猶兩足斬而寶乃論，	Nonetheless, both his feet were amputated before the treasure was properly assessed.
論寶若此其難也。	You can see how difficult it is to assess a treasure.
今人主之於法術也，	Now, the ruler treats the laws and techniques of rule
未必和璧之急也；	not necessarily with the urgency of Mr He's jade-disc,
而禁群臣士民之私邪。	but he prevents the self-interested treachery of the ministers, gentlemen and the common people.

10	然則有道者之不僇也，	And so, if those who have the right Way are not executed,
	特帝王之璞未獻耳。	it is only because they have not yet proffered the uncarved jade of sovereigns and kings.²
	主用術，	When a ruler uses the right techniques,
	則大臣不得擅斷，	senior ministers will not be permitted to make decisions on their own authority,
	近習不敢賣重；	and cronies will not dare to sell their influence.
15	官行法，	When officials implement laws,
	則浮萌趨於耕農，	the shiftless will rush to [take up] agricultural work,
	而游士危於戰陳；	and peripatetic gentlemen will expose themselves to danger on the battle lines;³
	則法術者乃群臣士民之所禍也。	thus the laws and techniques of rule are exactly what the ministers, gentlemen, and the common people regard as a disaster.⁴
	人主非能倍大臣之議，	If a ruler of men is unable to go against the propositions of senior ministers,
20	越民萌之誹，	if he cannot override disapproval among the common people,
	獨周乎道言也，	and if he cannot lend his ear exclusively to proposals based on the Way,
	則法術之士雖至死亡，	then, even if gentlemen upholding laws and techniques of rule go as far as to give their lives (for him),
	道必不論矣。	the Way will certainly not be appreciated.

10 僇 is read as 戮.　11 （持）〔特〕(校注 125).

---

2   That is to say, those who possessed the Way still did not present precious strategies that would turn the ruler into a "sovereign and king" or a Thearch 帝 and Monarch 王 (i.e. the unifier of All-under-Heaven). Presenting their ideas would only endanger them, just like He and his jade.

3   Peripatetic – or roving – gentlemen (*you shi* 遊士) are those men qualified for service who travelled from one court to another seeking patronage and employment. Because of their cross-state mobility and independence, they were anathema to many thinkers committed to strengthening the ruler's authority over all subjects, especially to the authors of the *Book of Lord Shang* and *Han Feizi*.

4   It is a disaster from the point of view of these groups' private interests, the pursuit of which would be thwarted by the ruler's effective administrative techniques.

HF 13.3 (*Xilun* 213, *Xin jiaozhu* 275)

昔者吳起教楚悼王以楚國之俗曰：	In the past, Wu Qi taught King Dao of Chu[5] the customs of Chu,[6] saying:
"大臣太重，	"Your senior ministers are too powerful
封君太眾。	and so are your enfeoffed rulers.[7]
若此，	When this is the case,
則上偪主而下虐民，	they will coerce the ruler above and oppress the people below.
此貧國弱兵之道也。	This is the way to impoverish the state and weaken the army.
不如使封君之子孫三世而收爵祿，	It would be best to make the descendants of enfeoffed rulers forfeit their ranks and stipends after three generations,
絕滅百吏之祿秩，	to discontinue or reduce the emoluments and salary ranks of the various officials,
損不急之枝官，	and to reduce non-essential sub-offices
以奉選練之士。"	in order to promote gentlemen who have been recruited and trained."
悼王行之期年而薨矣，	King Dao practised this for an entire year, but then he died,[8]
吳起枝解於楚。	and Wu Qi was dismembered in Chu.[9]

---

5 Wu Qi (d. 381; mentioned in chapter 3; see note 17 there) was one of the most eminent statesman and military leaders of the early Warring States period. He distinguished himself first in Wei 魏, where he is credited with successfully repelling Qin incursions and securing the country's western frontier. Later, he immigrated to Chu, where he orchestrated reforms aimed at strengthening royal power and pursued a policy of southward expansion. In *Han Feizi* (especially in chapters 13–14), Wu Qi and Shang Yang (see note 10 below) epitomise the rare type of selfless ministers who were wholly devoted to the interests of their ruler and the state. Their tragic destiny anticipates Han Fei's own.

6 "Customs" here refer to the political situation in Chu, not to popular customs. The word "customs" has a pejorative meaning in Warring States texts (see Lewis 2006a: 202–212).

7 Enfeoffed rulers were high-ranking aristocrats who were granted territorial allotments in Chu. This stratum of exceptionally powerful nobles distinguished Chu from most contemporaneous polities. See Zheng Wei 2012.

8 In reality, Wu Qi's tenure in Chu was longer (approximately ten years).

9 Wu Qi was not dismembered (which was the fate of Shang Yang), but rather assassinated by disgruntled nobles at the funeral of his patron, King Dao 楚悼王 (r. ca. 400–381).

商君教秦孝公以連什伍，	Lord Shang taught Lord Xiao of Qin[10] to organise the people in squads of ten and five,[11]
設告坐之過，	and instituted the offence of failing to denunciate crimes;
15 燔詩書而明法令，	he burnt the *Poems* and the *Documents*,[12] and made clear the laws and ordinances;
塞私門之請而遂公家之勞，	he blocked the avenues for private families to present special requests and opened the way for efforts in support of the ruling house;
禁游宦之民而顯耕戰之士。	he banned roving employees and extolled gentlemen engaged in agriculture and warfare.
孝公行之，	Lord Xiao put this into practice,
主以尊安，	and the ruler, by this means, was honoured and secure
20 國以富強，	and the state became rich and strong.
八年而薨，	After eight years, Lord Xiao died,[13]
商君車裂於秦。	and Lord Shang was quartered by chariots in Qin.[14]
楚不用吳起而削亂，	Chu did not use Wu Qi, and the country was decimated and reduced to chaos;[15]

---

10   Lord Shang (or, more precisely, the Lord of Shang) is Shang Yang 商鞅 (d. 338), the famous reformer who headed the Qin government during the reign of Lord Xiao (r. 361–338). Han Fei's intellectual debt to Shang Yang is undeniable (despite his mild criticism of Shang Yang in chapter 43). *Han Feizi* is one of a very few texts that laud this controversial statesman (see Pines 2017: 100–114 for further details).

11   This refers to establishing a universal system of surveillance and conscription. The members of the squads were mutually liable, whether for desertion or for crimes committed by family members. The squads became the basic social units in Qin, greatly enhancing social control by the state.

12   There is no corroboration of this claim elsewhere. The *Book of Lord Shang*, associated with Shang Yang, denounces the canons of *Poems* and *Documents* as "parasites" (chapters 3.5, 4.3, 13.4) but does not advocate their burning.

13   Again, a mistake. Lord Shang's reforms lasted a full twenty years.

14   Here Han Fei is correct. See the details in "The Biography of Lord Shang" in *Records of the Historian*.

15   Wu Qi's reforms were discontinued after his death, and Chu retained the most powerful aristocracy of any of the Warring States. Han Fei considers this (perhaps correctly) as the reason for the eventual decline of Chu and its weakness vis-à-vis Qin.

秦行商君法而富強。	Qin practiced the laws of Lord Shang and became rich and strong.
25 二子之言也已當矣，	These two men's proposals were very much to the point,
然而枝解吳起而車裂商君者，	and yet Wu Qi was dismembered and the Lord of Shang was pulled apart by chariots –
何也？	why was that?
大臣苦法而細民惡治也。	It was because the senior ministers felt embittered towards the laws and the petty people hated orderly rule.
當今之世，	If, in our age,
30 大臣貪重，	the senior ministers' craving for influence
細民安亂，	and the petty people's acceptance of chaos
甚於秦、楚之俗，	are greater than what was customary in Qin and in Chu,
而人主無悼王、孝公之聽，	whereas the rulers do not have the open-mindedness of King Dao and Lord Xiao,
則法術之士，	then how can gentlemen upholding laws and techniques of rule
35 安能蒙二子之危也而明己之法術哉？	submit themselves to the dangers like these two Masters (Wu Qi and Lord Shang) and openly advocate their laws and techniques of rule?
此世所以亂無霸王也。	This is why our age is in chaos and has no hegemonic king.

6 〈貪〉〔貧〕（校注 125）.　8 〈減〉〔减〕《韓子淺解》頁100　28 C mistakenly has 若 for 苦.　36 〔以〕（校注 125）.

CHAPTER 14

姦劫弒臣 Ministers Who Betray, Coerce or Assassinate Their Rulers

HF 14.1 (*Xilun* 217, *Xin jiaozhu* 278)

凡姦臣皆欲順人主之心以取親幸之勢者也。	As a rule, treacherous ministers all wish to play to the ruler's heart in order to obtain the strategic position of being a favourite.
是以主有所善， 臣從而譽之； 主有所憎， 5　臣因而毀之。 凡人之大體， 取舍同者則相是也，	Therefore, whom the ruler approves, the ministers will consequently praise; whom the ruler dislikes, the ministers will malign. In general, the situation of men is such that when they have the same preferences, they approve of each other,
取舍異者則相非也。	and when they have different preferences, they disapprove of each other.
今人臣之所譽者， 10　人主之所是也， 此之謂同取；	Now when what the ministers praise is what the ruler approves, this is called having the same positive preferences;
人臣之所毀者， 人主之所非也， 此之謂同舍。	when what the minister vilifies is what the ruler disapproves of, this is called having the same negative preferences.
15　夫取舍合而相與逆者，	For preferences to be concordant, but the people concerned to be at odds with each other,
未嘗聞也。 此人臣之所以取信幸之道也。	is quite unheard of. This is how ministers come to take the path of trusted favourites.
夫姦臣得乘信幸之勢以毀譽進退群臣者，	Now, when wicked ministers are allowed to avail themselves of their strategic position as trusted favourites in order to vilify or praise, promote or demote other subjects,[1]

---

[1] The *qunchen* "various ministers" are always public servants of minor ranks. One must remem-

姦劫弒臣 MINISTERS WHO BETRAY, COERCE OR ASSASSINATE   173

人主非有術數以御之也，	this is because the ruler does not have techniques and procedures to lead them,[2]
20 非參驗以審之也，	and because he does not check evidence to examine them.
必將以曩之合己信今之言，	Inevitably, because they were previously in agreement with him, the ruler will believe their current proposals:
此幸臣之所以得欺主成私者也。	this is how favoured ministers are able to cheat their rulers and achieve their private aims.
故主必欺於上，	In this way, the ruler is bound to be cheated above
而臣必重於下矣，	and the ministers are bound to gain importance below.
25 此之謂擅主之臣。	This is called "ministers who usurp the ruler's position."

8 C mistakenly has 合 for 舍.   17 〔取〕(校注 141).   19 (所)〔非〕(校注 141).

HF 14.2 (*Xilun* 219, *Xin jiaozhu* 279)

國有擅主之臣，	When a state has ministers who usurp the ruler's position,
則群下不得盡其智力以陳其忠，	subordinates will be unable to exhaust their intellect and strength in displaying their loyalty,
百官之吏不得奉法以致其功矣。	and the officials in the various departments will be unable to uphold laws to bring their contributions to fruition.
何以明之？	How can I make that clear?
5 夫安利者就之，	Security and gain, one strives for;
危害者去之，	danger and harm, one avoids:
此人之情也。	this is basic human instinct.
今為臣盡力以致功，	Now, if ministers commit all their force to bring their contributions to fruition,

ber that the customary translation of *chen* 臣 as "minister" is misleading in that the word refers to any servant, public or private.

2 It is customary to regard *shu* 數 "method" and *shu* 術 "technique, art" as synonymous, but the combination of these two concepts (which were not homophonous in pre-Buddhist Chinese) here suggests that in Han Fei's eyes they were distinct.

竭智以陳忠者，	if they exhaust their intelligence to display their loyalty,
10　其身困而家貧，	then they will suffer hardship personally, their families will be poor,
父子罹其害；	and their fathers and sons will suffer harm;
為姦利以弊人主，	if they aim for wicked gains and keep the ruler ignorant,
行財貨以事貴重之臣者，	if they use their wealth and resources to serve the noble and powerful ministers,
身尊家富，	then they will be honoured themselves, their families will be wealthy,
15　父子被其澤；	and their fathers and sons will be draped in abundance.
人焉能去安利之道而就危害之處哉？	How could anyone avoid the path of security and gain and strive for a place of danger and harm?
治國若此其過也，	To administer a state as wrongly as this,
而上欲下之無姦，	but, as their superior, to desire that your subordinates were anything other than wicked
吏之奉法，	and that your minor officials upheld the law –
20　其不可得亦明矣。	the futility of this is clear.
故左右知貞信之不可以得安利也，	Thus the members of the ruler's entourage, understanding that honesty and trustworthiness cannot be used to get security and gain,
必曰：	are bound to say:
"我以忠信事上，	"If we serve the ruler with loyalty and trustworthiness,
積功勞而求安，	accumulating achievements and toil in pursuit of security,
25　是猶盲而欲知黑白之情，	this is like being blind and wishing to understand the essence of black and white.
必不幾矣；	We would certainly not achieve our aims.
若以道化行正理，	If we use transformation by means of the Way to implement correct principles,
不趨富貴，	and do not scurry after wealth and honour,
事上而求安，	in this way serving our sovereign and aiming for security,
30　是猶聾而欲審清濁之聲也，	this is like being deaf and wanting to distinguish "pure" and "turbid" notes –
愈不幾矣。	we are even less likely to achieve our aims.

姦劫弒臣 MINISTERS WHO BETRAY, COERCE OR ASSASSINATE 175

二者不可以得安，	If neither of these methods will achieve security,
我安能無相比周、蔽主上、為姦私以適重人哉？"	how could we not form cliques, keep the ruler ignorant and work for wicked self-interest by pleasing the political heavyweights?"
此必不顧人主之義矣。	Such people are bound to take no note of their duties towards the ruler.
35 其百官之吏亦知方正之不可以得安也，	The officials in the various public offices will also know that they cannot achieve security by straight methods;
必曰：	they will be bound to say:
"我以清廉事上而求安，	"Serving the sovereign with moral purity and seeking security,
若無規矩而欲為方圓也，	is like being without a T-square or a compass and wanting to make something square or round:
必不幾矣；	we will certainly not achieve our aims.
40 若以守法不朋黨治官而求安，	If we conduct our official duties by safeguarding the law and not forming factions, seeking security in that way,
是猶以足搔頂也，	this is like trying to scratch the top of your head with your feet:
愈不幾也。	we are even less likely to achieve our aims.
二者不可以得安，	Since neither of these methods will achieve security,
能無廢法行私以適重人哉？"	can we fail to abandon the law and act according to self-interest, by pleasing the political heavyweights."
45 此必不顧君上之法矣。	Such people are bound to disregard the law laid down by the ruler above.
故以私為重人者眾，	So those who, out of private interest, act for the sake of political heavyweights will be many,
而以法事君者少矣。	and those who serve the ruler in accordance with law will be few.
是以主孤於上而臣成黨於下，	Therefore, the ruler will be isolated above and the ministers will form factions below.
此田成之所以弒簡公者也。	This is how Tian Cheng assassinated Lord Jian.[3]

12 弊 is read as 蔽.　28 趂 is read as 趨.

---

[3] Tian Cheng is usually referred to by his name Heng 恆 (or Chang 常); his alternative lin-

HF 14.3 (*Xilun* 221, *Xin jiaozhu* 282)

夫有術者之為人臣也，	Now when someone who understands the techniques of governance is a minister,
得效度數之言，	he manages to put into effect measured and principled proposals:
上明主法，	he brings clarity to the laws laid down by the ruler above
下困姦臣，	and makes trouble for wicked ministers below,
5 以尊主安國者也。	thereby making the ruler honoured and the state safe.[4]
是以度數之言得效於前，	Thus when measured and principled proposals are checked beforehand,
則賞罰必用於後矣。	rewards and punishments are inevitably applied after the event.
人主誠明於聖人之術，	When the ruler is truly clear about the techniques of the sages
而不苟於世俗之言，	and does not disgrace himself with the vulgar talk of the current age,
10 循名實而定是非，	then he makes titles and performance accord and determines right and wrong,
因參驗而審言辭。	and, checking the evidence, he examines proposals and their formulations.
是以左右近習之臣，	Under such circumstances, his entourage and cronies
知偽詐之不可以得安也，	understand that pretence and fraud cannot ensure security,
必曰：	and they are bound to say,
15 "我不去姦私之行，	"If we do not get rid of our wicked, self-interested behaviour,

---

eage name is Chen 陳; Cheng 成 is his posthumous name. On this figure, see chapter 7, note 3.

4 It is significant that the mastery of techniques of government (or art of statecraft, *shu* 術) is presented here as primarily the domain of specialists or ministers and not of the ruler himself (which contrasts with other discussions of *shu* in *Han Feizi*, e.g., chapters 30 and 43). Here, as elsewhere, the text skirts the question of how these specialists in the art of government are to be distinguished from the political heavyweights. In particular, one would like to know why these specialists in the techniques of government should be the only ones who do not act in their own interests.

姦劫弒臣 MINISTERS WHO BETRAY, COERCE OR ASSASSINATE

盡力竭智以事主，	even if we do our utmost and deploy all our intelligence to serve the ruler
而乃以相與比周妄毀譽以求安，	and then band together, vilifying and praising [others] baselessly in order to gain security,
是猶負千鈞之重陷於不測之淵而求生也，	it will be like lifting something the weight of a tonne on your shoulders, and throwing yourself into an unfathomably deep abyss and hoping to stay alive:
必不幾矣。"	we will certainly not achieve our aims."
20 百官之吏亦知為姦利之不可以得安也，	The officials in the various offices will also know that if they go for wicked profit, they cannot obtain security,
必曰：	and they are bound to say:
"我不以清廉方正奉法，	"If we fail to be morally pure and straight, so as to uphold the law,
乃以貪汙之心枉法以取私利，	but instead proceed to pervert the law with a profligate heart in order to obtain our private gain,
是猶上高陵之顛墮峻谿之下而求生，	this is like climbing to the top of a high mountain and plunging oneself into a craggy ravine and hoping to stay alive:
25 必不幾矣。"	we will certainly not achieve our aims."
安危之道若此其明也，	When the paths of security and danger are as clear as this,
左右安能以虛言惑主，	how can his entourage lead the ruler astray with empty words?
而百官安敢以貪漁下？	And how would his officers dare to exploit and seek profit from their inferiors?
是以臣得陳其忠而不弊，	In this way, the ministers will be able to display their loyalty and not be worn out,
30 下得守其職而不怨，	and those below will be able to attend to their duties without resentment.
此管仲之所以治齊，	This is the method by which Guan Zhong governed Qi
而商君之所以強秦也。	and how the Lord of Shang made Qin strong.[5]

8 張抄 has 成 for 誠.   13 C suggests emending 之 to 而. We see no need to emend.

---

5 The text details both examples below.

HF 14.4 (*Xilun* 223, *Xin jiaozhu* 282)

從是觀之，	From this it can be seen
則聖人之治國也，	that, in his governing of the state, the sage
固有使人不得不愛我之道，	has a sure way of making people have no choice but to love him,
而不恃人之以愛為我也。	and that he does not depend on others' caring for him out of love.
5 恃人之以愛為我者危矣，	Anyone who depends on others' caring for him out of love will be in danger;
恃吾不可不為者安矣。	anyone who relies on the fact that he cannot but be cared for will be secure.
夫君臣非有骨肉之親，	After all, rulers and ministers have no closeness due to blood relationship.
正直之道可以得利，	If, by walking the straight path, he can obtain advantages,
則臣盡力以事主；	a minister will do his utmost to serve the ruler;
10 正直之道不可以得安，	if, by walking the straight path, he cannot obtain security,
則臣行私以干上。	a minister will engage in selfish practices in order to gain advantages from the ruler.
明主知之，	The clear-sighted ruler knows this,
故設利害之道以示天下而已矣。	and therefore establishes the way of profit versus harm to show these things to the world – that is all.[6]
夫是以人主雖不口教百官，	Now, therefore, even if the ruler does not personally instruct the officials by word of mouth,
15 不目索姦衺，	even if he does not personally seek out the wicked with his own eyes,
而國已治矣。	the state will already be well-governed.
人主者，	As for the ruler,
非目若离婁乃為明[A 陽/庚 mjiaŋ/mjeŋ]也，	when his eyes are as good as those of Li Lou, he is not for that reason clear-sighted;

---

6 This is the basis of the "techniques" or "arts" of governance as employed by the ruler do not alter the ministers' selfishness itself, but rather orchestrate a situation whereby their pursuit of selfish interests will inevitably lead them to carry out their assigned tasks properly.

姦劫弒臣 MINISTERS WHO BETRAY, COERCE OR ASSASSINATE

非耳若師曠乃為聰[A 東/東 tshuŋ > tshuaŋ ?/tshuŋ]也。	when his ears are as good as those of Master Kuang, he does not for that reason have a sharp hearing.[7]
20 目必不任其數，	As for the eyes, if he is determined not to rely on proper strategic calculations,
而待目以為明，	but relies on the eyes [themselves] to be clear-sighted,
所見者少矣，	then what he sees will be little –
非不蔽之術也。	that is not the technique of not being beclouded.
耳必不因其勢，	As for the ears, if he is determined not to rely on his strategic position,
25 而待耳以為聰，	but relies on the ears [themselves] in order to be keen of hearing and always well-informed
所聞者寡矣，	then what he hears will be little,
非不欺之道也。	and that is not the Way not to be cheated.
明主者，	The clear-sighted ruler
使天下不得不為己視，	brings it about that the world cannot but look out on his behalf,
30 天下不得不為己聽。	and the world cannot but listen on his behalf.
故身在深宮之中而明照四海之內，	Therefore his body may be deep inside his palace, but his clarity of mind elucidates everything within the Four Seas,
而天下弗能蔽弗能欺者，	and no one under Heaven can becloud him, no one can cheat him.
何也？	Why is this?
闇亂之道廢而聰明之勢興也。	It is because he dismisses the way of darkness and chaos and elevates the strategic position of keen hearing and clear-sightedness.
35 故善任勢者國安，	Thus, if you are good at relying on your strategic position, your state will be safe,
不知因其勢者國危。	but if you do not understand how to use your strategic position, your state will be in danger.

---

7   Li Lou was a paragon of clear-sightedness. Master Kuang was a mid-sixth century master musician in the state of Jin, renowned for his sharp ears.

古秦之俗，	Qin's ancient customs were[8]
君臣廢法而服私，	that rulers and ministers abandoned the law and followed their private interests,
是以國亂兵弱而主卑。	and as a result the state was in chaos, the army weak, and the ruler debased.
40 商君說秦孝公以變法易俗而明公道，	Then the Lord of Shang persuaded Lord Xiao of Qin to change the laws, to alter the customs and to clarify the Way of impartiality,
賞告姦，	to reward those who report treachery,
困末作而利本事。	to make things difficult for those engaged in marginal occupations, and to make it profitable to engage in basic occupations.[9]
當此之時，	At that stage,
秦民習故俗之有罪可以得免，	the people of Qin were habituated, according to their old customs, that criminals would get away,
無功可以得尊顯也，	and those without merit could obtain honour and fame,
45 故輕犯新法。	so they thought nothing of violating the new laws.
於是犯之者其誅重而必，	Then the punishments for offenders were made heavy and inevitable,
告之者其賞厚而信，	the rewards for informers abundant and reliable,
故姦莫不得而被刑者眾，	and as a result wicked people were all caught and those who suffered punishments were many.
民疾怨而眾過日聞。	The people were full of resentment and every day there was news about many transgressions.
50 孝公不聽，	Lord Xiao did not listen to any complaints,
遂行商君之法。	but went on carrying out the laws of Lord Shang.
民後知有罪之必誅，	The people afterwards came to understand that criminals were sure to be punished,
而告私姦者眾也，	and more and more people informed on private treachery.
故民莫犯，	Thus the people did not violate the new laws,
55 其刑無所加。	so that there was no one to apply the punishments to.[10]

---

8   As in chapter 13 (see note 6 there), "customs" refers to negative political habits.

9   On Lord Shang, see chapter 13, note 10. His reforms are summarised in chapter 68 of *Shiji*; see also Pines 2017, chapter 1.

10 This exemplifies the concept, promulgated throughout the *Book of Lord Shang* (e.g., in chapters 7.4 and 17.3), of "eradicating punishments with punishments."

姦劫弑臣 MINISTERS WHO BETRAY, COERCE OR ASSASSINATE

是以國治而兵強，	As a result, the state of Qin became well-governed and its army became strong;
地廣而主尊。	its territory was enlarged and its ruler became honoured.
此其所以然者，	The reason why this came about
匿罪之罰重，	was that the punishments for concealing crimes were heavy
60 而告姦之賞厚也。	and the rewards for informing on acts of treachery were abundant.
此亦使天下必為己視聽之道也。	This is exactly the way to ensure that all under Heaven look and listen for their own sake.
至治之法術已明矣，	The laws and techniques of the perfectly ordered governance is already clear,
而世學者弗知也。	but the learned men of our age do not understand this.

5 〔為〕(校注 141). 23 弊 is read as 蔽. 24 (固)〔因〕(校注 141). 42 張抄 has 未 for 末. 53 〔告〕(校注 141).

HF 14.5 (*Xilun* 226, *Xin jiaozhu* 287)

且夫世之愚學，	Moreover, the stupid 'learned men' of our time
皆不知治亂之情，	all fail to understand the true conditions of order and turmoil;
讘䛦多誦先古之書，	they babble along, rehearsing and reciting ancient writings,
以亂當世之治；	thereby wreaking havoc on the orderly rule of our time.
5 智慮不足以避穽井之陷，	Their intellect and foresight are not sufficient to avoid holes and traps,
又妄非有術之士。	and they go on wildly to criticise gentlemen who understand techniques.
聽其言者危，	Those who listen to the their proposals are in danger;
用其計者亂。	those who use their plans will encounter turmoil.
此亦愚之至大而患之至甚者也。	These are surely the most egregious of fools, and their disastrous influence is of the most extreme kind.

10 俱與有術之士有談說之名，	Much like the men who understand techniques, they have the name as argumentative persuaders,
而實相去千萬也，	but in fact the two groups are infinitely removed from each other:
此夫名同而實有異者也。	this is what is meant by being the same in name, but being different in fact.
夫世愚學之人比有術之士也，	The stupid 'men of learning' of our age, in comparison with the gentlemen who understand techniques,
猶螘垤之比大陵也，	are like anthills in comparison to a large mound:
15 其相去遠矣。	the difference is vast,
而聖人者，	However, the sage
審於是非之實，	examines carefully the facts of right and wrong
察於治亂之情也。	and investigates the real conditions of orderly rule and chaos.
故其治國也，	Therefore, when he rules a state,
20 正明法，	he corrects and clarifies laws
陳嚴刑，	and lays out strict punishments
將以救群生之亂，	in order to save all living creatures from chaos,
去天下之禍，	to remove disasters from the world,
使強不陵弱，	to see to it that the strong do not lord it over the weak,
25 眾不暴寡，	that the many do not oppress the few,
耆老得遂，	that the elderly and the aged live out their days,
幼孤得長，	that the young and the orphaned are able to grow up,
邊境不侵，	that the border regions are not invaded,
君臣相親，	that rulers and ministers are close to each other,
30 父子相保，	that fathers and sons take good care of each other,
而無死亡係虜之患，	and that there are no disasters such as death or capture [on the battlefield].
此亦功之至厚者也！	This surely is the most substantial of meritorious achievements,[11]

---

11 This is an exceptional passage in the *Han Feizi* which speaks of the blissful results of the sage's rule. The outlined results are fundamentally coterminous with the common vision of orderly rule shared by the vast majority of contemporaneous thinkers. Some aspects of this vision – e.g., the proximity between the ruler and his ministers – are curiously at odds with the common situation of intrinsic mistrust between the two as repeatedly depicted in *Han Feizi*.

姦劫弒臣 MINISTERS WHO BETRAY, COERCE OR ASSASSINATE

愚人不知，	but these stupid people do not understand this;
顧以為暴。	rather, they consider [gentlemen who understand statecraft] as cruel.
35 愚者固欲治而惡其所以治，	The stupid insist on wishing for order, while they hate that which brings about order;
皆惡危而喜其所以危者。	they all hate danger, while they delight in that which brings about danger.
何以知之？	How do I know this?
夫嚴刑重罰者，	Severe punishments and heavy fines
民之所惡也，	are what the people hate,
40 而國之所以治也；	but they are the means by which the state is well governed;
哀憐百姓輕刑罰者，	feeling loving sympathy for the hundred clans and making punishments and fines light,
民之所喜，	these are what the people delight in,
而國之所以危也。	but they are what imperil the state.
聖人為法國者，	The sage, when administering a state governed by laws,
45 必逆於世，	is bound to act contrary to his own age,
而順於道德。	yet he complies with the Way and Virtue.[12]
知之者，	Those who understand this
同於義而異於俗；	will conform to what is right and differ from what is customary;
弗知之者，	those who do not understand this
50 異於義而同於俗。	will deviate from what is right and conform to what is customary.
天下知之者少，	When there are few in the world who understand this,
則義非矣。	what is right will count as wrong.

3 C mistakenly has 唊 for 詼.　6〔非〕(校注 141).　11（於）〔相〕(校注 141).　14 We have 螳 for 堂 with 吳本、趙本 and 陳奇猷、張覺.

12　This passage closely parallels the *Book of Lord Shang*, chapter 7.4–7.5.

HF 14.6 (*Xilun* 228, *Xin jiaozhu* 289)

處非道之位，	If you occupy a position in which the Way is rejected,
被眾口之譖，	you will be exposed to slander from many,
溺於當世之言，	and drowned in the words of the age;
而欲當嚴天子而求安，	if you then wish to take seriously the role of Son of Heaven and seek security,
5 幾不亦難哉！	would that not be difficult?
此夫智士所以至死而不顯於世者也。	This is why intelligent gentlemen of service,[13] until they die, never become illustrious in the world.
楚莊王之弟春申君有愛妾曰余，	The younger brother of King Zhuang of Chu, the Lord of Chunshen,[14] had a favoured concubine by the name of Yu.
春申君之正妻子曰甲。	The son of the Lord of Chunshen's regular wife was called Jia.
余欲君之棄其妻也，	Yu wanted his father to discard his main wife,
10 因自傷其身以視君而泣，	so she injured herself, showed her injuries to the ruler and, sobbing,
曰：	she said:
"得為君之妾，	"Becoming your concubine, my lord,
甚幸。	is something very fortunate.
雖然，	However,
15 適夫人非所以事君也，	pleasing your wife is not a way of serving you, my lord,
適君非所以事夫人也。	and pleasing you, my lord, is not a way of serving your wife.
身故不肖，	I am surely unworthy:

---

13   *Zhi shi* 智士 is customarily translated as "the wise," but in the context of Han Fei's thought this is quite misleading. For him what counts is not traditional wisdom acquired from the sages of the past but the professionalism acquired through the close study of *shu* 術, "techniques of government," thus it is more apt to think of them as "intellectuals."

14   There has been much historical speculation concerning this episode. The Lord of Chunshen, the powerful Chu statesman Huang Xie 黃歇, was Han Fei's contemporary, but he was not the king's brother. King Zhuang of Chu (r. 613–591) did not have a brother by this name, because enfeoffed rulers called "Lord of X" (X-*jun* 君) did not appear in Chu before the fifth century. In any case, in the context of the anecdote, the protagonist's identity is not important.

姦劫弒臣 MINISTERS WHO BETRAY, COERCE OR ASSASSINATE

力不足以適二主，	my strength is not enough to please two masters.
其勢不俱適，	The circumstances are such that I cannot please both masters.
20 與其死夫人所者，	Instead of dying at your wife's place,
不若賜死君前。	it is better to offer my death in front of you, my lord.
妾以賜死，	After I have offered my life,
若復幸於左右，	if you again show your favours to one of your entourage,
願君必察之，	I hope you, my lord, will make sure to examine the matter closely:
25 無為人笑。"	lest you be ridiculed by others."
君因信妾余之詐，	So the lord believed concubine Yu's deception
為棄正妻。	and, for her sake, discarded his regular wife.
余又欲殺甲而以其子為後，	In addition, Yu wanted to have (the heir) Jia killed so as to establish her own son as heir.
因自裂其親身衣之裏，	So she tore her own undergarments,
30 以示君而泣，	showed them to the lord, and, sobbing,
曰：	she said:
"余之得幸君之日久矣，	"I have long enjoyed your favours, my lord,
甲非弗知也，	and (your son) Jia will not have failed to understand this.
今乃欲強戲余。	Now he wishes to sport with me by force.
35 余與爭之，	I struggled against him,
至裂余之衣，	but he went so far as to tear my garments.
而此子之不孝，	No offence against filial piety
莫大於此矣。"	could be greater than this."
君怒，	The lord flew into a rage
40 而殺甲也。	and he killed Jia.
故妻以妾余之詐棄，	Thus his wife was abandoned because of concubine Yu's deceit
而子以之死。	and his son died on her account.
從是觀之，	From this it can be seen
父之愛子也，	that even a father's loving care for his son
45 猶可以毀而害也。	can still be damaged through slander.
君臣之相與也，	The association between ruler and minister
非有父子之親也，	is not as close as that between father and son,
而群臣之毀言，	and the slanderous words of a crowd of ministers

非特一妾之口也，
are not merely the mouth of a single concubine,

50 何怪夫賢聖之戮死哉！
so why should it be surprising that sages and worthies are executed?

此商君之所以車裂於秦，
This is why Lord Shang was rent by chariots in Qin

而吳起之所以枝解於楚者也。
and Wu Qi was dismembered in Chu.[15]

凡人臣者，
In general, when it comes to ministers,

有罪固不欲誅，
when they are guilty they naturally do not wish to be punished,

55 無功者皆欲尊顯。
and those who have no achievements all desire honour and fame.

而聖人之治國也，
However, the sage, in governing a state,[16]

賞不加於無功，
will not give rewards to those who have no achievements

而誅必行於有罪者也。
and will be certain to apply punishments to the guilty.

然則有術數者之為人也，
And so, by their very nature, specialists in the techniques and methods of governance

60 固左右姦臣之所害，
will inevitably be harmed by the wicked ministers among the ruler's entourage.

非明主弗能聽也。
and only a clear-sighted ruler will be able to pay proper heed.

17 故 is read as 固.　**22** 以 is read as 已.　**23** The C editors note: 「復」下疑有「有」字。「若復有幸於左右」謂如再有美人，得幸於左右。. We see no reason to emend.　**45** 〔毀〕(校注 141).

15　Wu Qi was not dismembered by the ruler, but rather assassinated by consipring nobles at the funeral of his master, King Dao. Here Han Fei seems to abandon historical accuracy for the sake of strengthening the parallelism between the cases of Shang Yang and Wu Qi. See also chapter 13.3 and note 9 there.

16　The "sage who governs the state" here refers to a sagacious minister of the Shang Yang variety. That he is personally in charge of deciding punishments and rewards contradicts Han Fei's insistence (e.g. in chapter 7) that these two levers of governance remain firmly in the hands of the ruler. This is yet another marked difference between the content of chapter 14 and that of the bulk of *Han Feizi*.

姦劫弒臣 MINISTERS WHO BETRAY, COERCE OR ASSASSINATE

HF 14.7 (*Xilun* 231, *Xin jiaozhu* 293)

世之學者說人主，	When the learned men of our age persuade rulers,
不曰"乘威嚴之勢以困姦衺之臣"，	they do not say "Avail yourself of your strategic position of awe-inspiring authority to make things difficult for wicked ministers."
而皆曰"仁義惠愛而已矣"。	Rather, they all say: "It is a matter of benevolence, righteousness, generosity, and loving care, and that is all."
世主美仁義之名而不察其實，	The rulers of our time admire a reputation for benevolence and righteousness, yet fail to investigate the corresponding reality.
5 是以大者國亡身死，	This is why, in major cases, their state is lost and they die,
小者地削主卑。	or, in lesser cases, lands are pared away and the ruler humiliated.
何以明之？	How can I make that clear?
夫施與貧困者，	Giving succour to the poor and the troubled,
此世之所謂仁義；	is what our world calls benevolence and righteousness;
10 哀憐百姓不忍誅罰者，	showing sympathy for the hundred clans and being unable to bear the idea of punishing or fining them
此世之所謂惠愛也。	is what our world calls kindness and loving care.
夫有施與貧困，	However, if you give succour to the poor and the troubled,
則無功者得賞；	then those without achievements will be rewarded;
不忍誅罰，	if you cannot bear to mete out punishments and fines,
15 則暴亂者不止。	then the violent and unruly will not cease.
國有無功得賞者，	If those who have no achievements are rewarded in a state,
則民不外務當敵斬首，	then, externally, its people will not undertake to face enemies and sever heads,
內不急力田疾作，	and, domestically, they will not devote themselves to energetic fieldwork and diligent production.

皆欲行貨財事富貴，	They will all want to go after valuables and work for wealth and nobility;
20 為私善立名譽，	they will work for their private good and establish their fame
以取尊官厚俸。	in order to attain high office and a substantial salary.
故姦私之臣愈眾，	As a result, wicked and selfish ministers will increase in number,
而暴亂之徒愈勝，	and the adherents of violence and chaos will become more dominant:
不亡何待？	and if that does not lead to ruin, what will?
25 夫嚴刑者，	Stern physical punishments
民之所畏也；	are what the people fear;
重罰者，	heavy fines
民之所惡也。	are what the people hate.
故聖人陳其所畏以禁其衺，	Therefore the sage will openly exhibit what they fear in order to preempt their deviance,
30 設其所惡以防其姦，	he will openly establish what they hate in order to prevent their wickedness:
是以國安而暴亂不起。	and as a result, the state will be in peace, and violence and chaos will not arise.
吾以是明仁義愛惠之不足用，	This is how we come to see clearly that benevolence, righteousness, kindness, and loving care are not sufficient for use,
而嚴刑重罰之可以治國也。	whereas stern punishments and heavy fines can bring order to the state.
無箠策之威，	Without the deterrent authority of the rod and whip,
35 銜橛之備，	or the provision of the horse's bit,
雖造父不能以服馬；	even [paragon charioteer] Zaofu would be unable to tame horses;
無規矩之法，	without the model of the compass and the T-square
繩墨之端，	or the ends of the ink line,
雖王爾不能以成方圓；	even [paragon carpenter] Wang Er would be unable to produce square and round shapes;
40 無威嚴之勢，	without the position of authority and sternness

姦劫弒臣 MINISTERS WHO BETRAY, COERCE OR ASSASSINATE

賞罰之法，	or the laws governing rewards and punishments,
雖堯舜不能以為治。	even [sage thearchs] Yao and Shun could not bring about good government.
今世主皆輕釋重罰嚴誅，	The rulers of our time all lighten or discard heavy fines and stern punishments
行愛惠，	and practise loving care and kindness,
45 而欲霸王之功，	and if they aim for the achievements of a hegemonic king in this way,
亦不可幾也。	they will be unable even to come close.
故善為主者，	Therefore, those who are good at acting as rulers
明賞設利以勸之，	clarify rewards and establish benefits to encourage people.
使民以功賞而不以仁義賜；	They bring it about that people are rewarded for their achievements, but do not receive gratuitous gifts for benevolence and righteousness;
50 嚴刑重罰以禁之，	they make punishments stern and fines heavy in order to inhibit [transgressions],
使民以罪誅而不以愛惠免。	and bring it about that people are punished for their crimes and not exempted out of loving kindness.
是以無功者不望，	Therefore, those without achievements will have no hopes,
而有罪者不幸矣。	and those guilty of crimes will look forward to no favours.
託於犀車良馬之上，	If you entrust yourself to a chariot covered by rhinoceros hide and driven by good horses,
55 則可以陸犯阪阻之患；	then, on land, you can manage all threats in a dangerous territory;
乘舟之安，	if you ride on a stable boat
持楫之利，	and avail yourself of the advantage of oars,
則可以水絕江河之難；	then, on water, you can make difficult river crossings;
操法術之數，	if you wield the arts of the laws and techniques of rule
60 行重罰嚴誅，	and practise heavy fines and stern punishments,
則可以致霸王之功。	then you can attain the achievements of a hegemonic king.

治國之有法術賞罰，	Having rewards and punishments by laws and techniques of rule in governing a state
猶若陸行之有犀車良馬也，	is like having well-protected carts and good horses when travelling by land
水行之有輕舟便楫也，	and light boats and convenient oars when travelling by water:
65　乘之者遂得其成。	one who avails himself of these things will achieve his aims.
伊尹得之，	Yi Yin attained these methods,
湯以王；	and Tang thereby became the king;[17]
管仲得之，	Guan Zhong attained them,
齊以霸；	and Qi thereby became the hegemon;
70　商君得之，	Lord Shang attained them,
秦以強。	and Qin thereby became strong.
此三人者，	These three men
皆明於霸王之術，	were all clear about the techniques of a hegemonic king;
察於治強之數，	they had a subtle understanding of the methods of good government and empowerment,
75　而不以牽於世俗之言；	and were not pulled about by the customary words of their time;
適當世明主之意，	they adapted to the ideas of the clear-sighted rulers of their time,
則有直任布衣之士，	so the rulers directly entrusted plain-clothed gentlemen[18]
立為卿相之處；	who were established in the office of senior minister and chancellor,
處位治國，	and when these held high office and governed the country,
80　則有尊主廣地之實：	they attained the real achievement of making the ruler honoured and territory vast;

17　Tang's establishment of the Shang dynasty in ca. 1600 is presented here as entirely indebted to Yi Yin's mastery of the proper methods of statecraft (For Yi Yin, see chapter 3, notes 9–10). The success of Tang, just like that of Qi and Qin (mentioned in the subsequent lines) is attributed squarely to wise ministers.

18　By the end of the Warring States period, "plain-clothed" (*buyi*, wearing coarse clothes) had become a symbol for the poor but aspiring man of service.

姦劫弒臣 MINISTERS WHO BETRAY, COERCE OR ASSASSINATE

此之謂足貴之臣。	these are called ministers that were worth holding in high honour.
湯得伊尹，	When Tang got hold of Yi Yin,
以百里之地立為天子；	he was established as Son of Heaven from a territory of one hundred *li* square.[19]
桓公得管仲，	When Lord Huan got hold of Guan Zhong,
立為五霸主，	he was established as one of the five hegemonic rulers;
九合諸侯，	nine times he assembled the regional lords
一匡天下；	and he unified and rectified the entire realm.[20]
孝公得商君，	When Lord Xiao got hold of Lord Shang,
地以廣，	his territory expanded
兵以強。	and his army grew stronger.
故有忠臣者，	So, one who has a loyal minister
外無敵國之患，	will have no threats from rival states abroad
內無亂臣之憂，	nor rebellious ministers to worry about at home;
長安於天下，	he will enjoy lasting security under Heaven
而名垂後世，	and his name will be handed down to later generations.
所謂忠臣也。	That is what I call a loyal minister.[21]
若夫豫讓為智伯臣也，	Yu Rang acted as a minister to Zhi Bo;[22]
上不能說人主使之明法術度數之理以避禍難之患，	above, he was unable to persuade the ruler and cause him to understand the laws and techniques

---

[19] The story of the righteous dynastic founders – kings Tang of the Shang dynasty and Wen of the Zhou – starting with a tiny domain of one hundred *li* squared (ca. 1600 km², i.e. smaller than present Luxembourg) and eventually attaining "All-under-Heaven" is fairly widespread in Warring States period texts; but in *Han Feizi* this mention is exceptional. It recurs, in a very different context, in 49.4.

[20] This is a standard reference to Lord Huan's achievements, first seen in the *Analects* (*Lunyu*) 14.16–17. Lord Huan did indeed establish his hegemony in the northeastern part of the Zhou world (but fell short of "uniformly rectifying" All-under-Heaven). "Nine assemblies" stands for "many assemblies" (Lord Huan assembled the regional lords no fewer than 15 times during his rule).

[21] The three paragon ministers – Yi Yin, Guan Zhong, and Shang Yang (as well as Wu Qi, mentioned above in this chapter) – are rare examples of ministers described in the *Han Feizi* using the adjective "loyal." Note that their loyalty is manifested exclusively through bringing about tangible achievements for their masters.

[22] On Zhi Bo (Zhi the Elder, named Yao), see chapter 10.5 and note 23 there. The story of Yu

下不能領御其眾以安其國。	of rule, standards and methods, so that he could avoid the worries of disaster and troubles, and below, he was unable to lead the multitudes to bring peace to the state.
100 及襄子之殺智伯也， 豫讓乃自黔劓，	When [Zhao] Xiangzi killed Zhi Bo, Yu Rang blackened his own face and cut off his nose;
敗其形容， 以為智伯報襄子之仇。 是雖有殘形殺身以為人主之名，	he ruined his body and facial appearance in order to avenge Xiangzi on behalf of Zhi Bo. Yet although he maimed his body and sacrificed himself in order to gain a name as someone who acted for the sake of his ruler,[23]
105 而實無益於智伯若秋毫之末。	he was, in fact, of no use to Zhi Bo, being as insignificant as the tip of an autumn hair.
此吾之所下也， 而世主以為忠而高之。	This is what I think little of, yet what the rulers of our time consider loyalty and value highly.
古有伯夷叔齊者， 武王讓以天下而弗受，	In ancient times, there were Boyi and Shuqi. King Wu left the rule of the realm to them, but they would not accept:
110 二人餓死首陽之陵。 若此臣， 不畏重誅， 不利重賞， 不可以罰禁也， 115 不可以賞使也，	the two starved to death on Mount Shouyang.[24] Subjects of this kind do not fear heavy punishments; they do not regard heavy rewards as profitable; they cannot be interdicted through fines; they cannot be made to perform tasks through rewards.

Rang, told below, parallels that in *Zhanguo ce* 18.4 ("Zhao 趙 1"). Han Fei, however, makes a significant digression by depicting Yu Rang's failure as a minister to Zhi Bo.

23 The *Zhanguo ce* story relates how Yu Rang, having failed to avenge Zhi Bo, was concerned primarily with attaining a name for himself as Zhi Bo's loyal servant. Before dying, he asked Zhao Xiangzi to give him Zhao's garments, which he stabbed, claiming to have thereby avenged Zhi Bo.

24 The story of the righteous purists, Boyi and Shuqi, who refused to eat what they regarded as the morally contaminated grain of the Zhou house, circulated widely in Warring States texts. The classic version of the story is found in the first of the "Arrayed Traditions" (*lie zhuan* 列傳) in Sima Qian's *Records of the Historian* (*Shiji* 61). According to the usual narrative, these righteous brothers rejected the legitimacy of King Wu's assault on his ruler, the Shang tyrant Zhòu 紂. The story of King Wu's desire to yield All-under-Heaven to Boyi and Shuqi is, in all likelihood, Han Fei's invention.

姦劫弑臣 MINISTERS WHO BETRAY, COERCE OR ASSASSINATE   193

此之謂無益之臣也。	These are called useless subjects.
吾所少而去也，	Such people I regard as being of little value and shun them,
而世主之所多而求也。	but they are the ones whom the rulers of our time admire and seek out.

1 學〔術〕者 (校注 141). 8 〔與〕(校注 141). 25 〔刑〕(校注 141). 29 張抄 has 衰 for 衺. 91 〔臣〕(校注 142). 98 說〔人〕主使〔人〕之 (校注 142). 104 C has 刑 for 形 with 校注. We follow 吳勉學本 and 王先慎、張覺. 陳奇猷 regard 刑 and 形 as interchangeable in HF.

HF 14.8 (*Xilun* 236, *Xin jiaozhu* 297)[25]

諺曰：	As the saying goes:
"厲憐王"。	"The lepers feel pity for the king."
此不恭之言也。	This are irreverent words.
雖然，	Nevertheless,
5 古無虛諺，	as the ancients had no empty proverbs,
不可不察也。	we should investigate them.
此謂劫殺死亡之主言也。	This statement refers to a king who is doomed to coercion and assassination.
人主無法術以御其臣，	If a ruler does not have laws and techniques of rule by which to steer his ministers,
雖長年而美材，	then, even if he lives long and has impressive talents,
10 大臣猶將得勢擅事主斷，	his powerful ministers will gain positions of power all the same; they will act without authorisation and take charge of decisions,
而各為其私急。	and each one will be urgently concerned for his private interests.
而恐父兄豪傑之士，	And then it is to be feared that elders and eminent and powerful gentlemen
借人主之力，	will borrow the ruler's power
以禁誅於己也，	to prevent punishments from being applied to themselves;

---

25   On the problematic nature of this section, which does not seem to connect naturally with what precedes it, see Chen Qianjun 1974: 378. The section reads like a separate chapter.

15 故弒賢長而立幼弱， and as a result, they will assassinate their worthy seniors and establish junior weaklings in their stead;

  廢正的而立不義。 they will set aside the upright and establish those without moral principles.

  故《春秋》記之曰： Thus, the *Springs-and-Autumns Annals*[26] records:
  "楚王子圍將聘於鄭， "Prince Wei of Chu was about to make a formal visit to Zheng.
  未出境， Before he had left his country,
20 聞王病而反， he heard that the king had fallen ill and returned,
  因入問病， and then he went in to ask how [the king] was.
  以其冠纓絞王而殺之， With the strap of his bonnet he strangled the king to death,
  遂自立也。" and then established himself as ruler."

  齊崔杼其妻美， "The wife of Cui Zhu of Qi was handsome
25 而莊公通之， and Lord Zhuang had intercourse with her.[27]
  數如崔氏之室。 Several times he went to Cui's residence.
  及公往， When the lord went there,
  崔子之徒賈舉率崔子之徒而攻公。 Master Cui's follower, Jia Ju, led Master Cui's men to attack the lord.[28]
  公入室， The lord entered Cui's home
30 請與之分國， and asked to divide the state between himself and Cui,
  崔子不許； but Master Cui did not go along with this.
  公請自刃於廟， The lord asked permission to kill himself in the ancestral temple,
  崔子又不聽； but Master Cui did not go along with this either.

---

26 The *Springs-and-Autumns Annals* here stands not for the canonical *Chunqiu* itself, but, as common in Warring States and Han literature, to one of its commentaries, namely *Zuozhuan*. The subsequent story slightly modifies the account in *Zuozhuan*, Zhao 1.12. Prince Wei, who murdered his nephew, King Jia'ao 郟敖, became one of the most powerful – and most controversial – Chu rulers, King Ling of Chu 楚靈王 (r. 540–529).

27 Once again, the entire story, even in its minor details, closely follows the narrative in *Zuozhuan* (Xiang 25.2). In light of this and the previous anecdote it is likely that Han Fei had read *Zuozhuan* itself and not just its sources or derivative texts.

28 This is the only place in which *Han Feizi* deviates from the *Zuozhuan* version of events: there Jia Ju is Lord Zhuang's eunuch, who, humiliated by the lord, avenged himself by helping Cui Zhu to advance his plot.

姦劫弒臣 MINISTERS WHO BETRAY, COERCE OR ASSASSINATE

公乃走，	Then the lord attempted to flee,
35 踰於北牆。	jumping over the northern curtain wall.
賈舉射公，	Jia Ju shot an arrow at the lord
中其股，	and hit him in the thigh.
公墜，	The lord fell to the ground;
崔子之徒以戈斫公而死之，	Master Cui's followers cut down the lord with a poleaxe, killing him,
40 而立其弟景公。"	and [Cui Zhu] established Lord [Zhuang's] younger brother as Lord Jing."
近之所見：	To take what we have seen closer to our own time:
李兌之用趙也，	When Li Dui took control of Zhao,
餓主父百日而死，	he left the Sovereign-Father famished for one hundred days, until he died.[29]
淖齒之用齊也，	When Nao Chi had taken control in Qi,
45 擢湣王之筋，	he had the sinews plucked out of King Min
懸之廟梁，	and had him suspended from a beam in the ancestral temple,
宿昔而死。	so that he died a slow death, which took a whole night.[30]
故厲雖癰腫疕瘍，	Now a leper may have all sorts of swellings and boils,
上比於《春秋》，	but if you compare his fate with what is reported in the Annals,
50 未至於絞頸射股也；	he does not quite fare as badly as being strangled or shot in the thigh;

---

[29] In 299, King Wuling of Zhao 趙武靈王 retired from his position of rulership, adopting the title of Sovereign-Father (主父). Soon enough, a power struggle engulfed the state of Zhao. The defeated rebel, King Wuling's son, Prince Zhang 章, escaped to the Sovereign-Father's mansion. Li Dui, who assisted Prince Cheng in quelling the rebellion, entered the mansion, seized Zhang, and had him executed (in 295). To avoid the Sovereign-Father's potential revenge, he encircled the mansion and starved the former king to death.

[30] King Min of Qi 齊湣王 was a powerful and arrogant ruler who alienated his neighbours and other regional lords. In 284, an anti-Qi coalition led by the King of Yan 燕 inflicted a heavy defeat on Qi, forcing King Min to flee to the southern district of Ju 莒. Nao Chi, a Chu military commander who had been dispatched to assist Qi, decided that the position of King Min was indefensible; he murdered the king and sued for peace with the Yan forces.

下比於近世，	or if you compare him with what is closer to our age,
未至饑死擢筋也。	he does not starve to death or have his sinews plucked out.
故劫殺死亡之君，	So, in a ruler who is doomed to coercion, assassination and death,
此其心之憂懼，	the worries and fears in his mind
55　形之苦痛也，	and the hardship and pain in his body
必甚於厲矣。	are certainly worse than those of a leper.
由此觀之，	From this point of view,
雖"厲憐王"可也。	even the saying "the leper feels pity for the king" is justified.

2, 48, 56, 58 厲 is read as 癩.　8〔主〕(校注 142).　44 C notes the reading 卓 for 淖.　48 C has 癱 for 癰.　47 昔 is read as 夕.　49 張抄 has 止 for 上.　50〔射〕(校注 142).　56〔於〕(校注 142).

CHAPTER 15

亡徵 Signs of Ruin

HF 15.1.1 (*Xilun* 240, *Xin jiaozhu* 300)[1]

凡人主之國小而家大，	In general, if a ruler's state is small by comparison to its large families,[2]
權輕而臣重者，	and if the ruler's leverage is slight but his ministers powerful,
可亡也。	then his state is likely to be ruined.

HF 15.1.2 (*Xilun* 240, *Xin jiaozhu* 300)

簡法禁而務謀慮，	If he is sparing in the use of laws and prohibitions and focusses on consultation and planning,
荒封內而恃交援者，	if he leaves domestic territories uncultivated and relies on the help of foreign ties,
可亡也。	then his state is likely to be ruined.

HF 15.1.3 (*Xilun* 242, *Xin jiaozhu* 300)

群臣為學，	If his ministers cultivate learning,
門子好辯，	his retinue is fond of disputation,
商賈外積，	if peddlers and merchants amass wealth abroad
小民右仗者，	and petty commoners care most about their sticks,
可亡也。	then his state is likely to be ruined.

---

1 This chapter is divided into 47 items that enumerate 73 reasons for the state's potential ruination (the number 73 is borrowed from Zheng Liangshu 1993: 141–152). Unlike many other chapters that discuss political failures on the basis of historical anecdotes (e.g., chapter 10, ["Ten faults"]), the present chapter speaks in general terms. This distinguishes the "Signs of ruin" chapter from parallel texts, such as the "Shiji" 史記 (Scribal records) chapter from the *Leftover Zhou Documents* (*Yi Zhou shu* 逸周書) and the parallel text from the manuscript fragment of the *Liu tao* 六韜 compendium (Grebnev 2024; see also Yanaka 1985).

2 *Guo* ("state") may refer here not only to the territory of the state, but the state apparatus as distinct from that of a ministerial household, or to the capital as distinct from the ministerial allotments. It is possible that all these three meanings are implied.

HF 15.1.4 (*Xilun* 242, *Xin jiaozhu* 300)

好宮室臺榭陂池，	If he is fond of palaces, raised wooden platforms, as well as dykes and artificial lakes,
事車服器玩，	if he cares about carriages, garments, vessels and playthings,
好罷露百姓，	if he likes to enervate the hundred clans
煎靡貨財者，	and waste goods,
5 可亡也。	then his state is likely to be ruined.

HF 15.1.5 (*Xilun* 243, *Xin jiaozhu* 300)

用時日，	If he employs hemerology,[3]
事鬼神，	if he serves ghosts and spirits,
信卜筮，	if he trusts prognostication by shell and milfoil,
而好祭祀者，	and he has a liking for sacrifices,
5 可亡也。	then his state is likely to be ruined.

1 C mistakenly has 曰 for 日.   3 張抄 has 十筮 for 卜筮.

HF 15.1.6 (*Xilun* 243, *Xin jiaozhu* 300)

聽以爵不待參驗，	If he follows advice according to [the speaker's] rank and has not checked the evidence,
用一人為門戶者，	if he employs but one person to guard the gates of power,
可亡也。	then his state is likely to be ruined.

1 〈以〉〔不〕(校注 151).

HF 15.1.7 (*Xilun* 244, *Xin jiaozhu* 300)

官職可以重求，	If offices and appointments are sought on the basis of [social] weight,
爵祿可以貨得者，	if ranks and stipends are obtained through bribes,
可亡也。	then his state is likely to be ruined.

---

3 This refers to divinatory calendar arrangements. See Kalinowski 2008.

亡徵 SIGNS OF RUIN

HF 15.1.8 (*Xilun* 244, *Xin jiaozhu* 300)

緩心而無成，	If he is slow of mind and does not carry things through to completion,
柔茹而寡斷，	if he is weak, fretful, and indecisive,
好惡無決，	if he is not definite in his likes and dislikes
而無所定立者，	and has nothing to which he is firmly committed,
可亡也。	then his state is likely to be ruined.

1 〈無而〉〔而無〕(校注 151).

HF 15.1.9 (*Xilun* 245, *Xin jiaozhu* 300)

饕貪而無饜，	If he is insatiably gluttonous and full of greed,
近利而好得者，	if he tends towards profit and is fond of acquisitions,
可亡也。	then his state is likely to be ruined.

HF 15.1.10 (*Xilun* 245, *Xin jiaozhu* 300)

喜淫辭而不周於法，	If he delights in wanton formulations and does not conform consistently to the laws,
好辯說而不求其用，	if he favours sophistry and does not probe its usefulness,
濫於文麗而不顧其功者，	if he is excessive in stylishness and disregards achievement,
可亡也。	then his state is likely to be ruined.

1 〔辭〕(校注 151).

HF 15.1.11 (*Xilun* 246, *Xin jiaozhu* 300)

淺薄而易見，	If he is shallow and superficial and easily given to expressing feelings,
漏泄而無藏，	if he lets things leak out and does not hide anything,
不能周密，	if he cannot keep things completely secret

而通群臣之語者，
可亡也。

and allows ministers' talk to be disseminated,
then his state is likely to be ruined.

HF 15.1.12 (*Xilun* 246, *Xin jiaozhu* 300)

很剛而不和，
愎諫而好勝，
不顧社稷而輕為自信者，

可亡也。

If he is hard and uncompromising,
if he is stubborn in the face of remonstrance and loves to keep the upper hand,
if he shows no proper concern for the altars of the soil and grain[4] and acts arbitrarily, relying on himself alone,[5]
then his state is likely to be ruined.

HF 15.1.13 (*Xilun* 247, *Xin jiaozhu* 300)

恃交援而簡近鄰，
怙強大之救，
而侮所迫之國者，
可亡也。

If he relies on help from foreign ties but ignores his close neighbours,
if he relies on succour from the strong and the great
and humiliates states that are in distress,
then his state is likely to be ruined.

HF 15.1.14 (*Xilun* 247, *Xin jiaozhu* 300)

羈旅僑士，
重帑在外，
上閒謀計，
下與民事者，
可亡也。

If itinerants and gentlemen of service living away from home
have stashed abroad substantial amounts of the state's funds,
but, above, they interfere with policy-making,
and, below, they interfere with the business of the people,
then his state is likely to be ruined.[6]

---

4 The "altars of the soil and grain" are symbolic centres of the state.

5 That is, the ruler is overly reliant on his own judgement and does not heed the advice of his ministers. Han Fei objects both to following ministers slavishly and disengaging from them completely.

6 This is a warning against "roving persuaders" whose machinations and unscrupulousness ignited the ire of many Warring States-era Masters (see also chapter 13, note 3).

亡徵 SIGNS OF RUIN

HF 15.1.15 (*Xilun* 248, *Xin jiaozhu* 300)

民信其相，	If the people have faith in the chancellor
下不能其上，	and those below do not regard the one on top as a capable person,
主愛信之而弗能廢者，	if the ruler cares for and trusts [the chancellor] and cannot dismiss him,
可亡也。	then [the ruler] is likely to be ruined.

HF 15.1.16 (*Xilun* 248, *Xin jiaozhu* 301)

境內之傑不事，	If outstanding men from within the boundaries are not employed,
而求封外之士，	yet he seeks to enfeoff men from outside,
不以功伐課試，	if he does not judge performance according to achievement,
而好以名問舉錯，	but likes to elevate and place people according to their reputation,
羈旅起貴以陵故常者，	if itinerants rise to noble status and dominate the permanent residents,
可亡也。	then his state is likely to be ruined.

4 問 is read as 聞.　　5 陵 is read as 凌.

HF 15.1.17 (*Xilun* 249, *Xin jiaozhu* 301)

輕其適正，	If he does not pay proper respect to the direct heir,
庶子稱衡，	whereas sons by secondary wives throw their weight around,
太子未定而主即世者，	if the ruler passes away before the crown prince is determined,
可亡也。	then the state is likely to be ruined.

HF 15.1.18 (*Xilun* 249, *Xin jiaozhu* 301)

大心而無悔，	If he is full of himself and lacks regret,
國亂而自多，	if the state is in chaos but he is full of praise for himself,
不料境內之資而易其鄰敵者，	if he does not assess the resources within his borders and underestimates his neighbouring rivals,
可亡也。	then his state is likely to be ruined.

HF 15.1.19 (*Xilun* 249, *Xin jiaozhu* 301)

國小而不處卑，	If his state is small but he does not take a humble stance,
力少而不畏強，	if his power is slight but he does fear the strong,
無禮而侮大鄰，	if he is impolite and rude to his sizeable neighbours,
貪愎而拙交者，	if he is greedy and stubborn and inept at striking good relations,
5　可亡也。	then his state is likely to be ruined.

HF 15.1.20 (*Xilun* 250, *Xin jiaozhu* 301)

太子已置，	If, the crown prince having been established,
而娶於強敵以為后妻，	the ruler takes a wife from a strong rival state,
則太子危，	then the position of the crown prince will be precarious,
如是則群臣易慮；	and under such conditions ministers will change their tactics;
5　群臣易慮者，	and if ministers change their tactics,
可亡也。	then the ruler is likely to be ruined.

　　5 〔群臣易慮〕(校注 151).

HF 15.1.21 (*Xilun* 250, *Xin jiaozhu* 301)

怯懾而弱守，	If he is fretful and weak at defending himself,
蚤見而心柔懦，	if he discloses his opinions early but his mind is weak and dithering,

亡徵 SIGNS OF RUIN

知有謂可，	if he knows that something is acceptable,
斷而弗敢行者，	makes decisions but does not dare to carry them through,
5　可亡也。	then his state is likely to be ruined.

HF 15.1.22 (*Xilun* 251, *Xin jiaozhu* 301)

出君在外而國更置，	If someone else is established within the state when the ruler is away,
質太子未反而君易子，	if the crown prince serves as hostage abroad and has not yet returned and the ruler appoints another son as his heir,
如是則國攜，	then the state will be of two minds.
國攜者，	If the state is of two minds,
5　可亡也。	then it is likely to be ruined.

1 〔更〕(校注 151).

HF 15.1.23 (*Xilun* 251, *Xin jiaozhu* 301)

挫辱大臣而狎其身，	If, having humiliated senior ministers, he treats them with improper familiarity,
刑戮小民而逆其使，	if, having punished petty people, he nonetheless employs them,
懷怒思恥而專習則賊生；	then they will think of their anger and ponder their shame, and if he becomes specially proximate to them, then brigandage will arise,
賊生者，	and if brigandage arises,
5　可亡也。	then his state is likely to be ruined.[7]

---

[7] Chen Qiyou expounded on this clause using the story from *Zuozhuan* (referred to in chapter 14.8): Lord Zhuang of Qi whipped his attendant Jia Ju, but continued to keep him close; Jia Ju later betrayed Lord Zhuang by allowing Cui Zhu to assassinate him in 549 (*Zuozhuan*, Xiang 25.2).

HF 15.1.24 (*Xilun* 252, *Xin jiaozhu* 301)

大臣兩重，	If two senior ministers hold powerful positions,
父兄眾強，	if the elders are numerous and strong,
內黨外援以爭事勢者，	and if factions within the state solicit outside help in contending for power,
可亡也。	then the ruler is likely to be ruined.

HF 15.1.25 (*Xilun* 252, *Xin jiaozhu* 301)

婢妾之言聽，	If the words of female slaves and concubines are heeded,
愛玩之智用，	if the intellect of beloved ones and playmates is put to use,
外內悲惋而數行不法者，	and if, in spite of sighs of sadness outside and inside the court, he frequently acts against the law,
可亡也。	then the ruler is likely to be ruined.

HF 15.1.26 (*Xilun* 252, *Xin jiaozhu* 301)

簡侮大臣，	If he slights and humiliates senior ministers,
無禮父兄，	if he is impolite to his elders,[8]
勞苦百姓，	if he makes the hundred clans toil bitterly
殺戮不辜者，	and executes the innocent,
可亡也。	then his state is likely to be ruined.

HF 15.1.27 (*Xilun* 253, *Xin jiaozhu* 301)

好以智矯法，	If he likes to twist laws in accordance with his own intelligence,
時以行雜公，	if he repeatedly dilutes impartial practice with private initiatives,
法禁變易，	if laws and prohibitions are changed

---

[8] Specifically uncles and cousins on the paternal side.

亡徵 SIGNS OF RUIN

| 號令數下者， | and commands and ordinances are frequently issued, |
| 5 可亡也。 | then his state is likely to be ruined. |

HF 15.1.28 (*Xilun* 253, *Xin jiaozhu* 301)

無地固，	If his lands do not provide natural security,
城郭惡；	if his inner and outer city walls are in disrepair,
無畜積，	if he has not accumulated supplies,
財物寡，	if his material resources are sparse,
5 無守戰之備而輕攻伐者，	and if, without defensive preparations, he thinks lightly of launching an attack,
可亡也。	then his state is likely to be ruined.

HF 15.1.29 (*Xilun* 254, *Xin jiaozhu* 301)

種類不壽，	If relatives do not live long lives,
主數即世，	and rulers pass away quickly, one after the other,
嬰兒為君，	if small children become rulers
大臣專制，	and senior ministers monopolise political control,
5 樹羈旅以為黨，	if he establishes itinerant ministers so they form factions
數割地以待交者，	and frequently gives away pieces of territory for the sake of good relations,
可亡也。	then his state is likely to be ruined.

HF 15.1.30 (*Xilun* 254, *Xin jiaozhu* 301)

太子尊顯，	If the crown prince is honoured and illustrious
徒屬眾強，	and his adherents are numerous and strong,
多大國之交，	if he frequently cultivates relations with other big states
而威勢蚤具者，	and if his awe-inspiring authority and positional power is firmly established before the proper time,
5 可亡也。	then the ruler is likely to be ruined.

HF 15.1.31 (*Xilun* 254, *Xin jiaozhu* 301)

變褊而心急，	If he is unsteady and hot-headed,
輕疾而易動發，	if he easily flies into a rage and lightly takes action,
心怓忿而不訾前後者，	if he is irascible and does not care in the least about[9] precedents and consequences,
可亡也。	then his state is likely to be ruined.

HF 15.1.32 (*Xilun* 255, *Xin jiaozhu* 301)

主多怒而好用兵，	If the ruler often is angered and is prone to use military force,
簡本教而輕戰攻者，	if he is negligent about basic training and thinks lightly of launching military attacks,
可亡也。	then his state is likely to be ruined.

2 本（欲）教 (校注 151).

HF 15.1.33 (*Xilun* 256, *Xin jiaozhu* 301)

貴臣相妒，	If the ennobled ministers are envious of one another,
大臣隆盛，	if the senior ministers are domineering,
外藉敵國，	externally relying on rival states
內困百姓，	and internally troubling the hundred clans,
5 以攻怨讎，	all in order to attack their hated enemies,
而人主弗誅者，	if the ruler will not[10] punish them for this,
可亡也。	then his state is likely to be ruined.

---

9   The use of *zi* 訾 in this sense of "to think warily about" is striking and unusual, although there is a vaguely comparable isolated example of this usage in *Records of the Rites* (*Liji* 禮記), chapter 4 ("Tan Gong xia" 檀弓下) (Sun Xidan 1995: 272).

10 The grammatical emphatic and deliberate nuance of *fu* 弗 as "refuse to, will not" is crucial for a proper understanding of the dynamics of this passage.

亡徵 SIGNS OF RUIN

HF 15.1.34 (*Xilun* 256, *Xin jiaozhu* 301)

君不肖而側室賢，	If the ruler is unworthy, whereas his sons by concubines are worthy,
太子輕而庶子伉，	if the crown prince is a lightweight, whereas the other princes are big shots,[11]
官吏弱而人民桀，	if the officials are weak, whereas the people take the lead –
如此則國躁；	under these conditions the state is in a hustle;
5 國躁者，	and if the state is in a hustle,
可亡也。	then the ruler is likely to be ruined.

HF 15.1.35 (*Xilun* 257, *Xin jiaozhu* 301)

藏怨而弗發，	If he stores his wrath inside and refuses to let it out,
懸罪而弗誅，	if he suspends action on crimes and will not punish [the perpetrators],
使群臣陰憎而愈憂懼，	if he makes the ministers secretly resentful and increasingly worried and fearful,
而久未可知者，	so that, for a long time, they cannot know what he will do,[12]
5 可亡也。	then his state is likely to be ruined.

HF 15.1.36 (*Xilun* 257, *Xin jiaozhu* 301)

出軍命將太重，	If, in sending out armies, if he gives too much power to the generals,
邊地任守太尊，	if the governors in the border regions are overly respected,
專制擅命，	if they take sole control and issue orders without authorisation,

---

11 What is translated as "big shots" here is a very unusual word to use in this meaning. I strongly suspect it has a very colloquial flavour, hence my provocative translation.

12 It is remarkable how in this particular context Han Fei advises against keeping one's cards close to one's chest, which is an approach he recommends elsewhere (e.g. in chapter 5).

徑為而無所請者，	if they act immediately and do not ask about any proposed action,
5 可亡也。	then the ruler is likely to be ruined.

HF 15.1.37 (*Xilun* 258, *Xin jiaozhu* 301)

后妻淫亂，	If the royal wife is wanton and disorderly,
主母畜穢，	if the ruler's mother cultivates indecent relations,
外內混通，	if there are improper relations outside and inside the court,
男女無別，	and no distinction between men and women,
5 是謂兩主；	that is called having two rulers;
兩主者，	and if there are two rulers,
可亡也。	then [the real one] is likely to be ruined.[13]

HF 15.1.38 (*Xilun* 258, *Xin jiaozhu* 301)

后妻賤而婢妾貴，	If the queenly consort enjoys humbler status than slaves and concubines,
太子卑而庶子尊，	if the crown prince is less honoured than the other princes,
相室輕而典謁重，	if the chancellor has less influence than the impresario in charge of receptions,[14]
如此則內外乖；	if things are in such a state, then those within and outside the court are at variance;
5 內外乖者，	and if those inside and outside the court are at variance,
可亡也。	then the ruler is likely to be ruined.

---

[13] It is difficult to avoid the suspicion that Han Fei here refers to the infamous events in the state of Qin, when the mother of the First Emperor engaged in illicit relations with the chancellor (and her former lover), Lü Buwei, and later with a preternaturally endowed ragamuffin named Lao Ai. The resulting intrigue almost ruined the state of Qin a few years before Han Fei's death there.

[14] An official in charge of receptions has the potential to open alternative routes of communication with the ruler, and could overshadow the chancellor as a result.

亡徵 SIGNS OF RUIN

HF 15.1.39 (*Xilun* 259, *Xin jiaozhu* 301)

大臣甚貴，	If the senior ministers are excessively honoured,
偏黨眾強，	if their factions are numerous and strong,
壅塞主斷而重擅國者，	if they block the ruler's decisions and with their power usurp authority over the state,
可亡也。	then his state is likely to be ruined.

HF 15.1.40 (*Xilun* 259, *Xin jiaozhu* 301)

私門之官用，	If people from private gates[15] are employed as officials,
馬府之世絀，	but those with distinguished military records are dismissed,
鄉曲之善舉，	if locals with good reputation are promoted,
官職之勞廢，	but those who toil at their official duties are dismissed,
5　貴私行而賤公功者，	if the ruler values selfish actions over unselfish achievements,
可亡也。	then his state is likely to be ruined.

2 〔絀〕(校注 151).

HF 15.1.41 (*Xilun* 260, *Xin jiaozhu* 301)

公家虛而大臣實，	If the lord's house is an empty name and senior ministers hold real power,
正戶貧而寄寓富，	if the regular taxpaying households are poor and the itinerant people wealthy,[16]
耕戰之士困，	if men engaged in agriculture or war are in dire straits,

---

15　That is, those who enjoy patronage of high ministers and do not follow the proper route into employment.

16　"Regular taxpaying households" refers to peasants; "the itinerant people" are probably those merchants and artisans whose prosperity is lamented in the next sentence. Cf. *Book of Lord Shang*, chapter 6.6.

	末作之民利者，	while people engaged in non-productive work reap a profit,
5	可亡也。	then the ruler is likely to be ruined.

HF 15.1.42 (*Xilun* 261, *Xin jiaozhu* 301)

	見大利而不趨，	If he sees great profit but does not rush for it,
	聞禍端而不備，	if he learns about the beginnings of disaster, but does not guard against it;
	淺薄於爭守之事，	if he pays scant attention to matters of combat and defence,
	而務以仁義自飾者，	but strives to embellish his image with benevolence and righteousness,
5	可亡也。	then his state is likely to be ruined.

HF 15.1.43 (*Xilun* 261, *Xin jiaozhu* 301)

	不為人主之孝，	If he does not practise the filial piety befitting a ruler,
	而慕匹夫之孝，	but shows admiration for the filial piety of a commoner,[17]
	不顧社稷之利，	if he does not pay attention to the interests of the altars of the soil and grain,
	而聽主母之令，	but obeys orders from the ruler's mother,
5	女子用國，	if women are in charge of the state
	刑餘用事者，	and eunuchs in charge of the administration,
	可亡也。	then the ruler is likely to be ruined.

HF 15.1.44 (*Xilun* 262, *Xin jiaozhu* 301)

	辭辯而不法，	If his formulations are sophisticated but do not accord with the law,

---

[17] From the context it is clear that devotion to one's mother – the form of filial piety prescribed for a "commoner" – would not be acceptable on the ruler's part because this would create an alternative locus of power in the palace.

亡徵 SIGNS OF RUIN

心智而無術，	if his mind is sharp, but without the techniques of governance,
主多能而不以法度從事者，	if the ruler has many abilities, but does not conduct affairs according to laws and standards,
可亡也。	then his state is likely to be ruined.

HF 15.1.45 (*Xilun* 262, *Xin jiaozhu* 302)

親臣進而故人退，	If the ministers close to him[18] advance and old ones are removed,
不肖用事而賢良伏，	if unworthy people are in charge and men of worth lie in hiding,
無功貴而勞苦賤，	if those without achievements are honoured, while those who work hard are disparaged,
如是則下怨；	if things are like this, then those below will be resentful;
下怨者，	if when those below are resentful,
可亡也。	then the ruler is likely to be ruined.

HF 15.1.46 (*Xilun* 263, *Xin jiaozhu* 302)

父兄大臣祿秩過功，	If the emoluments of [the ruler's] elders and senior ministers surpass their achievements,
章服侵等，	if their insignia and their dress illegally exceed their rank,
宮室供養大侈，	if [their] palaces and provisions are excessive
而人主弗禁，	and the ruler fails to prohibit this,
則臣心無窮；	then the ministers' ambitions will be unending;
臣心無窮者，	if the ministers' ambitions are unending,
可亡也。	then the ruler is likely to be ruined.

3 大 is read as 太.

---

18 Many commentators have wanted to emend the text to read *xin*, "new." The emendation is tempting at first sight but ultimately unnecessary. Here, ministers who are currently powerful are contrasted with old friends.

HF 15.1.47 (*Xilun* 263, *Xin jiaozhu* 302)

公壻公孫與民同門， If the lord's sons-in-law and grandchildren live next door to the people

暴慠其鄰者， and if they are violent and arrogant toward their neighbours,

可亡也。 then the ruler is likely to be ruined.

HF 15.2 (*Xilun* 264, *Xin jiaozhu* 302)

亡徵者， If there are signs of ruin,
非曰必亡， this is not to say that the state is bound to be ruined;
言其可亡也。 it means that the state may be ruined.

夫兩堯不能相王[A 陽/陽 gwjaŋ/jwaŋ]， Now, two Yaos cannot make each other monarchs,

兩桀不能相亡[A 陽/陽 mjaŋ/mjaŋ]； nor can two Jies ruin each other;[19]

亡、王之機[B 微/微 kjəd/kjěi]， the mechanism that causes ruin or kingship

必其治亂、其強弱相踦[B 歌/支 khjar/-jei/khjě]者也。 must be that order and chaos, weakness and strength are unevenly distributed.

木之折也必通蠹[C 魚/暮 tagh/tuo]， When a tree breaks, this is bound to be because of wood-boring insects;

牆之壞也必通隙[C 魚/陌 khjiak/khjɛk]。 when a wall collapses, this is bound to be because there are cracks in it.

然木雖蠹， However, even if there are wood-boring insects in a tree,

無疾風不折； without strong winds it will not break;

牆雖隙， and even if there are cracks in a wall,

無大雨不壞。 it will not collapse without a great storm.

萬乘之主， If a ruler of a large state with an armed force of ten thousand war chariots

---

19   This goes back to Han Fei's repeated insistence that the personal qualities of the rulers – be they as perfect as Yao or as doomed as Jie – are of no relevance to the ruler's success and failure, which instead solely depend on the techniques of government and law.

15 有能服術行法,   has the ability to devote himself to the techniques of governance and to practise the law,

以為亡徵之君風雨者,   so that he may be a thunderstorm for rulers with symptoms of ruin,

其兼天下不難矣。   he will have no trouble uniting the world.

CHAPTER 16

三守 Three Defences

HF 16.1.0 (*Xilun* 265, *Xin jiaozhu* 316)

人主有三守。	The ruler has three defences.
三守完，	If the three defences are in place,
則國安身榮；	then the state will be at peace and his person will be assured glory.
三守不完，	If the three defences are not in place,
5 則國危身殆。	then the state will be in a precarious situation and his person in danger.
何謂三守？	What is meant by "the three defences"?

HF 16.1.1 (*Xilun* 266, *Xin jiaozhu* 316)

人臣有議當途之失、用事之過、舉臣之情，	If ministers bring up, in formal consultation, oversights of those in command, offences of those who carry out the administration, and the real conditions of ministers who have been elevated to high position,
人主不心藏而漏之近習能人，	and the ruler does not hide this in his mind, but leaks it to favourites who are close to him,
使人臣之欲有言者，	this will cause ministers who want to speak up
不敢不下適近習能人之心，	not to dare but to please the minds of the cronies and the malevolent below,
5 而乃上以聞人主。	and only then to go on to make themselves heard by the ruler above.
然則端言直道之人不得見，	Then, under such circumstances, straight-talking and honest men will not be received in audience by him,
而忠直日疏。	and the loyal and straight will become more and more distant from him.

三守 THREE DEFENCES

HF 16.1.2 (*Xilun* 267, *Xin jiaozhu* 316)

愛人，	When [the ruler] is fond of someone
不獨利也，	and does not single-handedly benefit him,
待譽而後利之；	but waits for him to win praise before benefitting him,
憎人，	or when [the ruler] dislikes someone
5　不獨害也，	and does not single-handedly harm him,
待非而後害之。	but waits for him to be denounced before harming him –
然則人主無威而重在左右矣。	under such circumstances, the ruler will have no authority, whereas the political weight will reside with his entourage.

HF 16.1.3 (*Xilun* 267, *Xin jiaozhu* 316)

惡自治之勞憚，	If [the ruler] dislikes the overwork of governing in person,
使群臣輻湊之變，	and lets the ministers transform from being the spokes to being the hub,
因傳柄移藉，	thus passing on the handles of control and shifting the [royal] regalia [to the ministers],
使殺生之機、奪予之要在大臣，	and if [the ruler] lets the trigger of life and death and the crucial power to give and to take away rest with the senior ministers –
5　如是者侵。	with things like this, [the ruler] will be encroached upon.

1 憚 is read as 癉.

HF 16.1.4 (*Xilun* 268, *Xin jiaozhu* 316)

此謂三守不完。	This is what is called not having the three defences in place.
三守不完，	Not having the three defences in place
則劫殺之徵也。	is a symptom of impending arrogation and assassination.

HF 16.2.0 (*Xilun* 268, *Xin jiaozhu* 319)

凡劫有三：	Altogether, there are three arrogations:
有明劫，	there is arrogation of a title;
有事劫，	there is arrogation of executive authority;
有刑劫。	and there is arrogation of the authority over punishments.

HF 16.2.1 (*Xilun* 269, *Xin jiaozhu* 319)

人臣有大臣之尊，	When a minister enjoys the honour of a great minister,
外操國要以資群臣，	and externally holds the keys to the state, turning thereby all other ministers into his assets,
使外內之事非己不得行。	and brings it about that internal and external matters cannot be undertaken without him,
雖有賢良，	then even if there are worthy and good people,
5 逆者必有禍，	those who oppose him are bound to meet with disaster,
而順者必有福。	whereas those who obey him are bound to meet with good fortune.
然則群臣直莫敢忠主憂國以爭社稷之利害。	Under such circumstances, none of the forthright ministers would dare to be loyal to the ruler or worry about the state, or struggle about the harm or benefit to the altars of the soil and grain.
人主雖賢，	If the ruler, however worthy,
不能獨計，	is unable to calculate independently,
10 而人臣有不敢忠主，	and the ministers moreover do not dare to be loyal to their ruler,
則國為亡國矣。	then the state is a ruined state.
此謂國無臣。	This is what is called "there are no ministers in the state."
國無臣者，	[When we say] "there are no ministers in the state,"
豈郎中虛而朝臣少哉？	is it just that the corridors are empty and few ministers are present at court?

三守 THREE DEFENCES 217

15	群臣持祿養交，	If the ministers maintain their emoluments and cultivate their connections,
	行私道而不效公忠，	if they practise their selfish ways and do not do their best in being impartial and loyal,
	此謂明劫。	this is what is called arrogation of title.

10 有 is read as 又.　14 郎 is read as 廊.　17 明 is read as 名.

HF 16.2.2 (*Xilun* 270, *Xin jiaozhu* 319)

	鬻寵擅權，	When [the ministers] sell favours and usurp power,
	矯外以勝內，	make pretences of foreign [support] in order to overcome domestic [rivals],
	險言禍福得失之形，	when they risk to speak of what bodes disaster or fortune, success or failure,
	以阿主之好惡。	thus pandering to the likes and dislikes of the ruler –
5	人主聽之，	then, if the ruler heeds their advice,
	卑身輕國以資之，	he will humiliate his person and make light of his state, and thereby strengthen them.
	事敗與主分其禍，	When an undertaking fails, these ministers share responsibility for disasters with the ruler,
	而功成則臣獨專之。	but when it succeeds, then the ministers claim the merit solely for themselves.
	諸用事之人，	When those in charge of the administration
10	壹心同辭以語其美，	unanimously, and using identical phrases, talk about someone's good points,
	則主言惡者必不信矣，	the ruler will not believe anyone who speaks of his bad points.
	此謂事劫。	This is what is called arrogation of the executive authority.

HF 16.2.3 (*Xilun* 270, *Xin jiaozhu* 319)

至於守司囹圄，	Regarding the administration of prisons,
禁制刑罰，	prohibitions, regulations, punishments and penalties:
人臣擅之，	when ministers usurp authority over these matters,
此謂刑劫。	it is called the arrogation of punitive authority.

HF 16.2.4 (*Xilun* 271, *Xin jiaozhu* 319)

三守不完，	When the three defences are not in place,
則三劫者起;	the three arrogations will arise;
三守完，	when the three defences are in place,
則三劫者止。	the three arrogations will be stopped.
5 三劫止塞，	When the three arrogations are stopped and blocked,
則王矣。	one can become a true king.

2 張抄 has 超 for 起.

CHAPTER 17

備內 Guarding against the Enemy within

HF 17.1 (*Xilun* 272, *Xin jiaozhu* 321)

人主之患在於信人。	The threat to the ruler lies in placing faith in others.
信人，	When you place your faith in others,
則制於人。	you will be controlled by them.
人臣之於其君，	With regard to the ruler, ministers
非有骨肉之親也，	are not as close as the his flesh and blood;
縛於勢而不得不事也。	they are tied by [his] power and have no choice but to serve.
故為人臣者，	So, someone who serves as a minister
窺覘其君心也無須臾之休，	will not cease for a single moment to observe his ruler's attitudes,
而人主怠傲處其上，	while the ruler presides above him in an indolent and arrogant manner –
此世所以有劫君、弒主也。	this is why in our time there are cases where the power of ruler is arrogated and the ruler is assassinated.
為人主而大信其子[A 之/止 tsjəgx/-jaǐ/tsǐ]，	When you are a ruler and place great faith in your sons,
則姦臣得乘於子以成其私[A 脂/脂 sjid/-jiəi/sji]，	wicked ministers will avail themselves of your sons to achieve their selfish aims.
故李兌傅趙王而餓主父。	Thus Li Dui acted as tutor to the King of Zhao and starved the Sovereign-Father to death.[1]
為人主而大信其妻[A 脂/齊 tshid/tshiei]，	When you are a ruler and place great faith in your wife,
則姦臣得乘於妻以成其私[A 脂/脂 sjid/-jiəi/sji]，	wicked ministers will avail themselves of her to achieve their selfish aims.

---

1 See chapter 14, note 29 for details.

故優施傅麗姬殺申生而立奚齊[A 脂/齊 dzid/-iei/dziei]。

Thus Entertainer Shi acted as tutor to Li Ji, [instructing her] to kill Shensheng and establish Xiqi.[2]

夫以妻之近[B 文/隱 gjənx/gjən]與子之親[B 真/真 tshjin/-jiən/tshjěn]而猶不可信[B 真/震 sjinh/-jiən/sjěn],
則其餘無可信[B 真/震 sjinh/-jiən/sjěn]者矣。

Now, in the case of close relations like a wife and a son, if you cannot even place your faith in them,

then none of the others can be trusted!

HF 17.2 (*Xilun* 273, *Xin jiaozhu* 322)

且萬乘之主,

Moreover, in the case of a ruler of a ten-thousand chariot state

千乘之君,
后妃、夫人、適子為太子者,

or a ruler of one-thousand chariot state,
then among his consorts, wives, and those among the prospective heirs who can become crown prince,

或有欲其君之蚤死者。

there will probably be those who hope that the ruler will die early.

5 何以知其然?
夫妻者,
非有骨肉之恩也,

How do I know this to be so?
With a wife
you do not have the gratitude that goes with blood relations.

愛則親,
不愛則疏。

If you love her, you bring her close;
if you do not love her, you keep her at a distance.

10 語曰:
"其母好⟨A 幽/晧 həgwx/xâu⟩者其子抱⟨A 幽/晧 bəgwx/bâu⟩。"

As the saying goes:
"When the mother is liked, the son is hugged."

然則其為之反也,
其母惡[B 魚/暮 ʔagh/ʔuo]者其子釋[B 魚/昔 sthjiak/śjäk],

And so there is also the opposite:
"When the mother is detested, her son will be rejected."

---

2 Li Ji, a favourite concubine of Lord Xian of Jin 晉獻公 (r. 676–651), acted to depose the crown prince Shensheng and replace him with her own son. The plot is narrated in great detail in *Zuozhuan* (Zhuang 28.2, Xi 4.6, Xi 5.2) and *Discourses of the States* (*Guoyu* 7–8; [Jin 1–2]). The figure of Entertainer Shi as Li Ji's secret lover and the mastermind of her plot appears only in the *Discourses of the States* version.

備內 GUARDING AGAINST THE ENEMY WITHIN

丈夫年五十而好色未解也，	When a man has reached fifty, his taste for female beauty has not yet vanished,
15 婦人年三十而美色衰矣。	but when a woman is thirty, her beauty has already declined.
以衰美之婦人事好色之丈夫，	If a woman of declining beauty serves a husband who is fond of female beauty,
則身見疏賤，	then her person will be kept at a distance and she will be held in low esteem,
而子疑不為後，	and her son will held in suspicion and will not be made successor.
此后妃、夫人之所以冀其君之死者也。	This is why primary and secondary consorts wish that their ruler will die.
20 唯母為后而子為主，	When the mother has become dowager and her son is the ruler,
則令無不行，	her orders are invariably carried out,
禁無不止，	her prohibitions invariably followed.
男女之樂不減於先君，	Her sexual desires will be no less than with the former master,
而擅萬乘不疑，	and there is no doubt that she will assume control over the ten-thousand chariot state.
25 此鴆毒扼昧之所以用也。	This is why poison, strangulation and murder are used.
故《桃左春秋》曰：	That is why the *Springs-and-Autumns of Tao Zuo*[3] says:
"人主之疾死者不能處半。"	"Rulers who die of natural diseases cannot make up even one half (of rulers who die in office)."
人主弗知⟨C 佳/支 trig/-jiei/tjě⟩，	If the ruler refuses to understand this,
則亂多資⟨C 脂/脂 tsjid/-jiai/tsji⟩。	rebellion will have much support.

---

[3] "Springs-and-Autumns" was a generic term for historical (and quasi-historical anecdotal) writings in pre-imperial and early imperial China. The title *Springs-and-Autumns* is most commonly applied to the canonical *Springs-and-Autumns Annals* of Lu. Recall though that well into the Han dynasty it was routinely applied to commentaries on the *Annals*, whereas earlier the same term was applied to a great variety of unrelated texts (see also chapter 14, note 26). Nothing is known about *Springs-and-Autumns of Tao Zuo*. Yu Yue suggested that Tao Zuo should be read as *Taowu* 桃兀, the alleged name of the chronicle of the state of Chu.

30 故曰：	So it is said:
"利君死者眾，	"When those who profit from the ruler's death are many,
則人主危。"	the ruler will be imperilled."
故王良愛馬，	So, when Wang Liang took good care of his horses
越王勾踐愛人，	and King Goujian of Yue took good care of his people,
35 為戰與馳。	they did so in order to wage war and travel fast.[4]
醫善吮人之傷，	If a doctor is adept at sucking the wounds of the injured,
含人之血，	and takes people's blood into his mouth,
非骨肉之親也，	it is not because they are kin of flesh and blood,
利所加也。	but because he will derive added benefits from this.
40 故輿人成輿，	Thus, when a cartwright make carts,
則欲人之富貴；	he hopes that people will become rich and noble;
匠人成棺，	when the carpenter makes coffins,
則欲人之夭死也。	he hopes that people have untimely deaths.
非輿人仁而匠人賊也，	This is not because the cartwright is kind-hearted and the carpenter a villain;
45 人不貴，	it is just that, if people do not achieve noble status,
則輿不售；	elaborate carriages will not be sold,
人不死，	and if people do not die,
則棺不買。	coffins will not be bought.
情非憎人也，	His real feelings are not feelings of hatred for people,
50 利在人之死也。	but his profit lies in people's death.
故后妃、夫人、太子之黨成而欲君之死也，	When the factions of the primary and secondary consort and the crown prince are formed, and they hope for the ruler's death,

---

4 Wang Liang is a legendary horse driver. King Goujian of Yue (r. 496–464) is one of the most celebrated heroes of the rags-to-riches type in early China: having been utterly defeated by his Wu rivals shortly upon his ascendancy, he was able to painstakingly restore the fortunes of his state by adopting "people-oriented" policies. Eventually, in 473, he extinguished Wu and attained hegemony in the east. See also chapter 23, note 20.

備內 GUARDING AGAINST THE ENEMY WITHIN

君不死，	this is because, if the ruler does not die,
則勢不重。	their strategic position will not be great.
情非憎君也，	Their real feelings are not feelings of hatred for the ruler,
55 利在君之死也。	but their profit lies in the ruler's death.
故人主不可以不加心於利己死者。	Therefore, the ruler must be mindful of those who would profit from his death.
故日月暈圍於外[D 祭/泰 ŋwadh/ŋwâi]，	The sun and moon are surrounded by haloes,
其賊在內[D 微/隊 nədh/nuậi]，	but their nemesis lies within them.[5]
備其所憎，	People prepare for those whom they hate,
60 禍在所愛[D 微/代 ʔədh/ʔậi]。	but their misfortune comes from those whom they love.
是故明王不舉不參之事[E 之/志 tsrjəgh/tṣï]，	Therefore, the clear-sighted ruler does not undertake uninvestigated tasks
不食非常之食[E 之/職 grjək/dźjək]；	and does not eat extraordinary foods.
遠聽而近視以審內外之失[F 脂/質 sthjit/śjĕt]，	He listens for things distant and watches for things close at hand, so that he may examine errors inside and outside the court;
省同異之言以知朋黨之分，	he looks closely into variations between proposals in order to understand the divisions between different factions;
65 偶參伍之驗以責陳言之實[F 脂/質 djit/dźjĕt]；	he conducts surprise inspections in order to take people to task for the performance of their proposals.
執後以應前[G 元/先 dzian/dzien]，	He takes final results as a basis for responding to earlier proposals;
按法以治眾，	he relies on law to order the multitudes;
眾端以參觀[G 元/桓 kwan/kuân]；	he takes many elements into account when testing and observing.
士無幸賞[H 陽/養 sthjaŋx/śjaŋ]，	When gentlemen do not get rewards by sheer luck,

---

5 They are threatened by the crow in the sun and the rabbit in the moon, respectively (see for example Crump 1996: 364n2).

CHAPTER 17

70 無踰行[H 陽/映 graŋh/ɣeŋ]；	they will not transgress;
殺必當，	when executions unfailingly accord with the acts committed
罪不赦；	and crimes are not forgiven,
則姦邪無所容其私。	the wicked will find no place for their selfish pursuits.

17 身（死）見（校注 160).　35（馳）〔馳〕（校注 160).　49 張抄 has 增 for 憎.

HF 17.3 (*Xilun* 277, *Xin jiaozhu* 323)

徭役多則民苦，	When there is much corvée labour, the people suffer hardship;
民苦則權勢起，	when the people suffer hardship, political power-play will increase;
權勢起則復除重，	when political power-play increases, the powerful will be exempted from taxes;
復除重則貴人富。	when the powerful are exempted from taxes, the noble will be enriched.
5 苦民以富貴人，	Bringing hardship to the people in order to enrich the noble,
起勢以藉人臣，	and increasing political power-play in order to appease the ministers,
非天下長利也。	are not of long-term benefit to the world.
故曰：	Therefore it is said:
徭役少則民安，	When corvée is limited, the people are at peace;
10 民安則下無重權，	when the people are at peace, subordinates have no political influence;
下無重權則權勢滅，	when subordinates have no political influence, political power-play will be eroded;
權勢滅則德在上矣。	when political power-play is eroded, virtue will be on top.
今夫水之勝火亦明矣，	Now it is evident that water wins out against fire;
然而釜鬵間之，	however, if you put pots and pans between the two,
15 水煎沸竭盡其上，	above, the water evaporates by boiling,

備內 GUARDING AGAINST THE ENEMY WITHIN

而火得熾盛焚其下，	and below, the fire is able to burn abundantly:
水失其所以勝者矣。	the water has lost that by which it conquers.
今夫治之禁姦又明於此，	Now, that proper governance prevents skulduggery is even clearer than this,
然守法之臣為釜鬵之行，	but if the ministers in charge of maintaining the law act like the pots and the pans,
20 則法獨明於胸中，	the laws will be clear only in one's breast,
而已失其所以禁姦者矣。	and will have lost their means of preventing treachery.
上古之傳言，	According to ancient transmitted accounts
《春秋》所記，	and what is recorded in *The Annals*,[6]
犯法為逆以成大姦者，	those who broke the law, committed crimes and perpetrated great treachery
25 未嘗不從尊貴之臣也。	were invariably the followers of respected and honoured ministers.
然而法令之所以備，	Yet those against whom laws and ordinances are provided,
刑罰之所以誅，	and those whom punishments and fines penalise,
常於卑賤，	are always the lowly and the base.
是以其民絕望，	This is why the people lose all hope
30 無所告愬。	and have no place to lodge their plaints.
大臣比周，	When senior ministers band together,
蔽上為一，	they are united in keeping their superior in the dark.
陰相善而陽相惡，	Secretly, they are on the best of terms, but openly, they display hatred of one another
以示無私，	in order to convey that they do not cultivate their private interests.
35 相為耳目，	They act as ears and eyes for one another
以候主隙，	and look for cracks in the ruler.
人主掩蔽，	When the ruler is kept in the dark and blocked from information,
無道得聞，	he has no way of hearing about things.

---

6 Again, "annals" may refer to the historical genre as a whole and not necessarily to the canonical Lu annals.

有主名而無實，	He is the ruler in name but not in reality.
40　臣專法而行之，	The ministers will monopolise the law and execute it.
周天子是也。	The Sons of Heaven of the Zhou were of this sort.[7]
偏借其權勢，	If the ruler lends his powers to others one-sidedly,
則上下易位矣，	superordinates and subordinates will change places.
此言人臣之不可借權勢也。	This is to say that ministers should not be lent political authority.[8]

18 〔於〕(校注 160).

---

[7] It is not clear which period Han Fei means here (but of course examples of kings who were overshadowed by their subordinates abound from ninth century on). Note that the line of the Sons of Heaven was finally extinguished in 255, probably before the composition of this chapter.

[8] This last line may be a commentary which has crept into the main text.

CHAPTER 18

南面 Facing South

HF 18.1 (*Xilun* 280, *Xin jiaozhu* 328)

人主之過，	The mistakes of the ruler
在已任臣矣，	are due to the minister he has already employed.
又必反與其所不任者備之，	If he still has to turn to someone whom he has not employed to guard against that minister,
此其說必與其所任者為讎，	then the latter's views are bound to be hostile to the former's,
5 而主反制於其所不任者。	and the ruler will in turn be controlled by the one he has not employed.
今所與備人者，	The one with whom he now guards against others
且曩之所備也。	will be the one against whom he was guarding himself before.
人主不能明法而以制大臣之威，	If the ruler is unable to clarify the law and thus to control the authority of the senior ministers,
無道得小人之信矣。	then there is no way for him to gain the confidence of ordinary people.
10 人主釋法而以臣備臣，	If the ruler discards the law and controls ministers through other ministers,
則相愛者比周而相譽，	then those who are fond of each other will band together and praise each other,
相憎者朋黨而相非。	while those who hate each other will form factions and criticise each other.
非譽交爭，	When criticism and praise compete with each other,
則主惑亂矣。	the ruler will be confounded.
15 人臣者，	Unless a minister
非名譽請謁無以進取，	is famous and can request special audiences, he will have no way to make progress and acquire clout;

非背法專制無以為威,   unless he turns his back on the law and monopolises political control, he has no way to exercise authority,

非假於忠信無以不禁,   unless he feigns loyalty and trustworthiness, he has no way of avoiding prohibitions against him.

三者,   The combination of these three

20 惛主壞法之資也。   is what helps to confuse the ruler and destroy the rule of law.

人主使人臣雖有智能,   The ruler will see to it that his ministers, even if they are knowledgeable and competent,

不得背法而專制;   will not be allowed to go against the law and monopolise control;

雖有賢行,   even if they are worthy in their demeanour,

不得踰功而先勞;   will not get to be rewarded beyond their achievements and before they have made them;

25 雖有忠信,   even if they are loyal and trustworthy,

不得釋法而不禁: they will not be allowed to disregard the law and avoid prohibitions.

此之謂明法。   This is what is called clarifying the rule of law.

2 任（在）臣 (校注 166, following 顧廣圻).

HF 18.2.0 (*Xilun* 282, *Xin jiaozhu* 330)

人主有誘於事者,   The ruler may be seduced by a project
有壅於言者,   or [his good senses] may be clogged by proposals:
二者不可不察也。   both of these points must be investigated.

HF 18.2.1 (*Xilun* 282, *Xin jiaozhu* 330)

人臣易言事者,   If a minister lightly brings up projects
少索資,   and asks for few resources,
以事誣主。   then he is cheating the ruler with this project.
主誘而不察,   If the ruler is seduced and does not investigate the matter closely,
5 因而多之,   and if, as a result, he greatly values him,
則是臣反以事制主也。   then the minister will control the ruler through his project.

如是者謂之誘，	This situation is called "being seduced."
誘於事者困於患。	If you are seduced by a project, you will be embroiled in the ensuing disaster.
其進言少，	If someone brings forward a proposal with few expenses,
10 其退費多，	but in the end the expenses turn out to be large,
雖有功，	though the project might have been successful,
其進言不信。	the proposal was not reliable.
不信者有罪，	The unreliable are guilty of a crime;
事有功者不賞，	even when the project is successful, the ruler should not reward them,
15 則群臣莫敢飾言以惛主。	so that no minister will dare to embellish his proposals in order to confuse the ruler.
主道者，	The Way of the ruler
使人臣前言不復於後，	is to see to it that when the first proposal does not correspond to the result,
後言不復於前，	and when later proposals do not correspond to the earlier ones,
事雖有功，	then even if a project is successful,
20 必伏其罪，	the minister must face criminal charges.
謂之任下。	This is called employing subordinates.

14 （必）〔不〕(校注 166, following 顧廣圻).

HF 18.2.2 (*Xilun* 283, *Xin jiaozhu* 330)

人臣為主設事而恐其非也，	When a minister wants to arrange something for the ruler, but is afraid that people will criticise him,
則先出說設言曰：	he will first circulate talk to the following effect:
"議是事者，	"Anyone who might discuss this undertaking
妒事者也。"	is just envious of it."
5 人主藏是言，	The ruler will keep these words in mind
不更聽群臣；	and will not go on to heed other ministers;
群臣畏是言，	the ministers will be frightened by these words
不敢議事。	and will not dare to discuss the undertaking.
二勢者用，	If these two tendencies take effect,

10	則忠臣不聽而譽臣獨任。	then loyal ministers will not be heeded and renowned ministers[1] will have the field to themselves.
	如是者謂之壅於言，	This situation is called 'being clogged by words';
	壅於言者制於臣矣。	when you are clogged by words, you are controlled by ministers.
	主道者，	The way of the ruler is such that
	使人臣必有言之責，	the ruler will make ministers always bear responsibility for what they propose
15	又有不言之責。	and also bear responsibility for not speaking up.[2]
	言無端末辯無所驗者，	If proposals are incoherent and arguments inconclusive,
	此言之責也；	this is a case where they have to bear responsibility for having spoken up;
	以不言避責持重位者，	if, through not speaking, they avoid responsibility and thus maintain their powerful position,
	此不言之責也。	this is a case where they have to bear responsibility for not speaking up.
20	人主使人臣言者必知其端以責其實，	The ruler should see to it that when ministers speak up, he is sure to understand their basic standpoint in order to hold them responsible for their results;
	不言者必問其取舍以為之責。	and that when they do not speak up, he interrogates them about their decisions in order to hold them responsible [for these decisions].
	則人臣莫敢妄言矣，	As a result, no ministers will dare to speak up recklessly,
	又不敢默然矣，	and similarly no minister will dare to remain quiet;
	言、默則皆有責也。	for both speaking up and remaining silent, they will be taken to task.

16 張抄 has 未 for 末.

---

1 These are, of course, unjustly renowned. Their renown stems from the fact that they effectively block criticism and by doing so mislead the ruler.
2 Han Fei is aware that ministers being held responsible for what they say will give rise to the temptation not to speak up. This is sidestepped by the simple fix of also holding people responsible for *not* speaking up when appropriate.

南面 FACING SOUTH

HF 18.3 (*Xilun* 285, *Xin jiaozhu* 331)

人主欲為事，	When a ruler personally wishes to undertake a project,
不通其端末，	and, before understanding the relevant points,
而以明其欲。	he already publicly makes clear his desire,
有為之者，	then, when he goes ahead with his undertaking,
5 其為不得利，	his action will not yield a profit;
必以害反。	he is bound to come out of it with harmful results.
知此者，	He who understands this properly
任理去欲。	will rely on principle and disregard personal desires.[3]
舉事有道，	There is a way of undertaking a project:
10 計其入多，	if you calculate that the benefit is great
其出少者，	and the costs are few,
可為也。	you should go ahead.
惑主不然，	However, the confused ruler is not like this:
計其入，	he will calculate the benefit,
15 不計其出，	but not the cost.
出雖倍其入，	Even if the costs are twice the benefits,
不知其害，	he will still not understand the harmfulness of [the undertaking].
則是名得而實亡。	As a result, he will gain on the face of it, but will in fact lose.
如是者功小而害大矣。	In this way, his achievements will be small and the harmful consequences large.
20 凡功者，	In general, with meritorious achievements,
其入多，	it is only when the benefits are relatively large
其出少，	and the costs are relatively small
乃可謂功。	that we may call them meritorious achievements.

---

[3] Here Han Fei touches on the very nerve of his intellectual *démarche*. The ruler must *ren* 任, "rely on," something, and must choose between relying on his *yu* 欲, "desires," or on the results of his political and philosophical analysis, the objective *li* 理, "underlying determining structural principles," which shape social reality. Choosing *li* comes close to choosing rationality, reason and analysis over emotion and sentimentality.

今大費無罪而少得為功，	Now, if excessive expenditure goes unprosecuted and small gain count as a meritorious achievement,
25　則人臣出大費而成小功，	then the minister will undertake great expenses in order to attain small meritorious achievements,
小功成而主亦有害。	and although the small achievements are realised the ruler will still suffer the harmful consequences.

2 張抄 has 未 for 末.

HF 18.4 (*Xilun* 286, *Xin jiaozhu* 334)

不知治者，	Those who do not understand orderly rule
必曰：	will inevitably say:
"無變古，	"Do not change the old [ways];
毋易常。"	do not replace the constant [pattern]."
5　變與不變，	As for changing or not changing,
聖人不聽，	the sage does not pay attention to that:
正治而已。	he gets the government right, and that is all.[4]
然則古之無變，	Whether you should not change the old,
常之毋易，	or replace the constant pattern
10　在常、古之可與不可。	depends on whether the old and the constant are acceptable.
伊尹毋變殷，	If Yi Yin had not changed the Yin (Shang),
太公毋變周，	and Grand Duke [Wang] had not changed the Zhou,
則湯武不王矣。	then Tang and Wu would not have become kings.[5]
管仲毋易齊，	If Guan Zhong had not changed Qi
15　郭偃毋更晉，	and Guo Yan had not revamped Jin,

4　The argumentation in this section closely parallels that adopted by Shang Yang in the famous debate over the launch of reforms in Qin in 359. See chapter 1 in the *Book of Lord Shang*.

5　Yi Yin and Grand Duke Wang 太公望 served as strategists for the founders of the Shang and Zhou dynasties, Kings Tang and Wu. Han Fei implies that their success derived from the ability to innovate and depart from traditional methods when necessary.

南面 FACING SOUTH

則桓、文不霸矣。	Lords Huan and Wen would not have become hegemons.[6]
凡人難變古者，	In general, when people object to changing the old,
憚易民之安也。	it is because they are wary of making changes to the comfort of the people.
夫不變古者，	Now, not to change the old
20　襲亂之迹；	is to continue in the footsteps of chaos;
適民心者，	satisfying the people's inclinations
恣姦之行也。	is to give free rein to treacherous conduct.
民愚而不知亂，	When the people are stupid and do not recognise chaos,
上懦而不能更，	when the superiors are fearful and cannot make reforms –
25　是治之失也。	this is a failure of good government.
人主者，	Now, if the ruler's
明能知治，	intelligence is such that he can understand good government,
嚴必行之，	and he is stern so as to carry it through invariably,
故雖拂於民，	then, as a result, even if he goes against his people,
30　必立其治。	he is bound to set up the right kind of government.[7]

6　Lords Huan of Qi and Wen of Jin. Guan Zhong's role as the architect of Lord Huan's hegemony is attested in a variety of sources (see also chapter 10, note 51). The role of Guo Yan (or Diviner Yan 卜偃) in the success of Lord Wen of Jin is not clear: in *Zuozhuan*, he is a prescient but still marginal personage, nor does he figure as a model minister in the fourth century manuscript *Fine Ministers* (*Liang chen* 良臣) from the Tsinghua University collection. By the late Warring States period, however, Guo Yan seems to have joined a series of exemplary ministers of the past. Note that his *Methods* (*fa* 法) are cited approvingly by Shang Yang in the court debate of 359 (*Book of Lord Shang* 1.2). A text attributed to him, *Guo Yan lun shi* 郭偃論士 (Guo Yan discusses gentlemen [or men-of-service]), was discovered in 1972 in Tomb 1, Yinqueshan, Linyi 臨沂銀雀山 (Shandong) (*Yinqueshan Hanmu zhujian* (*er*) 2010: 181–182; Yates 2004: 355–358).

7　Going against the people is by no means the same as not acting in the best interests of the

說在商君之內外而鐵殳，	This explains why[8] the Lord of Shang, inside and outside of court, was surrounded by iron lances
重盾而豫戒也。	and heavy shields as a precaution.
故郭偃之始治也，	Thus, when Guo Yan began to rule,
文公有官卒；	Lord Wen had official soldier guards;
35 管仲始治也，	when Guan Zhong began to rule,
桓公有武車：	Lord Huan had his armoured chariots:
戒民之備也。	these were precautionary measures to warn the people.[9]
是以愚戇窳惰之民，	Thus the people, being stupid, obtuse, slothful and lazy,
苦小費而忘大利也，	are bitter about small costs and heedless of great benefits,
40 故蚡虎受阿謗。	and consequently Yin Hu was maligned.[10]
而賑小變而失長便，	They are afraid of minor reforms and lose the advantages of longtime benefits,
故鄒賈非載旅，	and therefore Zou Jia criticised the raising of troops on the basis of landholding.
狃習於亂而容於治，	They are inured to chaos and neglect good government,
故鄭人不能歸。	and therefore the people of Zheng were unable to return.[11]

30 （心）〔必〕（校注 166）.　38 （遇）〔愚〕（贛）〔戇〕（校注 166）.

---

　　　　people. Han Fei is acutely aware that acting according to popular opinion and desire is not necessarily in the best interests of the people. See more in chapter 50.11.
8　　The standard meaning of *shuo zai* 說在, "the explanation lies in," does not seem to fit this context. The interpretation here is tentative.
9　　The precautionary steps taken by Guan Zhong, Guo Yan, and Shang Yang against potential assassins are not attested in other sources.
10　 The relevant story about Yin Hu is unknown.
11　 The last lines of this chapter aim to provide historical examples that demonstrate Han Fei's points, but seem garbled beyond comprehension.

CHAPTER 19

飭邪 Taking Measures against Deviance

HF 19.1 (*Xilun* 290, *Xin jiaozhu* 338)

鑿龜數筴，	They bored holes in tortoise shells and counted yarrow stalks,
兆曰"大吉"，	whereupon the prediction was "very auspicious,"
而以攻燕者，	and then, on this basis, they attacked Yan.
趙也。	Such was the case of Zhao.
5 鑿龜數筴，	They bored holes in tortoise shells and counted yarrow stalks,
兆曰"大吉"，	whereupon the prediction was "very auspicious",
而以攻趙者，	and then, on this basis, they attacked Zhao.
燕也。	such was the case of Yan.[1]
劇辛之事燕，	When Ju Xin served Yan,
10 無功而社稷危；	he was not successful and the altars of soil and grain were in danger;[2]
鄒衍之事燕，	When Zou Yan served Yan,
無功而國道絕。	he was not successful and the orderly ways of the state of Yan were disrupted.[3]

---

1 Yan and Zhao were enmeshed in intermittent skirmishes through much of the third century; it is pointless to try to identify which of the multiple invasions and counter-invasions is referred to here (see more in note 5 below). What matters is Han Fei's main point: both Zhao's attack on Yan and Yan's counterattack on Zhao were sanctioned as "auspicious" through divination. This speaks to the unreliability of divination.

2 Ju Xin is mentioned in the "Hereditary House of Yan" chapter of *Shiji*. He is said to have come to Yan from Zhao in the early years of King Zhao of Yan 燕昭王 (r. 312–279); later the chapter relates how he instigated a reckless attack on his former home state, which ended in a disastrous defeat in 242 or 241 (*Shiji* 34: 1558 and 1560). The anachronism is blatant and inexplicable (surely Ju Xin could not have led an army a full seventy years after the start of his career in Yan!).

3 The statement is unclear. Zou Yan is a famous philosopher who allegedly moved to Yan from Qi around the same time as Ju Xin (i.e. in the late fourth century, although the dates are disputed). Nothing is known of his failure in serving Yan.

趙代先得意於燕，	First, Zhao got their way with Yan,[4]
後得意於齊，	then they got their way with Qi.[5]
國亂節高，	Although the state was in chaos, their spirits were high;
自以為與秦提衡，	they even imagined they could be a counterweight to Qin.
非趙龜神而燕龜欺也。	This was not because the tortoise in Zhao was marvellously efficacious and the tortoise in Yan was fraudulent.[6]
趙又嘗鑿龜數筴而北伐燕，	Another time, Zhao bored holes in tortoise shells and counted yarrow stalks and then attacked Yan in the north.
將劫燕以逆秦，	They wanted to despoil Yan in order to oppose Qin,
兆曰"大吉"。	and the prediction was "very auspicious."[7]
始攻大梁而秦出上黨矣，	When they first attacked Daliang, Qin mustered her forces at Shangdang;[8]

---

4 In 260, Zhao was utterly defeated by Qin in Changping, allegedly losing more than 400,000 soldiers (chapter 1, note 20). This awful setback notwithstanding, Zhao reportedly succeeded in defeating Yan in a series of battles in the next decade. Ju Xin's plan to attack Zhao in 242 was prompted by the expectation that the new chief commander of the Zhao forces would be less experienced than his successful predecessor, Lian Po. Yan's defeat emboldened Zhao, which, in 241, launched a series of attacks against Qin (to no avail), and then against Qi, as mentioned in the following note.

5 In 241, Zhao launched a campaign against Qi and obtained a portion of territory.

6 The point is that all divination provides incoherent results. This sentence might have been misplaced: several commentators (such as Chen Qiyou) believe that its rightful place is after the mention of Zou Yan's failure.

7 A loose Qin-Yan alliance in the 240s, forged against Zhao, is reported in the *Stratagems of the Warring States* (*Zhanguo ce*) and other sources.

8 There must be some confusion in the text. Daliang is the capital of Wei, to the south of Zhao, whereas what Han Fei discusses here is Zhao's campaigns to the north against Yan. Shangdang was a territory in central Shanxi, which the state of Hán had yielded to Qin in 262, but the local governor opted to surrender to Zhao instead. This was the background of the Qin-Zhao war that culminated with the Changping campaign of 262–260 and the destruction of Zhao's army (chapter 1, note 20). The subsequent records are confused, but it seems that Qin's final annexation of Shangdang and the rest of central Shanxi came in the wake of Zhao's campaigns against Yan in the late 240s and early 230s. This point Han Fei is making is that every success of Zhao over Yan was marked by a loss of territory to Qin.

飭邪 TAKING MEASURES AGAINST DEVIANCE 237

兵至釐而六城拔矣；	when Zhao's forces had arrived at Li, six of her cities had been captured [by Qin],
至陽城，	and by the time they had arrived at Yangcheng,
秦拔鄴矣；	Qin had captured the city of Ye.[9]
25 龐援揄兵而南，	When Pang Yuan drew his weapon and marched south,
則鄣盡矣。	the city of Zhang was completely routed.[10]
臣故曰：	So I, your subject, say:[11]
趙龜雖無遠見於燕，	Even if the Zhao tortoise was not far-sighted enough to see Yan,
且宜近見於秦。	it ought to have seen Qin, which was close at hand,
30 秦以其"大吉"，	but Qin relied on its omen of "very auspicious";
辟地有實，	in opening up new territories there were real gains,
救燕有有名。	and in addition it enjoyed the good name of having saved Yan.[12]
趙以其"大吉"，	Zhao, on the other hand, relied on its omen of "very auspicious,"
地削兵辱，	but its lands were pared away and its army humiliated,
35 主不得意而死。	and its ruler[13] died in desperation.

---

9   This happened in 236. Both Li and Yangcheng are identified as Yan localities in central Hebei (i.e. to the northeast of Zhao). Ye, a major Wei stronghold (located near Linzhang 臨漳, to the north of modern Anyang), was seized by Zhao a few years before the narrated events. Zhao was expanding northeastward and eastward (toward Yan and Qi), and simultaneously losing its southern and western territories to Qin.

10 A tentative explanation for this is that Pang Yuan or Pang Juan 龐涓 was a Zhao general who moved from the Yan campaign southward toward the city of Ye to prevent its being routed; this, however, did not prevent Qin from absorbing the city of Zhang further to the east. The detailed events mentioned here are not famous episodes in Chinese history. They must have been current affairs that would have been remembered well during the 230s when Han Fei wrote his memorial. For a general account of the episode see *Shiji* 43: 1820–1821 ("Hereditary House of Zhao") which is also a confused record.

11 On Han Fei's self-reference as *chen* 臣 "I, your subject," which suggests that the present chapter was designed as a memorial to a king, see chapter 4, note 1.

12 Qin was loosely allied with Yan against Zhao (note 7 above).

13 King Daoxiang of Zhao 趙悼襄王, r. 244–236.

又非秦龜神而趙龜欺也。	This again was not because the Qin tortoise was divinely effective and the Zhao tortoise deceitful.[14]
初時者，	Before this,
魏數年東鄉攻盡陶、衛，	Wei turned towards the east, where it attacked and pillaged Tao and Wey several years in a row,
數年西鄉以失其國，	but when it turned towards the west several years in a row, the state was lost.[15]
40 此非豐隆、五行、太一、王相、攝提、六神、五括、天河、殷搶、歲星數年在西也，	This was not because Fenglong, Wuxing, Taiyi, Wangxiang, Sheti, Liushen, Wukuo, Tianhe, Yinqiang, and Suixing were due west for several years,[16]
又非天缺、弧逆、刑星、熒惑、奎台數年在東也。	nor was it because Tianque, Guni, Xingxing, Yinghuo, and Guitai[17] were in the east for several years.
故曰：	Thus it is said:
龜筴鬼神不足舉勝，	"The tortoise shells and yarrow stalks, the ghosts and deities are not sufficient to determine the course of battle;
左右背鄉不足以專戰。	the stars' being on the left or right, at your back or facing you, are not sufficient to guarantee the outcome of a battle."
45 然而恃之，	This being the case, to rely on them
愚莫大焉。	is utmost stupidity.[18]

---

14 Once again, the conclusion is not to rely on divination but rather on proper political and military calculations. Cf. Sunzi's 孫子 recommendation to prohibit divination before military campaigns (*Wu Sunzi fawei* 11: 107 ["Jiu di" 九地]).

15 The first two campaigns – against Qin's easternmost territory of Tao (or Dingtao 定陶) and against Wey – are dated by Yang Kuan (1998: 420) to 254 (chapter 6, note 8). In both cases, Wei advanced eastward, where Qin's presence was weak (especially in the aftermath of Qin's debacles depicted in chapter 1). From 242 onwards, Wei suffered a series of setbacks on an almost annual basis which resulted in the massive loss of territory to Qin (note, though, that the final collapse of Wei occurred only in 225, after Han Fei's death). Whether or not Wei's defeats after 242 were indeed prompted by its own aggressive actions against Qin as implied by Han Fei, is unverifiable.

16 All these were lucky stars.

17 These were unlucky stars. For early Chinese astronomy, see Sun Xiaochun 1997; Pankenier 2013.

18 This is arguably the single most devastating assault on his contemporaries for what Han Fei considers superstition. The proximity to Xunzi's views in chapters 6 ("Rejecting phys-

飭邪 TAKING MEASURES AGAINST DEVIANCE   239

14〔得〕(校注 179).   34（利）〔地〕(校注 180).   36 張抄 has 敗 for 欺.   41 星（非）數 (校注 180).   41 台（非）數 (校注 180, following 王先慎).

        HF 19.2 (*Xilun* 295, *Xin jiaozhu* 344)

古者先王盡力於親民，	In ancient times, the former kings did their best to be close to the people,[19]
加事於明法。	and made every effort to clarify the laws.
彼法明，	Now, if the rule of law is clear,
則忠臣勸；	loyal ministers will feel encouraged;
5 罰必，	if punishments are inescapable,
則邪臣止。	wicked ministers will be stopped.
忠勸邪止而地廣主尊者，	The loyal are encouraged, the wicked stopped; the territory is enlarged, the ruler held in esteem –
秦是也；	the state of Qin is like this.
群臣朋黨比周以隱正道行私曲而地削主卑者，	That ministers form factions and cliques so as to obscure the straight Way and to practice their selfish crookedness, lands being pared away and the ruler humbled –
10 山東是也。	the region East of the Mountain is like this.[20]
亂弱者亡，	That those who are unruly and weak will fail
人之性也；	is in accordance with human nature;
治強者王，	that those who are orderly and strong become kings
古之道也。	is the ancient way of things.

---

    iognomy" 非相) and 17 ("Discussing Heaven" 天論) is strongly evident, although Han Fei's style is much more explicit.

19 This opening phrase may sound rather alien in the context of Han Fei thought: for one thing, he quotes the former kings as models, whereas elsewhere he opposes this practice; for another, he commends these early kings for caring for the people. Perhaps this chapter's origins as a memorial to the ruler prompted Han Fei to adjust his arguments accordingly. Note also positive invocations of the "former kings" in chapters 6.3 and 25.2.

20 The area "East of the Mountain" refers here to all the states apart from Qin. The mountain in question is either Mt. Hua 華山 or Mt. Yao (Xiao) 崤山 on Qin's eastern frontier.

15 越王勾踐恃大朋之龜與吳戰而不勝，	King Goujian of Yue relied on divination using linked turtle plastrons and went to battle with Wu, but he failed to win:
身臣入宦于吳；	he was personally reduced to entering the service of Wu as a subject.
反國棄龜，	When [at last] he returned to his state, he discontinued the tortoise oracles,
明法親民以報吳，	clarified the rule of law, and cultivated close relations with the people in order to take revenge on Wu –
則夫差為擒。	as a result, Fuchai was taken prisoner.[21]
20 故恃鬼神者慢於法，	Thus those who rely on ghosts and spirits are lax about the rule of law;
恃諸侯者危其國。	those who rely on [other] regional lords endanger the state.[22]
曹恃齊而不聽宋，	Cao relied on Qi and did not listen to Song,
齊攻荊而宋滅曹。	but Qi attacked Jing (Chu) and Song routed Cao.[23]
荊恃吳而不聽齊，	Jing (Chu) relied on Wu and did not listen to Qi;
25 越伐吳而齊滅荊。	Yue attacked Wu and Qi routed Jing (Chu).[24]
許恃荊而不聽魏，	Xǔ relied on Jing (Chu) and did not listen to Wei;

---

21 This famous story of the twenty-year-long struggle between Yue, led by King Goujian, and Wu, which Goujian extinguished in 473, is one of the most celebrated sagas in Zhou history, retold (with extensive embellishment) in *Discourses of the States* (*Guoyu*), *Shiji*, and many other sources, including two recently discovered manuscripts (see chapter 17, note 4; on the new documents see chapter 7, note 8).

22 Here Han Fei outlines the dangers of relying on alliances (a point reiterated with greater clarity in chapter 49.14). The solution is to pursue policies of self-reliance: the only source of real strength is the individual wealth and power of the state itself, and not its network of alliances.

23 The tiny state of Cao was annihilated by Song in 487. There is no evidence that it relied on Qi before its extinction; Han Fei may be wrong here (and in any case, Qi did not attack Chu around 487; to the contrary, the two states were loosely allied at that time).

24 Scholars are perplexed by the obvious scribal error in the text, for Jing (i.e. Chu) was not extinguished by Qi. Of manifold solutions, the most convincing is that proposed by Zhang Jue (2011: 296–297n10). A statelet called Mao 茅 split off from Zhu 邾, another statelet in southern Shandong, in the early fifth century, during the apex of the Wu-Qi rivalry over dominance in Shandong. Although the fate of this statelet is not known, it might have been extinguished because of its reliance on Wu, which was in turn overpowered by Yue.

飭邪 TAKING MEASURES AGAINST DEVIANCE

荊攻宋而魏滅許。	Jing (Chu) attacked Song and Wei routed Xǔ.[25]
鄭恃魏而不聽韓，	Zheng relied on Wei and did not listen to Hán;
魏攻荊而韓滅鄭。	Wei attacked Jing (Chu) and Hán routed Zheng.[26]
30 今者韓國小而恃大國，	Now Hán is a small state and relies on a big state.
主慢而聽秦，	The ruler shows little energy and takes orders from Qin.
魏恃齊、荊為用，	If Wei relies on Qi and Jing (Chu) and makes use of them,
而小國愈亡。	then the small state [of Hán] will be all the more doomed to ruin.
故恃人不足以廣壤，	Thus relying on others is not sufficient for expanding territory,
35 而韓不見也。	but Hán does not realise this.
荊為攻魏而加兵許、鄢，	Jing (Chu) wanted to attack Wei and applied military force to Xǔ and Yan,
齊攻任、扈而削魏，	but Qi attacked Ren and Hu and decimated Wei.
不足以存鄭，	This was not sufficient to preserve Zheng intact,[27]
而韓弗知也。	but Hán does not understand this.
40 此皆不明其法禁以治其國，	These are all cases where [the actors] did not clarify laws and prohibitions when governing their state,
恃外以滅其社稷者也。	but relied on outside forces, thereby bringing ruin upon their altars of soil and grain.

25　The statelet of Xǔ was a Chu dependency from the sixth century; it was relocated several times by its Chu masters, moving very close to Chu's borders, near the modern city of Rongcheng, Henan, in 506. In 504, Xǔ was extinguished by Zheng, but restored soon thereafter. It is unknown whether or not Xǔ was ever occupied by Wei (if so, this would mean that Wei expanded well into Chu's defensive perimeter). Eventually, Xǔ was incorporated into Chu.

26　The destruction of Zheng by Hán occurred in 375.

27　Commentators are confused about these events; there is not even consensus as to whether "Zheng" here refers to the original state of Zheng, which was extinguished by Hán in 375, or to Hán itself (which was often called Zheng after it relocated its capital to the previous capital of Zheng). Chen Qiyou is probably right that the story should be related to the earlier mention of Zheng's over-reliance on Wei: when Wei was assaulted by Chu from the south (using its major city of Yan 鄢 [not to be confused with the state of Yan 燕] and the former state of Xǔ as a springboard for its attack) and from Qi from the east, this gave Hán the chance to extinguish Zheng.

15 （吾）〔吳〕(校注 180). 16 張抄 has 官 for 宦. 24–25 C emends 荊 to 邢, following 顧廣圻 (校注 180). See note to translation. 29 （攻魏）〔魏攻〕(校注 180).

HF 19.3 (*Xilun* 299, *Xin jiaozhu* 348)

臣故曰：	So I, your subject, say:
明於治之數，	If you are clear about the methods of orderly rule,
則國雖小，	then even if your state is small,
富；	it will be rich;
5 賞罰敬信，	if rewards and punishments are carefully considered and reliable,
民雖寡，	then even if your population is sparse,
強。	you will be strong.
賞罰無度，	If rewards and punishments are unsystematic,
國雖大，	though your state may be large,
10 兵弱者，	your armed forces will be weak –
地非其地，	the territory will not be your territory
民非其民也。	and the people will not be your people.
無地無民，	Without control of territory and people,
堯、舜不能以王，	even Yao or Shun could not come to rule as a king,
15 三代不能以強。	and the three dynasties could not have become strong.
人主又以過予，	And yet rulers confer [rewards] excessively
人臣又以徒取。	and ministers reap them undeservedly.
舍法律而言先王明君之功者，	Those who disregard laws and regulations and speak about the achievements of the former kings and clear-sighted rulers
上任之以國。	are employed by their superiors and put in charge of the state.
20 臣故曰：	So I say:
是願古之功，	This is to hope for the achievements of the ancients
以古之賞賞今之人也。	by giving men of our time rewards of the ancients.
主以是過予，	That is how rulers confer [rewards] excessively
而臣以此徒取矣。	and how the ministers reap them undeservedly.

飭邪 TAKING MEASURES AGAINST DEVIANCE

25	主過予，	If the ruler confers [rewards] excessively,
	則臣偷幸；	ministers will gain undeserved favours;
	臣徒取，	if the ministers reap undeserved rewards,
	則功不尊。	meritorious achievements will not be esteemed.
	無功者受賞，	If people without meritorious achievements receive rewards,
30	則財匱而民望；	then resources will be depleted, whereas the people will nourish [gratuitous] hopes;
	財匱而民望，	When resources are depleted, whereas the people nourish [gratuitous] hopes,
	則民不盡力矣。	then the people will not exhaust their strength.
	故用賞過者失民，	Therefore, one who excessively uses rewards will lose the people,
	用刑過者民不畏。	and one who excessively uses punishments, the people will not hold in awe.
35	有賞不足以勸，	If rewards do not suffice to encourage
	有刑不足以禁，	and punishments do not suffice to interdict,
	則國雖大，	then even if your state is large,
	必危。	you are bound to become imperilled.

23 （以主）〔主以〕(校注 180). 26 （人）〔臣〕(校注 180).

HF 19.4 (*Xilun* 300, *Xin jiaozhu* 349)

	故曰：	So it is said:
	小知不可使謀事，	Petty understanding cannot be deployed to plan [major] undertakings;
	小忠不可使主法。	men of petty loyalty cannot be put in charge of the administration of the rule of law.
	荊恭王與晉厲公戰於鄢陵。	King Gong of Jing (Chu) fought a battle against Lord Li of Jin at Yanling.[28]
5	荊師敗，	The Jing (Chu) army was defeated,
	恭王傷。	and King Gong was injured.

---

28   In 575. For another account of the same story see *Han Feizi* 10.1 and note 2 there.

酣戰，
而司馬子反渴而求飲，
其友豎穀陽奉卮酒而進之，

10　子反曰：
"去之，
此酒也。"
豎穀陽曰：
"非也。"
15　子反受而飲之。
子反為人嗜酒，
甘之，
不能絕之於口，
醉而臥。
20　恭王欲復戰而謀事，

使人召子反，
子反辭以心疾。
恭王駕而往視之，

入幄中，
25　聞酒臭而還，
曰：
"今日之戰，
寡人目親傷。
所恃者司馬，
30　司馬又如此，
是亡荊國之社稷而不恤吾眾
也。

寡人無與復戰矣。"
罷師而去之，
斬子反以為大戮。

In the heat of battle,
Marshal Zifan was thirsty and asked for a drink.
Young Servant Guyang held up a mug of ale and presented it.
Zifan said:
"Away with this.
This is ale."
Young Servant Guyang said:
"It is not ale."
Zifan took it and drank it.
Now Zifan was by nature fond of ale;
once he had got a taste for it,
he could not stop himself from drinking more.
He got drunk and fell asleep.
King Gong wanted to renew battle and make plans,
and he sent someone to summon Zifan.
Zifan declined on the grounds of chest pains.
King Gong rigged up his carriage and went to look at Zifan for himself.
When he entered the tent,
he smelled the stench of ale and turned back,
saying:
"In today's battle,
I was personally injured in the eye.
The person I relied on was the Marshal.
And now the Marshal behaves like this!
This is to ruin the altars of soil and grain in the state of Jing (Chu) and to show no concern for the multitude of my people.
I should never go to battle with him again."
He withdrew the army and left,
and had Zifan cut down in a great public execution.[29]

29　Note that according to *Zuozhuan* (Cheng 16.5l), Zifan committed suicide. Han Fei surely exaggerates here: high-ranking officials would not have been publicly executed in the aristocratic age.

飭邪 TAKING MEASURES AGAINST DEVIANCE   245

35 故曰：	So it is said:
豎穀陽之進酒也，	When Young Servant Guyang offered ale,
非以端惡子反也，	it was not that he fundamentally hated Zifan:
實心以忠愛之，	with all his heart, with loyalty, he cared for the man,
而適足以殺之而已矣。	but, as it turned out, this sufficed only to have Zifan lose his life.
40 此行小忠而賊大忠者也。	This is a case of practising petty loyalty but offending against great loyalty.
故曰：	So it is said:
小忠，	Petty loyalty
大忠之賊也。	is the foe of great loyalty.
若使小忠主法，	If you were to take charge of the rule of law by means of petty loyalties,
45 則必將赦罪以相愛，	then you would pardon criminals because of your affection for them.
是與下安矣，	In this way, you would have comfortable relations with your inferiors;
然而妨害於治民者也。	however, this is harmful to the government of the people.

HF 19.5 (*Xilun* 302, *Xin jiaozhu* 354)

當魏之方明立辟、從憲令之時，	When Wei first published the *Established laws* and followed *Foundational orders*,[30]
有功者必賞，	those who had achievements were sure to be rewarded,
有罪者必誅，	and those who had committed crimes were sure to be punished.
強匡天下，	With their strength, they kept order in the world,
5 威行四鄰；	and with authority, they conducted affairs with their neighbours,

---

30 Commentators (e.g. Chen Qiyou, 355n1) identify *Libi* 立辟 and *Xianling* 憲令 as names of a criminal law and the collection of the ruler's orders on foundational administrative principles adopted in the state of Wei, probably as part of the political and legal reforms introduced by the famous minister Li Kui 李悝 (fl. 400).

	及法慢，	but when the implementation of the law became negligent,
	妄予，	and they started making arbitrary bestowals,
	而國日削矣。	the state was progressively diminished.
	當趙之方明國律、從大軍之時，	When Zhao first published the *State Ordinances*, and followed the *Great Army*,[31]
10	人眾兵強，	the population was large and the army strong,
	辟地齊、燕；	and the state expanded its territory to Qi and Yan.[32]
	及國律慢，	When the application of the *State Ordinances* was relaxed,
	用者弱，	those who employed these regulations were weakened,
	而國日削矣。	and the state lost territory day by day.
15	當燕之方明奉法、審官斷之時，	When Yan first published its *Submitted Laws*[33] and examined the decisions of its officials,
	東縣齊國，	it made Qi its dependency in the east[34]
	南盡中山之地；	and took the entire territory of Zhongshan in the south,[35]
	及奉法已亡，	but when the *Submitted Laws* had fallen into disuse
	官斷不用，	and official decisions were not implemented,
20	左右交爭，	there was infighting in the entourage
	論從其下，	and assessments followed the advice of inferiors,
	則兵弱而地削，	so that the armed forces were weakened, lands pared away,
	國制於鄰敵矣。	and the state was effectively controlled by neighbouring enemies.[36]

---

31 In light of the parallel with the discussion of Wei above, Chen Qiyou avers that *The Great Army* 大軍 was another code, probably regulating military conduct.

32 This probably refers to Zhao's robust expansion in the late fourth to early third centuries (the apex of which was the annexation of the state of Zhongshan in 296).

33 The *Submitted Laws* (*fengfa* 奉法) might refer to a criminal code developed during the reign of King Zhao of Yan (r. 311–279), the king who restored Yan after the disastrous wars of 314–311.

34 In 284, Yan led a grand coalition against Qi. Qi was utterly defeated and the Yan general Yue Yi 樂毅 successfully occupied its capital, Linzi. This occupation came to an end in 279 due to domestic troubles in Yan.

35 This is a patent exaggeration. Zhongshan was annexed by Qi in 296.

36 Needless to say, the three examples of Wei, Zhao, and Yan are not historically accurate: the

飭邪 TAKING MEASURES AGAINST DEVIANCE

故曰：	So it is said:
25 明法者強，	Those who make clear the rule of law are strengthened;
慢法者弱。	those who are lax on the rule of law are weakened.
強弱如是其明矣，	When the conditions of strength and weakness are so clear,
而世主弗為，	yet the rulers of our day do not act accordingly,
國亡宜矣。	it is only fitting that their states should be ruined.

1 令（行）之 (校注 180, following 顧廣圻).

HF 19.6 (*Xilun* 303, *Xin jiaozhu* 355, 359)

語曰：	A proverb says:
"家有常業⟨A 葉/業 njap/njep⟩，	"When a family has a stable occupation,
雖飢不餓⟨B 歌/箇 ŋarh/ŋâ⟩；	even in famine it will not go hungry;
國有常法⟨A 葉/乏 pjap/pjwep⟩，	when a state has a stable rule of law,
5 雖危⟨B 歌/支 ŋwjar/ŋjwĕ⟩不亡。"	even in precarity, it will not be ruined."
夫舍常法而從私意，	If you set aside the stable rule of law and follow your personal opinions,
則臣下飾於智能；	ministers and subordinates will put on a show of intellect and ability.
臣下飾於智能，	When ministers and subordinates put on a show of intellect and ability,
則法禁不立矣。	laws and prohibitions will not be established.
10 是妄意之道行，	Under such conditions, the way of arbitrary thought is practised
治國之道廢也。	and the way of governing the state is abandoned.
治國之道，	According to the way of governing the state,
去害法者，	if you remove what is harmful to the rule of law,
則不惑於智能，	you will not be confused by intellect and ability
15 不矯於名譽矣。	or misled by fame.

successes and failures of these states did not follow the ups and downs in the implementation of their legal system as neatly as Han Fei asserts.

昔者舜使吏決鴻水，

先令有功而舜殺之；

In ancient times, when Shun ordered officials to control the huge floods,
if someone had an achievement before he was given orders, Shun had him killed.

禹朝諸侯之君會稽之上，

防風之君後至而禹斬之。

When Yu assembled the regional lords and rulers at Kuaiji,
the ruler of Fangfeng arrived late, and Yu had him cut down.

以此觀之，
先令者殺，
後令者斬，

則古者先貴如令矣。

From this it can be seen:
since those who acted without orders were killed
and those who were late in carrying out their orders were cut down,
the ancients prioritised and honoured conformity with the law.[37]

故鏡執清而無事[C 之/志 dzrjəgh/-jəï/dẓï]，

美惡從而比[C 脂/旨 pjidx/-jiəd/pi]焉，

衡執正而無事[C 之/志 dzrjəgh/-jəï/dẓï]，

輕重從而載[C 之/海 tsəgx/-əï/tsâi]焉。

Thus in a mirror that is kept clean and has no defect,
beauty and ugliness will come out in proper contrast;
through scales that are kept straight and are not interfered with,
relative weight will be recorded.

夫搖鏡[D 陽/映 kjiaŋh/kjeŋ]，
則不得為明[D 陽/庚 mjiaŋ/mjeŋ]；
搖衡[D 陽/庚 graŋ/-reŋ/γeŋ]，
則不得為正[D 耕/勁 tjiŋh/-jieŋ/tśjäŋ]，
法之謂也。

If you shake a mirror,
it cannot show things clearly;
if you shake the scales,
they cannot be exact.

The same applies to the laws.

故先王以道為常，

以法為本。

Thus the former kings took the Way as their constant standard
and took the rule of law as the basis.

---

37 Note again the uncharacteristic resort to former paragons as a means to justify rule by impartial standards/laws; see more in note 19 above.

飭邪 TAKING MEASURES AGAINST DEVIANCE 249

35 本治者名尊，	When the basis is properly ordered, your name will be esteemed;
本亂者名絕。	when the basis is in disarray, your name will not be handed down at all.
凡智能明通，	In general, if intellect, ability, clarity, and insight
有以則行，	have [this basis to build on], they can be put into practice;
無以則止。	if they lack it, they cannot be put into practice.
40 故智能單道，	So, intellect and ability are a way of a single person;
不可傳於人。	they cannot be passed on to others.
而道法萬全，	The Way and the law are all-encompassing,
智能多失。	whereas intellect and ability often fail.
夫懸衡而知平，	Now, by balancing scales you can tell what is even,
45 設規而知圓，	and by setting up a compass you can know what is round:
萬全之道也。	this is the all-encompassing Way.
明主使民飭於道之故，	The clear-sighted ruler causes the people to improve themselves on the basis of the Way.
故佚而有功。	In this way, he obtains his results with ease.
釋規而任巧，	Disregarding the rules and relying on skilfulness,
50 釋法而任智，	disregarding the rule of law and relying on intellect,
惑亂之道也。	this is the way of confusion and chaos.
亂主使民飭於智，	A ruler doomed to chaos causes the people to adorn themselves by intellect;
不知道之故，	he does not understand the underlying features of the Way,
故勞而無功。	and, as a result, he toils without results.

5 The role of 亡 in this (obviously rhymed) passage is unclear; possibly the line read: 雖不亡而危. 7〔下〕(校注 180). 48（佚而則）〔故佚而有〕(校注 180). 52（將）〔於〕(校注 180).

HF 19.7 (*Xilun* 306, *Xin jiaozhu* 362)

釋法禁而聽請謁，	If one disregards laws and prohibitions and agrees to special audiences,
群臣賣官於上，	ministers will sell offices above
取賞於下，	and get rewards from below.
是以利在私家而威在群臣。	Under such circumstances, profit lies with the private [ministerial] houses and authority with the ministers.
故民無盡力事主之心，	As a result, the people will not be inclined to do their best to serve their ruler
而務為交於上。	or strive to create good relations with their superiors.
民好上交，	When the people are given to striking up good relations with their superiors,
則貨財上流，	goods will flow upwards
而巧說者用。	and those who can make clever speeches will be employed.
若是，	If such things happen,
則有功者愈少。	those with real achievements will become fewer and fewer.
姦臣愈進而材臣退，	When treacherous ministers gain more and more advancement, and ministers of talent are demoted,
則主惑而不知所行，	the ruler will be confused and not know where to go,
民聚而不知所道。	and the people will form cabals and not know what Way to follow.
此廢法禁、後功勞、舉名譽、聽請謁之失也。	This is the mistake of dispensing with laws and prohibitions, demoting the meritorious and laborious, promoting the famous and illustrious, and agreeing to special audiences.
凡敗法之人，	In general, those who ruin the rule of law
必設詐託物以來親，	are bound to set up fraudulent ruses and use gifts in order to attract their associates.
又好言天下之所希有。	Moreover, they love to speak of extraordinary portentous events.

飭邪 TAKING MEASURES AGAINST DEVIANCE

此暴君亂主之所以惑也，	This is how the unruly and chaos-bound ruler becomes confused,
20 人臣賢佐之所以侵也。	and how servants and "worthy aides" trespass against their superiors.
故人臣稱伊尹、管仲之功，	Thus, if ministers praise the achievements of Yi Yin and Guan Zhong,
則背法飾智有資；	then those who turn their backs on the rule of law and adorn intellect are aided;
稱比干、子胥之忠而見殺，	if they mention Bigan's and Zixu's loyalty and readiness to face death,
則疾強諫有辭。	then those who are eager to make coercive remonstrance will have a pretext.[38]
25 夫上稱賢明，	When they first mention worthy and clear-sighted [advisors],
下稱暴亂，	and then go on to mention violent and confused [rulers],
不可以取類，	they are not to be taken as examples.
若是者禁。	Talk like this must be banned.
君之立法以為是也，	When the ruler establishes the rule of law, this is to promote what is right.
30 今人臣多立其私智以法為非者，	However, when nowadays most ministers make much of their personal intelligence and take the rule of law as wrong,
是邪以智，	this is to be wicked by means of intellect,
過法立智。	to transgress the law and establish one's own intellect.
如是者禁，	To ban behaviour like this
主之道也。	is the Way of the ruler.

28 〔者〕(校注 180).

---

38 *Han Feizi* frequently points out the hidden subversion behind the ostensibly innocent ministerial discourse (see chapter 51 in particular). For Yi Yin and Guan Zhong as two paradigmatic good ministers, see e.g. chapter 14.7; Bigan (chapter 3, note 11) and Wu Zixu (chapter 3, note 5) are paradigmatic martyrs of loyalty. Han Fei notes that invocations of these paragons can serve the ministers' sinister motives.

HF 19.8 (*Xilun* 307, *Xin jiaozhu* 366)

明主之道，	It is the Way of the clear-sighted ruler
必明於公私之分，	to make clear the distinction between the selfish and the impartial,
明法制，	to clarify laws and regulations,
去私恩。	and to do away with private favours.
5 夫令必行，	Now, that orders be invariably carried out
禁必止，	and prohibitions be invariably obeyed –
人主之公義也；	that is the impartial moral principles promoted by the ruler;
必行其私，	that they invariably carry out their private purposes,
信於朋友，	are faithful to their friends,
10 不可為賞勸，	and cannot be encouraged through rewards
不可為罰沮，	or hindered through fines –
人臣之私義也。	these are the selfish moral principles of the minister.
私義行則亂，	When selfish moral principles are practised, there is chaos;
公義行則治，	when impartial moral principles are practised, there is order –
15 故公私有分。	thus the impartial and the selfish are distinct.
人臣有私心，	A minister has selfish inclinations,
有公義。	but also has impartial moral principles.
脩身潔白而行公行正，	To cultivate oneself so as to become pure and to practise impartiality and uprightness
居官無私，	to conduct official duties without selfishness –
20 人臣之公義也；	these are the impartial moral principles of the minister.
汙行從欲，	To be turbid in conduct and to follow his desires,
安身利家，	to seek safety for his person and profit for his house –
人臣之私心也。	these are the selfish inclinations of a minister.
明主在上，	When there is a clear-sighted ruler on top,

飭邪 TAKING MEASURES AGAINST DEVIANCE   253

25 則人臣去私心行公義；	the ministers discard their selfish inclinations and practise impartial moral principles;
亂主在上，	when a chaos-bound ruler is in charge,
則人臣去公義行私心。	the ministers will discard impartial moral principles and act out their selfish inclinations.
故君臣異心，	Thus, ruler and minister having different inclinations,
君以計畜臣，	the ruler will domesticate his ministers through calculations,
30 臣以計事君，	and ministers will serve the ruler through calculations,
君臣之交，	relations between rulers and ministers
計也。	being based on calculations.
害身而利國，	Harming his personal interests to profit the state
臣弗為也；	is something a minister will refuse to do;
35 害國而利臣，	harming the state to profit his ministers
君不行也。	is something the ruler will not do.
臣之情，	The minister's basic sense is
害身無利；	that to harm his person is not profitable;
君之情，	the ruler's basic feeling is
40 害國無親。	that if he harms the state, he will have nobody close to him.
君臣也者，	The relationship between a ruler and his ministers
以計合者也。	is one of matching calculations.
至夫臨難必死，	When it comes to facing difficulties and being prepared to risk their lives,
盡智竭力，	exhausting their intellect and expending their strength –
45 為法為之。	this is something they do because of the law.
故先王明賞以勸之，	Therefore, the former kings clarified rewards in order to encourage [the people]
嚴刑以威之。	and made punishments severe in order to assert their authority over them.
賞刑明，	When rewards and punishments are made clear,

則民盡死；	the people will [be prepared to] exhaust themselves to death.
50 民盡死，	When the people [are prepared to] exhaust themselves to death,
則兵強主尊。	the army will be strong and the ruler respected.
刑賞不察，	When punishments and rewards are not seen clearly,
則民無功而求得，	the people will seek rewards without real achievements
有罪而幸免，	and will aim to escape punishment when they have committed a crime;
55 則兵弱主卑。	under such conditions, the army will be weak and the ruler debased.
故先王賢佐盡力竭智。	Thus the worthy aides of the former kings gave their best and exhausted their intelligence.
故曰：	So it is said:
公私不可不明，	"You must be clear about impartiality and selfishness;
法禁不可不審，	you must investigate laws and prohibitions."
60 先王知之矣。	The former kings understood this.

1（禁）〔明〕(校注 180). 35（富）〔害〕(校注 180, with 意林 quotation). 56 陳啓天 suspects that some text is missing here.

CHAPTER 20

解老 Explaining Laozi

HF 20.1.1 (*Xilun* 313, *Xin jiaozhu* 370)[1,2]

德者，	Virtue
內也。	is something within;
得者，	attainment
外也。	is something outside.
5 "上德不德"，	"The person of highest Virtue does not cultivate Virtue"
言其神不淫於外也。	means that your spirit does not dissipate itself outside.
神不淫於外，	When your spirit does not dissipate itself outside,
則身全。	your person remains whole.
身全之謂德。	Your person's remaining whole is called Virtue.
10 德者，	Virtue
得身也。	is attaining full possession of your person.
凡德者，	In general, Virtue
以無為集，	coalesces through non-assertive action
以無欲成，	and attains completion through the absence of desires;
15 以不思安，	it achieves its inner balance through the absence of reflection
以不用固。	and reaches firm self-assurance by not being exercised.
為之欲之，	If you assert yourself through action and desire things,

---

1 Chapters 20–21 present two very different versions of exegesis on *Laozi* – the earliest extant exegesis on this text. There is much debate about the authorship of the two (Lundahl 1992: 218–240; Zheng Liangshu 1993: 196–244; Queen 2013). It is highly likely that the two chapters were not penned by a single author, although it is of course possible that they were written by the same author at very different periods of his life. In any case, chapter 21, which "explicates" *Laozi* through historical anecdotes, is more closely aligned with the rest of *Han Feizi* than chapter 20.

2 Section 1 of the chapter comments on *Laozi* 38 (following the numeration of the stanzas in Wang Bi's edition).

則德無舍；	Virtue will have nowhere to dwell;
德無舍，	if Virtue has nowhere to dwell,
20 則不全。	you will not be whole.
用之思之，	If you exert yourself and reflect on things,
則不固；	you will not have firm self-assurance;
不固，	if you do not have firm self-assurance,
則無功；	you will have no merit.
25 無功，	To have no merit
則生於德。	comes from Virtue.
德則無德。	If you cultivate Virtue, you will lack Virtue.
不德則有德。	If you do not cultivate Virtue, you will possess Virtue.
故曰：	So it is said:
30 "上德不德，	"The highest Virtue does not assert itself as Virtue.
是以有德。"	Therefore one comes to possess Virtue."

28 張抄 has 得 for 德。　28 則（在）有 (校注 210, with 張榜本).

HF 20.1.2 (*Xilun* 314, *Xin jiaozhu* 372)

所以貴無為無思為虛者，	The reason for valuing non-assertiveness in action, lack of reflection and the cultivation of emptiness[3] so highly,
謂其意無所制也。	is that your innermost thoughts must not be controlled by anything.
夫無術者，	Now, those who do not have the proper technique
故以無為無思為虛也。	insist on using non-assertiveness and non-reflection to cultivate emptiness.
5 夫故以無為無思為虛者，	Now, if you insist on using non-assertiveness and non-reflection in order to cultivate emptiness,

---

3 Emptiness is unprejudiced openness and receptive sensibility to circumstance.

其意常不忘虛，	then your innermost thoughts will be constantly mindful of emptiness –
是制於為虛也。	this is to be controlled by the cultivation of emptiness.
虛者，	Emptiness
謂其意無所制也。	means having thoughts that are not controlled by anything.
10 今制於為虛，	Now, to be controlled by deliberate emptiness –
是不虛也。	this is not emptiness.
虛者之無為也，	When a person who is 'empty', he is non-assertive,
不以無為為有常。	but he does not make this non-assertiveness into a constant rule.
不以無為為有常，	If you do not make non-assertiveness your constant rule
15 則虛；	then you will be 'empty'.
虛，	When you are empty,
則德盛；	you will be suffused with Virtue.
德盛之謂上德。	When you are suffused with Virtue, that is called superior Virtue.
故曰：	So it is said:
20 "上德無為而無不為也。"	"The man of superior Virtue practises non-assertive action, but there is nothing that does not get done."

2 （所無）〔無所〕(校注 210, with 張榜本).   5 故 is read as 固.

HF 20.1.3 (*Xilun* 315, *Xin jiaozhu* 374)

仁者，	"Kind-heartedness"
謂其中心欣然愛人也；	means that you care for others with a glad heart,
其喜人之有福，	that you are delighted when others meet with good fortune,

而惡人之有禍也；	and that you are displeased when others meet with misfortune.[4]
5　生心之所不能已也，	It originates in what the mind cannot stop.
非求其報也。	And it does not, in fact, seek reward.
故曰：	So it is said:
"上仁為之而無以為也。"	"The man of superior kind-heartedness acts, but does not thereby take any assertive action."

HF 20.1.4 (*Xilun* 316, *Xin jiaozhu* 374)

義者，	"Righteousness"
君臣上下之事，	determines the interaction[5] between ruler and minister, superior and inferior;
父子貴賤之差也，	it determines the difference between father and son, the noble and the base;
知交朋友之接也，	it determines the interchange between acquaintances and friends;
5　親疏內外之分也。	it determines the distinctions between close and distant, inner and outer.
臣事君宜，	When the minister serves his ruler, that is appropriate;
下懷上宜，	when inferiors are concerned about superiors, that is appropriate;
子事父宜，	when sons serve their fathers, that is appropriate;
賤敬貴宜，	when the base show respect to the noble, that is appropriate;
10　知交友朋之相助也宜，	when acquaintances and friends help each other, that is appropriate;
親者內而疏者外宜。	when those who are close are kept on the inside and those who are distant are kept outside, that is appropriate.
義者，	"Righteousness"
謂其宜也，	is taken to refer this appropriateness.[6]

4　Han Fei provides a remarkably analytic definition of *ren* 仁 as a quintessentially psychological concept.

5　The use of the word "service" here is indeed unusual. Some editions have *li* 禮 "ritual" instead which makes for much easier reading.

6　It is generally assumed that *yi* 義 and *yi* 宜 are etymologically related.

解老 EXPLAINING LAOZI

宜而為之。	When something is appropriate, do it.[7]
15 故曰：	So it is said:
"上義為之而有以為也。"	"The man of superior moral principle acts and with a definite aim."

4 張抄 has 夫 for 知。 7 〔宜〕（校注 210, following 盧文弨）。 9 （眾）〔賤〕（校注 210–211）。

HF 20.1.5 (*Xilun* 318, *Xin jiaozhu* 376)

禮者，	"Ritual"
所以貌情也，	is that through which one gives perceptible form[8] to inner feelings;
群義之文章也，	it is the manifestation in visible patterns of the various forms of moral principle;
君臣父子之交也，	it is constitutive of the relation between rulers and ministers, fathers and sons;
5 貴賤賢不肖之所以別也。	it is that through which the noble and the base, the worthy and the unworthy are kept apart.
中心懷而不諭，	One feels things in one's heart, but does not verbalise them,
故疾趨卑拜而明之；	and so one expresses them through scuffling and low bowing.
實心愛而不知，	One really loves things in one's in one's heart, but does not understand them,
故好言繁辭以信之。	and so one likes to speak in prolix phrases in order to demonstrate one's faith in them.
10 禮者，	"Ritual"
外飾之所以諭內也。	is that through which external ornament expresses what is inside.

---

7 *Han Feizi* sees moral principle, or rectitude, as having its justification outside itself. It is justified through appropriateness of action. Thus moral principle is not technically an end in and of itself. It is justified in terms of something other.

8 Han Fei takes the crucial concept of ritual as something linked to outward expression rather than inner feeling. On this point many ritualists would deeply disagree with him.

故曰：
禮以貌情也。

凡人之為外物動也，
15 不知其為身之禮也。

眾人之為禮也，
以尊他人也，
故時勸時衰。

君子之為禮，
20 以為其身；
以為其身，
故神之為上禮；

上禮神而眾人貳，
故不能相應；
25 不能相應，
故曰：
"上禮為之而莫之應。"

眾人雖貳，
聖人之復恭敬盡手足之禮也不衰。

30 故曰：
"攘臂而仍之。"

So it is said:
"Ritual is designed to give perceptible form to inner feelings."

In general, a person motivated by mere external things
does not understand the ritual practices for governing his person.

When ordinary people practise ritual propriety,
it is in order to honour other people.
As a result, sometimes they are encouraged, sometimes they fail through negligence.

When the superior man practises ritual,
it is in order to govern his person.
Since he does it in order to govern his person,
he makes a spiritual practice of it and practises superior ritual.[9]

Superior ritual is spiritual, but the common people are unearnest.
That is why they cannot respond to each other [properly].
They cannot respond to each other properly;
so it is said:
"When you practise superior ritual no one will properly respond to it."

Although the common people are unearnest,
the sage, in his repeated demonstrations of veneration and respect, and in his consummate ritual movements of hands and feet, neglects not the slightest detail.

So it is said:
"He rolls up his sleeves and carries on the tradition."

2 〔情貌〕〔貌情〕(校注 211). 7 〔其〕〔故〕(校注 211). 11 張抄 has 論 for 外. 11 〔節〕〔飾〕(校注 211). 13 〔情貌〕〔貌情〕(校注 211). 19 〔以〕〔之〕(校注 211).

---

9 The notion of "superior ritual" is not present in ancient Chinese ritual literature.

解老 EXPLAINING LAOZI

HF 20.1.6 (*Xilun* 320, *Xin jiaozhu* 376)

道有積而積有功;	The Way has something it accumulates, and accumulation gives results.
德者,	"Virtue"
道之功。	is a result achieved through the Way.
功有實而實有光;	In this result there is a concrete reality, and from this concrete reality there emerges an outward radiation.
5 仁者,	"Kind-heartedness"
德之光。	is the outward radiation of Virtue.
光有澤而澤有事;	Behind this outward radiation there is an inner abundance, and from this there emerges realisation in action.
義者,	"Righteousness"
仁之事也。	is the realisation in action of kind-heartedness.
10 事有禮而禮有文;	Each form of action has its own ritual propriety, and for each form of ritual propriety there is decorous patterning.
禮者,	"Ritual"
義之文也。	is the decorous patterning of moral principle.
故曰:	So it is said:
"失道而後失德,	"Only when the Way is lost, is Virtue lost;
15 失德而後失仁,	only when Virtue is lost, is kind-heartedness lost;
失仁而後失義,	only when kind-heartedness is lost, is moral principle lost;
失義而後失禮。"	only when moral principle is lost, is ritual propriety lost."[10]

1 (德)〔積〕(校注 211, following 顧廣圻).

---

10 *Laozi* 38, tr. D.C. Lau 1982: 57 is radically different:
故失道而後德,   Hence when the way was lost there was Virtue;
失德而後仁,   when Virtue was lost there was benevolence;
失仁而後義,   when benevolence was lost there was rectitude;
失義而後禮。   when rectitude was lost there were the rites.

HF 20.1.7 (*Xilun* 321, *Xin jiaozhu* 379)

禮為情貌者也，	Ritual provides an outer shape for feelings;
文為質飾者也。	decorous patterning provides outer ornamentation for the inner substance.
夫君子取情而去貌，	Now, the superior man opts for inner reality or feeling and dismisses outer form;
好質而惡飾。	he is fond of substance and dislikes ornamentation.
5 夫恃貌而論情者，	Now, if you rely on outer form to assess inner feelings,
其情惡也；	that must be because the inner feelings are bad;
須飾而論質者，	if you wait to see outer ornaments to assess inner substance,
其質衰也。	that is because the inner substance has degenerated.
何以論之？	How does one explain this?
10 和氏之璧，	Mr He's jade disk[11]
不飾以五采；	was not decorated with the five colours;
隋侯之珠，	the Marquis of Sui's pearl[12]
不飾以銀黃。	was not decorated in "silver and yellow."[13]
其質至美，	These substances were so superbly exquisite
15 物不足以飾之。	that other things were not deemed sufficient to decorate them.

Han Feizi's version makes incisive analytical sense once one appreciates that only after the Way is lost does there arise any spiritual power that may or may not be lost, and the same goes for the other constituents of the chain.

11 For Mr He's jade disc, see chapter 13.

12 The story goes that a Lord of Sui (which is normally transcribed 隨), cured and saved the life of a giant injured snake or dragon. As a token of gratitude, the snake gave him a peerlessly beautiful pearl. Many versions of this story are told and alluded to across ancient Chinese literature. Sui was located near modern Suizhou Municipality 隨州, Hubei. It is an alternative name for the polity of Zeng 曾, familiar from the series of remarkable archeological discoveries there from the 1970s on.

13 There are conflicting views on what exactly "silver and yellow" refers to, but general agreement on the fact that it must refer to precious ornaments.

解老 EXPLAINING LAOZI

夫物之待飾而後行者， Anything that depends on decoration to become acceptable
其質不美也。 must not already have an exquisite basic substance.
是以父子之間， Therefore, between father and son,
其禮樸而不明， ritual is plain and simple, not shiny.
故曰禮薄也。 So it is said: "Ritual propriety is of slight importance."

凡物不並盛， In general, things do not thrive at the same time –
陰陽是也； Yin and Yang are cases in point.
理相奪予， Their principle is reciprocal giving and taking,
威德是也， and authority and Virtue are like this.
實厚者貌薄， When the inner reality is solid, the outer manifestation is of slight importance –
父子之禮是也。 the relation between father and son as expressed in ritual is a case in point.

由是觀之， From this point of view,
禮繁者， when ritual is elaborate,
實心衰也。 it is because the mind has deteriorated.

然則為禮者， And so those who created rituals
事通人之樸心者也， were people who comprehensively understood the plain and simple mind that is pervasive among men.

眾人之為禮也， When the common people practise ritual propriety,
人應則輕歡[A 元/桓 hwan/xuân]， they are elated and pleased when others respond;
不應則責怨[A 元/願 ?wjanh/?jwen]。 they recriminate and complain when they do not respond.

今為禮者事通人之樸心而資之以相責之分， Those who nowadays practice ritual propriety and whose task is to work at the simple mind common to all, on the contrary abet people in angrily blaming each other[14] –
能毋爭乎？ can that fail to lead to competition and conflict?

---

14 I find this phrase opaque, and my translation is tentative.

	有爭則亂，	If there is competition and conflict, then there is disorder.
	故曰：	So it is said:
	"夫禮者，	"'Ritual'
40	忠信之薄也，	is the attenuation of loyalty and good faith,
	而亂之首乎。"	and it is the beginning of disorder."

19 〔樸〕(校注 211). 35 分 is read as 忿.

HF 20.1.8 (*Xilun* 323, *Xin jiaozhu* 383)

	先物行先理動之謂前識。	If you act before things arise, if you move before principles are manifest – that is called foreknowledge.
	前識者，	Foreknowledge
	無緣而妄意度也。	is an arbitrary way of assessing without good reason.
	何以論之？	How can I explain this?
5	詹何坐，	Zhan He was sitting
	弟子侍，	with his disciple in attendance.
	牛鳴於門外。	An ox was lowing outside the gate.
	弟子曰：	The disciple said:
	"是黑牛也而白題。"	"This is a black ox with a white forehead."
10	詹何曰：	Zhan He said:
	"然，	"Yes,
	是黑牛也，	it is a black ox,
	而白在其角。"	but the white is on its horns."
	使人視之，	He sent someone out to have a look at it.
15	果黑牛而以布裹其角。	Indeed, it was a black ox with its horns wrapped in cloth.
	以詹子之術，	Now, to use the special skills of Master Zhan
	嬰眾人之心，	to impose yourself on the minds of the common people
	華焉殆矣。	is an ostentatious and dangerous course.

解老 EXPLAINING LAOZI

故曰：	So it is said:
20 "道之華也。"	"[Foreknowledge] is an ostentatious deployment of the Way."[15]
嘗試釋詹子之察，	Suppose you try to leave aside the astuteness of Zhanzi
而使五尺之愚童子視之，	and send a stupid five-foot boy to look at it,
亦知其黑牛而以布裹其角也。	even he would understand that it is a black ox with horns wrapped in cloth.
故以詹子之察，	Thus, with the astuteness of a Zhanzi,
25 苦心傷神，	this man overtaxed his mind and injured his spirit
而後與五尺之愚童子同功，	before achieving the same result as the stupid boy.
是以曰"愚之首也"。	Therefore it is said: "It is the beginning of stupidity."
故曰：	So it is said:
"前識者，	"Foreknowledge
30 道之華也，	is only an ostentatious display of the Way,
而愚之首也。"	and the beginning of stupidity."

3 C has 忘 for 妄.　17 嬰 is read as 攖.

HF 20.1.9 (Xilun 325, Xin jiaozhu 385)

所謂"大丈夫"者，	The "great man"
謂其智之大也。	refers to the greatness of his intellect.
所謂"處其厚不處其薄"者，	"Dwelling in what is thick in substance, not in what is flimsy"
行情實而去禮貌也。	means working with basic inner reality and rejecting the outer aspects of ritual.

15　Curiously, *Han Feizi* only quotes part of the relevant passage, which he quotes in full below. *Laozi* 38; tr. D.C. Lau 1982: 57:
　　前識者，　　　Foreknowledge
　　道之華　　　is the flowery embellishment of the way
　　而愚之始。　And the beginning of folly.

5 　所謂"處其實不處其華"者，	"Dwelling in realities and not in ostentatious ornamentation"
必緣理不徑絕也。	means making sure to cleave to the path of principle and not break off midway.
所謂"去彼取此"者，	"Rejecting that and opting for this"
去貌、徑絕而取緣理、好情實也。	means rejecting outer aspects and breaking off midway, and opting for cleaving to principle and favouring basic realities.
故曰：	So it is said:
10 　"去彼取此。"	"Reject this and opt for that."[16]

HF 20.2.1 (*Xilun* 326, *Xin jiaozhu* 386)

人有禍，	When you suffer a disaster,
則心畏恐；	you will feel fear in your heart;
心畏恐，	when you feel fear in your heart,
則行端直；	your actions will be upright and straight;
5 　行端直，	when your actions are upright and straight,
則思慮熟；	your reflections and plans will be mature;
思慮熟，	when your reflections and plans are mature,
則得事理。	you will apprehend the principles of things.
行端直，	When your actions are principled and straight,
10 　則無禍害；	there will be no disasters or harm;
無禍害，	when there are no disasters or harm,
則盡天年。	you will complete your allotted span of life.
得事理，	When you apprehend the principles of things,
則必成功。	you will be sure to attain achievements.
15 　盡天年，	If you complete your allotted span of life,
則全而壽。	you will be unharmed and long-lived.
必成功，	If you are sure to attain achievements,
則富與貴。	you will be wealthy and noble.

16　　*Laozi* 38; see also *Laozi* 12.

解老 EXPLAINING LAOZI

全壽富貴之謂福。 — Health and long life, wealth and nobility are called good fortune,

20 而福本於有禍。 — and good fortune has its basis in bad fortune.
故曰： — So it is said:
"禍⟨A 歌/果 gwarx/yuâ⟩兮福之所倚⟨A 歌/紙 ?jarx/?jě⟩。" — "Bad fortune is what good fortune depends on."[17]
以成其功也。 — This is how you achieve success.[18]

19 〔貴〕(校注 211).

HF 20.2.2 (*Xilun* 327, *Xin jiaozhu* 387)

人有福， — When a man has good fortune,
則富貴至[A 脂/至 tjidh/tśji]； — wealth and nobility will come to him;
富貴至， — when wealth and nobility come to him,
則衣食美[A 脂/旨 mjidx/mji]； — then clothing and food will be elaborate and beautiful;
5 衣食美， — when clothing and food are elaborate and beautiful,
則驕心生； — an arrogant attitude will arise;
驕心生， — when an arrogant attitude arises,
則行邪僻[B 佳/昔 phjik/-jiek/phjäk]而動棄理[B 之/止 ljəgx/lǐ]。 — one's conduct will be wicked and one's actions will disregard Principle.

行邪僻， — When your conduct is wicked,
10 則身死夭； — you will die an early death;
動棄理， — when your actions disregard Principle,
則無成功。 — you will not attain any achievement.

夫內有死夭之難， — Now if, close at hand, you suffer the adversity of dying early,
而外無成功之名者， — and, abroad, you are not famous for achieving anything,
15 大禍也。 — that is a disaster.

---

17 Section 2 of the chapter comments on *Laozi* 58. See also *Lüshi chunqiu* 6.4 ("Zhi yue" 制樂).
18 Tsuda Hōkei 津田鳳卿 and Ōta Hō 太田方 suspect that this line is an intrusion from later commentaries on *Han Feizi* (Zhang Jue 2011: 327).

而禍本生於有福。

故曰：

"福⟨C之/屋 pjək/pjuk⟩兮禍之所伏⟨C之/屋 bjək/bjuk⟩。"

And so the roots of disaster are born of having good fortune.
So it is said:
"Good fortune is where bad fortune hides."

4〔則〕(校注 211)．　8〔行〕(校注 211)．　9 The C editors note:「行」字上疑脫「衣食美則行邪辟」句。

HF 20.2.3 (*Xilun* 328, *Xin jiaozhu* 388)

夫緣道理以從事者，

無不能成。
無不能成者，
大能成天子之勢尊，

5　而小易得卿相將軍之賞祿。

夫棄道理而妄舉動者，

雖上有天子諸侯之勢尊，

而下有猗頓、陶朱、卜祝之富，
猶失其民人而亡其財資也。

10　眾人之輕棄道理而易妄舉動者，

Now, when you accord with the principles of the Way in conducting affairs,
there is nothing you cannot achieve.
If there is nothing you cannot achieve,
then, as the maximum, you may achieve the position and honour of the Son of Heaven,
and, as a minimum, you may easily obtain the rewards and stipends of a high minister or general.

Now, one who disregards the principles of the Way and takes arbitrary initiatives,
even if, at the top level, he has the position and honour of a Son of Heaven or regional lord,
or, on a lower level, he has the wealth of Yi Dun, Tao Zhu, diviners or ritual impersonators,[19]
he will still fail to have control of his population and will lose his resources.

If the common people easily disregard the principles of the Way, and lightly engage in arbitrary initiatives,

---

19　Both Yi Dun and Tao Zhu (actually, Sire Zhu from Tao 陶朱公) were renowned for their wealth. It is very odd, however, to see diviners and ritual impersonators presented as epitomising wealth.

解老 EXPLAINING LAOZI   269

不知其禍福之深大而道闊遠若是也，	then they do not understand the depth and extent of bad and good fortune, and how broad and far-reaching the Way is.
故諭人曰：	Therefore [the text] instructs people, saying:
"孰知其極？"	"Who understands the ultimate?"

1 張抄 has 天 for 夫.　6 張抄 has 忘 for 妄.　8 而（天）下（校注 211).　9 張抄 has 射 for 財.　10 張抄 has 忘 for 妄.

HF 20.2.4 (*Xilun* 329, *Xin jiaozhu* 388)

人莫不欲富貴全壽，	Everyone desires to be wealthy and noble and to have sound health and a long life,
而未有能免於貧賤死夭之禍也。	but no one can ever be sure to avoid poverty, turpitude, and early death.
心欲富貴全壽，	In their minds, they desire to be wealthy, noble and to have sound health and a long life,
而今貧賤死夭，	but now they are poor and downtrodden, and die early.
5　是不能至於其所欲至也。	This is because they are unable to reach what they wish to reach.
凡失其所欲之路而妄行者之謂迷，	In general, when you have lost the path that you seek and walk at random, it is called 'going astray'.
迷則不能至於其所欲至矣。	Having gone astray, you will be unable to reach what you wish to reach.
今眾人之不能至於其所欲至，	Now, the masses are unable to reach what they wish to reach,
故曰：	so it is said:
10　"迷。"	"They have gone astray."
眾人之所不能至於其所欲至也，	The masses have been unable to reach what they wish to reach
自天地之剖判以至于今。	from the separation of Heaven and Earth to the present time.
故曰：	So it is said:
"人之迷也，	"People have indeed been going astray
15　其日故以久矣。"	for a long time."

3 C mistakenly has 必 for 心; cf. 校注 189, 陳奇猷 and 張覺.   6 The C editors note:「欲」字下疑應有「至」字。.   15 張抄 has 曰 for 日.   15 故 is read as 固.   15 以 is read as 已.

HF 20.2.5 (*Xilun* 330, *Xin jiaozhu* 390)

所謂方者，	"Square"
內外相應[A 蒸/證 ʔjəŋh/ʔjəŋ]也，	means that the inner and the outer correspond to each other,
言行相稱[A 蒸/證 thjəŋh/tśhjəŋ]也。	that proposals and actions match each other.
所謂廉者，	"Modest"
5 必生死之命也，	means taking the fate of life and death as inevitable
輕恬資財也。	and thinking lightly of assets and goods.
所謂直者，	"Straight"
義必公正，	means that one's moral principles are inevitably impartial and straight
公心不偏黨也。	and that one's impartial attitude does not turn to factionalism.
10 所謂光者，	"Glory"
官爵尊貴，	means that one's office and rank are elevated and noble,
衣裘壯麗也。	and that one's robes and coats are stately.
今有道之士，	Now, the gentlemen who possess the Way,
雖中外信順，	even if they are inwardly faithful and outwardly obedient,
15 不以誹謗窮墮；	will not publicly criticise or slander those who are in straits and fail.
雖死節輕財，	Even if they are prepared to die for their morality and think little of material wealth,
不以侮罷羞貪；	they will not humiliate those who are exhausted or shame the greedy.
雖義端不黨，	Even if they are straight in their moral principles and not partisan,
不以去邪罪私；	they will not remove the wicked or condemn the selfish.

解老 EXPLAINING LAOZI

20 雖勢尊衣美，   Even if they hold distinguished positions of power and wear elaborate and beautiful clothes,
不以夸賤欺貧。   they will not show off to the humble or cheat the poor.
其故何也？   Why is this?
使失路者而肯聽習問知，   Suppose someone who has lost his way is willing to listen to the experienced or ask the knowledgeable –
即不成迷也。   he will not go completely astray.
25 今眾人之所以欲成功而反為敗者，   Now the fact that the common people want to achieve results, but, contrary to their desire, fail in their pursuits
生於不知道理而不肯問知而聽能。   arises from their failure to understand the principles of the Way and their unwillingness to ask the knowledgeable or listen to the capable.

眾人不肯問知聽能，   When the common people are unwilling to ask the knowledgeable and listen to the capable,
而聖人強以其禍敗適之，   and the sage insists on castigating them for the resulting disasters,
則怨。   they will be resentful.

30 眾人多而聖人寡，   The common people are many and sages are few.
寡之不勝眾，   That the minority do not overcome the majority
數也。   is a question of numbers.
今舉動而與天下之為讎，   Now to act and become the enemy of the whole world,
非全身長生之道也，   is not the way to keep your body intact and achieve a long life.

35 是以行軌節而舉之也。   That is why the sage acts according to established paths of behaviour when he undertakes things.
故曰：   So it is said:
"方而不割，   "He is square but does not scrape,
廉而不劌，   is modest but does not jab,
直而不肆，   is straight but not unrestrained,
40 光而不耀。"   shines but does not bedazzle."

28 適 is read as 謫.   38 〔穢〕〔劌〕(校注 211).

HF 20.3.1 (*Xilun* 333, *Xin jiaozhu* 394)

聰明睿智，	Sharp hearing, clarity, acuity and intellect
天[A 真/先 thin/thien]也；	depend on Heaven;
動靜思慮，	Taking action or desisting, reflecting and planning
人[A 真/真 njin/ńźjěn]也。	depend on man.
5 人也者，	People
乘於天明以視，	avail themselves of clarity from Heaven[20] in order to see,
寄於天聰以聽，	rely on sharp hearing from Heaven in order to hear,
託於天智以思慮。	and count on intellect from Heaven in order to reflect and plan.
故視強，	Now if, in looking, a person expends too much effort,
10 則目不明；	his eyes will not have clarity;
聽甚，	if, in listening, he strains too much,
則耳不聰；	his ears will not have sharp hearing;
思慮過度，	if, in reflecting and planning, he transgresses the proper measure,
則智識亂。	his intelligence and knowledge will be confused.
15 目不明，	If his eyes do not have clarity,
則不能決黑白之分；	he cannot determine the difference between black and white;
耳不聰，	if his ears do not have sharp hearing,
則不能別清濁之聲；	he cannot distinguish between pure and turbid tones;
智識亂，	if his intelligence and knowledge are confused,
20 則不能審得失之地。	he cannot distinguish the points of gain and loss.
目不能決黑白之色則謂之盲[B 陽/庚 mraŋ/meŋ]，	If his eyes cannot determine the colours black and white, he is called blind;
耳不能別清濁之聲則謂之聾[B 東/東 luŋ > luaŋ ?/luŋ]，	if his ears cannot distinguish between pure and impure tones, he is called deaf;
心不能審得失之地則謂之狂[B 陽/陽 gwjiaŋ/gjwaŋ]。	if his mind cannot distinguish the points of gain and loss, he is called mad.

---

20   That one possesses a feature "from Heaven" is a traditional way of saying that feature is "part of one's natural endowment."

解老 EXPLAINING LAOZI 273

盲，	If he is blind,
25 則不能避晝日之險；	he is unable to avoid dangers in broad daylight;
聾，	if he is deaf,
則不能知雷霆之害；	he is unable to understand the harm involved in thunder;
狂，	if he is mad,
則不能免人間法令之禍。	he is unable to avoid the disasters brought on by the laws and ordinances for men.
30 書之所謂"治人"者，	The person whom the book calls 'he who governs the people'[21]
適動靜之節，	adapts to the proper rhythm of action and inaction,
省思慮之費也。	and is sparing in the exercise of reflection and planning;
所謂"事天"者，	the person who is referred to as 'he who serves Heaven'
不極聰明之力，	does not exhaust his powers of hearing and sight
35 不盡智識之任。	nor the power of his intelligence and knowledge.
苟極盡，	If he exercises his abilities to the utmost,
則費神多；	he will expend a great deal of spiritual energy;
費神多，	if he expends a great deal of spiritual energy,
則盲聾悖狂之禍至：	the disasters of blindness, deafness, confusion and madness will arise.
40 是以嗇之，	This is why the sage uses them sparingly.
嗇之者，	That 'he is sparing'
愛其精神，	is because he is chary of[22] his subtle inner energies
嗇其智識也。	and sparing in the use of intelligence and knowledge.

21　The chapter thrice refers to *Laozi* as "the book," or "the text" (*shu* 書). Such a reference to *Laozi* (or, more generally, to the Masters' texts) is unattested in pre-Qin literature. It also serves as a clear indication that the author of "Jie Lao" chapter commented on a written text (Queen 2013: 202).

22　*Ai* 愛 "1. Take loving care of; 2. be stingy with" not only has these two meanings, but often combines them.

故曰：
45 "治人事天莫如嗇。"

So it is said:
"In governing others and serving Heaven it is best to be sparing."²³

HF 20.3.2 (*Xilun* 335, *Xin jiaozhu* 395)

眾人之用神也躁，

躁則多費，
多費之謂侈。
聖人之用神也靜，
5 靜則少費，
少費之謂嗇。
嗇之謂術也，
生於道理。

夫能嗇也，
10 是從於道而服於理者也。

眾人離於患，
陷於禍，
猶未知退，
而不服從道理。
15 聖人雖未見禍患之形，

虛無服從於道理，

以稱蚤服。

故曰：
"夫謂嗇⟨A 之/職 srjək/sjək⟩，
20 是以蚤服⟨A 之/屋 bjək/bjuk⟩。"

The common people are impatient in the exercise of their spirit.
If they are impatient, they expend too much.
Using up a great deal is called excessiveness.
The sage, in his exercise of his spirit, is calm.
If he is quiet, he uses up little.
Using up little is called being sparing.
The technique of being sparing
arises from the principles of the Way.

Someone who has the ability to be sparing
is someone who has decided to follow the Way and submit to Principle.

The common people are exposed to disasters
and trapped in misfortune,
but still do not know how to retreat
and do not follow the principles of the Way.
Even when he has not yet seen the manifestations of disaster, the sage
cultivates emptiness and nothingness, and decides to follow the principles of the Way,
so that it may be said that 'he submits in good time'.

So it is said:
"Now it is because he is sparing
that he submits in good time."

7 謂 is read as 為.   19 謂 is read as 唯.

---

23   Section 3 of the chapter comments on *Laozi* 59.

解老 EXPLAINING LAOZI

HF 20.3.3 (*Xilun* 336, *Xin jiaozhu* 396)

知治人者，	As for a person who knows how to govern others,
其思慮靜；	his reflections and plans are calm;
知事天者，	as for one who knows how to serve Heaven,
其孔竅虛。	his apertures are receptively empty.
5　思慮靜，	His reflections and plans are calm,
故德不去；	and therefore Virtue does not leave him;
孔竅虛，	his apertures are receptively empty,
則和氣日入。	and thus the harmonious cosmic energy will enter him every day.
故曰：	So it is said:
10　"重積德。"	"He builds up Virtue many times over."
夫能令故德不去，	A person who is able to ensure that the original Virtue does not depart
新和氣日至者，	and that the new harmonious vital energy arrives every day,
蚤服者也。	is one who has submitted (to the Way) in good time.
故曰：	So it is said:
15　"蚤服⟨A 之 / 屋 bjək/bjuk⟩是謂重積德⟨A 之 / 德 tək/tək⟩。"	"To submit in good time – this is called building up one's Virtue many times over."
積德而後神靜，	Only after you have accumulated Virtue does the spirit become calm;
神靜而後和多，	only after the spirit is calm does harmony increase;
和多而後計得，	only after harmony is increased can you achieve what you plan;
計得而後能御萬物，	only after you make plans and achieve your aims can you steer the myriad things.
20　能御萬物則戰易勝敵，	If you can steer the myriad things, then in battle you will easily overcome your opponents;
戰易勝敵而論必蓋世，	if you easily overcome your opponents in battle, then your views are bound to spread throughout the world.
論必蓋世，	Your views are bound to spread throughout the world,
故曰：	so that it is said,

"無不克₍A之/德 khək/khək₎"。　"There is nothing you cannot overcome."

25　無不克₍A之/德 khək/khək₎本於重積德₍A之/德 tək/tək₎，　[A state where] nothing cannot be overcome is based on accumulating Virtue.
故曰：　So it is said:
"重積德₍A之/德 tək/tək₎，　"Build up your Virtue many times over,
則無不克₍A之/德 khək/khək₎"。　so that there is nothing you cannot overcome."[24]

戰易勝敵，　If, in battle, it is easy to overcome your opponent,
30　則兼有天下；　then you will control All-under-Heaven;
論必蓋世，　when your views are bound to spread throughout the world,

則民人從。　the people will follow.
進兼天下而退從民人，　If, when advancing, you can annex All-under-Heaven, and, when retreating, you can make the people follow,

其術遠，　and if your technique of governance is concerned with the long term,
35　則眾人莫見其端末。　then none among the common people will see the beginning and the end of [your strategies].

莫見其端末，　No one sees the beginnings and ends [of your strategies],

是以莫知其極。　so no one knows your ultimate goal.[25]
故曰：　So it is said:
"無不克₍A之/德 khək/khək₎，　"If nothing cannot be overcome,
40　則莫知其極₍A之/職 gjək/gjək₎。"　none will know your ultimate goal.

35　〔末〕（校注 211）.

HF 20.3.4 (*Xilun* 337, *Xin jiaozhu* 397)

凡有國而後亡₍A 陽/陽 mjaŋ/mjaŋ₎之，　In general, when you have a state and then lose it,
有身而後殃₍A 陽/陽 ʔjaŋ/ʔjaŋ₎之，　when you have a body and then ruin it,

---

24　Here again, the more extensive quotation follows the shorter quotation.
25　The *ji* 極 "ultimate point" is the overall long-term and far-reaching significance or ambition of the ruler's undertakings.

解老 EXPLAINING LAOZI   277

　　不可謂能有其國、能保其身。　　you cannot be said to be capable of possessing a
　　　　　　　　　　　　　　　　　　state or capable of safeguarding your body.

　　夫能有其國[B之/德 kwək/kwək]，　　If you are able to control your state,
5　必能安其社稷[B之/職 tsjək/tsjək]；　then you must be able to ensure the safety of the
　　　　　　　　　　　　　　　　　　altars of soil and grain;26
　　能保其身[C 真/真 sthjin/śjĕn]，　　being able to safeguard your body,
　　必能終其天年[C 真/先 nin/nien]；　you must be able to live out your allotted span.
　　而後可謂能有其國[B之/德
　　　kwək/kwək]、能保其身[C 真/真
　　　sthjin/śjĕn]矣。   Only then can you be said to be able to possess
                                      the state and safeguard your body.
　　夫能有其國，   For one who is able to possess a state
10　保其身者，   and safeguard his body
　　必且體道。   must have embodied the Way.
　　體道，   If you have embodied the Way,
　　則其智深；   your intellect is deep;
　　其智深，   if your intellect is deep
15　則其會遠；   your calculations are far-reaching;
　　其會遠，   if your calculations are far-reaching,
　　眾人莫能見其所極。   none among the common people can see your
                                      ultimate goal.
　　唯夫能令人不見其事極[B之/職
　　　gjək/gjək]，   Only then can you can cause others not to see the
                                      ultimate goal of your undertakings –
　　不見其事極者為保其身、有其   not having others who see the ultimate goal of
　　　國[B之/德 kwək/kwək]。   your undertakings, is safeguarding your body and
                                      possessing the state.
20　故曰：   So it is said:
　　"莫知其極⟨B之/職 gjək/gjək⟩。   "No one knows your ultimate goal.
　　莫知其極⟨B之/職 gjək/gjək⟩，   When no one knows your ultimate goal,
　　則可以有國⟨B之/德 kwək/kwək⟩。"   you can possess the state."

18 張抄 has 天 for 夫.　19〔其〕(校注 211).

　　HF 20.3.5 (*Xilun* 338, *Xin jiaozhu* 398)

　　所謂"有國之母"：   When it says "the mother of controlling the state":
　　母者，   the mother in question

26　These altars are the ritual symbols of state.

道也；　　　　　　　　　　　is the Way.
道也者，　　　　　　　　　　The Way
5 生於所以有國之術，　　　　is born of the techniques by which you possess the state.

所以有國之術，　　　　　　They are the techniques by which you possess a state

故謂之"有國之母"。　　　　and they are therefore called "the mother of possessing the state."[27]

夫道以與世周旋者，　　　　If the Way is the means by which you interact with the people of the world,

其建生也長，　　　　　　　then you will be able to establish your life for a protracted time,

10 持祿也久。　　　　　　　and you will be able to maintain your emoluments for a long time.

故曰：　　　　　　　　　　So it is said:
"有國之母⟨A之/厚 məgx/mǎu⟩，　"With the mother of controlling the state,
可以長久⟨A之/有 kjəgx/kjŏu⟩。"　you can be long-lasting."

樹木有曼根，　　　　　　　A tree[28] has entwining roots
15 有直根。　　　　　　　　as well as straight roots.
直根者，　　　　　　　　　The straight roots
書之所謂"柢"也。　　　　　are what the book calls 'the basic root'.
柢也者，　　　　　　　　　The basic root
木之所以建生也；　　　　　is that through which the tree establishes its life;
20 曼根者，　　　　　　　　the intertwined roots
木之所以持生也。　　　　　are those through which it maintains its life.[29]

德也者，　　　　　　　　　Virtue
人之所以建生也；　　　　　is that by which a man establishes his life;
祿也者，　　　　　　　　　emoluments
25 人之所以持生也。　　　　are the means by which a man maintains his life.
今建於理者，　　　　　　　Now, someone who has his foundation in Principle[30]

27　Deriving the Way from the concept of the art of proper government deliberately overturns the conventional ways of understanding the relation between these two things.

28　Note the use of the explicitly general or abstract binome *shumu* 樹木 "a tree."

29　The Chinese use of the word *sheng* 生 "life" refers to the state of being alive rather than the subject of a "bio"graphy.

30　This notion of *li* 理 "Principle" is one of the conspicuous keywords in the present chap-

解老 EXPLAINING LAOZI

其持祿也久，	will maintain his emoluments for long.
故曰：	So it is said:
"深其根。"	"Set your roots deep."
30 體其道者，	As for someone who embodies the Way,
其生日長，	the days of his life will be long.
故曰：	So it is said:
"固其柢。"	"Make firm your roots."
柢固，	When the basic roots are firm,
35 則生長，	life will be long;
根深，	when the roots are deep,
則視久。	existence will be long-lasting.
故曰：	So it is said:
"深其根，	"Setting the roots deep
40 固其柢，	and making firm the basic roots,
長生久視之道也。"	is the way of long life and long-lasting existence."[31]

16 〔直〕(校注 211, following 俞樾). 21 〔以〕(校注 211). 41 張抄 has 不 for 長.

HF 20.4.1 (*Xilun* 340, *Xin jiaozhu* 400)

工人數變業則失其功，	When a craftsman repeatedly changes his trade, he will lose his effectiveness;
作者數搖徙則亡其功。	when a labourer repeatedly wavers and moves about, he will have no results.
一人之作，	When one man doing labour
日亡半日，	wastes half of every day,
5 十日則亡五人之功矣；	in the course of ten days he will have wasted the fruit of the labour of five men.
萬人之作，	When ten thousand men doing labour
日亡半日，	waste half of every day,
十日則亡五萬人之功矣。	in ten days they will have wasted the fruit of the labour of fifty thousand men.

---

ter. It refers to the underlying pattern things make, the underlying structure of things that determines their superficial appearance.

31 Again, the partial quotations precede the complete quotation.

然則數變業者，
其人彌眾，
其虧彌大矣。

凡法令更則利害易，

利害易則民務變，

務變之謂變業。
故以理觀之：
事大眾而數搖之，

則少成功；
藏大器而數徙之，

則多敗傷；
烹小鮮而數撓之，
則賊其澤；
治大國而數變法，

則民苦之。
是以有道之君貴靜，

不重變法。
故曰：
"治大國者若烹小鮮。"

18 張抄 has 徒 for 徙.

Thus, when it comes to those who change their trade,
the more people who do this
the greater the loss.

In general, when the laws and ordinances are altered, the conditions of advantage and disadvantage will change.
When conditions of advantage and disadvantage change, the people will seek political change.
Seeking change is called 'changing the agenda'.
Thus if you look at this in terms of Principle:
when employing the great multitudes, if you make them waver frequently,
their achievements will be few;
when you hide a great vessel but you shunt it about frequently,
it will often be ruined or damaged;
when you fry a small fish and frequently stir it,
you destroy its visual richness;
when governing a large state, if you frequently change the laws,
the people will find this hard to bear.
Therefore the ruler who has grasped the Way sets great store by calm
and will not repeatedly change the laws.[32]
So it is said:
"Governing a large state is like frying a small fish."[33]

---

32   This way of reading *jing* 靜 "mystical calm" as political conservatism and consistency represents pretty much exactly the kind of political reading of *Laozi* that one would expect from Han Fei.

33   Section 4 of the chapter comments on *Laozi* 60.

解老 EXPLAINING LAOZI

HF 20.4.2 (*Xilun* 341, *Xin jiaozhu* 402)

人處疾則貴醫，	When a person is beset by illness, he values doctors;
有禍則畏鬼。	if there is a disaster, he dreads ghosts.
聖人在上，	When a sage is at the top,
則民少欲；	the people will have few desires;
5 民少欲，	when the people have few desires,
則血氣治而舉動理；	their blood and vital spirits will be well settled and their actions principled;
舉動理則少禍害。	when their actions are principled, there will be few disasters.
夫內無痤疽癉痔之害，	When there is no harm from ulcers or boils internally,
而外無刑罰法誅之禍者，	and if there is no misfortune from punishment, fines, laws, or executions externally,
10 其輕恬鬼也甚。	they will very smugly disregard the ghosts.
故曰：	So it is said:
"以道涖天下，	"When you govern the world in accordance with the Way,
其鬼不神。"	the ghosts will not display their numinous force."
治世之民，	The people of an age in good order
15 不與鬼神相害也。	do not enter into harmful conflict with the ghosts and spirits.
故曰：	So it is said:
"非其鬼不神也，	"It is not that the ghosts have no numinous force –
其神不傷人也。"	it is that the spirits do not harm men."
鬼祟也疾人之謂鬼傷人，	When the ghosts wreak misfortune, those who are ill say that ghosts harm men;
20 人逐除之之謂人傷鬼也。	when men exorcise these ghosts and drive them away, it is said that men harm ghosts.
民犯法令之謂民傷上，	When the people offend against the laws and ordinances, it is said that the people harm their superiors;
上刑戮民之謂上傷民。	when superiors execute the people, it is said that superiors harm the people.
民不犯法，	When the people do not offend against the law,

則上亦不行刑；	their superiors will also not carry out punishments;
25 上不行刑之謂上不傷人。	when superiors do not carry out punishments, it is said that superiors do not harm the people.
故曰：	So it is said:
"聖人亦不傷民。"	"The sage will also not harm the people."
上不與民相害，	Superiors and people do not harm each other,
而人不與鬼相傷，	and men and ghosts do not hurt each other.
30 故曰：	So it is said:
"兩不相傷。"	"The two do not hurt each other."
民不敢犯法，	When the people do not dare to offend against the laws,
則上內不用刑罰，	superiors do not, on the inside, punish them,
而外不事利其產業。	and, outside, do not seek profit from the people's work.
35 上內不用刑罰，	If superiors do not employ punishments inside,
而外不事利其產業，	and do not seek profit from the people's work outside,
則民蕃息。	then the people will flourish.
民蕃息而畜積盛。	When the people flourish, their accumulated supplies will be plentiful.
民蕃息而畜積盛之謂有德。	When the people flourish and their accumulated supplies are plentiful, it will be said that you have Virtue.[34]
40 凡所謂祟者，	In general, what are called 'noxious influences'
魂魄去而精神亂，	happen when the *hun* and *po* souls have left the body and the subtle spirits are in disarray.[35]
精神亂則無德。	When the subtle spirits are confused, there is no Virtue.

---

34 The (untranslatable) *de* 德 "virtue" in the ruler, manifests itself in the flourishing of the general population. Han Fei relegates what is mysterious and profound to the status of a mere prerequisite for the political. And this is very much in accordance with his overall intellectual scheme.

35 The *hun* and *po* are respectively the anima and corporeal soul, the bifurcation between which is often conceptualised as the bifurcation between the *yang* and *yin* powers.

解老 EXPLAINING LAOZI

鬼不祟人則魂魄不去，	When the ghosts do not exercise their noxious influence on people, the souls do not leave the body.
魂魄不去而精神不亂，	When the souls do not leave the body, the subtle spirits are not confused.
45 精神不亂之謂有德。	When one's subtle spirits are not confused, it is said that there is Virtue.
上盛畜積而鬼不亂其精神，	If superiors have accumulated plentiful supplies and the ghosts do not confuse their subtle spirits,
則德盡在於民矣。	then Virtue will be fully present among all the people.
故曰：	So it is said:
"兩不相傷，	"When the two[36] do not hurt each other,
50 則德交歸焉。"	Virtue will assemble in that place."
言其德上下交盛而俱歸於民也。	This means that Virtue and benign influence among superiors and inferiors is bountifully knit together and completely converges on the people.

7 〔舉動理〕(校注 211–212). 18 〔人〕(校注 212). 19 張抄 has 崇 for 祟. 21 張抄 has 人 for 之. 40 張抄 has 崇 for 祟. 51 張抄 has 得 for 德.

HF 20.5.1 (Xilun 343, Xin jiaozhu 405)

有道之君，	A ruler who has mastered the Way
外無怨讎於鄰敵，	has no bitter enemies among his neighbouring rivals,
而內有德澤於人民。	and, within his state, he shows benign generosity towards the people.
夫外無怨讎於鄰敵者，	If he has no bitter enemies among his neighbouring rivals abroad,
5 其遇諸侯也外有禮義。	then when he meets the regional lords, he shows proper outward ritual propriety and righteousness.
內有德澤於人民者，	If, within his state, he shows benign generosity towards the people,

---

36 The sage and humans; see the previous line: 聖人亦不傷人 "The sage also does not harm other people."

其治人事也務本。	then, in ordering the business of others, he attends to the fundamentals.
遇諸侯有禮義，	If he shows ritual propriety and righteousness when he meets the regional lords,
則役希起；	then his conscript troops will rarely be brought out.
10 治民事務本，	If he attends to what is basic when ordering the business of the people,
則淫奢止。	then wantonness and extravagance will cease.
凡馬之所以大用者， 外供甲兵而內給淫奢也。	In general, the great usefulness of the horse is that outside [on the battleground], it delivers armour and weapons, and, inside [at court], it provides for wantonness and extravagance.
今有道之君，	Now, the ruler who mastered the Way
15 外希用甲兵，	will rarely deploy armoured forces on the battleground,
而內禁淫奢。	and, at court, he will prohibit wantonness and extravagance.
上不事馬於戰鬥逐北，	If those above do not employ their horses in war or in pursuit of the defeated,
而民不以馬遠淫通物，	and if the people[37] do not use horses to indulge in extravagance to reach special goods in distant places,
所積力唯田疇。	then what they concentrate all their efforts on is their fields.
20 積力於田疇， 必且糞灌。	If their efforts are concentrated on their fields, they are bound to fertilise and irrigate them.
故曰：	So it is said:
"天下有道，	"If the Way prevails in the world,
卻走馬以糞也。"	fleet-footed horses are used [to transport] nothing but fertiliser."[38]

20 〔積力於田疇〕 (校注 212).

---

[37] This nicely illustrates that the group referred to as *min* 民 "the people" could be wealthy enough to own and ride horses.

[38] Section 5 of the chapter comments on *Laozi* 46.

解老 EXPLAINING LAOZI

HF 20.5.2 (*Xilun* 345, *Xin jiaozhu* 406)

人君無道，	When the ruler has not mastered the Way,
則內暴虐其民，	he will be violent and cruel to the people within his state
而外侵欺其鄰國。	and he will invade and cheat the neighbouring states abroad.
內暴虐[A 宵/藥 ŋjakw/ŋjak]，	If he is violent and cruel within his state,
5 則民產絕[A 祭/薛 dzjuat/dzjwät]；	the people's productivity will be disrupted;
外侵欺[B 之/之 khjəg/khï]，	if he invades and cheats other states abroad,
則兵數起[B 之/止 khjəgx/khï]。	his armed forces will often be raised.
民產絕，	When the people's productive work is disrupted,
則畜生少；	domestic animals will be few;
10 兵數起，	when the army is repeatedly raised,
則士卒盡。	officers and men will be exhausted.
畜生少，	When domestic animals are few,
則戎馬乏；	warhorses will be in short supply;
士卒盡，	when officers and men are exhausted,
15 則軍危殆。	the military situation will be precarious.
戎馬乏，	When warhorses are in short supply,
則將馬出；	the commander's horses will be sent [into battle];
軍危殆，	when the military situation is precarious,
則近臣役。	courtiers will have to do military service.
20 馬者，	"Horses"
軍之大用；	are what the military uses on a large scale;
郊者，	"Suburb"
言其近也。	means that the place is close.
今所以給軍之具於將馬近臣。	Now, an army is equipped by its commander's horses and [the ruler's] courtiers –
25 故曰：	so it is said:
"天下無道⟨C 幽/晧 dəgwx/dâu⟩，	"When the Way does not prevail in the world,
戎馬生於郊⟨C 宵/肴 kragw/kau⟩ 矣。"	warhorses are born the suburbs."

1 無道（道）(校注 212).   17, 24 C emends 將 to 牸 with 顧廣圻 (校注 212). We see no reason to emend.

HF 20.5.3 (*Xilun* 346, *Xin jiaozhu* 407)

人有欲，	When men have strong desires,[39]
則計會亂；	their calculations and plans become confused;
計會亂，	when their calculations and plans are confused,
而有欲甚；	the strong desires they have grow even stronger;
5 有欲甚，	when the strong desires they have grow even stronger,
則邪心勝；	the wickedness in their minds wins the day;
邪心勝，	when the wickedness in their minds wins the day,
則事經絕；	they break of midway in their tasks;
事經絕，	when they break off midway in their tasks,
10 則禍難生。	disasters and troubles arise.
由是觀之，	From this point of view,
禍難生於邪心，	disasters and troubles arise from wickedness in the mind,
邪心誘於可欲。	and wickedness in the mind is provoked by what is desirable.
可欲之類，	When the sorts of things that are desirable
15 進則教良民為姦，	are promoted, they lead decent people to become evil;
退則令善人有禍。	when they are disapproved of, they cause good people to be led into calamity.
姦起，	When wickedness arises,
則上侵弱君；	then they will encroach upon weak rulers above;
禍至，	when disasters arrive,
20 則民人多傷。	then many among the people will be hurt.
然則可欲之類，	Thus, when it comes to the sort of things that are desirable,
上侵弱君而下傷人民。	above, they will encroach upon weak rulers and below, they will hurt the people.
夫上侵弱君而下傷人民者，	Now, to encroach upon weak rulers above and to hurt the people below
大罪也。	is the greatest of crimes.

---

39   *Yu* 欲 are typically non-essential desires, the essential ones being referred to as *qing* 情.

解老 EXPLAINING LAOZI

25　故曰： So it is said:
　　"禍莫大於可欲"。 "Nothing is more conducive to disaster than what is desirable."[40]
　　是以聖人不引五色， Therefore a sage is not seduced by the five colours;
　　不淫於聲樂； he is not made wanton by music.
　　明君賤玩好而去淫麗。 The clear-sighted ruler despises beautiful playthings and abjures wanton beauty.

HF 20.5.4 (*Xilun* 348, *Xin jiaozhu* 407)

　　人無毛羽， Man has neither fur nor feathers.
　　不衣則不犯寒； If he does not wear clothes, he cannot brave the cold.
　　上不屬天而下不著地， He does not belong to Heaven above and does not adhere to Earth below.
　　以腸胃為根本， The bowels and the stomach are the root and trunk of his existence;
5　不食則不能活； if he does not eat, he cannot survive.
　　是以不免於欲利之心。 Therefore, he inevitably has a mind preoccupied with material benefits.
　　欲利之心不除， That his urge for material benefits is not removed
　　其身之憂也。 is a consequence of his concern for his body.
　　故聖人衣足以犯寒， Therefore, if the sage has enough clothes to brave the cold
10　食足以充虛， and enough food to fill what is empty in him,
　　則不憂矣。 then he will not have serious cause for concern.
　　眾人則不然， The common people are not like this.
　　大為諸侯， Even if they become as distinguished as regional lords,
　　小餘千金之資， or at least have assets of over a thousand pieces of gold,
15　其欲得之憂不除也。 their greedy concerns are still not removed.
　　胥靡有免， A minor culprit may escape punishment;

40　*Laozi* 46, according to the Mawangdui version, has 罪莫大於可欲, which one might try to render as "nothing is more guilty than that which is desirable." This would fit our context better than what we read. Indeed, it has been suggested that the *huo* 禍 in all editions should be emended to *zui* 罪.

死罪時活， a criminal guilty of death will at times survive.
今不知足者之憂終身不解。 However, the worries of someone who does not know what is enough are never dispelled.

故曰： So it is said:
20 "禍莫大於不知足。" "No misfortune is greater than not knowing what is enough."

HF 20.5.5 (*Xilun* 349, *Xin jiaozhu* 407)

故欲利甚於憂， Therefore, if the urge for material benefits is excessively strong, there is concern;

憂則疾生； if there is concern, exigency arises;
疾生而智慧衰； and when exigency arises, intelligence declines;
智慧衰， if intelligence declines,
5 則失度量； you lose your ability to make assessments;
失度量， if you lose your ability to make assessments,
則妄舉動； you will take reckless initiatives;
妄舉動， if you take reckless initiatives,
則禍害至； then disaster and harm will come your way;
10 禍害至而疾嬰內； when disaster and harm come your way, exigency will tie you down inside;

疾嬰內， when exigency ties you down inside,
則痛禍薄外； painful disasters will assail you from the outside;
痛禍薄外， when painful disasters assail you from the outside,

則苦痛雜於腸胃之間； bitterness and pain are commixed in your bowels and stomach;
15 苦痛雜於腸胃之間， when bitterness and pain are commixed in your bowels and stomach,

則傷人也憯。 this will hurt a person severely;
憯則退而自咎， if you are severely afflicted, you will withdraw and blame yourself.

退而自咎也生於欲利。 Withdrawing and blaming yourself arises from concupiscence.

故曰： So it is said:
20 "咎莫憯於欲利。" "No disaster is more severe than that of concupiscence."

1 於 of all editions is read as 則, with 于鬯 and 張覺.　11 嬰 is read as 纓.

解老 EXPLAINING LAOZI

HF 20.6 (*Xilun* 350, *Xin jiaozhu* 411)

道[A 幽/晧 dəgwx/dâu]者，	The Way
萬物之所然也，	is what makes the myriad things what they are
萬理之所稽也。	and what gives the myriad Principles coherence.
理[A 之/止 ljəgx/lǐ]者，	Principle
成物之文也；	is the pattern that brings things to completion;[41]
道[A 幽/晧 dəgwx/dâu]者，	the Way
萬物之所以成也。	is that through which the myriad things are completed.
故曰：	So it is said:
"道⟨A 幽/晧 dəgwx/dâu⟩，	"The Way
理⟨A 之/止 ljəgx/lǐ⟩之者也。"	is what gives pattern and Principle to things."[42]
物有理，	If things have inherent Principles,
不可以相薄；	they cannot interfere with each other.
物有理不可以相薄，	Things have Principles and cannot interfere with each other,
故理之為物之制。	and that is why Principle acts as the organising force of things.[43]
萬物各異理，	Each of the myriad kinds of things has its different Principles
而道盡稽萬物之理，	and the Way thoroughly coordinates the Principles of the myriad things,
故不得不化；	and so they will inevitably be transformed.
不得不化，	They are inevitably transformed,
故無常操。	so they have no constant standard of behaviour.
無常操，	They have no constant standard of behaviour;
是以死生氣稟焉，	therefore they receive the cosmic energies of death and life from the Way.
萬智斟酌焉，	All forms of intellect and deliberations are based on it [the Way].
萬事廢興焉。	All undertakings are come to naught or flourish on the basis of the Way.

---

41 This definition of principle clearly makes the term into a metaphysical concept, indeed bringing it surprisingly close to Platonism. See Lau 1989.

42 This sentence does not appear in the current recensions of *Laozi*.

43 As Chen Qiyou has noticed, the first *zhi* 之 is redundant and has somehow crept into the text. As it stands I would say the text is ungrammatical.

天得之以高，	By obtaining the Way, Heaven is high,
25 地得之以藏[B 陽/唐 dzaŋ/dzâŋ]，	By obtaining the Way, Earth stores her energies.
維斗得之以成其威[C 微/微 ʔwjəd/-jəd, -jəiʔ/ʔjwěi]，	By obtaining the Way, the Great Dipper achieves its authority.
日月得之以恆其光[B 陽/唐 kwaŋ/kwâŋ]，	By obtaining the Way, the sun and moon shine eternally.
五常得之以常其位[C 微/至 gwjədh/jwi]，	By obtaining the Way, the Five Constants constantly hold their places.
列星得之以端其行[B 陽/庚 graŋ/γeŋ]，	By obtaining the Way, the stars hold to their courses.
30 四時得之以御其變氣[C 微/未 khjədh/khjěi]，	By obtaining the Way, the four seasons control the vital transforming energies.
軒轅得之以擅四方[B 陽/陽 pjaŋ/pjaŋ]，	By embodying the Way, Xuanyuan (the Yellow Thearch)[44] was able to participate in it and assumed control of the Four Regions.
赤松得之與天地統，	By embodying the Way, Red Pine achieved unity with Heaven and Earth.[45]
聖人得之以成文章[B 陽/陽 tjaŋ/tśjaŋ]。	By embodying the Way, the sages achieved the decorous patterning of public display.
道，	The Way
35 與堯、舜俱智，	manifests itself as intellect insofar as it is attached to Yao and Shun,
與接輿俱狂[B 陽/陽 gwjiaŋ/gjwaŋ]，	as madness insofar as it is attached to Jieyu,
與桀、紂俱滅，	destruction insofar as it is attached to Jie and Zhòu,
與湯、武俱昌[B 陽/陽 thjaŋ/tśhjaŋ]，	as a constructive element insofar as it is attached to Tang and Wu.
以為近乎，	Should it be considered close?
40 遊於四極[D 之/職 gjək/gjək]；	It roams among the four extremities of the universe.
以為遠乎，	Should it be considered far?
常在吾側[D 之/職 tsrjək/tsjək]；	It is always at your side.
以為暗乎，	Should it be considered dark?
其光昭昭；	It shines resplendently.
45 以為明乎，	Should it be considered bright?

---

44 Xuanyuan is the personal name of the Yellow Thearch (chapter 8, note 15).

45 The Red Pine Master 赤松子 is a famous immortal, eventually incorporated into Daoist religion (Smith 2014).

解老 EXPLAINING LAOZI

其物冥冥[E 耕/青 miŋ/mieŋ]。 　　　　Its nature is dark and mysterious.
而功成天地, 　　　　　　　　　　And so the works of Heaven and Earth are achieved,
和化雷霆[E 耕/青 diŋ/dieŋ], 　　　　and the Way soothes and transforms even violent thunder.
宇內之物, 　　　　　　　　　　　　All creatures in the universe
50 恃之以成[E 耕/清 djiŋ/źjäŋ]。　　 depend on it to be completed.

凡道之情, 　　　　　　　　　　　　In general, it is the essence of the Way
不制不形[E 耕/青 giŋ/γieŋ], 　　　 that it does not dominate things or take definite shape.
柔弱隨時, 　　　　　　　　　　　　It is pliable and soft, follows the seasons,
與理相應[E 蒸/證 ʔjəŋh > -ʔjiəŋh ʔ/ʔjəŋ]。 and corresponds to the inherent principles of things.
55 萬物得之以死, 　　　　　　　　　 By obtaining the Way, the myriad things die;
得之以生[E 耕/庚 sriŋ/ṣeŋ]; 　　　 by obtaining it, they live.
萬事得之以敗, 　　　　　　　　　　By obtaining it, the myriad undertakings fail;
得之以成[E 耕/清 djiŋ/źjäŋ]。 　　 by obtaining it, they succeed.

道譬諸若水, 　　　　　　　　　　　The Way may be likened to water:
60 溺者多飲之即死, 　　　　　　　　if a drowning man drinks too much of it, he will die;
渴者適飲之即生[E 耕/庚 sriŋ/ṣeŋ]; if someone is thirsty and drinks moderately, he will live.
譬之若劍戟, 　　　　　　　　　　　The Way may be likened to a sword or a halberd:
愚人以行忿則禍生[E 耕/庚 sriŋ/ṣeŋ], when the foolish act out their anger with it, disaster arises;
聖人以誅暴則福成[E 耕/清 djiŋ/źjäŋ]。 when the sage punishes the violent with it, good fortune is achieved.

65 故得之以死, 　　　　　　　　　　Thus one obtains it so as to die,
得之以生[E 耕/庚 sriŋ/ṣeŋ], 　　　one obtains it so as to live,
得之以敗, 　　　　　　　　　　　　one obtains it so as to be defeated,
得之以成[E 耕/清 djiŋ/źjäŋ]。 　　 one obtains it so as to succeed.

26, 27〔之〕(校注 212). 　　**44**〔其〕(校注 212).

HF 20.7 (*Xilun* 354, *Xin jiaozhu* 413)

人希見生象也，	People rarely see a live elephant
而得死象之骨，	but they get the bones of a dead elephant,
案其圖以想其生也，	and on the basis of visual representations, they imagine it alive.
故諸人之所以意想者皆謂之"象"也。	Thus, the means by which people imagine things are all called "elephant."[46]
5　今道雖不可得聞見，	Now, although the Way cannot be heard or seen,
聖人執其見功以處見其形，	the sage takes hold of its visible results and, by inference from a local instance,[47] visualises its general form.
故曰：	So it is said:
"無狀之狀⟨A 陽/漾 dzrjaŋh/dzjaŋ⟩，	"A shape without a shape,
無物之象⟨A 陽/養 rjaŋx/zjaŋ⟩。"	an image without a physical object."[48]

HF 20.8 (*Xilun* 355, *Xin jiaozhu* 414)

凡理者，	In general, Principles
方圓、短長、麤靡、堅脆之分也，	are the distinguishing features of the square or round, the short or the long, the coarse or fine, the hard or soft.
故理定而後可得道也。	Thus only after the principles are determined can you obtain the Way.[49]
故定理有存亡，	Thus among the determined principles, there are those of preservation and ruin;
5　有死生，	there are those of death and of life;
有盛衰。	there are those of flourishing and of decay.

46　The word *xiang* 象 means both "image" and "elephant," presumably because ivory images were thought of as typical cases of a material image.

47　The meaning of the character 處 here is obscure. My translation is tentative, based on a suggestion by Gao Heng quoted by Chen Qiyou.

48　Section 7 of the chapter comments on *Laozi* 14.

49　The Way has to be understood as that which brings about the Principles of things. If one has not grasped these Principles, then one cannot get to the Way. Epistemologically the Principles are primary, but metaphysically, it is the Way that is primary.

解老 EXPLAINING LAOZI

    夫物之一存一亡，   Things, now preserved, now ruined,
    乍死乍生，   suddenly dying, suddenly being born,
    初盛而後衰者，   first flourishing and then decaying,
10 不可謂常。   cannot be called constant.

    唯夫與天地之剖判也具生，   Only that which was born together with the separation of Heaven and Earth
    至天地之消散也不死不衰者
    謂"常"。   and which until the dissolution of Heaven and Earth will neither die nor decay, can be called 'constant'.

    而常者，   However, the constant,
    無攸易，   does not undergo change,
15 無定理，   has no fixed principles.
    無定理，   Since it has no fixed principles,
    非在於常所，   it is not in a constant place.
    是以不可道也。   Therefore it cannot be spoken of.

    聖人觀其玄虛，   The sage observes its mysterious emptiness
20 用其周行，   and avails himself of its revolutions.
    強字之曰"道"，   When forced to use a word for it, he says, "The Way."[50]

    然而可論。   In that manner, it can be discussed.[51]
    故曰：   So it is said:
    "道之可道，   "When the Way can be taken as the Way[52]
25 非常道也。"   it is not the constant Way."

11 天（與）地 (校注 212).   12 謂「常」（者）。(校注 212).   13 〔者〕 (校注 212).

HF 20.9.1 (*Xilun* 356, *Xin jiaozhu* 416)

    人始於生而卒於死。   Man originates in birth and ends in death.
    始之謂出，   The beginning is called "coming out."

---

50 See *Laozi* 25.
51 *Han Feizi* brings up the keyword, the technical term *lun* 論, that is, "the discussion that sorts things out and aims at passing a judgment on them."
52 *Han Feizi* provides a most interesting variant to one of the most famous lines in Chinese philosophy (*Laozi* 1): he makes the subordinate status of this phrase linguistically explicit by the addition of the nominalising *zhi* 之.

卒之謂入。 The ending is called "going in."
故曰： So it is said:
"出生入死。" "They come out and are born, go in and die."[53]

人之身三百六十節， The human body has 360 joints,[54]
四肢、九竅， four limbs, and nine apertures:
其大具也。 that is its great panoply.
四肢與九竅十有三者， The four limbs and the nine apertures make thirteen.
十有三者之動靜盡屬於生焉。 The activity and quietude of these thirteen all belong to the realm of life.

屬之謂徒也， Belonging to it is called "being a follower."
故曰： So it is said:
生之徒也十有三者。 "Of the followers of life there are thirteen."[55]

至死也， When you die,
十有三具者皆還而屬之於死， all thirteen revert to their origins, and are placed under the rubric of death.
死之徒亦有十三。 There are also thirteen "followers" of death.
故曰： So it is said:
"生之徒十有三， "There are thirteen followers of life
死之徒十有三。" and there are thirteen followers of death."

凡民之生生， In general, the people keep reproducing themselves,
而生者固動， and those who live must be active.
動盡則損也； When activity is exhausted, they suffer loss.
而動不止， So if they keep being active without end,
是損而不止也。 they will keep being reduced.
損而不止， If they keep being reduced,
則生盡； their life will be exhausted.
生盡之謂死， The exhaustion of life is called death.
則十有三具者皆為死死地也。 And so all the thirteen components are places of death in which one dies.[56]

---

53 Section 9 of the chapter comments on *Laozi* 50.
54 A microcosm of the ca. 360 days of the year.
55 Very probably, the correct interpretation in *Laozi* 50 is "three out of ten are adherents of life."
56 *Han Feizi* is playing on *sheng sheng* 生生 "cause the life in the living" in *Laozi* 50.

故曰：
"民之生，
生而動，
動皆之死地，
之十有三。"

So it is said:
"People are born.
Since they are born they are active,
and in their activity they all move towards their place of death.
These are thirteen."[57]

是以聖人愛精神而貴處靜。

So the sage is chary of his refined spirit and sets store by dwelling in quietude.

HF 20.9.2 (*Xilun* 358, *Xin jiaozhu* 416)

不愛精神、不貴處靜，
此甚大於兕虎之害。
夫兕虎有域，
動靜有時。
避其域，
省其時，
則免其兕虎之害矣。
民獨知兕虎之有爪角也，
而莫知萬物之盡有爪角也，
不免於萬物之害。
何以論之？
時雨降集，
曠野閒靜，
而以昏晨犯山川，
則風露之爪角害之。

Not to be chary of the refined spirit and not to value dwelling in quietude –
this is greater than the harm from a rhinoceros or tiger.
Now the rhinoceros and tiger have their abode;
their activity and quietude have their season.
If you avoid their abode,
and are cognisant of their season,
you will avoid harm from the rhinoceros and tiger.
People understand only that rhinoceros and tigers have claws and horns,
but no one understands that all the myriad things have "claws and horns",
and so they do not avoid harm from the myriad things.
How can I explain this?
After the seasonal rains have brought downpour and flooding,
quiet returns to the open lands,
but if in the evening or morning you brave the mountains and rivers,
the "claws and horns" of the elements will harm you.

---

57   *Laozi* 50 reads 亦有三 "there are also three out of ten."

事上不忠，	When those who serve their superiors are disloyal,
輕犯禁令，	when they deprecate and violate prohibitions and orders,
則刑法之爪角害之。	the "claws and horns" of the penal and administrative law will harm them.
處鄉不節，	When those who dwell in their villages do not show restraint,
20 憎愛無度，	when they are immoderate in hate and love,
則爭鬥之爪角害之。	the "claws and horns" of competition and strife will harm them.
嗜慾無限，	When, in their predilections and desires, they have no limits,
動靜不節，	and when in their activity and quietude they show no restraint,
則痤疽之爪角害之。	the "claws and horns" of boils and ulcers will harm them.
25 好用其私智而棄道理，	When they are fond of using their private intelligence, and reject the principles of the Way,
則網羅之爪角害之。	they will be harmed by the "claws and horns" of traps and nets.
兕虎有域，	Rhinoceroses and tigers have their abode,
而萬害有原。	and the myriad forms of harm have their sources.
避其域，	If you avoid their abode,
30 塞其原，	and you block their sources,
則免於諸害矣。	you will avoid all forms of harm.
凡兵革者，	In general, arms and leather armour
所以備害也。	are the means to guard against harm.
重生者，	Those who value life,
35 雖入軍無忿爭之心；	even when they charge into an army, have no inclination to fight out of anger.
無忿爭之心，	If they have no inclination to fight out of anger,
則無所用救害之備。	there is no use for the means to save themselves from harm.
此非獨謂野處之軍也。	This refers not only to the army which is out in the countryside.
聖人之遊世也，	Because the sage, as he wanders in the world,

解老 EXPLAINING LAOZI

40 無害人之心，	has no inclination to harm others,
則必無人害；	he certainly avoids being harmed by others.
無人害，	If he is not harmed by others,
則不備人。	he does not guard against others.
故曰：	So it is said:
45 "陸行不遇兕虎。"	"When travelling on land, they do not run into rhinoceroses and tigers."
入山不恃備以救害，	When he enters mountains, he does not depend on precautions to save himself from harm.
故曰：	So it is said:
"入軍不備甲兵。"	"When he charges into an army he is not furnished with armour or weapons."
遠諸害，	Distance yourself from harm.
50 故曰：	So it is said:
"兕無所投其角，	"The rhinoceros finds no place in him to thrust its horn,
虎無所錯其爪，	nor the tiger a place to fix its claws,
兵無所容其刃。"	nor the weapon a place to admit its blade."
不設備而必無害，	Not taking precautionary measures, yet being certain not to suffer any harm
55 天地之道理也。	is the principles of the Way of Heaven and Earth.
體天地之道，	[The sage] understands and incorporates the Way of Heaven and Earth;
故曰：	so it is said:
"無死地焉。"	"There is no place of death for him there."[58]
動無死地，	When he acts, there is no place of death,
60 而謂之"善攝生"矣。	and he is called "good at holding onto life."

1–2 A lacuna before 此甚大於兕虎之害 was suspected by 松舉圓、陳奇猷 and 梁啟雄. The eight characters 不愛精神、不貴處靜 have been added conjecturally (據文意補) in 校注 204, following 松舉圓; 校注 is followed by C. 校注 and C begin the section with 是以聖人愛精神而貴處靜; this section division appears doubtful. 陳奇猷 does not start a new section and conjectures that 眾人 occurs before 不愛精神、不貴處靜. 張覺 disagrees that there is a lacuna and holds 此 to refer to 民之生，生而動 of the preceding section. We reluctantly follow 松舉圓 and 校注.   8 張抄 has 氏 for 民.   13 C has 間 for 閒.   15 （兕虎）〔風露〕（校注 212）.   24 則（虛）痤 (校注 212).   53 （害）〔容〕（校注 212）.

---

58   Laozi 50, tr. D.C. Lau 1982: 71 以其無死地 "because for him there is no realm of death."

HF 20.10.1 (*Xilun* 361, *Xin jiaozhu* 421)

愛子者慈於子，	One who loves a son will care for him;
重生者慈於身。	one who values life will care for his person;
貴功者慈於事。	one who esteems achievements will care for his tasks.
慈母之於弱子也，	A loving mother treats her helpless child
5　務致其福；	so that every effort is to bring it happiness;
務致其福，	when every effort is to bring it happiness,
則事除其禍；	her task will be to eliminate bad fortune for it;
事除其禍，	when her task is to eliminate bad fortune for it,
則思慮熟；	her reflections and plans will mature;
10　思慮熟，	when her reflections and plans mature,
則得事理；	she will grasp the principle of her tasks;
得事理，	when she grasps the principles of tasks,
則必成功；	she will be sure to succeed;
必成功，	when she is sure to succeed,
15　則其行之也不疑；	her actions will leave no place for doubt;
不疑之謂勇。	having no doubt is called "courage."
聖人之於萬事也，	The sage treats the myriad undertakings
盡如慈母之為弱子慮也，	exactly as a loving mother plans for her helpless child.
故見必行之道。	Therefore, he sees the path that he must take.
20　見必行之道則明，	Seeing the path that he must take, he is clear-sighted,[59]
其從事亦不疑；	and in conducting his affairs, he is not in doubt;
不疑之謂勇。	not being in doubt is called "courage."
不疑生於慈，	Not being in doubt comes from being deeply concerned.
故曰：	So it is said:
25　"慈，	"He is deeply concerned.
故能勇。"	Hence he is capable of being courageous."[60]

6〔務致其福〕(校注 212).　20〔見必行之道〕(校注 212).

---

[59] Again, enlightenment is not in theoretical or purely intellectual insight. It is in knowing what to do and how to do it.

[60] Section 10 of the chapter comments on *Laozi* 67.

HF 20.10.2 (*Xilun* 363, *Xin jiaozhu* 421)

周公曰：	The Duke of Zhou said:
"冬日之閉凍也不固，	"If, during the winter, the frost-lock is not complete,
則春夏之長草木也不茂。"	then in spring and in summer, when one grows herbs and trees, they will not flourish."
天地不能常侈常費，	Heaven and Earth cannot be always luxuriant or always lavish:
5 而況於人乎？	how much less can men?
故萬物必有盛衰，	Thus the myriad things must have their periods of flourishing and decline;
萬事必有弛張，	the myriad undertakings must have their slackening and tightening;
國家必有文武，	a state must have its civil and military activities;
官治必有賞罰。	in official administration, there must be rewards and penalties.
10 是以智士儉用其財則家富，	Thus, when intelligent gentlemen make sparing use of resources, their houses will be wealthy;
聖人愛寶其神則精盛。	when the sage is sparing with and treasures his spirit, his refined essence will flourish.
人君重戰其卒則民眾，	When the ruler does not send his soldiers into battle lightly, his people will multiply;
民眾則國廣。	when the population multiplies, the state will expand.
是以舉之曰：	This is why [the book] spells this out and says:
15 "儉，	"Be sparing,
故能廣。"	so that you can expand."

HF 20.10.3 (*Xilun* 363, *Xin jiaozhu* 422)

凡物之有形者易裁也，	In general, things with a shape are easy to slice
易割也。	and easy to carve up.
何以論之？	How can I explain this?
有形，	If something has a form,
5 則有短長；	it has a measurable length;
有短長，	if it has a measurable length,

則有小大；	it has a measurable size;
有小大，	if it has a measurable size,
則有方圓；	it has a certain round or square shape;
10 有方圓，	if it has a certain round or square shape,
則有堅脆；	it has a certain hardness;
有堅脆，	if it has a certain hardness,
則有輕重；	it has a measurable weight;
有輕重，	if it has a measurable weight,
15 則有白黑。	it has a measurable brightness.
短長、大小、方圓、堅脆、輕重、白黑之謂理。	Length, size, shape, hardness, weight, and brightness are called principles.
理定而物易割也。	When principles are well-defined, things are easily held apart.
故議於大庭而後言則立，	Thus, after major debates in the great court,[61] proposals are put forth –
權議之士知之矣。	gentlemen who weigh arguments know this.
20 故欲成方圓而隨其規矩，	If you want to establish square or round forms, and follow the circle and the T-square,
則萬事之功形矣。	success in all undertakings will manifest itself.
而萬物莫不有規矩，	The myriad things all have their "compasses and T-squares."[62]
議言之士，	The gentleman who speaks up in discussions
計會規矩也。	calculates according to "compasses and T-squares."
25 聖人盡隨於萬物之規矩，	The sage exhaustively follows all the compasses and T-squares of the myriad things.
故曰：	So it is said:
"不敢為天下先。"	"He does not presume to be the first in the world."
不敢為天下先，	If he does not presume to be first in the world,
則事無不事，	whatever he does will be done;
30 功無不功，	whatever he tries to achieve will be achieved,

---

61 The convention of public debate at the ruler's court ensures that when at last the ruler speaks he does so in the light of current opinion within his entourage.

62 *Han Feizi* moves from the literal meaning "compass and square" to the more abstract meaning of "standards" here.

解老 EXPLAINING LAOZI

而議必蓋世，	his arguments will be heard throughout his world –
欲無處大官，	even if he should desire not to occupy a great office,
其可得乎？	would he be able to succeed in this?
處大官之謂為成事長。	"Occupy a great office" refers to being the best at completing tasks.
35 是以故曰：	Thus it says:
"不敢為天下先，	"He does not presume to be first under Heaven;
故能為成事長。"	therefore, he is able to be best at completing tasks."

HF 20.10.4 (*Xilun* 365, *Xin jiaozhu* 423)

慈於子者不敢絕衣食，	A person who cares for his children will not dare to deprive them of clothes and food;
慈於身者不敢離法度，	a person who cares for his body will not dare to depart from the law and the standards;
慈於方圓者不敢舍規矩。	a person with the same care for square and round shapes will not dare to discard the compass and the T-square.
故臨兵而慈於士吏則戰勝敵，	Thus, in dealing with the armed forces, if you care for gentlemen and officers, you will defeat your opponents in war;
5 慈於器械則城堅固。	if you care for the instruments of war, your city walls will be solid and firm.
故曰：	So it is said:
"慈，	"If you care,
於戰則勝，	when waging war you will win;
以守則固。"	when defending, you will be firm and secure."
10 夫能自全也而盡隨於萬物之理者，	If you are able to remain unharmed and follow all the principles of the myriad things,
必且有天生。	this must be due to having qualities that are engendered by Heaven.
天生也者，	These "qualities engendered by Heaven"
生心也，	are engendered in your heart.

故天下之道盡之生也。	Thus the Way of the world exhausts what is engendered (by Heaven).
15　若以慈衛之也，	If you use care to guard yourself,
事必萬全，	your undertakings will be successful without exception,
而舉無不當，	and no initiative you take will fail to be appropriate;
則謂之寶矣。	then [this care] is called a treasure.
故曰：	So it is said:
20　"吾有三寶，	"I have three treasures;
持而寶之。"	I hold fast to them and treasure them."

14 Following 陳啓天, we read 之 as 其.

HF 20.11 (*Xilun* 366, *Xin jiaozhu* 424)

書之所謂"大道"也者，	What the book calls the Great Way
端道也。	is the correct Way;
所謂"貌施"也者，	what it calls 'deviant in outer appearance'
邪道也。	is the wicked Way.
5　所謂"徑大"也者，	When it says that the "paths are great"
佳麗也。	this refers to ostentatious beauty.[63]
佳麗也者，	Ostentatious beauty
邪道之分也。	is part of the Way of wickedness.
"朝甚除"也者，	As for "the courts are all filthy,"
10　獄訟繁也。	this means that litigation proliferates.[64]

63　Section 11 of the chapter comments on *Laozi* 53; but in the current edition the compound 徑大 ("paths are great") does not appear. See the next note.

64　Compare *Laozi* 53 (tr. D.C. Lau 1982: 77):

使我介然有知，	Were I possessed of the least knowledge,
行於大道，	I would, when walking on the great way,
唯施是畏。	fear only paths that lead astray.
大道甚夷，	The great way is easy,
而人好徑。	yet people prefer by-paths.
朝甚除，	The court is corrupt,
田甚蕪，	The fields are overgrown with weeds,
倉甚虛。	The granaries are empty;
服文綵，	Yet there are those dressed in fineries,

獄訟繁，	When litigation proliferates,
則田荒；	the fields lie neglected.
田荒，	When the fields lie neglected,
則府倉虛；	the storehouses are empty;
15 府倉虛，	when the storehouses are empty
則國貧；	the state will be poor;
國貧，	when the state is poor
而民俗淫侈；	the habits of the people will become wanton and lewd;
民俗淫侈，	when the customs of the people become wanton and lewd,
20 則衣食之業絕；	the production of clothing and food will be disrupted;
衣食之業絕，	when the production of clothing and food is disrupted,
則民不得無飾巧詐；	the people will become pretentious, crafty, and fraudulent;
飾巧詐，	when they are pretentious, clever, and fraudulent,
則知采文；	they become aware of colours and elegant patterns.
25 知采文之謂"服文采"。	Their awareness of colours and elegant patterns are referred to by "their clothes are patterned and colourful."
獄訟繁，	When litigation proliferates
倉廩虛，	and storehouses are empty
而有以淫侈為俗，	and there are those who make wantonness and lewdness their habit,
則國之傷也若以利劍刺之。	the harm to the state is as if someone were to stab it with a sharp sword.
30 故曰：	So it is said:
"帶利劍。"	"Gird yourself with a sharp sword."

帶利劍，	with swords at their sides,
厭飲食，	Filled with food and drink,
財貨有餘。	And possessed of much wealth.
是謂盜夸。	This is known as taking the lead in robbery.
非道也哉。	Far indeed is this from the way.

諸夫飾智故以至於傷國者，

其私家必富；
私家必富，

35　故曰：
　　"資貨有餘。"

國有若是者，
則愚民不得無術而效之；

效之，
40　則小盜生。

由是觀之，
大姦作則小盜隨[A 歌/支 sdjuar/zjwĕ]，
大姦唱則小盜和[A 歌/戈 gwar/ɣuâ]。

竽也者，
45　五聲之長者也，
故竽先則鍾瑟皆隨[A 歌/支 sdjuar/zjwĕ]，
竽唱則諸樂皆和[A 歌/戈 gwar/ɣuâ]。
今大姦作則俗之民唱，
俗之民唱則小盜必和[A 歌/戈 gwar/ɣuâ]。
50　故"服文采，
帶利劍，
厭飲食，

When all these fellows become pretentious and intelligent, to the point that they harm the state, private houses[65] are bound to become wealthy; Since private houses are bound to become wealthy,
so it is said:
"Of resources and goods there is superabundance."

When there are [scoundrels] like this in the state, the foolish populace will not fail to be tempted and imitate them.
When [the foolish populace] imitates them, petty thieves emerge.

From this point of view,
when great wickedness arises, petty thieves follow suit;
when great wickedness calls the tune, petty thieves chime in.

The mouth organ
is the leader of the Five Sounds.
Thus the mouth organ comes first, and the bells and zithers all follow suit;
the reed organ calls the tune and all the other musical instruments chime in.
Now when the great wickedness arises, vulgar people call the tune;
when vulgar people call the tune, petty thieves will inevitably chime in.
Therefore "they wear elegantly patterned and colourful clothes;
they are girded with sharp swords;
they drink and eat gluttonously;

---

65 *Han Feizi* reduces the meaning of *Laozi* to his own categories of analysis, like here: the category of "private families" is quite absent in *Laozi*, but the conflict of interest between private family and the public interests of the state (as represented by the ruler) is important in *Han Feizi*'s philosophy.

解老 EXPLAINING LAOZI

| 而貨資有餘者， | and still their goods and resources are superabundant. |
| 是之謂盜竽矣。" | These are called "thieves who play the mouth organ."⁶⁶ |

3 施 is read as 迆/迤 (to meander, to slant), following 王念孫 as equivalent to qi 其, following 陳啟天.   14 The second zhi 之 is taken   38 術 is read as 誠   42 〔則〕 (校注 213).

HF 20.12 (Xilun 369, Xin jiaozhu 428)

人無愚智，	No people, no matter how stupid or intelligent,
莫不有趣舍。	are invariably without priorities.
恬淡平安，	When you are calm and mild, and at peace,
莫不知禍福之所由來。	you will invariably understand where bad fortune and good fortune come from,
5 得於好惡，	but when you are dominated by likes and dislikes
怵於淫物，	and tempted by wanton things,
而後變亂。	then these things change to become all chaotic.
所以然者，	The reason for this
引於外物，	is that you are drawn in by external things,
10 亂於玩好也。	and confused by beautiful playthings.
恬淡有趣舍之義[A 歌/真 njarh/-jei/ŋjĕ]，	When calm and mild, you have the rightness of your priorities,
平安知禍福之計[A 脂/齊 kidh/-iei/kiei]。	When at peace, you understand the plans leading to good and bad fortune,
而今也玩好變之，	but now beautiful playthings have corrupted people,
外物引之；	external things draw them in.
15 引之而往，	They are drawn in and they set out,
故曰"拔"。	so they are said to be "seized."⁶⁷

---

66 In the middle of this most puzzling commentary on a puzzling choice of a chapter in *Laozi*, *Han Feizi* reverts to a whole sequence of Han Fei's pet ideas about injuring the state, about the shrewd and the clever, about the wicked causing the vulgar to take the lead, about private families becoming rich at the expense of the ruling house.

67 Section 12 of the chapter comments on *Laozi* 34. Being cajoled and seduced away from one's rational balanced "legalist" judgment is the interpretation Han Fei imposes on the *Laozi* text.

至聖人不然：	The sage is not like this.
一建其趣舍，	Once he has set up his priorities,
雖見所好之物[B 微/物 mjət/mjuɑt]，	even when he sees a thing he likes,
20　不能引，	it will not draw him in.
不能引之謂"不拔[C 祭/黠 briat/bwăt]"；	This inability to draw him in is referred to by "not being seized."
一於其情，	He is concentrated in his instincts;
雖有可欲之類[B 微/至 ljədh/ljwi]，	even when there is something desirable,
神不為動，	his spirit will not be moved.
25　神不為動之謂"不脫[C 祭/末 thuat/thuât]"。	His spirit's not being moved is referred to by "not letting go."
為人子孫者，	One's sons and grandsons
體此道以守宗廟，	will embody this Way so as to protect the ancestral temples.
宗廟不滅[C 祭/薛 mjiat/mjiät]之謂"祭祀不絕[C 祭/薛 dzjuat/dzjwät]"。	That the ancestral temples are not destroyed is referred to by "the sacrifices are not discontinued."
身以積精為德，	The person takes the accumulation of the subtle essence as its inherent Virtue;[68]
30　家以資財為德，	the house takes its resources and wealth as its inherent Virtue.
鄉國天下皆以民為德。	the district, the state, and the world all take the people to be [the source of] its inherent Virtue.
今治身而外物不能亂其精神，	Now, govern your person in such a way that external things cannot disturb your subtle essence and spirit –
故曰：	so it is said:
"脩之身⟨D 真/真 sthjin/śjĕn⟩，	"If you cultivate your person,
35　其德乃真⟨D 真/真 tjin/tśjĕn⟩。"	your Virtue will be genuine."
真者，	To be genuine
慎之固也。	is to be firmly attentive.

68　This *jing* 精 "subtle essence; semen" is assembled in a variety of ways that are described in detail in the ancient literature of physical self-cultivation. See Harper 1998.

解老 EXPLAINING LAOZI   307

	治家，	When you govern your house
	無用之物不能動其計，	in such a way that useless things do not interfere with your plans,
40	則資有餘，	its resources will be plenty.
	故曰：	So it is said:
	"脩之家⟨E 魚/麻 krag/ka⟩，	"If you cultivate it in your house,
	其德有餘⟨E 魚/魚 rag/jiwo⟩。"	your Virtue will be superabundant."
	治鄉者行此節，	If someone who governs a district practises this line of restraint,
45	則家之有餘者益眾，	then houses with surpluses will multiply.
	故曰：	So it is said:
	"脩之鄉⟨F 陽/陽 hjaŋ/xjaŋ⟩，	"If you cultivate it in your district
	其德乃長⟨F 陽/陽 drjaŋ/djaŋ⟩。"	your Virtue will grow."
	治邦者行此節，	If someone who governs a state[69] practises this line of restraint,
50	則鄉之有德者益眾，	then those who have Virtue in a district will multiply.
	故曰：	So it is said:
	"脩之邦⟨G 東/江 pruŋ/păŋ⟩，	"If you cultivate it in your state,
	其德乃豐⟨G 中/東 phjəŋw/phjuŋ⟩。"	your Virtue will be abundant."
	涖天下者行此節，	If someone who is in charge of the world practises this line of restraint,
55	則民之生莫不受其澤，	all the people in their lives will enjoy this bounty.
	故曰：	So it is said:
	"脩之天下⟨H 魚/馬 gragx/ɣa⟩，	"If you cultivate it throughout the world,
	其德乃普⟨H 魚/姥 phagx/phuo⟩。"	your Virtue will be universal."
	脩身者以此別君子小人，	If those who cultivate their persons in this way distinguish between superior men and petty men,

---

69 Note the usage of *bang* 邦 here and frequently in chapter 21 with the meaning of "the state." In the vast majority of the extant editions of pre-imperial texts, the Han editors replaced the tabooed *bang* (the name of the Han founder, Liu Bang 劉邦 [d. 195]) with *guo* 國. In *Han Feizi*, the term *bang* appears altogether 22 times, of which five instances are found in the "Jie Lao" chapter and 13 in "Yu Lao."

60　治鄉治邦涖天下者各以此科適觀息耗，	if those who govern a district, a country or are in charge of the world, each using these divisions, compare and observe the flourishing and overspending of things,
則萬不失一。	they will not fail even one time in ten thousand.
故曰： "以身觀身， 以家觀家， 65　以鄉觀鄉， 以邦觀邦， 以天下觀天下。 吾奚以知天下之然也？ 以此。"	So it is said: "Observe the persons as proper for a person, observe the families as proper for a family, observe the districts as proper for a district, observe the countries as proper for a country, observe the world as proper for the world. How do we know that the world is as it is? Because of this."

16, 21 C has 校 for 拔, but notes the reading 拔. 藏本 has 校; 陳奇猷 regards 校 as a mistake. 25 C has 悅 for 脫.　28〔宗廟〕(校注 213).　65〔以鄉觀鄉〕(校注 213).

CHAPTER 21

喻老 Illustrating Laozi

HF 21.1.1 (*Xilun* 374, *Xin jiaozhu* 431)

天下有道，	When the Way prevails in the world
無急患，	and there are no emergencies or disasters,
則曰靜，	this is called a state of undisturbed calm,
遽傳不用。	and there is no need for quick communications.
5 故曰：	So it is said:
"卻走馬以糞。"	"Fleet-footed horses are used for nothing but their dung."[1]
天下無道，	When the Way does not prevail in the world,
攻擊不休，	attacks and assaults are incessant,
相守數年不已，	for years on end all sides hold their positions,
10 甲冑生蟣虱，	flea's eggs hatch in armour and helmets,
鷰雀處帷幄，	swallows and sparrows settle in tents and canopies,
而兵不歸。	but still the armies do not return home.[2]
故曰：	So it is said:
"戎馬生於郊。"	"War-horses breed in the outskirts of the capital."

10 C has 冑 for 冑.

HF 21.1.2 (*Xilun* 375, *Xin jiaozhu* 432)

翟人有獻豐狐、玄豹之皮於晉文公。	A man of the Di[3] presented a long-haired fox skin and a dark leopard skin to Lord Wen of Jin

---

1 Section 1 of this chapter comments on *Laozi* 46.
2 These lengthy campaigns were indeed characteristic of the late Warring States period (Miyake 2018). Suffice here to mention the Changping campaign, during which the Qin and Zhao forces faced off for three years before the decisive battle (chapter 1, note 20).
3 Di (usually written 狄) was a designation for ethnic groups in northern China.

文公受客皮而歎曰：	Lord Wen accepted the furs from the stranger and said with a sigh:
"此以皮之美自為罪。"	"I have now committed a crime because of the beauty of these furs."[4]
夫治國者以名號為罪，	Those who govern a state commit crimes for the sake of fame.
5　徐偃王是也。	King Yan of Xú is a case in point.[5]
以城與地為罪，	Or they commit crimes for the sake of cities and territories.
虞、虢是也。	Yu and Guo were such cases.[6]
故曰：	So it is said:
"罪莫大於可欲。"	"No crime is greater than avarice."

6　(則)以(校注 231).

HF 21.1.3 (*Xilun* 376, *Xin jiaozhu* 433)

智伯兼范、中行而攻趙不已，	Zhi Bo annexed [the territories of] Fan and of Zhonghang and relentlessly attacked [those of] Zhao.
韓、魏反之，	When Hán and Wei turned against him,
軍敗晉陽，	his army was defeated at Jinyang
身死高梁之東，	and he himself died east of Gaoliang,
5　遂卒被分，	and in the end he was carved up
漆其首以為溲器。	and they lacquered his skull and made it into a chamberpot.[7]

4　The moral is that excessive gifts call for unwarranted favours which in turn constitute a crime.

5　The explanation of this enigmatic statement appears in chapter 49; see note 9 there. King Yan of Xu is told there to promulgate the policy of "benevolence and righteousness," igniting thereby the ire of King Wen of Chu who reportedly annihilated Xu.

6　The Yu and Guo examples are discussed below in this chapter. In *Zuozhuan*, both polities are presented as being led by short-sighted leaders. Guo was engaged in territorial expansion and neglected its defences; it had further alienated the neighbouring Yu polity, which cooperated with Jin in its elimination of Guo. Once Guo was extinguished, that same Jin army annexed Yu as well (see *Han Feizi* 10.2).

7　The story follows the same erroneous identification of the Zhi Bo who overpowered the Fan and Zhonghang lineages, with the Zhi Bo who was defeated by Zhao Xiangzi (see the vari-

喻老 ILLUSTRATING LAOZI

故曰：
"禍莫大於不知足。"

So it is said:
"No disaster is greater than not knowing sufficiency."

HF 21.1.4 (*Xilun* 377, *Xin jiaozhu* 434)

虞君欲屈產之乘與垂棘之璧，
不聽宮之奇，
故邦亡身死。

故曰：
"咎莫憯於欲得。"

The ruler of Yu coveted the horse-teams bred in Qu as well as the jade disks from Chuiji, and did not listen to the advice of Gong Zhi Qi. As a result, the county was ruined and he himself died.[8]

So it is said:
"No disaster is more severe than that of concupiscence."

HF 21.1.5 (*Xilun* 377, *Xin jiaozhu* 434)

邦以存為常，
霸王其可也；
身以生為常，
富貴其可也。
不以欲自害，
則邦不亡，
身不死。

故曰：
"知足之為足矣。"

If a country takes survival as its constant concern, it would be possible [for its ruler] to become a hegemonic king;
if a person takes his life as constant concern, it would be possible [for him] to become rich and noble.
If you do not harm yourself because of desires, your country will not be ruined and you will not die.

So it is said:
"Knowing sufficiency is sufficient."

2 〔王〕(校注 231).　5 〔以〕(校注 231).

---

ant that appears in Chapter 10.5 and comments there). As for the usage of Zhi Bo's skull: *Zhanguo ce* 18.4 ("Zhao 1") mentions his lacquered skull being used as a drinking vessel. Han Fei evidently aims to exaggerate Zhi Bo's humiliation by turning the lacquered skull into a chamberpot.

8 Here Han Fei opts for a short summary of a tale rather than a narrative to explain the text. The episode recurs in greater detail in Chapter 10.3.

HF 21.2 (*Xilun* 378, *Xin jiaozhu* 435)

楚莊王既勝，	After King Zhuang of Chu had won his victory,
狩于河雍，	he conducted a hunt at Heyong.[9]
歸而賞孫叔敖，	When he returned, he rewarded Sunshu Ao,
孫叔敖請漢間之地，	who asked for the territory of Hanjian,
5 沙石之處。	which was a sandy and rocky place.[10]
楚邦之法，	According to the laws of the land of Chu
祿臣再世而收地，	ministers with stipends had their lands confiscated after two generations.
唯孫叔敖獨在。	Only Sunshu Ao still occupied his place.
此不以其邦為收者，	The reason why they did not confiscate his land
10 瘠也，	was that it was barren.
故九世而祀不絕。	So for nine generations the ancestral sacrifices were performed without interruption.[11]
故曰：	So it is said:
"善建不拔⟨A 祭/黠 briat/bwăt⟩，	"If you are good at establishing things, they will not be uprooted;
善抱不脫⟨A 祭/末 thuat/thuât⟩，	if you are good at embracing things, they will not slip loose.
15 子孫以其祭祀世世不輟⟨A 祭/祭 trjuadh/tjwäi⟩。"	Sons and grandsons will offer their sacrifices, for generations, uninterrupted.[12]
孫叔敖之謂也。	This refers to Sunshu Ao.

15 張抄 has 叔 for 孫.

---

9   The reference is to the victory at Bi 邲 over the Jin army in 597: the apex of Chu's military successes. Heyong or Hengyong 衡雍 is a location near the Bi battleground, in the proximity of the Yellow River.

10 Sunshu Ao acted as Chu's prime minister (*lingyin* 令尹) at the time of the Bi battle. By the Warring States period, he became the paragon of a loyal and efficient minister who benefitted the state of Chu tremendously. See more in Durrant, Li, and Schaberg 2016: 634n166. Hanjian is supposed to be located near the Han river. For an alternative version of this story, see *Lüshi chunqiu* 10.4 ("Yi bao" 異寶).

11 Their offering sacrifices would mean that the territory remained the hereditary possession of the Sunshu lineage, since only an enfeoffed grandee had the right to maintain an ancestral temple.

12 Section 2 of the chapter comments on *Laozi* 54 (tr. D.C. Lau 1982: 77):
    善建者不拔。 What is firmly rooted cannot be pulled out;
    善抱者不脫。 What is tightly held in the arms will not slip loose;
    子孫以祭祀不輟。 Through this the offering of sacrifice by descendants will never come to an end.
    Note that is quite likely that at the time Han Fei was commenting on the *Laozi* text, the chapters were not in their present sequence and possibly being circulated separately.

喻老 ILLUSTRATING LAOZI

HF 21.3 (*Xilun* 380, *Xin jiaozhu* 436)

制在己曰重，	If control lies within yourself, this is called being heavyweight;
不離位曰靜。	if you do not leave your position, this is called being at ease.
重，	If you are weighty,
則能使輕；	you can command the light;
靜，	if you are tranquil,
則能使躁。	you can command those who act with haste.
故曰：	So it is said:
"重為輕根⟨A 文/痕 kən/kən⟩，	"The weighty is the root of the light;
靜為躁君⟨A 文/文 kwjən/kjuən⟩。"	the tranquil is the ruler of those who act with haste."
故曰，	So it is said:
"君子終日行，	"The true gentleman, when travelling all day,
不離輜重"也。	does not leave his baggage wagon"
邦者，	As for the country,
人君之輜重也。	it is the ruler's baggage wagon.
主父生傳其邦，	When the Sovereign-Father passed on power in his country,
此離其輜重者也，	this was leaving the baggage wagon.
故雖有代、雲中之樂，	He may still enjoy the delights of Dai and Yunzhong,
超然已無趙矣。	but he has already been cleanly stripped of his kingdom of Zhao.[13]
主父，	The Sovereign-Father
萬乘之主，	was the ruler over ten thousand war chariots
而以身輕於天下。	but made himself a lightweight in the world.

13　For the abdication of King Wuling of Zhao in 299 and his subsequent reign as "Sovereign-Father," see chapter 14, note 29. In 296, after successfully expanding Zhao territory northward (in particular toward the Dai and Yunzhong commanderies in northern Shanxi and Inner Mongolia of today), the "Sovereign-Father" returned to the capital of Zhao, then under the reign of his son, arranged big feasts and announced a general amnesty. A year later he was starved to death by his ministers following an unsuccessful intervention in the succession struggles of the state.

無勢之謂輕，   Having no position of power is called being a lightweight;

離位之謂躁，   leaving your position is called acting in haste.
是以生幽而死。   Therefore, your life is dusky, and then you die.

25 故曰：   So it is said:
"輕則失臣⟨B 真/真 grjin/-jiən/źjĕn⟩，   "If you are a lightweight, you will lose your ministers;

躁則失君⟨B 文/文 kwjən/kjuən⟩。"   if you act in haste, you will lose the ruler's position."[14]

主父之謂也。   This refers to the Sovereign-Father.

HF 21.4.1 (*Xilun* 381, *Xin jiaozhu* 437)

勢重者，   The power of position,
人君之淵也。   is the wellspring of rulership.
君人者，   He who rules over others
勢重於人臣之間，   has a powerful position among the ministers.
5 失則不可復得也。   When he loses this position, it cannot be won back.

簡公失之於田成，   Lord Jian [of Qi] lost it to Tian Cheng;[15]
晉公失之於六卿，   the lords of Jin[16] lost it to the Six Senior Ministers;
而邦亡身死。   and their states were ruined while they themselves died.[17]

---

14   Section 3 of this chapter comments on *Laozi* 26. In the current version of *Laozi* 26, we have *gen* 根 "root" for *Han Feizi*'s *chen* 臣 "minister."

15   For this paradigmatic ministerial usurpation by Tian Chang (here referred to by his posthumous name, Cheng), see chapter 7, note 3.

16   The lords of Jin started losing power to the ministerial lineages soon after the demise of Lord Wen (r. 636–628). The six top ministers (*qing* 卿) were commanders or second-in-command in the three Jin armies (Jin experimented with the number of armies but the default number was three). By the mid-sixth century the term "six ministers" designated six powerful lineages which sidelined the lords of Jin. These were Wei, Zhao, and Hán (who eventually formed their independent polities in 403), Zhi (eliminated in 453), Fan and Zhonghang (eliminated in 490); see chapter 1, note 33, and chapter 11, note 13.

17   Characteristically, Han Fei gives a highly concrete political reading to the abstract discourse in the *Laozi*.

喻老 ILLUSTRATING LAOZI

故曰：	So it is said:
10 "魚不可脫於深淵。"	"A fish must not be removed from the depths."[18]
賞罰者，	Rewards and punishments
邦之利器也。	are the country's sharp tools.
在君，	If these are in the hands of the ruler,
則制臣；	he will control the ministers;
15 在臣，	if these are under the control of ministers,
則勝君。	they will overcome the ruler.
君見賞，	If the ruler openly sets out to give rewards,
臣則損之以為德；	the ministers will try to undermine him by turning it into a show of their own generosity;
君見罰，	when the ruler openly sets out to mete out punishments,
20 臣則益之以為威。	the ministers will try to outdo him by turning it into a show of their own authority.
人君見賞，	When the ruler of men openly sets out to give rewards,
而人臣用其勢；	the ministers avail themselves of his position of power;
人君見罰，	when the ruler of men openly metes out punishments,
人臣乘其威。	the ministers avail themselves of his authority.
25 故曰：	So it is said:
"邦之利器，	"The sharp tools of the country
不可以示人。"	cannot be shown to the people."

3–5 The C editors note: 此文應作「人君者失勢重於人臣之間，則不可復得也」。.

HF 21.4.2 (*Xilun* 382, *Xin jiaozhu* 438)

越王入宦於吳，	The King of Yue[19] entered the service of Wu as a lowly servant;
而觀之伐齊以弊吳。	in order to ruin Wu, he convinced it to attack Qi.

---

18   Section 4 of the chapter comments on *Laozi* 36.
19   On King Goujian of Yue, see chapter 17, note 4. The apocryphal story of Goujian becoming the personal servant of King Fuchai of Wu became popular from the Warring States period on (chapter 23, note 20).

吳兵既勝齊人於艾陵，

張之於江、濟，

強之於黃池，

故可制於五湖。

故曰：
"將欲翕之，
必固張⟨A 陽/陽 trjaŋ/tjaŋ⟩之；
將欲弱之，
必固強⟨A 陽/陽 gjaŋ/gjaŋ⟩之。"

晉獻公將欲襲虞，

遺之以璧馬；
知伯將襲仇由，

遺之以廣車。

After the Wu army had won a victory at Ailing against the people of Qi,[20]

they spread out their forces on the Yangzi and the Ji rivers,

and dominated [the other regional lords] at Huangchi:

as a result, the Wu army could be brought under control at Wuhu.[21]

So it is said:
"If you want to contain someone,
you must surely cause him to expand;
if you want to weaken someone,
you must surely strengthen him."

When Lord Xian of Jin was about to launch a secret attack on Yu,

he gave them presents of jade disks and horses;[22]

when Zhi Bo was about to launch a secret attack on Chouyou,

he gave them presents of wide-bodied chariots.[23]

---

20 This happened in 484, and the story is told in *Zuozhuan*, Ai 11.3.

21 The events depicted here are largely paralleled in *Zuozhuan* and later texts, especially the "Discourses of Wu" 吳語 section of *Discourses of the States* (*Guoyu*), except one aspect which appears to be Han Fei's invention, namely that King Goujian himself enticed Wu to attack Qi and thereby weaken its southern frontiers (from which it would be duly attacked by Yue). The depicted events are: after Wu's victory over Qi in Ailing in 484, Wu expanded its influence all the way from the Yangzi shores to the Ji River (the modern course of the Yellow River in Shandong province). In 482 it participated in a major interstate meeting in Huangchi at which it allegedly successfully fought for precedence in smearing sacrificial blood at the covenant (i.e. being recognised as a new hegemonic power) with the Jin representatives. Alredady during the Huangchi meeting, Yue started to harass Wu. In 478, Yue defeated the Wu armies near Wuhu (modern Taihu lake in the vicinity of the Wu capital). Wu was extinguished in 473.

22 See chapter 10.2 for details.

23 See chapter 23.28 for details. As is explained there, the present was not of chariots but of a huge bell. To enable its delivery, the ruler of Chouyou had to clear the paths for the Jin transportation chariots, which were in due course followed by the Jin military.

喻老 ILLUSTRATING LAOZI   317

    故曰：   So it is said:
    "將欲取⟨B侯/麌 tshjugx/-juo/tshju⟩之，   "If you want to take something from someone,
    必固與⟨B魚/語 ragx/-jo/jiwo⟩之。"   you must surely give something to him."

    起事於無形，   To start working on the level of the shapeless and invisible
20 而要大功於天下，   and to work for great success in the world –
    "是謂微明。"   this is called "a fine sense for subtleties."
    處小弱而重自卑損，   To strike a posture of weakness and to keep humiliating yourself –
    謂"弱勝強"也。   this is called "the weak overcoming the strong."

2 張抄 has 獘 for 弊.   22 〔損〕(校注 231).   23 謂(損)弱 (校注 231).

HF 21.5.1 (*Xilun* 384, *Xin jiaozhu* 440)

    有形之類[A微/至 ljədh/ljwi]，   Things that have a physical shape,
    大必起於小[B宵/小 sjagwx/sjäu]；   even if they are large, are bound to arise from the small;
    行久之物[A微/物 mjət/mjuət]，   things that are long-lasting,
    族必起於少[B宵/小 sthjagwx/śjäu]。   even if they are many, are bound to start as few.
5 故曰：   So it is said:
    "天下之難事必作於易⟨C佳/寘 righ/-jiei/jiĕ⟩， The difficult things in the world invariably start with the easy;
    天下之大事必作於細⟨C脂/霽 sidh/-iei/siei⟩。" the large things invariably start with the slight."[24]

    是以欲制物者於其細也。   Therefore, if you wish to control things, the point is in their subtle beginnings.

    故曰：   So it is said:
10 "圖難於其易⟨C佳/寘 righ/-jiei/jiĕ⟩也，   "Making plans for the difficult depends on what is easy;

---

24 Section 5 of the chapter comments on *Laozi* 63.

為大於其細⟨C 脂/齊 sidh/-iei/siei⟩也。"	undertaking large things depends on what is slight."

HF 21.5.2 (*Xilun* 385, *Xin jiaozhu* 441)

千丈之堤以螻蟻之穴潰，	A thousand-pole long dyke collapses because of the holes of termites;
百尺之室以突隙之熛焚。	a hundred-foot house is burnt down because of the spark from a crack in the chimney.
故曰：	So it is said:
白圭之行堤也塞其穴，	Bai Gui[25] walked along the dyke in order to plug the holes,
5 丈人之慎火也塗其隙，	old people, being cautious about fire, plaster the cracks.
是以白圭無水難，	Accordingly, Bai Gui faced no difficulties from floods,
丈人無火患。	And for old people fires do not create difficulties.
此皆慎易以避難，	These are all cases of being cautious about what is easy in order to avoid difficulties,
敬細以遠大者也。	to pay diligent attention to what is slight in order to keep at bay what is large.

2 We emend 煙 of all editions to 熛, following 王引之.

HF 21.5.3 (*Xilun* 386, *Xin jiaozhu* 441)

扁鵲見蔡桓公，	Bian Que paid a visit to Lord Huan of Cai.[26]
立有間，	After he had been standing for a while,
扁鵲曰：	Bian Que said:

---

25 Nothing is known about Bai Gui. One commentator's guess is that he was a fourth century personality in Wei who was renowned for his hydraulic projects.
26 Bian Que is the famous doctor whose biography appears in *Shiji* 105. There is much confusion about when he lived, and this figure may be a conflation of different personalities. The current mention in *Han Feizi* only exacerbates the confusion. The lords of Cai were normally referred to as Marquises even posthumously, hence, it should be Marquis Huan of Cai 蔡桓侯 (r. 714–695) later in the chapter (if it is indeed Marquis Huan).

"君有疾在腠理，	"My lord, you have an acute disease on the surface of your skin.
不治將恐深。"	If you do not treat this, I am afraid the condition will worsen."
桓侯曰：	Marquis Huan said:
"寡人無。"	"I have nothing of the kind."
扁鵲出。	Bian Que left,
桓侯曰：	and Marquis Huan said:
"醫之好治不病以為功。"	"The reason why doctors like to treat those who have nothing wrong with them is that they want to count this as their success."
居十日，	After ten days,
扁鵲復見曰：	Bian Que went to pay another visit and said:
"君之病在肌膚，	"My lord, your disease is now in the skin itself.
不治將益深。"	Unless you treat this, it will get even worse."
桓侯不應。	Marquis Huan made no reply.
扁鵲出。	Bian Que left.
桓侯又不悅。	Marquis Huan again felt dissatisfied.
居十日，	After ten days,
扁鵲復見曰：	Bian Que went to pay another visit and he said:
"君之病在腸胃，	"My lord, the disease is in your bowels and stomach.
不治將益深。"	Unless you treat this, it will get even worse."
桓侯又不應。	Marquis Huan, again, made no reply.
扁鵲出。	Bian Que left.
桓侯又不悅。	Marquis Huan was still more dissatisfied with the doctor's skills.
居十日，	After ten days,
扁鵲望桓侯而還走，	Bian Que looked at Marquis Huan from a distance, turned round and ran away.
桓侯故使人問之。	Marquis Huan then sent someone to ask him about this.
扁鵲曰：	Bian Que said:
"疾在腠理，	"When the disease was in the surface of the skin,
湯熨之所及也；	it could be reached by medicated liquid and by hot pressure;
在肌膚，	when it was in the skin itself,
鍼石之所及也；	it could be reached by metal and stone needles;
在腸胃，	when it was in the bowels and stomach,
火齊之所及也；	it could be reached with boiled medicines;

35	在骨髓，	but when it is in the bone and marrow
	司命之所屬，	it is a matter for the Master of Fate,[27]
	無奈何也。	and there is nothing we can do.
	今在骨髓，	Now it is in the bones and marrow,
	臣是以無請也。"	and that is why I have nothing to recommend."
40	居五日，	After five days,
	桓侯體痛，	Marquis Huan felt a pain in his limbs.
	使人索扁鵲，	He sent someone to seek out Bian Que,
	已逃秦矣。	but [Bian] had already fled to Qin.
	桓侯遂死。	Then Marquis Huan died.
45	故良醫之治病也，	Thus, a fine doctor, when treating a disease,
	攻之於腠理，	will attack it on the surface of the skin.
	此皆爭之於小者也。	These are all cases of fighting something at the stage where it is small.
	夫事之禍福亦有腠理之地，	Among disaster and misfortune in undertakings, there is also that which corresponds to the skin surface.
	故聖人蚤從事焉。	Therefore, a sage will make an early start.

8〔出〕(校注 231). 30〔也〕(校注 231). 34 齊 is read as 劑. 35 張抄 has 體 for 髓. 49 故（曰）聖人 (校注 231).

HF 21.6 (*Xilun* 389, *Xin jiaozhu* 444)

	昔晉公子重耳出亡，	In ancient times, Chong'er, the Prince of Jin, went into exile.
	過鄭，	When he passed through Zheng,
	鄭君不禮。	the ruler of Zheng did not treat him with decorum.
	叔瞻諫曰：	Shuzhan remonstrated, saying:
5	"此賢公子也，	"This is a worthy prince.
	君厚待之，	If you, my lord, treat him with generosity,
	可以積德。"	you can build up goodwill."
	鄭君不聽。	The ruler of Zheng did not listen.
	叔瞻又諫曰：	Shuzhan again remonstrated, saying:
10	"不厚待之，	"If you will not treat him with generosity,

---

27 The god-administrator of deaths.

喻老 ILLUSTRATING LAOZI

不若殺之，	then it is best to kill him,
無令有後患。"	lest there be disaster later."
鄭君又不聽。	The ruler of Zheng again did not listen.[28]
及公子返晉邦，	When the prince returned to the country of Jin,
舉兵伐鄭，	he raised an army and attacked Zheng,
大破之，	and he greatly crushed it,
取八城焉。	taking eight walled cities from them.[29]
晉獻公以垂棘之璧假道於虞而伐虢，	Lord Xian of Jin used jade rings from Chuiji to request right of way from Yu and attack Guo.[30]
大夫宮之奇諫曰：	The grandee Gong Zhi Qi remonstrated, saying:
"不可。	"That is not acceptable.
脣亡而齒寒，	As the proverb has it: when the lips are gone, the teeth will be cold.
虞、虢相救，	Yu and Guo are mutually dependent for defence,
非相德也。	but they do not by any means have a mutually generous relationship.
今日晉滅虢，	If Jin destroys Guo today,
明日虞必隨之亡。"	then tomorrow Yu is bound to follow suit and be ruined."
虞君不聽，	The ruler of Yu did not listen.
受其璧而假之道。	He accepted the jade rings and granted right of way.
晉已取虢，	After Jin had conquered Guo,
還，	on their way back
反滅虞。	they turned round to destroy Yu.

---

28 The story of Chong'er's mistreatment by the Zheng ruler and Shuzhan's remonstrance is told in *Zuozhuan* Xi 23.6; see also an alternative version in *Han Feizi* 10.10. Han Fei's addition here is of advice to kill the prince as an alternative to merely alienating him. For a similar odd advice (either elevate this person or detain/kill him), see, for instance, an anecdote about the Wei minister Gongshu Cuo 公叔痤 and Gongsun Yang (future Shang Yang), *Lüshi chunqiu* 11.5 ("Chang jian"); *Zhanguo ce* 12.9 ("Wei 魏 1"); *Shiji* 68. Perhaps it was a common trope in late Warring States stories.

29 This is surely an exaggeration. According to the detailed account in *Zuozhuan* (Xi 30.3), the Jin assault on Zheng in 630 was terminated when Jin's ally, Qin, shifted sides and decided to support Zheng.

30 See chapter 10.2 for another version of this story.

此二臣者皆爭於腠理者也，	These two ministers (i.e. Shuzhan and Gong Zhi Qi) joined the discussions forcefully when the problem was on the surface of the skin
而二君不用也。	but the two rulers did not use their advice.
然則叔瞻、宮之奇亦虞、鄭之扁鵲也，	Thus Shuzhan and Gong Zhi Qi are surely the Bian Ques of Yu and Zheng.
而二君不聽，	However, the two rulers did not listen,
35 故鄭以破，	and therefore Zheng was defeated,
虞以亡。	and Yu was ruined.
故曰：	So it is said:
"其安易持⟨之/之 drjəg/dï⟩也，	"In peace, things are easy to sustain;
其未兆易謀⟨之/尤 mjəg/mjə̂u⟩也。"	when there are as yet no symptoms, it is easy to make plans."[31]

13　（公）〔君〕（校注 231）.

HF 21.7 (*Xilun* 390, *Xin jiaozhu* 445)

昔者紂為象箸[A 魚/御 trjagh/tjwo]，	In ancient times, [King] Zhòu had chopsticks made of ivory,
而箕子怖[A 魚/暮 phagh/phuo]。	and Jizi was terrified.[32]
以為象箸必不加於土鉶，	He considered: "Ivory chopsticks are not used with earthenware *xing*-vessels;
必將犀玉之杯[B 之/灰 pəg/puə̂i]。	they go with drinking bowls of rhinoceros horn and jade.
5　象箸、玉杯必不羹菽藿，	With ivory chopsticks and jade bowls, it is certain that broth will not be made of beans and leaves;
必旄、象、豹胎[B 之/咍 thəg/thə̂i]。	it has to be yak, elephant or leopard foetus.
旄、象、豹胎必不衣裋褐而食於茅屋之下，	With yak, elephant and leopard foetus, it is certain that one will not wear coarse clothes and eat under thatched roofs;
則錦衣九重，	rather, one will have many-layered rich brocade,
廣室高臺[B 之/咍 dəg/də̂i]。	spacious dwellings, and high terraces.

31　Section 6 of the chapter comments on *Laozi* 64.
32　Zhòu was the last, tyrant king of the Shang dynasty; Jizi was his virtuous uncle.

10	吾畏其卒，	I am afraid of how this will end;
	故怖其始。	therefore, I am terrified of these beginnings."
	居五年，	After five years,
	紂為肉圃，	Zhòu made a grove of hanging meat;[33]
	設炮烙，	he set up red-hot grills for roasting people;
15	登糟丘，	he ascended mountains of dregs
	臨酒池，	and looked out over his lake of ale,
	紂遂以亡。	and Zhòu was subsequently ruined.
	故箕子見象箸以知天下之禍。	So, when Jizi saw the ivory chopsticks, he understood the impending disaster for the world.
	故曰：	So it is said:
20	"見小曰明。"	"Noticing what is small is called clear-sightedness."[34]

2 C emends 怖 to 唏, with 史記 and 淮南子. We see no reason to emend, since 唏[微/未 hjədh/xjẽi] (or 怖[希 微/微 hrəd/xjẽi]) does not rhyme.　　7 The C editors note:「食」應依〈說林〉作「舍」。「食」與「舍」聲形並近，因而致誤。. We regard 舍 as a loan for 食; cf. HF 22.24.　　7 短 is emended to 裋, following 劉堅.　　11 C emends 怖 to 唏, with 史記 and 淮南子. We see no reason to emend; cf. above.

HF 21.8 (*Xilun* 392, *Xin jiaozhu* 447)

	勾踐入宦於吳，	Goujian became a servant in Wu.
	身執干戈為吳王洗馬，	In person he held the shield and the halberd, and washed horses for the King of Wu.[35]
	故能殺夫差於姑蘇。	As a result, he was able to kill Fuchai at Gusu.
	文王見詈於玉門，	When King Wen was insulted at the Jade Gate,
5	顏色不變，	his facial expression did not change,
	而武王擒紂於牧野。	and King Wu captured Zhòu at Muye.[36]

33　There are many lurid accounts of this tyrant's depravity in ancient Chinese literature. See Pines 2008 for details.
34　Section 7 of the chapter comments on *Laozi* 52.
35　See note 19 above.
36　The details of King Wen's (or, in alternative version, future King Wu's) humiliation at the Jade Gate 玉門 (or Royal Gate 王門?) are not clear.

CHAPTER 21

故曰：	So it is said:
"守柔曰強。"	Preserving weakness is called strength."
越王之霸也不病臣，	King [Goujian] of Yue, in order to become the hegemon, was not aggrieved by serving as a functionary.
10　武王之王也不病詈。	King Wu, in order to become king, was not upset by being insulted.
故曰：	So it is said:
"聖人之不病也，	"The fact that the sage is not upset about things,
以其不病，	is because there is nothing upsetting about them;
是以無病也。"	and that is why he has no reactions of being upset."[37]

1 張抄 has 官 for 臣.　　4 王 is emended to 玉, following 盧文弨.　　9 張抄 has 官 for 臣.

HF 21.9.1 (*Xilun* 393, *Xin jiaozhu* 449)

宋之鄙人得璞玉而獻之子罕，	A country bumpkin from Song found a piece of uncarved jade and presented it to Zihan,
子罕不受。	but Zihan did not accept the gift.
鄙人曰：	The country bumpkin said:
"此寶也，	"This is a treasure.
5　宜為君子器，	It is suitable to be made into a fine instrument for a superior man;
不宜為細人用。"	it is not suitable to be used by a slight person."
子罕曰：	Zihan said:
"爾以玉為寶，	"You consider the piece of jade as a treasure;
我以不受子玉為寶。"	I, for my part, consider it a treasure not to accept your jade."[38]
10　是鄙人欲玉，	In this way, the country bumpkin had a desire for jade,
而子罕不欲玉。	but Zihan had no desire for jade.

37　Section 8 of the chapter comments on *Laozi* 71.
38　See *Zuozhuan*, Xiang 15.8. Zihan is an appellative of the Song minister, Yue Xi 樂喜. Do not confuse him with the infamous usurper, Zihan, from the fourth century (chapter 7, note 5).

喻老 ILLUSTRATING LAOZI

故曰：
"欲不欲，
而不貴難得之貨。"

So it is said:
"Desire not to desire,
and do not value items that are hard to get."[39]

HF 21.9.2 (*Xilun* 394, *Xin jiaozhu* 449)

王壽負書而行，
見徐馮於周塗。
馮曰：
"事者，
為也；
為生於時，
知者無常事。

書者，
言也；
言生於知，
知者不藏書。
今子何獨負之而行？"
於是王壽因焚其書而儛之。
故知者不以言談教，
而慧者不以藏書篋。

此世之所過也，
而王壽復之。
是學不學也。

故曰：
"學不學，
復歸眾人之所過也。"

Wang Shou was travelling, carrying his books on his back.
He met Xu Feng on the road to Zhou.[40]
Feng said:
"Undertakings
are things we do.
Doing is determined by the season.
He who understands things, has no inflexible undertakings.

As for books,
they are words.
Words are determined by understanding;
he who understands does not store books.
Now why do you travel with these things on your back, of all things."
Then, Wang Shou went on to burn his books in and danced on them.
Thus he who understands things does not use words to discuss his teachings,
and the wise person has no use for boxes to store books.

This is something that everyone regards as wrong,
but Wang Shou turned to it.
This is to learn non-learning.

So it is said:
"Learn non-learning,
and turn to what the multitudes regard as wrong."

---

39 Section 9 of the chapter comments on *Laozi* 64.
40 Wang Shou and Xu Feng are unattested outside of *Han Feizi*.

HF 21.9.3 (*Xilun* 395, *Xin jiaozhu* 451)

夫物有常容，
因乘以導之。
因隨物之容，
故靜則建乎德，
5　動則順乎道。

宋人有為其君以象為楮葉者，

三年而成。
豐殺莖柯，
毫芒繁澤，

10　亂之楮葉之中而不可別也。

此人遂以功食祿於宋邦。

列子聞之曰：
"使天地三年而成一葉，

則物之有葉者寡矣。"

15　故不乘天地之資而載一人之身，

不隨道理之數而學一人之智，

此皆一葉之行也。

故冬耕之稼，
后稷不能羨也；

Now, things have constant appearances,
and so you rely on these to guide them.
You follow the appearances of things,
and as a result, when inactive, you are established in inner integrity;
and when moving, you follow the Way.

Once a man from Song made a mulberry leaf of ivory for his ruler.
After three years, it was finished.
Lavishly, he evened out the stems and stalks;
the pattern of its fibres and filaments was intricate.
Were you to mix it in with mulberry leaves, it would have been indistinguishable.
This man then drew stipends in the country of Song because of his contributions.
When Liezi[41] heard about this, he said:
"Suppose Heaven and Earth took three years to finish one leaf;
things with leaves would be few indeed."

Thus, if you do not rely on the resources of Heaven and Earth, but put your trust in one person,
if you do not follow the methods of the principles of the Way, but study from the knowledge of one man –
these are all practices like those of the single leaf.

Thus, if he worked his fields during the winter, even Hou Ji would not reap a rich [harvest].[42]

41　Liezi is usually identified as a Daoist sage. A book attributed to him was compiled after the end of the Han dynasty.

42　Hou Ji (Lord Millet) is a cultural hero and the legendary progenitor of the Zhou house.

喻老 ILLUSTRATING LAOZI

20	豐年大禾，	In a rich year with a bumper grain harvest,
	臧獲不能惡也。	even a slave cannot come out badly.
	以一人力，	If one uses one person's strength,
	則后稷不足；	even Hou Ji is inadequate;
	隨自然，	if one follows the natural course of events,
25	則臧獲有餘。	even a slave would have more than enough.
	故曰：	So it is said:
	"恃萬物之自然而不敢為也。"	"Rely on the natural course of the myriad things,
		and do not presume to take assertive action."

16 〔之〕(校注 232).   21 C has 藏 for 臧, with 張抄.

HF 21.10.1 (*Xilun* 397, *Xin jiaozhu* 453)

	空竅者，	The apertures
	神明之戶牖也。	are the doors and windows of the spirit and the supernatural intelligence.
	耳目竭於聲色，	Ears and eyes are exhausted by sounds and colours;
	精神竭于外貌，	the subtle spirit is exhausted by external appearances.
5	故中無主。	That is why there is no ruling element within.
	中無主，	When there is no ruling element within,
	則禍福雖如丘山，	even if disasters and good fortune pile up like mounds and mountains,
	無從識之。	people have no way to recognise these.
	故曰：	So it is said:
10	"不出於戶⟨A 魚/姥 gagx/ɣuoˀ⟩，	"Without going out through the door,
	可以知天下⟨A 魚/馬 gragx/ɣaˀ⟩；	you can know the world;
	不闚於牖⟨B 幽/有 rəgwx/jiəuˀ⟩，	without peering out of the window,
	可以知天道⟨B 幽/晧 dəgwx/dâuˀ⟩。"	you can know the way of Heaven."[43]
	此言神明之不離其實也。	This means that supernatural intelligence is not separable from the actual.

---

43   *Laozi* 47.

HF 21.10.2 (*Xilun* 397, *Xin jiaozhu* 454)

趙襄主學御於王子於期，	Xiang, ruler of Zhao,[44] was studying charioteering with Wangzi Yuqi.
俄而與於期逐，	One day, he was in a competition with Wangzi Yuqi.
三易馬而三後。	Three times he changed horses, but three times he finished behind.
襄主曰：	Ruler Xiang said:
5 "子之教我御，術未盡也？"	"Are the techniques of chariot driving that you, Sir, have taught me not yet complete?"
對曰：	Wang Ziqi replied politely:
"術已盡，	"The techniques are complete.
用之則過也。	It is in its implementation that the mistake lies.
10 凡御之所貴：	In general, the most important points in driving are these:
馬體安于車，	The limbs of the horse must be comfortably placed before the vehicle;
人心調于馬，	the human mind must be attuned to the horses;
而後可以進速致遠。	only then can you advance fast and reach far.
今君後則欲逮臣，	Now when you, my lord, are behind, you desire to catch up with me,
15 先則恐逮于臣。	and when you are ahead, you are afraid to be overtaken by me.
夫誘道爭遠，	When you egg the horses on and struggle to reach far,
非先則後也，	you are either ahead or behind,
而先後心皆在于臣，	but, no matter whether you are ahead or behind, if your mind is always fixed on me,
上何以調於馬？	how can your excellency be attuned to the horses?
20 此君之所以後也。"	This is why you, my lord, finish behind."
白公勝慮亂，	The Duke of Bai named Sheng[45] was plotting a rebellion.

---

44 Zhao Xiangzi (d. ca. 442), the head of the Zhao lineage and the de facto founder of the independent Zhao polity. Referring to him not as Xiangzi but as "ruler Xiang" is unusual, but such references are found elsewhere in *Han Feizi* and *Zhanguo ce* (see chapter 1, note 33).

45 The Duke of Bai named Sheng was the son of the former crown prince of Chu, Jian 建,

喻老 ILLUSTRATING LAOZI

罷朝，	When he left the court,
倒杖而策銳貫頤，	he inverted his weapon and, with the sharp end, pierced his cheek.
血流至于地而不知。	Blood dripped to the ground without his knowing.
25 鄭人聞之曰：	When the people of Zheng heard about this, they said:
"頤之忘，	"If he disregards his cheek,
將何不忘哉？"	what will he not disregard?"
故曰：	So it is said:
"其出彌遠者，	"The further you go,
30 其智彌少。"	the lesser is your intellect."
此言智周乎遠，	This means that when your intellect ranges everywhere into the distance,
則所遺在近也。	what you miss is close at hand.
是以聖人無常行也。	Therefore the sage is not a man who constantly moves.
能並智，	He is able to know by analogical inference.
35 故曰：	So it is said:
"不行而知。"	"Without travelling, he knows."
能並視，	He is able to see by analogical inference.
故曰：	So it is said:
"不見而明。"	"Without seeing, he has insight."
40 隨時以舉事，	He follows the right times in all his undertakings,
因資而立功，	and avails himself of resources to establish results.
用萬物之能而獲利其上，	He avails himself of the potential of the myriad things and so reaps his profit from them.[46]

---

who was ousted from his state in 522. Jian stayed for a while in the state of Zheng, but once his plot against his hosts was discovered, he was put to death. His son Sheng fled to the state of Wu, but was later summoned back to Chu and given the fief of Bai there. In 479, he launched a rebellion that almost toppled King Hui of Chu. According to the *Han Feizi* anecdote cited here, he already harboured "rebellious thoughts" as early as his father's stay in Zheng, when the would-be Duke of Bai was but a youngster. Needless to say, the historicity of this anecdote is questionable.

46   The use of *shang* 上 here is opaque to me.

330   CHAPTER 21

故曰：
"不為而成。"

So it is said:
"He does not take assertive action but succeeds."

1 張抄 has 王 for 主.　1〔於〕(校注 232).　4 張抄 has 王 for 主.　13 The C editors note:「進速」疑應作「追速」,〈難勢〉正作「追速致遠」.　18〔皆〕(校注 232).　27（為）〔不〕(校注 232).　42 張抄 has 土 for 上.

HF 21.11 (*Xilun* 400, *Xin jiaozhu* 456)

楚莊王蒞政三年，

無令發，
無政為也。
右司馬御座而與王隱曰：

5　"有鳥止南方之阜，

三年不翅，
不飛不鳴[A 耕/庚 mjiŋ/mjeŋ]，
嘿然無聲[A 耕/清 hrjiŋ/śjäŋ]，
此為何名[A 耕/清 mjiŋ/mjäŋ]？"
10　王曰：
"三年不翅，
將以長羽翼[B 之/職 rək/jiək]；
不飛不鳴，
將以觀民則[B 之/德 tsək/tsək]。
15　雖無飛，
飛必沖天[C 真/先 thin/thien]；
雖無鳴，
鳴必驚人[C 真/真 njin/ńźjĕn]。
子釋之，
20　不穀知之矣。"
處半年，

King Zhuang of Chu[47] had been leading his government for three years,
without issuing an ordinance
or engaging in administration.
The Marshal on the Right was in attendance and told the King a riddle:
There is a bird that has settled on the hills in the southern regions.
For three years now, it has not flapped its wings;
it has not flown; it has made no song;
all quiet, it has made no sound.
What shall we call this bird."
The King said:
"If, in three years, it has never flapped its wings, this was in order to let its feathers grow.
If it has not flown or sung,
this must be in order to view the rules that the people obey.
It may never have flown,
but if it should fly, it will surely surge to Heaven;
it may never have sung,
but if it should sing, it will surely astonish men.
You had better set him free, Sir.
I understand this very well."[48]
Half a year went by,

---

47 King Zhuang of Chu (r. 613–591) was the singularly successful ruler of Chu under whose reign Chu attained hegemony in most areas south of the Yellow River.
48 Many variants of this story appear in texts from the late Warring States period onwards. Most of these deal with King Zhuang (and a variety of his advisors), but at least in one case

喻老 ILLUSTRATING LAOZI

乃自聽政。	and he personally attended to administrative matters.
所廢者十，	He dismissed ten courtiers
所起者九，	and elevated nine.
25 誅大臣五，	He punished five senior ministers
舉處士六，	and elevated six reclusive gentlemen to high position.
而邦大治。	As a result, the country was eminently well-ordered.
舉兵誅齊，	He raised his army for a punitive expedition against Qi
敗之徐州，	and defeated Qi at Xuzhou;[49]
30 勝晉於河雍，	he defeated Jin in Heyong,[50]
合諸侯於宋，	assembled the regional lords at Song,[51]
遂霸天下。	and ended by being the hegemon of all under Heaven.
莊王不為小害善，	King Zhuang would not hurt the good cause for petty reasons;
故有大名；	that is why he had a great name.
35 不蚤見示，	He did not show his hand too early;
故有大功。	that is why he had great success.
故曰：	So it is said:
"大器晚成⟨D 耕/清 djiŋ/ʑjän⟩，	"A great tool takes time to be fashioned;
大音希聲⟨D 耕/清 hrjiŋ/śjän⟩。"	a great tone is a slight sound."[52]

12 以（觀）長（校注 232). 15 The C editors note:「雖」字讀作「唯」。《莊子·齊物論》：「是唯无作，作則萬竅怒呺。」句法與此相同。《韓非子·內儲說下》：「唯毋一戰，戰必不兩存。」《淮南子·兵略》：「唯無一動，動則淩天振地。」並其例。下「雖」字同。

(*Shiji* 126), the protagonist is the fourth century King Wei of Qi. See a summary in Chen Qiyou's gloss (457n2).

49 This is surely a historical inaccuracy: Han Fei probably conflates King Zhuang's military exploits with those of King Wei of Chu (who did indeed fight Qi at Xuzhou in 333 [*Shiji* 40: 1721]).

50 A reference to Chu's major defeat of Jin at Bi 邲 in 597.

51 It is not clear to which event Han Fei refers. King Zhuang of Chu fought with Song in 596–595 and was victorious, but no major regional meeting there in the aftermath of the battle is recorded.

52 Section 11 of the chapter comments on *Laozi* 41.

HF 21.12.1 (*Xilun* 402, *Xin jiaozhu* 457)

楚莊王欲伐越，	King Zhuang of Chu wanted to attack Yue.
杜子諫曰：	Duzi remonstrated:[53]
"王之伐越，	"Your Majesty is going to attack Yue,
何也？"	why is that?"
5 曰：	[The king] said:
"政亂兵弱。"	"Their government is in turmoil and their army is weak."
杜子曰：	Duzi said:
"臣愚患之。	"Stupid as I am, I consider this as a disastrous thing to do.
智如目也，	Intellect is like the eye.
10 能見百步之外而不能自見其睫，	It can see further than one hundred paces, but cannot see its own eyelashes.
王之兵自敗於秦、晉，	Through your own fault, Your Majesty's armed forces were beaten by Qin and Jin;
喪地數百里，	you have lost a territory of several hundred *li* square.[54]
此兵之弱也；	This was because of the weakness of your own armed forces.
莊蹻蹻為盜於境內而吏不能禁，	Zhuang Qiqiao has been practising his banditry within our borders,[55] and the officials are unable to quell to his activities.
15 此政之亂也。	This was because the government is in turmoil.
王之弱亂，	The weakness and turmoil on Your Majesty's part

---

53 There is some confusion in this story, either due to Han Fei's inaccuracy or a later scribal error that resulted in the attribution of the debate to the time of King Zhuang. Clearly, the information in the text is relevant, if at all, to third century events and not to the time of King Zhuang (who died in 591).

54 This statement may refer to Chu's military setbacks in the late fourth or, more likely, early third century, in which case Jin would be an alias of the state of Wei. However, it is equally possible that the statement was messy from the beginning, reflecting Han Fei's (or this chapter's other authors) imperfect knowledge of the past.

55 Here the character "Qi" 蹻 is almost certainly redundant, although Zhang Jue (2011: 402–403) considers it to be Zhuang Qiao's appellative (*zi* 字). The information about Zhuang Qiao is confusing, but he was most probably a Chu general who wreaked havoc in the state of Chu following its disastrous defeat at the hands of Qin armies in 278. If the passage above has any historical background at all, it may hint at Chu king's desire to expand eastward toward Yue in the aftermath of the 278 debacle. Needless to say, this is purely conjectural.

喻老 ILLUSTRATING LAOZI

非越之下也，	is no less than that of Yue,
而欲伐越，	and still you are inclined to attack Yue.
此智之如目也。"	This is because intellect is like the eye."
20 王乃止。	Then the King desisted.
故知之難，	Thus the difficulty with knowing
不在見人，	is not in seeing others;
在自見。	it is in seeing yourself.
故曰：	So it is said:
25 "自見之謂明。"	"Seeing yourself is called clear insight."[56]

18 〔而〕欲伐越 (校注 232).

HF 21.12.2 (*Xilun* 403, *Xin jiaozhu* 460)

子夏見曾子。	Zixia visited Zengzi.[57]
曾子曰：	Zengzi said:
"何肥也？"	"I say, why are you looking so sleek?"
對曰：	Zixia replied:
5 "戰勝，	"I have won in battle.
故肥也。"	That is why I look sleek."
曾子曰：	Zengzi said:
"何謂也？"	"What do you mean."
子夏曰：	Zixia said:
10 "吾入見先王之義，	"Looking inwards, I have seen the moral principles of the Former Kings,
則榮之；	and I found them tremendous.
出見富貴之樂又榮之。	Looking outwards, I have seen the delights of wealth and honour, and these I found imposing too.
兩者戰於胸中，	The two were at war in my breast,[58]

---

56 In this instance, Han Fei seems to have seen a different *Laozi* text from the transmitted versions we have. *Laozi* 33 speaks of "knowing oneself" 子知 and not "seeing yourself." Alternatively, as suggested by Chen Qiyou, the substitution of "knowing" for "seeing" may be the work of the author of the chapter.

57 Both were among the most famous disciples of Confucius.

58 This is one of the few occasions where inner conflict is dramatised in an almost personified way in ancient Chinese literature.

未知勝負，	and I did not yet know which would win and which would lose.
15 故臞。	So I was emaciated.
今先王之義勝，	Now the moral principles of the Former Kings have won.
故肥。"	That is why I look sleek."
是以志之難也，	Therefore, the difficulty for aspirations
不在勝人，	is not in overcoming others;
20 在自勝也。	it is in overcoming yourself.
故曰：	So it is said:
"自勝之謂強。"	"overcoming oneself is called 'strength'."[59]

15 張抄 has 曜 for 臞。   18 張抄 has 忘 for 志。

HF 21.13 (*Xilun* 405, *Xin jiaozhu* 460)

周有玉版，	Once there was a jade tablet in Zhou.
紂令膠鬲索之，	[King] Zhòu [of Shang] ordered Jiao Ge to ask for it,
文王不予；	but (the future) King Wen of the Zhou would not give it away;
費仲來求，	Fei Zhong came to try to get it,
5 因予之。	and [King Wen] gave it to him.
是膠鬲賢而費仲無道也。	This is because Jiao Ge was worthy and Fei Zhong did not have the Way.[60]
周惡賢者之得志也，	The Zhou were disinclined to let a worthy get his will,
故予費仲。	so they gave the tablet to Fei Zhong.

59　Section 12 of the chapter comments on *Laozi* 33.

60　Jiao Ge is commonly referred to as a worthy follower of King Zhòu, the Shang tyrant, who failed to make use of him. Fei Zhong appears in *Han Feizi* altogether four times. In the extract above he appears as an immoral official, an image which is supported in chapter 31.6.1, where Fei Zhong acts as a Zhou agent at King Zhòu's court (a point hinted at in *Shiji* 4: 116). Elsewhere, however (39.4.3), Fei Zhong is hailed as a worthy minister who, despite his worthiness, failed to save his master. This point is elucidated in *Han Feizi* 33.3.7, in which Fei Zhong gives King Zhòu correct (if immoral) advice to annihilate the righteous King Wen of Zhou, but is not heeded.

喻老 ILLUSTRATING LAOZI

文王舉太公於渭濱者， When King Wen raised Grand Duke [Wang] to high office on the banks of River Wei,
10 貴之也； it is because he valued him;
而資費仲玉版者， and when he gave Fei Zhong the jade tablet,
是愛之也。 this was because he was fond of him.[61]

故曰： So it is said:
"不貴其師⟨A 脂/脂 srjid/ʂji⟩， "If you do not value your teacher
15 不愛其資⟨A 脂/脂 tsjid/tsji⟩， and are not fond of this resource,
雖知大迷⟨A 脂/齊 mid/miei⟩， then although you might be knowledgeable, you will be greatly misguided.
是謂要妙。" This is called the crucial mystery."[62]

---

61 As a future resource for the dynasty he was to establish, Grand Duke Wang was valued as a teacher, and Fei Zhong was valued as suitable "material" to work on (as is explained in *Han Feizi* 31.6.1).
62 Section 13 of the chapter comments on *Laozi* 27.

CHAPTER 22

說林上 A Forest of Persuasions, Part 1

HF 22.1 (*Xilun* 407, *Xin jiaozhu* 461)

湯以伐桀，	Tang, because he attacked Jie,
而恐天下言己為貪也，	was afraid that all the world would say that he was greedy for power,[1]
因乃讓天下於務光。	so he yielded the world to Wuguang,
而恐務光之受之也，	but then he was afraid that Wuguang would accept the offer,
5 乃使人說務光曰：	so he sent an emissary to Wuguang, advising him:
"湯殺君而欲傳惡聲于子，	"Tang has killed the ruler and wants to pass on the bad reputation to you.
故讓天下於子。"	That is why he has yielded the empire to you."
務光因自投於河。	Wuguang thereupon threw himself into the [Yellow] River.[2]

HF 22.2 (*Xilun* 408, *Xin jiaozhu* 462)

秦武王令甘茂擇所欲為於僕與行事。	King Wu of Qin ordered Gan Mao to choose whether he wanted to be his servant or his manager of affairs.
孟卯曰：	Meng Mao said:
"公不如為僕。	"You had better become his servant![3]

---

1   This is one of the rare cases of indirect speech in pre-Han Chinese. Tang, the founder of the Shang dynasty, rebelled against the "last bad king" of the Xia dynasty, Jie.

2   This story is remarkable for its focus on the fear of public opinion, and particularly the public expression of negative opinions. It is also an epitome of Han Fei's cynical views of history. Tang the Successful, who is clearly greedy for power, pretends to yield his rule to a lofty recluse Wuguang. However, he also hints that by accepting the offer, Wuguang would forever sully his reputation. To protect his name, Wuguang opts to commit suicide. One short story ridicules everybody – the paragon of good rule, the lofty recluse, and the ideal of selfless abdication, which Han Fei views as nothing but cynical manipulation (cf. his take on the latter topic in 35.3.4).

3   Gan Mao (fl. 310–300), a native of Chu, was one of Qin's famous "guest ministers" (*ke qing* 客卿). His service started under King Huiwen 秦惠文王 (r. 337–311), but it was under Huiwen's

說林上 A FOREST OF PERSUASIONS, PART 1

公所長者，	Your strong point
使也。	is serving as his commissioner.
公雖為僕，	Even if you are a servant,
王猶使之於公也。	the king will still give you a formal mission.
公佩僕璽而為行事，	If you wear the seal of a servant[4] and act on the king's behalf,
是兼官也。"	this will be "holding down two offices at the same time."

HF 22.3 (*Xilun* 408, *Xin jiaozhu* 463)

子圉見孔子於商太宰。	Ziyu saw Confucius at the place of the Grand Steward of Shang (i.e. the state of Song).[5]
孔子出，	When Confucius left,
子圉入，	Ziyu went in:
請問客。	"May I ask about the stranger?"
太宰曰：	The Grand Steward said:
"吾已見孔子，	"Having met Confucius,
則視子猶蚤虱之細者也。	I find you as insignificant as a louse.
吾今見之於君。"	Today I shall present him to the ruler."
子圉恐孔子貴於君也，	Ziyu was afraid that Confucius would win honour with the ruler,
因謂太宰曰：	so he said to the Grand Steward:
"君已見孔子，	"Once the ruler has seen Confucius,
亦將視子猶蚤虱也。"	he will also look upon you as a louse."
太宰因弗復見也。	The Grand Steward accordingly refused to make any contact with Confucius again.

10 （請）〔謂〕(校注 250).　12 （孔子）亦 (校注 250).

---

son, King Wu 秦武王 (r. 310–307) that he was appointed to the top ministerial position. Meng Mao was a travelling persuader; in *Han Feizi* 50.5 he is blamed for offering disastrous advice to the king of Wei.

4　In Warring States-period China, offices were conferred along with an official seal, which could later be withdrawn when the commission ended.

5　The state of Song was established by descendants of the vanquished Shang dynasty and was occasionally referred to by that prestigious name. *Taizai* (Grand Steward) was an ad hoc appointment to a senior ministerial position. There is no early supporting evidence of Confucius' visit to the Song Grand Steward; nor anything is known about Ziyu.

HF 22.4 (*Xilun* 409, *Xin jiaozhu* 463)

魏惠王為臼里之盟，	When King Hui of Wei organised the covenant at Jiuli[6]
將復立於天子。	and wanted to reestablish the authority of the Son of Heaven,
彭喜謂鄭君曰：	Peng Xi said to the ruler of Zheng (i.e. Hán):[7]
"君勿聽。	"Do not take his advice!
大國惡有天子，	The great states dislike having a Son of Heaven,
小國利之。	whereas the small states regard having a Son of Heaven as advantageous.
若君與大不聽，	If, together with the great ones, you refuse to listen,
魏焉能與小立之？"	how could Wei, together with the small ones, reestablish the Son of Heaven?[8]

HF 22.5 (*Xilun* 410, *Xin jiaozhu* 464)

晉人伐邢，	When the people of Jin attacked Xing,[9]
齊桓公將救之。	Lord Huan of Qi was going to come to its rescue.

---

6 The covenant at Jiuli, in the vicinity of the Zhou capital at Luoyang, was organised by King Hui of Wei in 342, when he was at the apex of his power. The details are disputed, but there is no doubt that the king assembled the leaders of small- and medium-sized states in an ostensible display of deference to the Son of Heaven, so as to strengthen his own hegemonic position in the Zhou world. This attempt backfired: in 341 and 340 the state of Wei suffered humiliating defeats by Qi in the east and Qin in the west, after which its power permanently declined.

7 Having extinguished Zheng in 375, Han Fei's ancestral state of Hán moved its capital to the site of the former Zheng capital, hence it is called "Zheng" in many Warring States-period sources.

8 Peng Xi boldly speaks the unspeakable, namely that the powerful states have no interest in restoring the position of the Zhou king as arbiter in interstate relations. Hence, they will thwart Wei's plans. Hán was in an intermediary position: its joining of the Jiuli covenant would greatly bolster the prestige of King Hui of Wei, but would also mean presenting itself as a small state. To retain its pretensions as a major power, Hán had to refrain from assisting Wei. Note that the only thing which matters is Hán's self-interest, not the issue of the legitimacy of the Zhou ruling house. For an alternative (and less accurate) version of this episode, see *Zhanguo ce* 28.20 (Hán 3).

9 Han Fei characteristically abuses the evidence. In 661, the Di extinguished the statelet of Xing (in southern Hebei). Soon thereafter, Xing was reestablished by Lord Huan of Qi. By Han Fei's time, the idea of the Di being powerful had vanished from living memory, whereas the aggression could be easily ascribed to the major power of the Springs-and-Autumns period, namely Jin.

說林上 A FOREST OF PERSUASIONS, PART 1

	鮑叔曰：	(His minister) Bao Shu said:
	"太蚤。	"This is too early.
5	邢不亡，	If Xing is not ruined,
	晉不敝；	Jin will not exhaust its strength in subduing it.
	晉不敝，	If Jin does not exhaust its strength,
	齊不重。	Qi will not gain correspondingly in strength.
	且夫持危之功，	The achievement of helping someone in danger
10	不如存亡之德大。	is not as great as the virtue acquired by preserving a ruined state.
	君不如晚救之以敝晉，	You should postpone saving Xing so as to ensure that Jin exhausts its strength.
	齊實利。	It will be Qi that profits from that.
	待邢亡而復存之，	Wait until Xing is ruined and then restore it –
	其名實美。"	that will give you an illustrious name."
15	桓公乃弗救。	As a result, Lord Huan decided not to rescue Xing.

HF 22.6 (*Xilun* 411, *Xin jiaozhu* 465)

	子胥出走，	When Zixu fled [from Chu],
	邊候得之。	a border official arrested him.[10]
	子胥曰：	Zixu said;
	"上索我者，	"When the ruler was seeking me out,
5	以我有美珠也。	it was because I possessed a beautiful pearl.
	今我已亡之矣。	Now I have already lost it.
	我且曰：	I am going to tell the ruler
	子取吞之。"	that you've taken [the pearl] and swallowed it."
	候因釋之。	The border official thereupon set him free.

HF 22.7 (*Xilun* 412, *Xin jiaozhu* 465)

	慶封為亂於齊而欲走越。	Qing Feng set Qi in turmoil and wanted to flee to Yue.[11]

---

10   Wu Zixu (see chapter 3, note 5) was son of a Chu minister who was slandered and executed by King Ping of Chu 楚平王 (r. 528–516). Wu Zixu fled to Chu's arch-enemy, the state of Wu, for which he eventually oversaw a spectacular victory over Chu in 506.

11   Qing Feng, a leading Qi minister, first joined forces with Cui Zhu 崔杼 to carry out the assassination of Lord Zhuang of Qi in 548. Two years later, Qing Feng exterminated the

其族人曰：His kinsman said:
"晉近[A 文/隱 gjənx/gjən]，"Jin is close.
奚不之晉[A 真/震 tsjinh/-jiən/tsjĕn]？" Why don't you go to Jin."
慶封曰：Qing Feng said;
"越遠[B 元/阮 gwjanx/jwɐn]，"Yue is far away,
利以避難[B 元/翰 nanh/nân]。" and it is most suitable to keep out of trouble."
族人曰：His kinsman said:
"變是心也，"If you change this (rebellious) heart of yours,
居晉而可；staying in Jin will be just fine;
不變是心也，if you do not change this attitude of yours,
雖遠越，then even if you move away as far as Yue,
其可以安乎？" will you be able to stay safe?"

HF 22.8 (*Xilun* 412, *Xin jiaozhu* 465)

智伯索地於魏宣子，Zhi Bo demanded territory from Wei Xuanzi,
魏宣子弗予。and Wei Xuanzi would not give it to him.[12]
任章曰：Ren Zhang said:
"何故不予？" "Why didn't you give it to him."
宣子曰：Xuanzi said:
"無故請地，"With no good reason, he asked me for territory,
故弗予。" that's why I refused to give it to him."
任章曰：Ren Zhang said:
"無故索地，"Since he is demanding territory without reason,
鄰國必恐。the neighbouring states[13] are bound to be afraid (that they will be next).

彼重欲無厭，If that man has heavy insatiable ambitions,
天下必懼。the whole world will certainly be afraid of him.
君予之地，If you, my lord, give him territory,
智伯必驕而輕敵，Zhi Bo is bound to become arrogant and make light of his enemies,

---

Cui lineage and became the sole dictator of Qi. However, other aristocratic lineages joined forces against Qing Feng and caused him to flee to Wu (not to Yue) in 545. In 538, King Ling of Chu invaded Wu, seized Qing Feng, and had him executed.

12 For the story of Zhi Bo and his fall, see chapter 10.5.
13 Note that throughout the anecdote, Wei, Zhao, and Hán are treated as "states" (*guo* 國, or once *bang* 邦) and not as parts of the Jin polity. The anecdote recurs in *Zhanguo ce* 22.1 (Wei 1).

說林上 A FOREST OF PERSUASIONS, PART 1

15 鄰邦必懼而相親。	and the neighbouring states are bound to move more closely to us out of fear.
以相親之兵待輕敵之國，	If we face a state which makes light of its enemies with closely allied forces,
則智伯之命不長矣。	Zhi Bo's fortunes will not last long.
《周書》曰：	The *Zhou Documents* say:
'將欲敗⟨A 祭/夫 bradh/bai⟩之，	'If you want to defeat someone,
20 必姑輔⟨A 魚/襲 bjagx/bju⟩之。	you must first help him;
將欲取⟨B 侯/襲 tshjugx/-juo/tshju⟩之，	if you want to take from someone,
必姑予⟨B 魚/語 ragx/-jo/jiwo⟩之。'	you must first give to him.'[14]
君不如與之以驕智伯。	You should rather hand over the territory to make Zhi Bo arrogant.
且君何釋以天下圖智氏，	Moreover, why should you not plot against the Zhi Bo with the whole world,
25 而獨以吾國為智氏質乎？	and just give a piece of our country to Zhi Bo as a token gift?
君曰：	The ruler said:
"善。"	"Very good."
乃與之萬戶之邑。	And he handed over settlements of ten thousand households.
智伯大悅，	Zhi Bo felt greatly satisfied,
30 因索地於趙，	and went on to demand territory from Zhao.
弗與，	They would not hand over territory,
因圍晉陽。	so he besieged Jinyang.
韓、魏反之外，	Hán and Wei revolted against him on the outside,
趙氏應之內，	the Zhao lineage responded from the inside,
35 智氏以亡。	and the Zhi lineage was thereby annihilated.

35 (自)〔以〕(校注 250).

HF 22.9 (*Xilun* 413, *Xin jiaozhu* 467)

秦康公築臺三年。	Lord Kang of Qin had been building terrace for three years.
荊人起兵，	The people of Jing (Chu) raised an army

---

14 The quotation appears in the current version of *Laozi* 36.

將欲以兵攻齊。	and wanted to use the army to launch an attack on Qi.15
任妄曰：	Ren Wang said:
5　"饑召兵，	"Famine attracts armed attacks,
疾召兵，	disease attracts armed attacks,
勞召兵，	exhaustion attracts armed attacks,
亂召兵。	and disorder attracts armed attacks.
君築臺三年，	You have been building this terrace for three years,
10　今荊人起兵將攻齊，	and when the people of Jing (Chu) now raise an army and are about to attack Qi,
臣恐其攻齊為聲，	I am afraid that their attack on Qi is for show,
而以襲秦為實也，	and that in reality they are invading Qin.
不如備之。"	We had better make preparations for this."
戍東邊，	They garrisoned the eastern border
15　荊人輟行。	and the people of Jing (Chu) ceased their march.16

15 張抄 has 輒 for 輟. The reading preferred by 王念孫 is followed.

HF 22.10 (*Xilun* 414, *Xin jiaozhu* 468)

齊攻宋，	Qi launched a formal attack on Song
宋使臧孫子南求救於荊。	and Song sent Mr Zangsun to seek help from Jing (Chu) in the south.17
荊大說，	Jing (Chu) was greatly satisfied by this request.

15　This is another instance of anachronism. The Qin-Chu-Qi triangle characterised military competition in ca. 300, but during the time of Lord Kang of Qin (r. 620–606), Qin and Chu had formed a loose alliance against their common enemy, Jin.

16　Geographically speaking, the story is ridiculous: the army mobilised against Qi could not be easily redeployed westward against Qin; hence no surprise attack was imminent. Ren Wang possibly offers indirect criticism: he suggests that the platform should never have been built, and that the people should not have had to exhaust themselves for three years in order to build it. However, Lord Kang does not stop the laborious project; instead, he makes appropriate military preparations, which is enough to stop Chu's advance.

17　The story appears in *Zhanguo ce* 32.1 ("Song 宋"). The details of the events are unclear (many commentators point to a date in the late fourth or early third centuries, but these are just guesses). Zangsun was a leading aristocratic lineage from Lu, some members of which may have crossed the border to serve the neighbouring Song.

説林上 A FOREST OF PERSUASIONS, PART 1

	許救之,	They agreed to come to the rescue,
5	甚勸。	and greatly encouraged Song.
	臧孫子憂而反。	Mr Zangsun returned home, looking worried.
	其御曰:	His driver asked:
	"索救而得,	"You demanded support and you got it,
	今子有憂色,	and now you look worried.
10	何也?"	Why is this?"
	臧孫子曰:	Mr Zangsun said:
	"宋小而齊大。	"Song is small and Qi is large.
	夫救小宋而惡於大齊,	Rescuing little Song and creating bad feelings with great Qi –
	此人之所以憂也,	this is something to be worried about.
15	而荊王說,	The reason why the King of Jing (Chu) is pleased
	必以堅我也。	is bound to be that he wants to strengthen us.
	我堅而齊敝,	If we are strengthened and Qi is weakened,
	荊之所利也。"	that will be to the advantage of Jing (Chu)."[18]
	臧孫子乃歸。	Mr Zangsun then returned,
20	齊人拔五城於宋而荊救不至。	and when Qi took five walled cities from Song, no relief arrived from Jing (Chu).[19]

5 甚(歡)〔勸〕(校注 250). 7 張抄 has 禦 for 御.

HF 22.11 (*Xilun* 415, *Xin jiaozhu* 468)

魏文侯借道於趙而攻中山,	Marquis Wen of Wei asked for right of way through Zhao in order to attack Zhongshan,
趙肅侯將不許。	but Marquis Su of Zhao was about to refuse.[20]
趙刻曰:	Zhao Ke said;

---

18 The point is that Chu supports Song out of self-interest and as part of its strategy to weaken Qi wherever possible. It is not really in Chu's interest to support Song for its own sake.

19 It is difficult not to think of this anecdote as a version of the story told in *Zuozhuan* (Xuan 15.2) of Chu's attack against Song. Song asks for Jin's help and is promised it, provided they stay firm, whereas in reality Jin simply aims to exhaust Chu's army and fight Chu using Song without having to dispatch its own military forces. For the resultant series of tricks and cheating on all sides, see Li Wai-yee 2023: 141–149.

20 Another blatant anachronism. It is true that in 408, Marquis Wen of Wei (r. 445–396) launched an attack on Zhongshan, passing through the territory of Zhao (then still a close ally). Yet the reign of Marquis Su of Zhao (r. 349–326) was sixty years thereafter. The story is told in *Zhanguo ce* 18.5 (Zhao 1), but there the Marquis of Zhao is not identified.

"君過矣。	"You are making a mistake.
5　魏攻中山而弗能取，	If Wei attacks Zhongshan and is unable to take it out,
則魏必罷。	Wei will be exhausted.
罷則魏輕，	If Wei is exhausted, it will have little clout,
魏輕則趙重。	and if Wei has little clout, Zhao will gain in influence.
魏拔中山，	If Wei takes Zhongshan,
10　必不能越趙而有中山也。	she will be unable to control the place from across Zhao.
是用兵者，	Under such circumstances, the one who uses military force
魏也；	is Wei,
而得地者，	but the one who gains territory
趙也。	is Zhao.
15　君必許之。	You, my lord, must absolutely accede to the request.
許之而大歡，	If you accede, he [Marquis Wen] will be greatly elated,
彼將知君利之也，	but he will come to understand that the advantages from his campaign belong to you,
必將輟行。	and he is bound to discontinue it.
君不如借之道，	You had better grant him right of way,
20　示以不得已也。"	and pretend that you have no alternative."

16 〔許之〕(校注 251).

HF 22.12 (*Xilun* 416, *Xin jiaozhu* 469)

鴟夷子皮事田成子。	Chiyi Zipi[21] was in the service of Tian Chengzi.
田成子去齊，	Tian Chengzi left Qi,
走而之燕，	fleeing to Yan.[22]

21　The reference is to Fan Li 范蠡, the semi-legendary wise advisor to King Goujian of Yue, who, following Goujian's victory over Wu in 473, prudently escaped to Qi to avoid Goujian's wrath. For his story, see *Shiji* 41: 1751–1753 ff.

22　Tian Chengzi (Tian Heng, or Tian Chang) was the head of the Tian/Chen lineage in the state of Qi who orchestrated the takeover of power in that state in 481 (chapter 7, note 3). The story of his flight to Yan is in all likelihood an invention.

說林上 A FOREST OF PERSUASIONS, PART 1

鴟夷子皮負傳而從。	Chiyi Zipi followed along, carrying the travel permit.
5　至望邑，	When they got to Wangyi,
子皮曰：	Zipi said:
"子獨不聞涸澤之蛇乎？	"Have you, by any chance, never heard of the snake in the parched swamp?
澤涸，	When the swamp gets parched,
蛇將徙。	the snake will relocate.
10　有小蛇謂大蛇曰：	There was a small snake who told a big snake:
'子行而我隨之，	'If you go along and I follow you,
人以為蛇之行者耳，	people will suppose that we are just snakes moving along,
必有殺子。	and there is bound to be someone who will kill you.
不如相銜負我以行，	You had better take me in your mouth and walk along like that, carrying me along.
15　人以我為神君也。'	Then people will think I am a god.'
乃相銜負以越公道。	So the large snake took the small snake in its mouth and carried it along, and in such a way they crossed a public road.
人皆避之，	People all got out of their way
曰：	and said to each other:
'神君也。'	'This is a god!'
20　今子美而我惡。	Now you are more handsome than I;
以子為我上客，	if I treat you as my honoured retainer,
千乘之君也；	I will count as the ruler of a thousand chariots;
以子為我使者，	if I take you as my ambassador,
萬乘之卿也。	I will count as the chief minister of ten thousand chariots.
25　子不如為我舍人。"	It will be best if you follow me as a member of my retinue."
田成子因負傳而隨之。	And so Tian Chengzi took the passport and followed Chiyi Zipi.
至逆旅，	When they got to a guest house,
逆旅之君待之甚敬，	the proprietor treated him with great respect
因獻酒肉。	and accordingly served him ale and meat.

8（涸澤）〔澤涸〕(校注 251)．　25 張抄 has 予 for 子．

HF 22.13 (*Xilun* 418, *Xin jiaozhu* 471)

溫人之周，	A man from Wen[23] went to Zhou,
周不納客。	but Zhou did not take in foreigners.
問之曰：	They asked him:
"客耶？"	"Are you a foreigner."
5　對曰：	He replied:
"主人。"	"I am a native of the place."
問其巷人而不知也，	They asked him about his neighbours, but he did not know any,
吏因囚之，	so the magistrate put him in prison.
君使人問之曰：	The ruler sent someone over to him to question him:
10　"子非周人也，	"You are not a man from Zhou,
而自謂非客，	but you say you are not a foreigner.
何也？"	Why is this."
對曰：	He replied:
"臣少也誦《詩》曰：	"When I was young, I recited the *Poems*:
15　'普天之下，	'Everywhere under Heaven,
莫非王土；	there is nothing but the King's land;
率土之濱，	all between the shores,
莫非王臣。'	there are none but the King's subjects.'[24]
今君，	Now you, my ruler,
20　天子，	are the Son of Heaven,
則我天子之臣也。	so I must be the Son of Heaven's subject.
豈有為人之臣而又為之客哉？	How can one be someone's subject and still be regarded as a foreigner?
故曰：	So I said,
主人也。"	'I am a native of the place.'"
25　君使出之。	The ruler ordered him to be released.

11 張抄 has 容 for 客.

23　Wen is located to the north of Zhou capital of Luoyang. The anecdote appears in *Zhanguo ce* 1.12 ("Dong Zhou" 東周).

24　These lines from "Bei shan" ode in the *Classic of Poems* (Mao 205) are among the most widely quoted in early Chinese literature. Their citation is of course ironic: by the time of the anecdote the Zhou royal domain was divided into two principalities and the Son of Heaven was a ruler of just a few tiny settlements beyond his capital.

說林上 A FOREST OF PERSUASIONS, PART 1

HF 22.14 (*Xilun* 419, *Xin jiaozhu* 471)

韓宣王謂樛留曰：	King Xuan of Hán said to Jiu Liu:
"吾欲兩用公仲、公叔，	"I wish I could employ both Gongzhong and Gongshu.
其可乎？"	Would that be acceptable?"[25]
對曰：	He replied:
"不可。	"That is not advisable.
晉用六卿而國分；	Jin employed six senior ministers, and the state disintegrated;[26]
簡公兩用田成、闞止而簡公殺；	Lord Jian [of Qi] employed both Tian Cheng and Kan Zhi, and Lord Jian was killed.[27]
魏兩用犀首、張儀，	Wei employed both Xishou and Zhang Yi,
而西河之外亡。	and the area beyond the Western River was lost.[28]
今王兩用之，	Now, if Your Majesty employs both these men,
其多力者樹其黨，	the one who has the greater power will establish cliques,
寡力者借外權。	and the one who has lesser power will seek support from foreign powers.
群臣有內樹黨以驕主，	If some ministers establish cliques and are arrogant towards the ruler,
有外為交以削地，	and others maintain connections outside and decimate the state's territory,
則王之國危矣。"	then your state will be in danger."

13 主（內）(校注 251). 14 C has 列 for 削, following 王念孫.

---

25 King Xuan of Hán reigned from 332 to 312; Gongzhong Peng 公仲朋 and Gongshu Boying 公叔伯嬰 were two of his chancellors in succession.

26 For the six senior ministers of Jin, see chapter 11, note 13.

27 Kan Zhi was a personal favourite of Lord Jian of Qi, whose position threatened the powerful minister Tian Heng (Tian Chang, Tian Chengzi; chapter 7, note 3). In 481, Tian Chang orchestrated a coup, killing both Kan Zhi and Lord Jian. See *Zuozhuan*, Ai 14.3; see also chapter 3, note 25.

28 This is a double anachronism. The rivalry of Xishou (Gongsun Yan 公孫衍) and Zhang Yi erupted parallel to the rivalry of Gongshu and Gongzhong in Hán, so this example could not have been employed in Jiu Liu's speech. Second, the loss of Wei's territory west of the Yellow River to Qin took place *before* the rivalry between Zhang Yi and Xishou.

HF 22.15 (*Xilun* 420, *Xin jiaozhu* 473)

紹績昧醉寐而亡其裘。

宋君曰：
"醉足以亡裘乎？"

對曰：
"桀以醉亡天下，

而《康誥》曰'毋彝酒'者，

彝酒，
常酒也。
常酒者，
天子失天下，
匹夫失其身。"

Shao Xumei got drunk and fell asleep, and lost his coat.

The ruler of Song said:
"Does one lose one's coat just because one gets drunk?"

He replied:
"Jie lost All-under-Heaven because of drunkenness,

and the 'Declaration to Kang' says, "Do not perdurably drink."[29]

'Perdurably drink'
means 'constantly drink'.
If he constantly drinks,
the Son of Heaven will lose his domain,
and an ordinary fellow will lose his life."

HF 22.16 (*Xilun* 421, *Xin jiaozhu* 474)

管仲、隰朋從於桓公而伐孤竹。
春往冬反，

迷惑失道。
管仲曰：
"老馬之智可用也。"

乃放老馬而隨之，

遂得道。

Guan Zhong and Xi Peng followed Lord Huan [of Qi] when he attacked Guzhu.[30]
They went out on the campaign in the spring and returned in the winter,
but got lost on their way back.
Guan Zhong said:
"The intelligence of an old horse may be useful here."
And he set free an old horse, which he then trailed,
so that in the end he found the right way.

---

29 Shao Xumei confuses two chapters of the *Canon of Documents* (*Shang shu* 尚書): he cites "Declaration on Ale" ("Jiu gao" 酒誥) and not "Declaration to Kang" ("Kang gao" 康誥). In any case, both documents are closely related: they were supposedly issued simultaneously by the Duke of Zhou to his brother, Kangshu.

30 This attack is identified with the Qi assault on the Mountain Rong 山戎 ca. 663. Guan Zhong and Xi Peng were wise advisors to Lord Huan and the architects of his hegemony.

說林上 A FOREST OF PERSUASIONS, PART 1   349

行山中無水，	When they were marching in the mountains, there was no water,
隰朋曰：	and Xi Peng said:
10 "蟻冬居山之陽，	"Ants, in the winter, reside on the sunny side of a mountain;
夏居山之陰，	in the summer, they reside on the shady side of a mountain.
蟻壤一寸而仭有水。"	If there is one inch of earth with ants in it, then at a depth of one fathom there is water.
乃掘地，	And so they dug in the ground,
遂得水。	and did in fact find water.
15 以管仲之聖而隰朋之智，	A person as much of a sage as Guan Zhong and a person as intelligent as Xi Peng,
至其所不知，	when they arrived at something they did not understand,
不難師於老馬與蟻。	had no qualms about being instructed by old horses or by ants.
今人不知以其愚心而師聖人之智，	People nowadays do not understand this, with their foolish minds, but venerate the intellect of sages –
不亦過乎？	is that not wrong?

12 張抄 has 兩 for 而.   18 〔師〕(校注 251).

HF 22.17 (*Xilun* 422, *Xin jiaozhu* 475)

有獻不死之藥於荊王者，	Someone handed a pill of immortality to the King of Jing (Chu);
謁者操之以入。	the butler brought it in.[31]
中射之士問曰：	A palace guard asked him:
"可食乎？"	"Can this be eaten?"
5 曰：	He said:
"可。"	"It can."
因奪而食之。	So the guard seized the pill and ate it.
王大怒，	The King flew into a rage
使人殺中射之士。	and sent someone to put the guard to death.

---

31   The story is told in *Zhanguo ce* 17.8 ("Chu 楚 4").

10 中射之士使人說王曰：	The guard sent someone to persuade the King, saying:
"臣問謁者，	"I asked the butler,
曰'可食'，	who said: 'This can be eaten',
臣故食之，	and so I ate it.
是臣無罪，	I am innocent,
15 而罪在謁者也。	and it is all the butler's fault.
且客獻不死之藥，	Moreover, since the guest offered an immortality pill,
臣食之而王殺臣，	if you kill me after I have eaten it,
是死藥也，	then this was a mortality pill,
是客欺王也。	which means that the guest has swindled you.
20 夫殺無罪之臣，	Now that would be to kill an innocent servant
而明人之欺王也，	and to show people that you were swindled.
不如釋臣。"	You had better set me free."
王乃不殺。	The King did not have him put him to death.

HF 22.18 (*Xilun* 423, *Xin jiaozhu* 475)

田駟欺鄒君，	Tian Si had bullied the ruler of Zou
鄒君將使人殺之。	and the ruler of Zou was going to send a person to kill him.[32]
田駟恐，	Tian Si was terrified
告惠子。	and reported the matter to Master Hui.[33]
5 惠子見鄒君曰：	Master Hui went to see the ruler of Zou and said:
"今有人見君，	"Suppose there was a person who went to see you
則眹其一目，	and kept one eye closed.
奚如？"	How would you deal with him."
君曰：	The ruler said:
10 "我必殺之。"	"I would certainly kill him."

---

32 Tian Si is sometimes identified as a minister at the court of Zhao (this is inferred from a single reference in *Zhanguo ce*). Zou was a tiny polity to the south of Lu that survived as an independent entity into the early third century. However, these two identifications are probably wrong. Tian Si, judging from his family name, was a member of the ruling lineage in the state of Qi. Zou was intermittently subjugated by Qi and Chu; it is likely that the "ruler of Zou" here is another Qi potentate. That would explain why Tian Si was terrified.

33 Master Hui (Huizi) is the famous sophist, Hui Shi 惠施 (frequently mentioned in *Zhuangzi*, especially in chapter 33, "Tianxia" [The world]).

說林上 A FOREST OF PERSUASIONS, PART 1

惠子曰：	Master Hui said:
"瞽，	"Being blind
兩目眹，	is having both eyes closed.
君奚為不殺？"	Why don't you kill a blind person."
15 君曰：	The ruler said:
"不能勿眹。"	"He cannot help keeping his eyes closed!"
惠子曰：	Master Hui said:
"田駟東慢齊侯，	"To the East, Tian Si has hoodwinked the Marquis of Qi,[34]
南欺荊王。	and in the South he has cheated the King of Jing (Chu).
20 駟之於欺人，	For Si, bullying others
瞽也，	is the same as being blind.[35]
君奚怨焉？"	Why are you so resentful of him."
鄒君乃不殺。	The ruler of Zou then did not have Tian Si killed.

HF 22.19 (*Xilun* 425, *Xin jiaozhu* 476)

魯穆公使眾公子或宦於晉，	Lord Mu of Lu sent his many sons to serve either in Jin
或宦於荊。	or in Jing (Chu).[36]
犁鉏曰：	Li Ju said:
"假人於越而救溺子，	"If you had to hire a person from Yue when trying to save a son who is about to drown,[37]
5 越人雖善游，	even if the man from Yue is a good swimmer,
子必不生矣。	the son is bound not to survive.
失火而取水於海，	When fire breaks out and you fetch water from the sea,
海水雖多，	even though there is plenty of water in the sea,
火必不滅矣。	the fire is bound not to be extinguished.

---

34 Note another anachronism: by the time of Hui Shi (late fourth century), Qi's ruler was titled "king" and not "marquis."
35 That is to say, it is an affliction that Tian Si cannot control.
36 Lord Mu of Lu reigned ca. from 416 to 383 (the exact dates are disputed).
37 Yue (as a geographic entity, which usually refers to the areas along the southeastern coast to the south of the Yangzi estuary) is very far away. Note, however, that during Lord Mu of Lu's reign, the capital of the state of Yue was located in Langya 琅琊, relatively close to Lu.

10 遠水不救近火也。	This is because water in some distant place will not help against a fire nearby.
今晉與荊雖強， 而齊近，	Now Jin and Jing (Chu) may be strong, but Qi is close at hand.
魯患其不救乎？"	Does Lu worry that they will not come to her rescue?"[38]

5 C has 遊 for 游.　7 張抄 has 少 for 火.

HF 22.20 (*Xilun* 425, *Xin jiaozhu* 477)

嚴遂不善周君，	Yan Sui was not on good terms with the ruler of Zhou,[39]
患之。	who was upset about this.
馮沮曰：	Feng Ju said:
"嚴遂相，	"Yan Sui acts as the prime minister,
5 而韓傀貴於君。	but Han Gui is more esteemed by the ruler [of Hán].
不如行賊於韓傀，	It is best to assassinate Han Gui,
則君必以為嚴氏也。"	so that the ruler [of Hán] will treat Yan as the culprit."[40]

HF 22.21 (*Xilun* 426, *Xin jiaozhu* 477)

張譴相韓，	Zhang Qian was prime minister in Hán.
病將死。	He was ill and about to die.

38　Unlike Jin and Chu, Qi was Lu's immediate neighbour and major rival at the time.

39　Yan Sui was a powerful official at the court of Lord Ai of Hán (r. 377–371). The "ruler of Zhou" refers here not to the Zhou king but to the ruler of the Western Zhou principality: a statelet carved out of the Zhou royal domain in the late fifth century.

40　This is an interesting alternative narrative of the famous story of Yan Sui's plot to assassinate Han Gui (or Han Kui). According to a better known narrative from the *Stratagems of the Warring States* (*Zhanguo ce* 27.22 ["Hán 2"]) and *Records of the Historian*, Yan Sui planned the assassination of his rival, the Hán chancellor Han Gui, hiring one of the most famous assassin-retainers, Nie Zheng 聶政. Han Fei has a different take on this clandestine plot: an enemy can be neutralised by committing a crime that can subsequently be attributed to him.

說林上 A FOREST OF PERSUASIONS, PART 1

公乘無正懷三十金而問其疾。	Gongcheng Wuzheng took along thirty pieces of gold and called on him on account of his illness.
居一日，	A day went past,
君問張譴曰：	and the ruler[41] asked Zhang Qian:
"若子死，	"If you die,
將誰使代子？"	whom shall we employ to replace you."
答曰：	He immediately replied:
"無正重法而畏上，	"Wuzheng takes the law seriously and shows fearful reverence of superiors.
雖然，	Nonetheless,
不如公子食我之得民也。"	Prince Shiwo is the better man to win over the people."
張譴死，	When Zhang Qian died,
因相公乘無正。	the ruler made Gongcheng Wuzheng prime minister.[42]

3 張抄 has 士 for 十。 4 居一（月）〔日〕（校注 251, following 顧廣圻）。 5 （自）〔君〕問張譴曰 (校注 251, following 盧文弨).

HF 22.22 (Xilun 427, Xin jiaozhu 478)

樂羊為魏將而攻中山，	When Yue Yang was a general in Wei and attacked Zhongshan,
其子在中山。	his son was in Zhongshan.[43]
中山之君烹其子而遺之羹，	The ruler of Zhongshan broiled Yue Yang's son and sent the broth to his father.
樂羊坐於幕下而啜之，	Yue Yang sat down in front of his tent and slurped the broth,
盡一杯。	emptying the whole bowl.
文侯謂堵師贊曰：	Marquis Wen, addressing Du Shi, commended Yue Yang, saying:

---

41 It is unclear who this ruler is supposed to be.
42 Zhang Qian means to recommend one of the men, but the kind of information he provides makes it clear that the other man is preferable. Popularity with the people would only make the alternative candidate a dangerous competitor to the ruler, as the ruler understands.
43 This is the same attack on Zhongshan mentioned in section 22.11 above. The story is told in *Zhanguo ce* 22.3 ("Wei 1").

"樂羊以我故而食其子之肉。"
答曰：
"其子而食之，
且誰不食？"
樂羊罷中山，
文侯賞其功而疑其心。

孟孫獵得麑，
使秦西巴持之歸，
其母隨之而啼。
秦西巴弗忍而與之。

孟孫歸，
至而求麑。
答曰：
"余弗忍而與其母。"
孟孫大怒，
逐之。
居三月，
復召以為其子傅。
其御曰：
"曩將罪之，
今召以為子傅，
何也？"
孟孫曰：
"夫不忍麑，
又且忍吾子乎？"

"Yue Yang ate the flesh of his own son for my sake."
Du Shi replied:
"If he will even eat his son,
whom will he not eat?"
Yue Yang relented in his siege of Zhongshan,
and Marquis Wen rewarded his achievements but was suspicious of his motives.[44]

When [one of the clan of the] Mengsun caught a fawn in a hunt,
he asked Qin Xiba to take it home.
The fawn's mother followed behind, weeping.
Qin Xiba could not bear this and gave the fawn back.

When Mengsun got back,
he went to Qin Xiba to ask for the fawn.
He replied:
"I was unable to bear the sight, and gave it back to its mother."
Mengsun flew into a rage
and banished the man.
Three months passed by,
and he summoned back Qin Xiba to make him his son's tutor.
Mengsun's driver said:
"A little time ago you were about to accuse him of a crime,
and now you summon him as your son's tutor. Why is this."
Mengsun said:
"If he cannot bear the sight of the fawn suffering, can he bear the sight of my son suffering."

---

44 It is strategically dangerous to display extremes of callous disregard for human feelings. Han Fei may have approved of Yue Yang's dedication to his military task, but at the same time such a display of dedication raises suspicions of ulterior motives.

說林上 A FOREST OF PERSUASIONS, PART 1   355

故曰：	So it is said;
"巧詐不如拙誠。"	"Breaking promises skilfully is not as good as being stupidly trustworthy."
樂羊以有功見疑，	Yue Yang was held in suspicion because he had achievements;
35 秦西巴以有罪益信。	Qin Xiba, because of his crime, was more trusted.

14 （載之持）〔持之〕歸 (校注 251, following 王先慎).

HF 22.23 (*Xilun* 428, *Xin jiaozhu* 480)

曾從子，	Zeng Congzi
善相劍者也。	was an expert on swords.
衛君怨吳王。	The ruler of Wey resented the King of Wu[45]
曾從子曰：	and Zeng Congzi said:
5 "吳王好劍，	"The King of Wu is fond of swords
臣相劍者也。	and I am an expert on swords.
臣請為吳王相劍，	May I act as an expert of swords for the King of Wu,
拔而示之，	pull out a sword to show to him,
因為君刺之。"	and then kill him on your behalf?"
10 衛君曰：	The ruler of Wey said:
"子之為是也，	"If you do such a thing,
非緣義也，	it is not in accordance with moral principle;
為利也。	it would be for the sake of gaining advantage.
吳強而富，	Wu is strong and rich,
15 衛弱而貧。	and Wey is weak and poor.
子必往，	Since you insist on going,
吾恐子為吳王用之於我也。"	I am afraid you will use the same dishonesty against me."
乃逐之。	Then the ruler banished him.

11 （為之）〔之為〕(校注 251, following 陶鴻慶).   18 〔之〕(校注 251).

---

45 A logical inference is that the resented King of Wu is Fuchai 吳王夫差 (r. 495–473), the only Wu ruler who tried to expand northward in the direction of Shandong. This could reasonably cause the resentment of the current Wey ruler, either Lord Chu 衛出公 (r. 492–481 and 477–470), or his father, Lord Zhuang 衛莊公 (r. 480–478).

356　　　　　　　　　　　　　　　　　　　　　　　　　　　　CHAPTER 22

HF 22.24 (*Xilun* 429, *Xin jiaozhu* 481)

紂為象箸而箕子怖， [King] Zhòu had chopsticks made of ivory, and Jizi was terrified.

以為象箸必不盛羹於土鉶， He considered: "Ivory chopsticks are not used with earthenware *xing*-vessels;

則必犀玉之杯， they go with drinking bowls of rhinoceros horn and jade.

玉杯象箸必不盛菽藿， With ivory chopsticks and jade bowls, it is certain that beans and leaves will not be eaten;

5　則必旄象豹胎； it has to be yak, elephant or leopard foetus.

旄象豹胎必不衣短褐而舍茅茨之下， With yak, elephant and leopard foetus, it is certain that one will not wear short coarse clothes and eat under thatched roofs;

則必錦衣九重， rather, one will have many-layered rich brocade,

高臺廣室也。 high terraces and spacious dwellings.

稱此以求， If you make such demands,

10　則天下不足矣。 all the resources of the world will not be sufficient.

聖人見微以知萌， The sage notices subtle points and understands incipient signs.

見端以知末， He sees the beginnings and understands thereby the ends.

故見象箸而怖， Therefore Jizi was terrified when he saw the ivory chopsticks,

知天下不足也。 and knew that the world would not suffice to satisfy Zhòu.

1 〔而〕(校注 251). 1, 13 C has 唏 for 怖, against 校注. 吳本、張抄、錢抄、趙本、藏本 and 張本 have 怖; 陳本 has 悑. See note to HF 21.7.　2 張抄 has 為 for 箸.　2〔必〕(校注 251).　2（簋）〔鉶〕(校注 251).　2 張抄 has 美 for 羹.　3 吳本、張抄、藏本、張本、陳本 and 趙本 have 玉; 錢抄 has 王.　6 We read 舍 as 食, with HF 21.7 parallel.

HF 22.25 (*Xilun* 431, *Xin jiaozhu* 482)

周公旦已勝殷， After the Duke of Zhou, Dan, had won his victory over Yin,[46]

將攻商蓋。 he intended to attack Shanghe.[47]

46　The latter period of the Shang dynasty is often referred to as Yin 殷 after its capital's name.
47　The attack on Shanghe 商蓋, alternatively identified as Shangyan 商奄, was mentioned

說林上 A FOREST OF PERSUASIONS, PART 1

辛公甲曰：	Patriarch Xin Jia said:[48]
"大難攻，	"A large place is hard to attack;
小易服。	a small place is easy to subdue.
不如服眾小以劫大。"	It is best to subdue many small places in order to take one large one."
乃攻九夷而商蓋服矣。	Then the Duke of Zhou attacked the Nine Yi and Shanghe submitted to him.[49]

HF 22.26 (*Xilun* 431, *Xin jiaozhu* 483)

紂為長夜之飲，	King Zhòu drank all night long,
懽以失日，	enjoying himself so much that he forgot what day it was.
問其左右，	He asked his entourage,
盡不知也。	but none of them knew.
乃使人問箕子。	Then he sent someone to ask Jizi.
箕子謂其徒曰：	Jizi told his followers:
"為天下主而一國皆失日，	"He is the ruler of All-under-Heaven, and everyone in the whole state has forgotten what day it is:
天下其危矣。	All-under-Heaven is in danger!
一國皆不知而我獨知之，	And if no one in the whole state knows, and I alone know,
吾其危矣。"	then I must be in danger!"
辭以醉而不知。	He pretended that he was drunk and did not know.

2 (懽)〔懼〕以失日 (校注 251, following 顧廣圻).

---

in different sources, but its context became clearer with the publication of the bamboo manuscript *Xinian* from the Tsinghua University collection. According to *Xinian* 3, Shanghe (located in the vicinity of the future Lu capital, Qufu) became the stronghold of Shang loyalists after their failed rebellion in the Shang capital. According to *Xinian*, the Duke of Zhou and his protégé, King Cheng, invaded Shanghe and relocated its defeated defenders to the far west, where they became the founders of the Qin polity. See Pines 2020a: 109–112.

48 Xin Jia is usually identified as a Shang noble who submitted to the Zhou and became the Great Scribe of the Zhou house. His identification as *gong* 公 is perplexing (he was neither a duke in the Zhou government, nor a regional lord). Here the early meaning of *gong* as "patriarch" is most appropriate.

49 Nine Yi may refer either to nine entities of the Yi ethnicity or of a single entity as is implied in *Analects* 9.14.

HF 22.27 (*Xilun* 432, *Xin jiaozhu* 483)

魯人身善織屨，	A man from Lu who was good at pleating sandals
妻善織縞，	and whose wife was good at weaving fine gauze
而欲徙於越。	wanted to move to Yue.
或謂之曰：	Somebody told him:
5 "子必窮矣。"	"You are in trouble."
魯人曰：	The man from Lu said:
"何也？"	Why is that."
曰：	He said:
"屨為履之也，	"Sandals are for wearing on the feet,
10 而越人跣行；	but the people of Yue walk barefoot;
縞為冠之也，	gauze is for making hats,
而越人被髮。	but the people of Yue keep their hair undone.
以子之所長，	If, with your specialities,
游於不用之國，	you travel to a place where they are of no use,
15 欲使無窮，	then if you wished to avoid penury,
其可得乎？"	would you be able?[50]

HF 22.28 (*Xilun* 433, *Xin jiaozhu* 484)

陳軫貴於魏王。	Chen Zhen held a high position with the King of Wei.[51]
惠子曰：	Master Hui said:[52]
"必善事左右。	"You have to be good at cultivating the King's entourage.
夫楊，	As for the aspen tree,
5 橫樹之即生，	if you plant it sidewise, it will still grow;
倒樹之即生，	if you plant it upside-down, it will still grow;
折而樹之又生。	and if you break off a branch and plant it, it will still grow.

---

50 The lesson from Han Fei's point of view is that even political and strategic skills are not of universal application: such skills, like all other skills, apply differently in different places and may be completely different in some.

51 Chen Zhen is a travelling persuader active in the second half of the fourth century.

52 Once again, Master Hui should be Zhuangzi's friend and rival, Hui Shi.

然使十人樹之而一人拔之，	However, if you employ ten people to plant them, and one person to pull them up,
則毋生楊。	there will be no aspens growing.
10 至以十人之眾，	Even as many as ten people
樹易生之物，	planting aspen trees, which are easy to grow,
而不勝一人者，	cannot overcome one person –
何也？	why is this?
樹之難而去之易也。	Planting trees is difficult, but removing them is easy.
15 子雖工自樹於王，	Although you are proficient at establishing yourself with the King,
而欲去子者眾，	those who wish to remove you are many.
子必危矣。"	You are bound to be in danger."

1 張抄 has 正 for 王.

HF 22.29 (*Xilun* 434, *Xin jiaozhu* 485)

魯季孫新弒其君，	Jisun of Lu had just assassinated his ruler,[53]
吳起仕焉。	and Wu Qi was in his service.
或謂起曰：	Someone said to Wu Qi,
"夫死者，	"Now when someone who is dead
5 始死而血，	has died recently, he has blood in him,
已血而衂，	but as the blood goes, he will become desiccated.
已衂而灰，	After he is desiccated, he will turn to ashes,
已灰而土。	and from ashes, he will turn into earth.
及其土也，	By the time he has turned into earth,
10 無可為者矣。	there is nothing anyone can do for him.
今季孫乃始血，	Now in the case of Jisun, the blood is recent,

---

[53] Jisun was the most powerful of the so-called Three Huan lineages (the other being Mengsun 孟孫 and Shusun 叔孫, all descendants of Lord Huan of Lu 魯桓公 [r. 711–694]). The heads of the Jisun lineage held power in Lu from the early sixth century. There is no clear indication that the head of Jisun lineage had ever assassinated a Lu ruler (but twice the Jisun orchestrated the expulsion of Lu sovereigns: in 517 and 468). However, very little is known about Lu history during the middle-to-late fifth century, when this story is set. Zhang Jue (2011: 435n1) avers that the assassinated ruler was Lord Dao of Lu 魯悼公, r. 467–432.

360　　　　　　　　　　　　　　　　　　　　　　　　　　　　CHAPTER 22

其毋乃未可知也。" 　　　and I'm afraid we do not yet know how things will turn out."
吳起因去之晉。　　　　As a result, Wu Qi left and went to Jin.[54]

6 〔而〕(校注 251).　　9 張抄 has 反 for 及.

HF 22.30 (*Xilun* 435, *Xin jiaozhu* 485)

隰斯彌見田成子，	Xi Simi went to see Tian Chengzi.[55]
田成子與登臺四望。	Tian Chengzi climbed up on a platform with him to enjoy the view in all directions.
三面皆暢。	In three directions, they had an unimpeded view.
南望，	When they looked towards the south,
5　隰子家之樹蔽之。	a tree in the estate of the Xi family blocked the view.
田成子亦不言。	Nonetheless, Tian Chengzi did not bring the matter up.
隰子歸，	When Master Xi went home,
使人伐之。	he ordered a man to fell the tree,
斧離數創，	but when the axe had cut several gashes in the tree,
10　隰子止之。	Xizi stopped him.
其相室曰：	His Senior Secretary said:
"何變之數也？"	"Why did you change your mind so abruptly."
隰子曰：	Master Xi said:
"古者有諺曰：	"In ancient times there was a saying:
15　'知淵中之魚者不祥。'	'It bodes ill for he who understands the fish living in the deep.'
夫田子將有大事，	Master Tian is planning a great undertaking,
而我示之知微，	and if I reveal that I know his subtle motives,
我必危矣。	I am bound to be in danger.
不伐樹，	Not to fell a tree
20　未有罪也；	is no crime;

54　The story of Wu Qi, a brilliant military commander, thinker, and strategist, departing from Lu to Jin (more precisely to Wei 魏) is told in his biography in the *Records of the Historian*, where, however, the reason for his departure is the Lu's ruler's lack of trust in him.

55　Tian Chengzi is the usurper of the power in the state of Qi, Tian Chang (chapter 7, note 3). Xi Simi should be a descendant of the righteous Qi minister, Xi Peng (fl. 650).

說林上 A FOREST OF PERSUASIONS, PART 1

知人之所不言，	but to know what someone has not yet said –
其罪大矣。」	that crime is truly big."
乃不伐也。	So he did not fell the tree.[56]

22 張抄 has 眾 for 罪.

HF 22.31 (*Xilun* 436, *Xin jiaozhu* 486)

楊子過於宋東之逆旅。	Master Yang stopped at a guesthouse in Eastern Song,[57]
有妾二人，	where there were two concubines:
其惡者貴，	the uglier one was honoured,
美者賤。	the more beautiful one was held in low esteem.
5 楊子問其故。	Master Yang asked the reason for this.
逆旅之父答曰：	The old man in the guesthouse said:
"美者自美，	"The beautiful one considers herself beautiful,
吾不知其美也；	so we do not see her as beautiful;
惡者自惡，	the uglier one considers herself ugly,
10 吾不知其惡也。」	so we do not see her as ugly."
楊子謂弟子曰：	Master Yang said to his disciples:
"行賢而去自賢之心，	"If your behaviour is worthy, yet you abandon the mindset of considering yourself worthy,
焉往而不美？」	you will be considered beautiful no matter where you go."

1 張抄 has 柬 for 東.

HF 22.32 (*Xilun* 437, *Xin jiaozhu* 487)

衛人嫁其子而教之曰：	A man from Wey married off his daughter and instructed her as follows:

---

56 Xi Simi is afraid that by obliging his neighbour and politely cutting down the tree he will raise suspicion, as if he already knew what he does know, namely that Tian Chengzi is the coming usurper of power.

57 Some commentators speculate that this Master Yang is the famous thinker Yang Zhu 楊朱 (whose changing image is discussed in Defoort and Lee 2022). The story also appears in the "Shan mu" 山木 chapter of *Zhuangzi*.

"必私積聚。	"Make sure that you accumulate private savings.
為人婦而出，	For a wife to be thrown out of the house
常也；	is a common thing;
5　其成居，	for her to establish a permanent household with her husband
幸也。"	is a matter of luck."
其子因私積聚，	Accordingly, the daughter accumulated private savings.
其姑以為多私而出之。	Her mother-in-law thought she was selfish and threw her out,
其子所以反者倍其所以嫁。	but what the daughter returned home with was twice the amount of her dowry.
10　其父不自罪於教子非也，	The father did not blame himself for giving the wrong instructions;
而自知其益富。	on the contrary, he noted that she had become much wealthier.
今人臣之處官者，	Nowadays, ministers occupying offices
皆是類也。	are all like this.[58]

12 （今）〔今〕 (校注 252).

HF 22.33 (*Xilun* 438, *Xin jiaozhu* 488)

魯丹三說中山之君而不受也，	Lu Dan attempted to persuade the ruler of Zhongshan three times, but [his advice] was never accepted.[59]
因散五十金事其左右。	Consequently, he distributed fifty pieces of gold to cultivate the ruler's entourage.
復見，	Then he had another audience,
未語，	and before he had even spoken,
5　而君與之食。	the ruler invited him to a meal.
魯丹出，	When Lu Dan left,

58　Han Fei implies that selfishness pays off: even if a selfish minister is dismissed, he still benefits from his pre-dismissal corruption. The ruler should understand this well.

59　From the context it is clear that the story is set in the resurrected state of Zhongshan, which reached the apex of its power in the late fourth century before being extinguished by Zhao in 296.

說林上 A FOREST OF PERSUASIONS, PART 1

而不反舍，	he did not return to his dwelling
遂去中山。	but instead departed from Zhongshan.
其御曰：	His driver said:
10 "反見，	"When you went back for your audience,
乃始善我。	the ruler was beginning to treat us well.
何故去之？"	Why are you leaving him."
魯丹曰：	Lu Dan said:
"夫以人言善我，	"Since he treats me well because of what people say,
15 必以人言罪我。"	he is bound to treat me as a criminal because of what people say."
未出境，	Before he had even left the territory,
而公子惡之曰：	one of the princes of Zhongshan maligned him and said:
"為趙來間中山。"	"He has come to Zhongshan in order to spy for Zhao."
君因索而罪之。	The ruler accordingly sought him out and accused him of the crime.

HF 22.34 (*Xilun* 439, *Xin jiaozhu* 488)

田伯鼎好士而存其君，	Tian Boding was fond of retainers and thereby saved his ruler,
白公好士而亂荊。	but the Duke of Bai was fond of retainers and thereby wreaked havoc in Jing (Chu).[60]
其好士則同，	In their love of retainers, they were the same,
其所以為則異。	but their motivation was different.
5 公孫友自刖而尊百里，	Gongsun You cut off his own feet in order to show his respect for Baili;
豎刁自宮而諂桓公。	Young Servant Diao castrated himself to curry favour with Lord Huan.[61]
其自刑則同，	In their self-mutilation they were the same,
其所以自刑之為則異。	but their motivation for self-mutilation was different.

---

60   Nothing is known of Tian Boding. For the rebellious Duke of Bai 白公勝, see chapter 21, note 45.
61   The first of the stories is not known. For Young Servant Diao, see chapter 7, note 10.

慧子曰：
"狂者東走，
逐者亦東走。
其東走則同，
其所以東走之為則異。"

Master Hui[62] said:
"A madman may run eastwards;
his pursuers may also run eastwards.
In running eastwards they agree,
but their motivation for running eastwards is different."[63]

故曰：
"同事之人，
不可不審察也。"

So it is said:
"When two people do the same thing,
you must not fail to investigate this carefully."

6 （諂）〔謟〕(校注 252).　7 張抄 has 荊 for 刑.　8 張抄 has 荊 for 刑.　8 〔以〕(校注 252).　9 張抄 has 往 for 狂.　13 張抄 has 畢 for 異.

62　Huizi 慧子 (Master Hui) here stands for Huizi 惠子, i.e. Hui Shi (see note 33 above).
63　At this point our text enters into a jocular variant of the logic-chopping mode of thinking that is well-attested in the "dialectical chapters" of the *Mozi* and also in *Gongsunlongzi*. Such evidence is important because it demonstrates the impact of ancient Chinese logic on narrative culture and intellectual history in ancient China. See Harbsmeier 1998: 298–344.

CHAPTER 23

說林下 A Forest of Persuasions, Part 2

HF 23.1 (*Xilun* 441, *Xin jiaozhu* 490)

伯樂教二人相踶馬，	Bole was teaching two people how to judge the quality of horses that tended to kick,
相與之簡子廄觀馬。	and he went with them to [Zhao] Jianzi's stable to look at the horses.[1]
一人舉踶馬。	One of them picked out a horse that kicked,
其一人從後而循之，	while the other man went up to it from behind.
5 三撫其尻而馬不踶。	Three times he patted its back, yet the horse did not kick.
此自以為失相。	The man who had chosen the horse considered that he had made a mistake,
其一人曰：	but the other man said:
"子非失相也。	"You have not made a mistake in your judgment.
此其為馬也，	The condition of this horse is such
10 踒肩而腫膝。	that it has a bruised collarbone and swollen knees.
夫踶馬也者，	As for a horse that tends to kick,
舉後而任前，	it must lift its backside and rest on its front legs,
腫膝不可任也，	but the swollen knees of this horse knees provide no support –
故後不舉。	that is why it cannot lift its backside and kick.
15 子巧於相踶馬而拙於任腫膝。"	You are good at judging horses that tend to kick, but you are inept when it comes to 'relying on the swollen knee.'"
夫事有所必歸，	Matters have their basic categories under which they must be classified,
而以有所腫膝而不任，	but that they cannot be applied because of a swollen knee –
智者之所獨知也。	that is something that a wise man alone understands.

---

1 Bole was renowned as exceptionally good at raising horses. Judging from this anecdote, he was a contemporary of Zhao Jianzi 趙簡子 (d. 476), the head of the Jin government and one of the forefathers of Zhao as an independent polity.

惠子曰：
"置猿於柙中⟨A中/東 trjəŋw/tjuŋ⟩，
則與豚同⟨A東/東 duŋ/duŋ⟩。"
故勢不便，
非所以逞能也。

Master Hui said:
"If you place a monkey in a cage,
he is no different from a piglet."
Thus, when conditions are not conducive,
they do not provide the opportunity to show one's skill.

4（其一人舉踶馬）其一人 (校注 270).　　7〔曰〕(校注 270).　　15 於任（在腫膝而不任拙於）腫膝 (校注 270).

HF 23.2 (*Xilun* 443, *Xin jiaozhu* 493)

衛將軍文子見曾子，

曾子不起而延於坐席，

正身於奧。

文子謂其御曰：
"曾子，
愚人也哉！
以我為君子也，
君子安可毋敬也？
以我為暴人也，
暴人安可侮也？
曾子不僇，

命也。"

Wenzi, a general from Wey, paid a visit to Zengzi,[2]
but Zengzi did not rise and asked [Wenzi] to sit,
while he himself sat upright in the seat of honour.
Wenzi told his driver:
"Zengzi –
what a stupid man he is!
If he considers me a noble man,
how can one fail to respect a noble man?
If, on the other hand, he considers me a bully,
how can one humiliate a bully?
The fact that Zengzi has still not met a violent death
is by the grace of fate.

HF 23.3 (*Xilun* 443, *Xin jiaozhu* 494)

鳥有翢翢者，
重首而屈尾，
將欲飲於河，
則必顛。

Among birds, there is a certain *zhouzhou*.
It has a heavy head and a short tail,
and when it wants to drink from a stream,
it invariably tips over.

---

2 General Wenzi is Gongsun Mimou 公孫彌牟, a high-ranking Wey noble, who played a crucial role in ousting his cousin, the "Ousted Lord of Wey" 衛出公, from the state in 470. Zengzi (505–432) is one of Confucius's most famous disciples.

說林下 A FOREST OF PERSUASIONS, PART 2

5	乃銜其羽而飲之，	And so the bird drinks by sucking water from its plumage.
	人之所有飲不足者，	When someone cannot satisfy his thirst,
	不可不索其羽也。	he needs to turn to his "feathers." (i.e. helpers and friends).³

HF 23.4 (*Xilun* 444, *Xin jiaozhu* 494)

	鱣似蛇，	The eel is like a snake;
	蠶似蠋。	the silk-worm is like a maggot.
	人見蛇，	When people see a snake,
	則驚駭；	they are terrified;
5	見蠋，	when they see a maggot,
	則毛起。	their hair stands on end.
	漁者持鱣，	However, fishermen catch eels,
	婦人拾蠶，	and women handle silk-worms –
	利之所在，	where there is profit to be found,
10	皆為賁、諸。	people all turn into [paragons of courage] like [Meng] Ben and [Zhuan She] Zhu.⁴

HF 23.5 (*Xilun* 445, *Xin jiaozhu* 495)

	伯樂教其所憎者相千里之馬，	The [horse-connoisseur] Bole was teaching someone he hated to judge which horses are excellent,
	教其所愛者相駑馬。	and was teaching someone he liked how to judge which horses are bad.
	千里之馬時一，	The good horses were sold at a rate of one per season,
	其利緩；	and the profit was sluggish;
5	駑馬日售，	the bad horses were sold at a rate of one per day,
	其利急。	and the profit was quick.

---

3 The force of this little joke depends on a pun of the word yu 羽 "1. feather; 2. helper" which I have found it impossible to reproduce in English.
4 Meng Ben 孟賁 (fl. 310) was renowned for his physical power and courage. Zhuan Shezhu 鱄設諸 is a famous assassin-retainer who assassinated king Liao of Wu 吳王僚 in 515.

此《周書》所謂"下言而上用者，	This is what the *Zhoushu* refers to as: "Taking words from a lower sphere and applying them to the higher sphere,
惑也。"	that is confusion."[5]

HF 23.6 (*Xilun* 445, *Xin jiaozhu* 496)

桓赫曰：	Huan Hao said:
"刻削之道，	"As for the way of carving a face,
鼻莫如大，	it is best to make the nose comparatively large
目莫如小。	and the eyes comparatively small.
5　鼻大可小，	When the nose is too large, it may be made smaller,
小不可大也。	but when it is too small, it cannot be made larger.
目小可大，	When the eyes are too small, they may be made larger,
大不可小也。"	but when they are too large, they cannot be made smaller."
舉事亦然。	Undertaking actions is also like this.
10　為其後可復者也，	If one does things which can be amended later,
則事寡敗矣。	one's undertakings will rarely fail.

10　（不）〔後〕（校注 270）.

HF 23.7 (*Xilun* 446, *Xin jiaozhu* 496)

崇侯、惡來知不適紂之誅也，	The Marquis of Chong and Elai understood that if they did not follow [the tyrant] Zhòu, they would be executed,
而不見武王之滅之也。	but they did not realise that King Wu would destroy Zhòu.[6]

5　The precise force of this final quotation has prompted a considerable amount of discussion. I take Han Fei's idea to be that whereas it may be profitable enough to be a good judge of mediocre horses, what matters in politics is the ability to develop a sound judgment of the top brass.

6　Both the Marquis of Chong and Elai were among the closest aides of the last Shang king, Zhòu. Both perished in the course of the overthrow of Zhòu and his Shang dynasty by the Zhou dynasty led by King Wu.

說林下 A FOREST OF PERSUASIONS, PART 2

比干、子胥知其君之必亡也，	Bigan and Zixu understood that their ruler was bound to be ruined,
而不知身之死也，	but they did not understand that they themselves would die.[7]
5 故曰：	Thus it is said:
"崇侯、惡來知心而不知事，	The Marquis of Chong and Elai understood minds but not action;
比干、子胥知事而不知心。"	Bigan and Zixu understood actions but not minds.[8]
聖人其備矣。	The sage has all these things put in place.

HF 23.8 (*Xilun* 446, *Xin jiaozhu* 497)

宋太宰貴而主斷。	The Grand Steward of Song held a high position and was in charge of decision-making.
季子將見宋君，	When Jizi was going to visit the ruler of Song,
梁子聞之曰：	Liangzi heard about it and said:[9]
"語必可與太宰三坐乎，	"When you talk [to the ruler], make sure that a third person is present, namely the Grand Steward.
5 不然，	Otherwise,
將不免。"	you cannot escape trouble."
季子因說以貴主而輕國。	So Jizi went ahead and advised on enhancing the status of the person in charge [i.e. the Grand Steward] and on taking the affairs of state lightly.[10]

1 張抄 has 與 for 宋.

---

7   Bigan and Wu Zixu are the opposite of the Marquis of Chong and Elai. The latter were collaborators who were willing to work with any ruler in order to survive. The former were forceful – actually suicidal – remonstrators. Bigan was an uncle of the same tyrant Zhòu mentioned above. Infuriated by Bigan's remonstrance, Zhòu ordered Bigan's heart cut out (chapter 3, note 11). For Wu Zixu, see chapter 3, note 5.
8   It never occurred to Bigan, for example, that Zhòu's mentality was such that he would have his heart cut out in return for his loyalty. Neither did it occur to Wu Zixu that the king of Wu would eventually force him to commit suicide.
9   None of the personages in this anecdote can be safely identified.
10 Some editors have chosen the conjecture *sheng* 生 "life" for *zhu* 主 "ruler" so that the advice would be to take good care of one's personal life and to put little weight on

HF 23.9 (*Xilun* 447, *Xin jiaozhu* 498)

楊朱之弟楊布衣素衣而出。	Yang Zhu's younger brother Yang Bu went out wearing white clothes.[11]
天雨，	Since it was raining,
解素衣，	he took off his white coat,
衣緇衣而反，	and returned wearing dark clothes.
5　其狗不知而吠之。	His dog did not recognise him at barked at him.
楊布怒，	Yang Bu got angry
將擊之。	and wanted to beat the animal.
楊朱曰：	Yang Zhu said:
"子毋擊也，	"Don't you hit him!
10　子亦猶是。	You are also like this.
曩者使女狗白而往，	Before this, if your dog had gone out white
黑而來，	and returned black,
子豈能毋怪哉？"	how could you have failed to be taken aback?"[12]

HF 23.10 (*Xilun* 448, *Xin jiaozhu* 498)

惠子曰：	Master Hui said:
"羿執決持扞，	"When Yi puts on the thumb rings and takes the shooting glove,
操弓關機，	when he wields the bow or cocks the crossbow,
越人爭為持的，	even the people of Yue compete to hold up the target;[13]
5　弱子扞弓，	However, when a little boy pulls the bow,
慈母入室閉戶。"	even his loving mother seeks refuge in the house and closes the door."[14]

---

state affairs. However, it seems that *zhu* 主 stands here for the Grand Steward (note that *Zuozhuan* refers several times to chief ministers as "masters" [*zhu* 主] of the people). Being aware of the Grand Steward's invisible presence, Jizi recommends the ruler to bestow honours on his chief aide and avoid interference in the state affairs. This advice actually helps the Grand Steward to further concentrate power in his hands at the sovereign's expense.

11　For the philosopher Yang Zhu, see also chapter 22, note 57.
12　It is only when one views situations from the differing points of views of the participants that one can involve oneself in a situation in a well-informed analytic and strategic way.
13　Yi is the legendary superb archer. Yue stands here for "remote, far away" people, who, in spite of their remoteness are still aware of Yi's prowess.
14　Note the psychological dramatisation: the mother, of course, just keeps at a safe distance, but she is so afraid that her child will get killed that she hides in her house.

說林下 A FOREST OF PERSUASIONS, PART 2

故曰：	Therefore it is said:
"可必，	"When one can be sure of the outcome,
則越人不疑羿；	the people of Yue do not distrust Yi;
不可必，	when one cannot be sure of the outcome,
則慈母逃弱子。"	even a loving mother runs away from her toddler."

2 C emends 鞅 to 決, following 王念孫.　5 張抄 has 若 for 弱.　5 C emends 扞 to 扜, following 王念孫.　6 張抄 has 閑 for 閉.

HF 23.11 (*Xilun* 449, *Xin jiaozhu* 499)

桓公問管仲：	Lord Huan [of Qi] asked Guan Zhong:
"富有涯乎？"	"Is there a natural limit to wealth?"
答曰：	Guan Zhong replied:
"水之以涯，	"The reason a river's water has a bank as limit
其無水者也；	is that there is no more water;
富之以涯，	The reason why wealth has a limit
其富已足者也。	is that the wealth is already enough.
人不能自止於足，	If a person cannot stop himself when he has enough,
而亡其富之涯乎！"	then he loses the limit to his wealth."

6（以）富 (校注 271).

HF 23.12 (*Xilun* 449, *Xin jiaozhu* 500)

宋之富賈有監止子者，	In Song there was a rich merchant by the name of Jian Zhizi
與人爭買百金之璞玉，	who was quarrelling about buying a piece of uncarved jade for a hundred pieces of gold.
因佯失而毀之，	For the purpose, he pretended to drop the piece of jade on the floor and to damage it in the process.
負其百金，	He compensated one hundred pieces of gold for it,
而理其毀瑕，	and polished away the flaw.

得千溢焉。	Then he got a thousand *yi*[15] for it.
事有舉之而有敗，	There are undertakings which start with a failure,
而賢其毋舉之者，	but that is still more intelligent than not undertaking them at all.[16]
負之時也。	Compensating [the damaged jade] was a case in point.

9 時 is read as 是.

HF 23.13 (*Xilun* 450, *Xin jiaozhu* 500)

有欲以御見荊王者，	There was someone who sought an audience as a driver with the King of Jing (Chu).
眾騶妒之。	All the grooms were envious of him.
因曰：	On the strength of his announcement,
"臣能撽鹿。"	"I can clap a deer (while driving)."[17]
5 見王。	he had an audience with the king
王為御，	When the King acted as driver
不及鹿；	he did not get close enough to any deer;
自御，	but when the man himself drove
及之。	he did get close enough.
10 王善其御也，	The King commended his driving
乃言：	and then went on to comment:
"眾騶妒之。"	"All these coachmen were just jealous of the new driver."

6 張抄 has 禦 for 御.

HF 23.14 (*Xilun* 451, *Xin jiaozhu* 501)

荊令公子將伐陳。	[The king of] Jing (Chu) ordered a prince to lead an attack against Chen.[18]

---

15 *Yi* is a measure of weight of twenty *liang* (ca. 320 grammes).
16 The omission of the preposition *yu* 於 in this construction is unusual. The text of this concluding remark is problematic, and the interpretation tentative.
17 His speed and steering was so good that he could drive right up to the hunted deer.
18 Chu fought several wars with Chen, and had subjugated this state twice: Chen was an-

說林下 A FOREST OF PERSUASIONS, PART 2　　　373

	丈人送之日：	His father-in-law sent him off saying:
	"晉強，	"Jin is powerful.
	不可不慎也。"	You had better be cautious."
5	公子曰：	The prince said:
	"丈人奚憂？	"What are you worried about, father-in-law?
	吾為丈人破晉。"	I shall smash Jin for you!"
	丈人曰：	The father-in-law said:
	"可。	"All right.
10	吾方廬陳南門之外。"	In that case I shall build a hut outside the south gate of Chen."[19]
	公子曰：	The prince said:
	"是何也？"	"Why is this?"
	曰：	He said:
	"我笑勾踐也。	"It is because I find Goujian ridiculous.
15	為人之如是其易也，	If it were so easy to deal with,
	已獨何為密密十年難乎？"	why did he have to go to the trouble of making secret plans for ten years?"[20]

HF 23.15 (*Xilun* 452, *Xin jiaozhu* 501)

堯以天下讓許由，　　When Yao yielded the rule over All-under-Heaven to Xu You,[21]

---

[19] nexed by Chu in 534, regained independence in 529, and was annexed again in 478. The anecdote is not related to any specific campaign, and the mention of King Goujian (r. 496–464) in the last phrases betrays its anachronistic nature (Goujian overpowered Wu five years after Chen had perished).

[19] The southern gate would be the gate through which the Chu army should enter. Promising to build a hut here buttresses the ridiculous nature of prince's promise: if it were so easy to smash the Jin army, then conquering Chen would indeed be the simplest thing, and the father-in-law could watch the conquest from near Chen's gate.

[20] King Goujian of Yue was defeated early in his reign by Yue's arch-enemy, the state of Wu. According to the popular legend from the Warring States period, he plotted his revenge for a decade (494–484), during which he even served King Fuchai of Wu as a personal retainer. Only after having accumulated sufficient power did Goujian rebel against Wu, and after another ten years of campaigns finally annihilated Wu and did not spare Fuchai. This enduring determination and persistence is juxtaposed with the facile grandiloquence of the prince who proposes to solve all problems in one fell swoop.

[21] The story of Yao's unsuccessful attempt to yield his rule over All-under-Heaven to a righteous recluse, Xu You, is first mentioned in *Zhuangzi* (chapter 1). By the late Warring States period this legend had become ubiquitous (Pines 2005: 282–285).

許由逃之，	Xu You fled from him,
舍於家人，	and lodged with a relative.
家人藏其皮冠，	The relative stowed away his own official leather cap.
5 夫棄天下而家人藏其皮冠，	Now, when one has relinquished All-under-Heaven, for one's relative to stow away his official leather cap –
是不知許由者也。	this is a case of not understanding Xu You.[22]

HF 23.16 (*Xilun* 452, *Xin jiaozhu* 502)

三虱相與訟，	Three lice were involved in a litigation.
一虱過之，	Another louse passed by
曰：	and said:
"訟者奚說？"	"What is the issue of the litigation?"
5 三虱曰：	The three lice said:
"爭肥饒之地。"	"We are quarrelling over a succulent piece of land."
一虱曰：	The fourth louse said:
"若亦不患臘之至而茅之燥耳，	"Don't you folks worry that when the winter sacrifice comes they will simply cover you with reeds and roast you?
若又奚患？"	What else do you have to worry about?"
10 於是乃相與聚嘬其母而食之。	Thereupon they sucked greedily at their "mother" together and fed on her.
彘臞，	The sow was emaciated,
人乃弗殺。	and its human owner decided not to kill it after all.[23]

HF 23.17 (*Xilun* 453, *Xin jiaozhu* 503)

蟲有虺者，	Among worms there is the [poisonous] *hui* snake,
一身兩口，	endowed with one body but two mouths.

---

22   The relative did not understand the lofty ideals that motivated Xu You, believing that Xu You might steal the cap that stood for his capacity as official.

23   The rhetoric of this is almost disconcertingly advanced. Note the delayed provision of the information that the territory is in fact a sow.

說林下 A FOREST OF PERSUASIONS, PART 2

爭食相齕也。	In their struggle to eat, these mouths bite each other
遂相殺，	and consequently kill each other,
5 因自殺。	and as a result, the worm kills itself.
人臣之爭事而亡其國者，	When ministers fight and ruin the state,
皆虺類也。	they are all like the *hui* snake.

1 C emends 就 to 虺 (校注 271). 吳本、張抄、錢抄 have 就; 藏本、張本、陳本、趙本 have 蚘. We follow 張覺 in emending to 虺. 就 is obviously the same character rendered as 蚘 below.   3 〔食〕(校注 271).   7 （蚘）〔虺〕(校注 271); see note above.

HF 23.18 (*Xilun* 454, *Xin jiaozhu* 504)

宮有堊，	If one plasters houses white
器有滌，	and rinses pots and pans,
則潔矣。	then things will be clean.
行身亦然，	Conducting oneself is also like this.
5 無滌堊之地，	When there are no places to rinse or plaster,
則寡非矣。	there will be few faults.

HF 23.19 (*Xilun* 454, *Xin jiaozhu* 504)

公子糾將為亂，	When Prince Jiu was about to stage his revolt,[24]
桓公使使者視之。	Lord Huan of Qi sent an emissary to observe him.
使者報曰：	The emissary reported back:
"笑不樂，	"He laughs without joy
5 視不見，	and has a blank look on his face:
必為亂。"	he is sure to start a revolt."
乃使魯人殺之。	So Lord Huan ordered the people of Lu to kill him.

---

24 Prince Jiu was a major rival of Lord Huan of Qi in the fratricidal struggle in the state of Qi in 686–685. He was initially supported by Guan Zhong, and by the state of Lu (from which his mother hailed). After the defeat of Lu armies by supporters of Lord Huan, the state of Lu yielded to Lord Huan's demands and executed Prince Jiu. *Han Feizi*'s anecdote messes the story up: the execution of Prince Jiu was not when he "was about" to stage his revolt but after his failure. See also chapter 3, note 7.

HF 23.20 (*Xilun* 455, *Xin jiaozhu* 505)

公孫弘斷髮而為越王騎，	Gongsun Hong cut off his long hair and became a knight with the King of Yue.[25]
公孫喜使人絕之曰：	Gongsun Xi sent someone to break off relations with him, saying:
"吾不與子為昆弟矣。"	"I am no longer your brother."
公孫弘曰：	Gongsun Hong said;
5 "我斷髮，	"I cut off my hair
子斷頸而為人用兵，	and you will have your head cut off in military service for others.
我將謂子何？"	What can I call you then?"
周南之戰，	At the battle of Zhounan[26]
公孫喜死焉。	Gongsun Xi died.[27]

7 張抄 has 伐 for 我.

HF 23.21 (*Xilun* 456, *Xin jiaozhu* 506)

有與悍者鄰，	There was a man with a violent neighbour
欲賣宅而避之。	who wanted to sell his house in order to get away from him.
人曰：	Someone else said:
"是其貫將滿矣，	"That man will soon have filled his measure of violent crime –
5 子姑待之。"	just wait a while."

---

25   Cutting off one's hair was a savage custom associated (together with tattooing one's body) with the southern kingdoms of Wu and Yue. For Yue's image see Brindley 2015: 113–190. Note that by the time depicted in the anecdote (ca. 294), the Yue kingdom had in all likelihood ceased to exist.

26   The battle of Zhounan is a reference to what is most commonly known as the Yique 伊闕 campaign of 294, which saw Qin armies under the famous general Bai Qi (d. 257) decisively defeat the coalition of Wei, Hán and the Eastern Zhou principality. Gongsun Xi was one of the commanders of the coalition army.

27   Gongsun Xi dismisses his brother's behaviour because by adopting savage customs of the Yue people, Hong abandoned the principle of preserving the wholeness of one's body. What Xi forgets is that when serving in the army one endangers one's body much more in other ways.

說林下 A FOREST OF PERSUASIONS, PART 2

答曰：	He replied:
"吾恐其以我滿貫也。"	"I am scared that he will fill his measure at my expense,"
遂去之。	and left.
故曰：	Therefore it is said:
10 "物之幾[A 微/微 kjəd/-jəi/kjěi]者，	"When matters have reached a crisis,
非所靡[A 歌/紙 mjiarx/-jei/mjě]也。"	action is not to be delayed."

4 「是其貫將滿（也），（遂去之）。」（故曰）：「（勿之）矣(校注 271).

HF 23.22 (Xilun 457, Xin jiaozhu 507)

孔子謂弟子曰：	Confucius addressed his disciples:
"孰能導子西之釣名也？"	"Who can guide Zixi away from his tendency to angle for fame?"28
子貢曰：	Zigong said:
"賜也能。"	"I can do it."
5 乃導之，	So he went ahead and guided him,
不復疑也。	and he was no longer held in suspicion.29
子西曰：	Zixi said:
"寬哉，	"How large-hearted I am!
不被於利！	I am not drawn by profit.
10 絜哉，	How pure I am!
民性有恆！	The people's nature has its constants.
曲為曲，	The crooked will be crooked,
直為直。"	and the straight will be straight."
孔子曰：	Confucius said:
15 "子西不免。"	"Zixi will not get out of this alive."
白公之難，	When Duke of Bai made trouble,
子西死焉。	Zixi was killed.

---

28   Zixi, a son of King Ping of Chu, was the chief minister of Chu under his brother, King Zhao, and his nephew, King Hui. He was killed during the rebellion of the Duke of Bai (chapter 21, note 45) in 479.

29   The usual portrait of Confucius' disciple Zigong is that of a skilled diplomat, and not a moral paragon. There is an ironic hint in the anecdote: Zixi pursues fame to a greater extent than before after having been "taught" by Zigong.

故曰：
"直於行者曲於欲。"

Thus it is said:
"Those who are straight in their actions are crooked in their desires."[30]

1 子（曰）謂, with 吳本、張抄、陳本 and 趙本, following 梁啟雄.　　7 孔子, attested in all editions, is here emended to 子西, following 王先慎.

HF 23.23 (*Xilun* 458, *Xin jiaozhu* 508)

晉中行文子出亡，
過於縣邑。
從者曰：
"此嗇夫，
5　公之故人。
公奚不休舍，
且待後車？"
文子曰：
"吾嘗好音，
10　此人遺我鳴琴；
吾好佩，
此人遺我玉環，
是振我過者也，
以求容於我者，
15　吾恐其以我求容於人也。"

乃去之。
果收文子後車二乘而獻之其君矣。

Zhonghang Wenzi of Jin went into exile[31]
and passed through the county seat.
His followers said:
"The bailiff of this place
is an old friend of yours.
Why don't you put up in his place
and wait for your trailing carriages?"
Wenzi said:
"I used to be fond of music
and this person gave me a resonant zither;
when I was fond of pendants,
this man gave me a jade ring;
he is someone who abets my faults.
Since he is pandering to me,
I am afraid that afterwards he will pander to others at my expense."
And so he departed.
In the event, the man confiscated two of Wenzi's trailing carriages and presented them to his ruler.

30　Zixi's pursuit of vanity ("name" 名) remained his malady. *Zuozhuan* (Ai 16.5) depicts how his excessive magnanimity and the trust of the Duke of Bai facilitated the latter's rebellion, the beginning of which saw Zixi murdered. Han Fei implies that the "crooked desire" to become famous was the reason for Zixi's suicidal pursuit of "straight action."

31　Zhonghang Wenzi (Xun Yin 荀寅) was the head of the Zhonghang lineage in Jin, which, together with the Fan lineage, was defeated during the epochal inter-ministerial feud of 497–490.

說林下 A FOREST OF PERSUASIONS, PART 2

HF 23.24 (*Xilun* 459, *Xin jiaozhu* 509)

周趮謂宮他曰：	Zhou Zao said to Gong Tuo:[32]
"為我謂齊王曰：	"Tell the King of Qi on my behalf:
以齊資我於魏，	'If you help me in Wei,
請以魏事王。"	I beg to serve you with Wei.'"
宮他曰：	Gong Tuo said:
"不可，	"That is not acceptable.
是示之無魏也，	This would be to indicate to him that you are not in control in Wei.
齊王必不資於無魏者，	The King of Qi will certainly not support someone who is not in control in Wei,
而以怨有魏者。	thereby arousing the resentment of those who are.
公不如曰：	You should say:
以王之所欲，	'In accordance with your desires,
臣請以魏聽王。	I beg permission to make Wei heed you.'
齊王必以公為有魏也，	Then the King of Qi is bound to consider you in control of Wei
必因公。	and he will surely rely on you.
是公有齊也，	In this way, you will gain the support of Qi,
因以有齊、魏矣。"	and, as a result, can gain control in both Qi and Wei."[33]

HF 23.25 (*Xilun* 459, *Xin jiaozhu* 508)

白圭謂宋大尹曰：	Bai Gui told the Song Senior Official:[34]
"君長自知政，	"When your ruler has grown up and taken charge of the affairs of government,

---

32 Zhou Zao is identified as Zhou Xiao 周霄, a travelling persuader from the state of Wei mentioned in *Mengzi* and *Zhanguo ce*. Another version of the anecdote appears in *Zhanguo ce* 25.19 ("Wei 4").

33 This is a classic exposition of the machinations of travelling persuaders. In a political situation peculiar to the Warring States (much lamented in *Han Feizi* and, earlier, in the *Book of Lord Shang*) certain ministers got promoted in the court of their states due to the support of foreign powers (usually the state's nominal allies). Naturally, this gave rise to a situation whereby these "servants to several masters" sought the support of foreign powers with an eye towards career advancement in their domestic states. The loyalties of these ministers, needless to say, lay with their own private interests alone.

34 In *Han Feizi* the unnamed official is identified as *lingyin* 令尹, which is the Chu term for

380   CHAPTER 23

公無事矣。	you will be out of work.
今君少主也而務名,	At this point, the ruler is still a minor and is concerned about his reputation.
5 不如令荊賀君之孝也,	You had better cause Jing (Chu) to congratulate the ruler on his filial piety.
則君不奪公位,	Then the ruler will not take away your position,
而大敬重公,	and will show you great reverence,
則公常用宋矣。"	so you may rule in Song for a long time."

1 張抄 has 為 for 謂.   1〔今〕〔大〕(校注 271).

HF 23.26 (*Xilun* 460, *Xin jiaozhu* 509)

管仲、鮑叔相謂曰:	Guan Zhong and Bao Shu[ya] said to each other:
"君亂甚矣,	"The ruler is doing very badly.[35]
必失國。	He is bound to lose his state.
齊國之諸公子其可輔者,	Among the princes of Qi, the one who can help him,
5 非公子糾,	apart from Prince Jiu,
則小白也。	is Xiaobai.
與子人事一人焉,	Now you and I each serve one of these men,

a chief minister. Commentators correct it to *dayin* 大尹 on the basis of the parallel passage in *Zhanguo ce* 32.5 ("Song"). The office of *dayin* is mentioned in the context of the state of Song once in *Zuozhuan* (Ai 26.2), from which it can be inferred that this was a very powerful man personally close to the reigning lord, but not a holder of a regular ministerial rank. From the *Han Feizi* and *Zhanguo ce* parallel anecdotes it is highly likely that the Senior Official acted as regent to the young lord of Song. *Zhanguo ce* commentators speculate that he was a confidant of the dowager, but it may be even speculated that he was the young ruler's biological father (think of Zaifeng, the father of the child emperor Puyi [r. 1908–1912] who was in charge of affairs in the twilight days of the Qing dynasty).

35 Lord Xiang was not behaving well. He had scandalously committed incest with his younger sister, the wife of Lord Huan of Lu, and alienated several nobles. His prospective heirs Xiaobai 小白 (the future Lord Huan of Qi), and Prince Jiu 公子糾 fled the country. In 686, Lord Xiang was assassinated by his half-brother Wuzhi who was then briefly established as a ruler only to be killed within a few weeks. It is not clear to which of the two rulers the remark refers. According to *Zuozhuan* (Zhuang 8.3), Xiaobai fled during the reign of Lord Xiang, whereas Jiu (on whom see note 24 above) fled in the aftermath of Wuzhi's seizure of power.

說林下 A FOREST OF PERSUASIONS, PART 2

先達者相收。" so let us say that the one who succeeds first will shelter the other."
管仲乃從公子糾, Guan Zhong then joined the party of Prince Jiu,
10 鮑叔從小白。 and Bao Shu[ya] the party of Xiaobai.
國人果弒君。 The capital dwellers did in fact assassinate the ruler.[36]
小白先入為君, Xiaobai entered [the capital] first to become the ruler,
魯人拘管仲而效之, and the people of Lu detained Guan Zhong and handed him over,[37]
鮑叔言而相之。 but Bao Shu[ya] spoke [on his behalf] and he was made chancellor.
15 故諺曰： Thus the proverb says:
"巫咸雖善祝, "Although Wu Xian was good at invoking the spirits,
不能自祓也； he was unable to exorcise them from himself;
秦醫雖善除, Although the Qin Doctor was be good at dispelling disease,
不能自彈也。" he is unable to apply moxibustion to himself."[38]
20 以管仲之聖而待鮑叔之助, Although he was a sage, being Guan Zhong, he still depended on the help of Bao Shu[ya].
此鄙諺所謂"虜自賣裘[A 之/尤 gjəg/gjə̆u]而不售[A 幽/宥 djəgwh/źjə̆u], This is what the popular saying refers to when it says: "If a slave peddles his own fur coat, it will not be sold,
士自譽辯[B 元/獮 bjianx/bjän]而不信[B 真/震 sjinh/sjĕn]"者也。 and if a scholar praises his own eloquence, he will not be believed."

8 （相）〔先〕(校注 271). 18 （養）秦 (校注 271).

---

36 This refers to the assassination of Wuzhi in 685.
37 Xiaobai stayed in the state of Ju (southeast of Qi's capital, Linzi), whereas Jiu stayed at Lu (southwest of Linzi). Xiaobai was the first to return and establish himself as a legitimate ruler. In the ensuing fight with the Lu troops who were trying to install Prince Jiu, the Lu armies were defeated, and Xiaobai was confirmed as the lord of Qi (posthumously known as Lord Huan). In keeping with Qi's demands, Lu had to execute its protégé, Prince Jiu, and turned Guan Zhong over to Qi. See *Zuozhuan*, Zhuang 9.5 and chapter 3, note 7.
38 Wu Xian a legendary shaman of the Shang dynasty. The Qin doctor is Bian He, who is hailed in *Zuozhuan* (Zhao 1.12) as an excellent physician; his abilities became proverbial.

HF 23.27 (*Xilun* 461, *Xin jiaozhu* 510)

荊王伐吳，	The King of Jing (Chu) attacked Wu,
吳使沮衛蹷融犒於荊師，	and Wu sent Juwei Juerong to offer friendly food offerings to the Jing (Chu) army[39]
而將軍曰：	but the general said:
"縛之，	"Tie him up!
殺以釁鼓。"	Kill him and smear the battle drums with his blood."
問之曰：	He asked him:
"女來，	"Before you came,
卜乎？"	did you consult the tortoise shells."
答曰：	He replied:
"卜。"	"I did."
"卜吉乎？"	"Did you get a favourable prognostication."
曰：	He said:
"吉。"	"Yes, I did."
荊人曰：	The men from Jing (Chu) said:
"今荊將欲女釁鼓，	"Now Jing (Chu) wants to smear the attack drums with your blood.
其何也？"	How can that be?"
答曰：	He replied:
"是故其所以吉也。	"That is exactly why the signs were favourable.
吳使臣來也，	When Wu sent me here,
固視將軍怒。	it was basically to observe whether you, general, would show anger.
將軍怒，	If you, general, were angry,
將深溝高壘；	you would build deep moats and high ramparts;
將軍不怒，	If you, general, were not angry,
將懈怠。	you would be lax and careless.
今也，	Now, on the other hand,
將軍殺臣，	if you, general, are having me killed,
則吳必警守矣。	Wu will surely be alarmed and defend itself.
且國之卜，	Moreover, a state prognostication
非為一臣卜。	is not a prognostication for a single individual.

---

39 This anecdote is based (with small modifications) on one told in *Zuozhuan* (Zhao 5.8). The king of Chu at hand is the infamous King Ling (r. 540–529), and the year is 537. The Wu envoy there is the younger brother of the king of Wu, called in *Zuozhuan* Jueyou (or Guiyou 蹷由).

說林下 A FOREST OF PERSUASIONS, PART 2   383

30 夫殺一臣而存一國，	Now, for one servitor to be killed but the whole state to survive –
其不言吉，	if that cannot be called auspicious,
何也？	what can?
且死者無知，	Moreover, if the dead have no awareness,[40]
則以臣釁鼓無益也；	using me to smear the attack drums with blood will be of no benefit,[41]
35 死者有知也，	but if the dead do have awareness,
臣將當戰之時，	then at the time of the battle,
臣使鼓不鳴。"	I will cause the drums not to sound."
荊人因不殺也。	Accordingly, the people of Jing (Chu) did not kill him.

19 C has 民 for 臣, with 校注 271; 錢抄. 錢抄、藏本、張本、陳本 read 臣; 吳本、張抄、趙本 read 人.

HF 23.28 (Xilun 463, Xin jiaozhu 511)

知伯將伐仇由，	Zhi Bo was about to invade Chouyou,[42]
而道難不通，	but the road was difficult and impassable.
乃鑄大鍾遺仇由之君。	He cast a large bell and presented it to the ruler of Chouyou.
仇由之君大說，	The ruler of Chouyou was greatly delighted;
5 除道將內之。	he had the road cleared and wanted to let in [Zhi Bo].
赤章曼枝曰：	Chizhang Manzhi said:
"不可。	"This is unacceptable.
此小之所以事大也，	This would be a way for a small state to serve a large one,
而今也大以來，	but now a large state is making such an approach,
10 卒必隨之，	and soldiers are bound to follow.

---

40 The question of whether the dead have consciousness was matter of debate in the Warring States period (see Goldin 2015). Note that the discussion of the consciousness of the dead mentioned here does not appear in the version of the story as presented in *Zuozhuan*.
41 Presumably, the blood of a dead person was thought to be devoid of magical efficacy.
42 For a reference to the same story, see chapter 21.4.2. *Zhanguo ce* 2.3 ("Xi Zhou" 西周) has embedded into it a version of this story which follows a quite different narrative. There, Chouyou is written Qiuyou 厹由. Han Fei is clearly working from a different source than that used by the editors of *Zhanguo ce*.

不可內也。"	It is not acceptable to let him in."
仇由之君不聽，	The ruler of Chouyou did not listen to this advice,
遂內之。	but proceeded to let him in.
赤章曼枝因斷轂而驅，	Chizhang Manzhi thereupon raced away with his axle-caps detached,[43]
15 至於齊，	he got to Qi.
七月而仇由亡矣。	After seven months, Chouyou was ruined.

1 C has 智 for 知, against 校注 271. 吳本、張抄、趙本 have 知; 錢抄、藏本、張本、陳本 have 智.   10 （以）〔必〕(校注 271).

HF 23.29 (*Xilun* 464, *Xin jiaozhu* 513)

越已勝吳，	After Yue had won a victory against Wu,
又索卒於荊而攻晉。	it went on to demand soldiers from Jing (Chu) to attack Jin.[44]
左史倚相謂荊王曰：	The Scribe of the Left, Yixiang, said to the King of Jing (Chu):[45]
"夫越破吳，	"Yue has destroyed Wu;
5 豪士死，	its finest officers have died;
銳卒盡，	its crack troops are all lost;
大甲傷。	and its heavy infantry are injured.
今又索卒以攻晉，	Now they go on to seek soldiers in order to attack Jin,
示我不病也。	demonstrating to us that they are not disabled.
10 不如起師與分吳。"	It would be best to raise an army and to divide the spoils of Wu [between them and us]."
荊王曰：	The King of Jing (Chu) said:
"善。"	"Very good."

43   So eager was he to leave that he paid no attention to his axle-caps being broken as he left.
44   King Goujian of Yue's victory over Wu was accomplished in 473. Nothing is known of his plans to assault Jin. To the contrary, from the bamboo manuscript *Xinian* we learn of a stable Jin-Yue axis directed against Qi (and potentially against Chu). See more in Pines 2020a: 113–116.
45   Scribe of the Left Yixiang is mentioned in *Zuozhuan* and *Discourses of the States* as a sagacious scribe, whose first appearance is under King Ling of Chu, in 530. The events depicted in the *Han Feizi* anecdote are from the reign of King Hui of Chu, and should have taken place after 473. That Yixiang remained active for more than 57 years is highly unlikely.

因起師而從越。	And so he raised an army which pursued Yue.[46]
越王怒，	The King of Yue was enraged
15 將擊之。	and wanted to launch an attack against Chu.
大夫種曰：	Grandee Zhong[47] said:
"不可。	"That is not acceptable.
吾豪士盡，	Our finest officers are all dead
大甲傷。	and our heavy infantry is injured.
20 我與戰，	If we join battle with them,
必不克，	we are bound not to succeed.
不如賂之。"	The best thing would be to bribe them."
乃割露山之陰五百里以賂之。	And so they carved out 500 *li* to the north of Mount Lu[48] to bribe them with.

3 〔謂〕; 錢抄 lacks 謂; 吳本、張抄、藏本、張本、陳本、趙本 have 謂; we follow 梁啟雄.

HF 23.30 (*Xilun* 466, *Xin jiaozhu* 514)

荊伐陳，	Jing (Chu) was attacking Chen
吳救之，	and Wu came to Chen's rescue.[49]
軍間三十里。	The armies of Chu and Wu were thirty *li* apart from each other.
雨十日，	It had rained for ten days,
5 夜星。	but overnight the weather became fine.
左史倚相謂子期曰：	The Chu Scribe of the Left, Yixiang, told Ziqi:[50]
"雨十日，	"It has been raining for ten days;
甲輯而兵聚。	the armour is collected and the weapons are stockpiled:
吳人必至，	the Wu people are bound to arrive.

---

46 It appears that having been asked for some military support, the powerful state of Chu sent off an entire threatening army.
47 Grandee Zhong and Fan Li are two great ministers of King Goujian (chapter 17, note 4), the architects of his astounding success.
48 The exact location of Mt. Lu is debatable, but it may conceivably refer to territory in the Huai River basin which formerly belonged to Wu and was now divided between Wu's two enemies, Yue and Chu.
49 The struggle between Wu and Chu over the allegiance of the intermediary state of Chen between 489–486 is recorded in *Zuozhuan* (Ai 6.2, 6.4, 9.3).
50 Ziqi was then acting as Chu's prime minister.

10 不如備之。"	We had better prepare for them."
乃為陳。	And so he arrayed the troops,
陳未成也而吳人至，	However, before the battle arrays were completely formed, the Wu people arrived,
見荊陳而反。	and when they saw that the Jing (Chu) battle arrays were being formed, they turned back.[51]
左史曰：	The Chu Scribe of the Left said:
15 "吳反覆六十里，	"Wu have travelled sixty *li* back and forth;
其君子必休，	their noble men are bound to have to rest,
小人必食。	and their petty men are bound to need something to eat.[52]
我行三十里擊之，	If we march thirty *li* and strike them,
必可敗也。"	they can certainly be defeated."
20 乃從之，	Ziqi followed [this advice],
遂破吳軍。	and subsequently routed the Wu army.

13 陳 is read as 陣.　14 張抄 has 思 for 史.

HF 23.31 (*Xilun* 467, *Xin jiaozhu* 515)

韓、趙相與為難。	Relations were strained between Hán and Zhao.[53]
韓子索兵於魏曰：	The ruler of Hán asked for troops from Wei, saying:
"願借師以伐趙。"	"I hope to borrow troops in order to launch a formal attack on Zhao."
魏文侯曰：	Marquis Wen of Wei said:
5 "寡人與趙兄弟，	"I have brotherly relations with Zhao,
不可以從。"	and cannot accede to this request."
趙又索兵以攻韓。	Zhao also asked for troops to attack Hán.

51　They had hoped to launch a surprise attack.

52　Note that here "noble" and "petty" are purely based on ascribed status, without moral connotations. This usage was common in the aristocratic Springs-and-Autumns age from which period this anecdote evidently originates.

53　The story is set during the reign of Marquis Wen of Wei (r. 445–396), i.e. precisely when Wei, Hán, and Zhao were recognised as independent polities and not just ministerial lineages of Jin. During that period, the three houses continued to succeed at maintaining a close alliance against Chu and Qi. For another version of the anecdote, see *Zhanguo ce* 22.2 ("Wei 1").

說林下 A FOREST OF PERSUASIONS, PART 2 387

文侯曰：	Marquis Wen said:
"寡人與韓兄弟，	"I have brotherly relations with Hán,
10 不敢從。"	and dare not accede to this request.
二國不得兵，	Neither Hán nor Zhao got any troops,
怒而反。	and, full of fury, they returned home.
已乃知文侯以構於己，	In the end, they realised that Marquis Wen was concerned to build peace with them,
乃皆朝魏。	and they all paid their respects at the court of Wei.

13 構 is read as 講.

HF 23.32 (*Xilun* 467, *Xin jiaozhu* 515)

齊伐魯，	Qi attacked Lu
索讒鼎，	and demanded the Chan cauldron.[54]
魯以其鴈往。	Lu sent a fake one.
齊人曰：	The people of Qi said:
5 "鴈也。"	"This is a fake."
魯人曰：	The people of Lu said:
"真也。"	"It is authentic."
齊曰：	The people of Qi said:
"使樂正子春來，	"Send Yuezheng Zichun here,[55]
10 吾將聽子。"	then[56] we shall accept your view."
魯君請樂正子春，	The ruler of Lu asked Yuezheng Zichun to go;
樂正子春曰：	Yuezheng Zichun said:
"胡不以其真往也？"	"Why didn't you send the authentic one?"
君曰：	The ruler said:
15 "我愛之。"	"I am very fond of it."
答曰：	He replied:
"臣亦愛臣之信。"	"I, your subject, am equally fond of my trustworthiness."

1 張抄 has 代 for 伐.   3, 5 鴈 is read as 贋.   15 之（信）(校注 271).

54　The Chan cauldron is mentioned in *Zuozhuan* Zhao 3.3; in later texts it is identified as *cen* 岑 cauldron.
55　Yuezheng Zichun was active in the late fifth century; he is sometimes identified as the disciple of Confucius's disciple, Zengzi 曾子.
56　If he confirms it.

388   CHAPTER 23

HF 23.33 (*Xilun* 468, *Xin jiaozhu* 516)

韓咎立為君未定也。 Han Jiu's establishment as the ruler was not yet secure.[57]

弟在周， His younger brother was in Zhou.[58]
周欲重之， The Zhou wanted to show their respect,
而恐韓咎不立也。 but were afraid that Han Jiu would not be established.[59]

5 綦毋恢曰： Qi Wuhui said:
"不若以車百乘送之。 "We had better send off [Jiu's brother] with a hundred chariots.

得立， If Han Jiu is established,
因曰為戒； we shall say: 'This was to be on guard.'
不立， And if he is not established,
10 則曰來效賊也。" then we shall say that we come with the chariots to hand over the villain."[60]

5 C has 母 for 毋.

HF 23.34 (*Xilun* 469, *Xin jiaozhu* 517)

靖郭君將城薛， Lord Jingguo (the Lord-Calming-the-State) was about to wall the city of Xue.[61]

---

57 Han Jiu is King Li 釐 of Hán, r. 295–273. That Han Fei refers to the former king of his home state by his personal name is odd. For another version of this anecdote, see *Zhanguo ce*, 27.20 ("Hán 2").

58 The tiny Zhou domain was effectively surrounded by the territories of the state of Hán.

59 An open show of respect to Han Jiu would make sense only if Han Jiu had become the king of Hán.

60 The details of the ploy are not clear. In particular, it is disputed whether Jiu's younger brother should be considered Jiu's supporter or rival. Taking the former as a tentative answer, we may surmise that Zhou's ploy was as follows: if Jiu is established, then the military escort for his brother would merely be an escort of honour and a precaution against possible assaults of the new king's close kin. If Jiu was not established, then his brother would be handed over to the new king of Hán as one of the potential rivals for the throne.

61 Another version of the anecdote, with variations, appears in *Zhanguo ce* 8.3 ("Qi 齊 1"). The Lord-Calming-the-State (alternatively, the Lord-who-Pacifies-Outer-Walls, Lord Jingguo 靖郭君) is the posthumous title of Tian Ying 田嬰 (d. ca. 298), one of the most important military and civilian leaders of the state of Qi. His biography is given in *Shiji* 75: 2353–2355, where it serves a preface to the biography of Tian Ying's famous son, Tian Wen

說林下 A FOREST OF PERSUASIONS, PART 2

客多以諫者。	Many of his retainers remonstrated against this.
靖郭君謂謁者曰：	The Lord-Calming-the-State told his steward:
"毋為客通。"	"Do not pass on messages from the retainers."
齊人有請見者曰：	A man from Qi requested an audience, saying:
"臣請三言而已。	"I beg to submit three words only.
過三言，	If I exceed three words,
臣請烹。"	I beg to be broiled."
靖郭君因見之。	So the Lord-Calming-the-State agreed to see him.
客趨進曰：	The retainer rushed forward and said:
"海大魚。"	"sea, great, fish."
因反走。	Then he turned round to run away.
靖郭君曰：	The Lord-Calming-the-State said:
"請聞其說。"	"May I hear the explanation?"
客曰：	The retainer said:
"臣不敢以死為戲。"	"I dare not play with my death."
靖郭君曰：	The Lord-Calming-the-State said:
"願為寡人言之。"	"I wish you would say it for me."
答曰：	He replied:
"君聞大魚乎？	"Have you heard about the great fish?[62]
網不能止，	Nets cannot stop it,
繳不能絓也，	nor can harpoons entangle it,
蕩而失水，	but when it goes astray and loses its watery element,
螻蟻得意焉。	maggots and ants have their way with it.
今夫齊亦君之海也。	Now the state of Qi is your "sea,"
君長有齊，	and since you possess Qi as its leader,
奚以薛為？	why should you be so concerned about Xue?
君失齊，	If you lose Qi,
雖隆薛城至於天，	then even if the imposing walls of Xue reach to Heaven,
猶無益也。"	they will still be of no avail."
靖郭君曰：	The Lord-Calming-the-State said:

田文, Lord Mengchang 孟嘗君, a renowned patron of itinerant gentlemen. According to the biography (which may contain several factual, especially chronological, inaccuracies), Tian Ying was a minor son of King Wei of Qi (r. 356–320); he rose to the position of prime-minister under his half-brother, King Xuan (r. 319–301) and served into the reign of King Min (r. 300–284). Xue was his fief, which, uncharacteristically of the Warring States period, was developing into a semi-independent polity. Another version of the anecdote appears in *Zhanguo ce* 8.3 ("Qi 1").

62 The reference is probably to whales.

390　　　　　　　　　　　　　　　　　　　　　　　　　CHAPTER 23

"善。"	"Good."
乃輟，	In the end he desisted
不城薛。	and did not wall Xue.

1 君（曰）將（校注 271）.

HF 23.35 (*Xilun* 471, *Xin jiaozhu* 518)

荊王弟在秦，	The younger brother of the King of Jing (Chu) was in Qin,
秦不出也。	and Qin would not let him out.[63]
中射之士曰：	An officer of the palace guard said:
"資臣百金，	"If you support me with one hundred pieces of gold,
5　臣能出之。"	I shall be able to get him out."
因載百金之晉，	So he took one hundred pieces of gold and went to Jin,
見叔向，	where he visited Shuxiang
曰：	and said:
"荊王弟在秦，	"The younger brother of the King of Jing (Chu) is in Qin,
10　秦不出也。	and Qin will not let him out.
請以百金委叔向。"	I would like to hand over one hundred pieces of gold to you."
叔向受金，	Shuxiang accepted the gold
而以見之晉平公曰：	and showed it to Lord Ping of Jin, saying:
"可以城壺丘矣。"	"We may now build a wall round Huqiu."[64]
15　平公曰：	Lord Ping said:
"何也？"	"Why is that."
對曰：	He replied:
"荊王弟在秦，	"The son of the King of Jing (Chu) is in Qin,
秦不出也，	and Qin will not let him out.
20　是秦惡荊也，	This is because Qin hates Jing (Chu).

63　The story has a clear Warring States flavour; but insofar as it mentions the Jin minister Shuxiang, it supposedly took place in the 540s or 530s.

64　Huqiu (alternatively written 瓠丘) was located to the north of Yellow River, in southwestern Shanxi, relatively close to Qin territory.

說林下 A FOREST OF PERSUASIONS, PART 2   391

必不敢禁我城壺丘。	They will surely not dare to forbid us to build walls at Huqiu,
若禁之，	but in case they do,
我曰：	we should say:
'為我出荊王之弟，	'If you hand over the younger brother of Jing (Chu),
25　吾不城也。'	we will not proceed with the walling of Huqiu.'
彼如出之，	If they let him out,
可以德荊；	we shall have built up good will with Jing (Chu);
彼不出，	if they do not,
是卒惡也，	then [relations between Qin and Chu] will finally be bad,
30　必不敢禁我城壺丘矣。"	and in that case, they will certainly not dare to forbid us to wall Huqiu."
公曰：	The lord said:
"善。"	"Excellent!"
乃城壺丘。	Then he started to build a city wall around Huqiu,
謂秦公曰：	and said to the lord of Qin:
35　"為我出荊王之弟，	"If you let out the younger brother of the king of Jing (Chu) for me,
吾不城也。"	I shall not wall [the city]."
秦因出之。	So then Qin let the man out.
荊王大說，	The king of Jing (Chu) was greatly satisfied
以鍊金百鎰遺晉。	and gave one hundred ounces of purified gold as a present to Jin.

27　（得）〔德〕（校注 271）.

HF 23.36 (Xilun 472, Xin jiaozhu 519)

闔廬攻郢，	Helu attacked Ying,[65]
戰三勝，	and won three victories in three battles.
問子胥曰：	He asked Zixu:[66]
"可以退乎？"	"May we withdraw?"
5　子胥對曰：	Zixu replied:

65　Helu is the king of Wu. The invasion of Chu's capital Ying took place in 506.
66　Wu Zixu (see chapter 3, note 5 and chapter 22, note 10) was a fugitive from Chu, who became the top strategist for Wu in their anti-Chu campaign.

"溺人者一飲而止， "If you are drowning someone and stop at one gulp,
則無遂者， you will not succeed,
以其休也。 because you will be relenting midway.
不如乘之以沉之。" We had better take the opportunity to sink them."

7（逆）〔遂〕(校注 271, following 顧廣圻).　8 其（不）休(校注 271, following 孫楷第).

HF 23.37 (*Xilun* 473, *Xin jiaozhu* 520)

鄭人有一子， There was a young man in Zheng
將宦， who was going to take office.
謂其家曰： He told his family:
"必築壞牆， "Be sure to repair the damaged wall.
5 是不善， If it is not in good shape,
人將竊。" people are going to break in and steal things."
其巷人亦云。 A neighbour said the same thing.
不時築， [The wall] was not repaired in time
而人果竊之。 and someone actually stole something from the family.
10 以其子為智， They considered their son wise,
以巷人告者為盜。 but the neighbour who had predicted this, they regarded as a thief.

CHAPTER 24

觀行 Observing Behaviour

HF 24.1 (*Xilun* 474, *Xin jiaozhu* 520)[1]

古之人，	In ancient times,
目短於自見[A 元/霰 gianh/γien]，	since people's eyes fell short of being able to see themselves,
故以鏡觀面[A 元/線 mjianh/mjiän]；	they used mirrors to look at their faces;
智短於自知[B 佳/支 trig/-jiəi/tjĕ]，	since their intelligence fell short of being able to know themselves,
5 故以道正己[B 之/止 kjəgx/-jəi/kĭ]。	they corrected themselves through the Way.
故鏡無見疵之罪，	You do not blame the mirror for showing flaws,
道無明過之怨。	nor do you resent the Way for clarifying mistakes.
目失鏡，	If your eyes lose their mirror,
則無以正鬚眉；	you will have no way of adjusting your beard and brows;
10 身失道，	if your lose the Way,
則無以知迷惑。	you will have no way of knowing when you have gone astray.
西門豹之性急，	Ximen Bao was hot-tempered by nature,
故佩韋以緩己；	so he wore a soft leather belt to tone himself down.[2]
董安于之心緩，	Dong Anyu had a slow frame of mind,

1　This is the first in a cluster of six chapters (24–29) which are very close to each other in terms of ideas, lexicon, and modes of argumentation. The ostensible proximity of these chapters to Confucian ideas (e.g., approving references to the past and to its paragons) and to *Laozi* (most notably, chapter 29) has given rise to considerable debate over their authorship. Yet, as many scholars have observed, differences of argumentation aside, these chapters present ideas that align with the rest of *Han Feizi* overall, apart from their lack of the aura of cynicism which is prominent elsewhere in the text. Some scholars have speculated that these chapters were produced by Han Fei at an early stage of his intellectual career. See more in Lundahl 1992: 241–260 and Zheng Liangshu 1993: 262–377.

2　Ximen Bao (fl. 400) was a leading official in the state of Wei under Marquis Wen 魏文侯.

15 故佩弦以自急。

　　故以有餘補不足[C 侯/燭 tsjuk/tsj-wok]，
　　以長續短之謂明主[C 侯/麌 tjugx/tśju]。

　　2 張抄 has 矩 for 短。

so he wore a bow-string as a belt to urge himself on.[3]

And so, to supplement what you lack with what you have in surplus,

to lengthen what is short with what is long, is called being a clear-sighted ruler.

HF 24.2 (*Xilun* 475, *Xin jiaozhu* 522)

　　天下有信數三：
　　一曰智有所不能立，

　　二曰力有所不能舉，

　　三曰強有所不能勝。

5　故雖有堯之智而無眾人之助，

　　大功不立；
　　有烏獲之勁而不得人助，

　　不能自舉；
　　有賁、育之強而無法術，

10　不得長勝。

　　故勢有不可得，

There are three reliable constants in the world:
First, there are things that your intellect cannot bring to fruition;

second, there are objects that your strength cannot raise up;

third, there are people that your force cannot overpower.

Thus, if you have the intellect of Yao but not the support of the multitudes,[4]

you will not establish great achievements;
if you have the strength of Wu Huo, but do not obtain the support of other people,

you cannot even lift yourself up;[5]
if you have the power of [Meng] Ben or [Xia] Yu,[6] but do not know the law and techniques of rule,

you cannot overpower others permanently.

Thus there are circumstances that make things impossible,

3　Dong Anyu (chapter 3, note 24) was a faithful servant of the Zhao lineage in Jin, who sacrificed himself in 496 by letting himself be used as the scapegoat amid Zhao's strife with the Fan and Zhonghang lineages.

4　The importance of the multitudes' support for political success is suggested also in 28.2, and, more provocatively, in 40.1.

5　Wu Huo (d. 306) was a renowned strongman from the state of Qin.

6　Meng Ben (fl. 310) and Xia Yu 夏育 (of whom next to nothing is known) are another pair of renowned strongmen. Meng Ben also epitomises peerless courage.

觀行 OBSERVING BEHAVIOUR

事有不可成。	and there are tasks that can never be achieved.
故烏獲輕千鈞而重其身，	Thus Wu Huo regarded a tonne as light, but found his own body too heavy to lift.
非其身重於千鈞也，	It is not that his body was heavier than a tonne,
15 勢不便也。	but the circumstances were not advantageous.[7]
離朱易百步而難眉睫，	Li Zhu found it easy to see across a hundred paces, but had difficulty seeing his own eyebrows and eyelashes.
非百步近而眉睫遠也，	It is not that a hundred paces is close and the eyebrows and eyelashes are far away,
道不可也。	but it is in the way of things that this is impossible.
故明主不窮烏獲以其不能自舉，	A clear-sighted ruler will not cause trouble for Wu Huo for not being able to lift himself up,
20 不困離朱以其不能自見。	nor make trouble for Li Zhu for not being able to see himself.
因可勢，	A clear-sighted ruler adapts to the circumstances of what is possible
求易道，	and seeks the way of ease,
故用力寡而功名立。	so that, using little effort, his success and fame[8] are established.
時有滿虛，	There are times full [of opportunity] and times devoid [of opportunity];
25 事有利害，	there are advantageous and disadvantageous undertakings;
物有生死，	among creatures there are those destined to live and those destined to die.
人主為三者發喜怒之色，	If the ruler shows emotion when faced with these three things,
則金石之士離心焉。	his staunch officers will become disaffected
聖賢之撲深矣。	and the sagacious and worthy will go into deep hiding.

---

7 What is translated here as "circumstances" is what elsewhere we render "positional power" (*shi* 勢).

8 This theme of success and fame, meritorious achievement and high reputation, reverberates throughout chapters 24–29 (and provides the name for chapter 28).

30	故明主觀人，	Hence the clear-sighted ruler should observe others,
	不使人觀己。	but not let others observe him.
	明於堯不能獨成，	He clearly understands that Yao cannot obtain his successes alone,
	烏獲不能自舉，	that Wu Huo cannot lift himself,
	賁、育之不能自勝，	and that [Meng] Ben and [Xia] Yu cannot overpower themselves.
35	以法術則觀行之道畢矣。	If he uses laws and techniques of rule, his way of observing behaviour will be perfect.

4 張抄 has 疆 for 彊 (here normalised to 強).　**10**（生）〔勝〕(校注 274, following 孫楷第).
11（世）〔勢〕(校注 274).　**29** C emends 撲淺深 of 吳本、張抄、錢抄、藏本、張本 and 趙本作 to 樸深. 張覺 has 測淺深 with 陳本. 陳奇猷 reads 撲 as a loan for 樸, glossed by 服虔 as 隱 (to go into hiding). We follow C and 服虔.　**32** The C editors note:「堯」字下應有「之」字。.

CHAPTER 25

安危 Security and Danger

HF 25.1.0 (*Xilun* 478, *Xin jiaozhu* 524)

安術有七，	There are seven techniques that are conducive to security
危道有六。	and six ways[1] that lead to danger.

HF 25.1.1 (*Xilun* 478, *Xin jiaozhu* 524)

安術[A 微/術 djət/dźjuĕt]：	As for the techniques that are conducive to security,
一曰，	the first is that
賞罰隨是非[A 微/微 pjəd/pjwěi]；	rewards and punishments follow right and wrong;
二曰，	the second is that
禍福隨善惡[B 魚/暮 ʔagh/ʔuo]；	misfortune and good fortune follow goodness or evil;
三曰，	the third is that
死生隨法度[B 魚/暮 dagh/duo]；	life and death follow laws and standards;
四曰，	the fourth is that
有賢不肖而無愛惡[B 魚/暮 ʔagh/ʔuo]；	account is taken of the degree of talent, not of likes and dislikes;
五曰，	the fifth is that
有愚智而無非譽[B 魚/御 ragh/jiwo]；	account is taken of stupidity or intelligence, not of slander and praise;
六曰，	the sixth is that
有尺寸而無意度[B 魚/暮 dagh/duo]；	account is taken of objective measurements, not of subjective assessments;
七曰，	The seventh is that
有信而無詐[B 魚/禡 tsragh/tṣa]。	trustworthiness is practised and not deceit.

---

1 Note the negative use of the normally positively laden concept of the Way. Note also that the word is used as a count noun here. There is not one Way, but many ways that are at issue.

HF 25.1.2 (*Xilun* 479, *Xin jiaozhu* 525)

危道：	As for the ways that lead to danger,
一曰，	the first is
斲削於繩之內[A 微/隊 nədh/nuậi]；	cutting within the ink-line;[2]
二曰，	the second is
5 斷割於法之外[A 祭/泰 ŋwadh/ŋwâi]；	cutting beyond the law;
三曰，	the third is
利人之所害[A 祭/泰 gadh/γâi]；	to profit from what harms others;
四曰，	the fourth is
樂人之所禍；	to delight in what causes others disaster;
10 五曰，	the fifth is
危人於所安；	to endanger others where they are secure;
六曰，	the sixth is
所愛不親，	to not be close with those that are liked,
所惡不疏。	and not to keep distant those that are disliked.
15 如此，	If you act in this way,
則人失其所以樂生，	people will lose their joy for life,
而忘其所以重死。	and forget why they should take seriously the threat of death.[3]
人不樂生，	If people do not enjoy their life,
則人主不尊：	the ruler will not be respected;
20 不重死，	if they do not take the threat of their death seriously,
則令不行也。	his orders will not be carried out.

5 （斲）〔斷〕（校注 280). 9 Rhyming appears to be given up at this point.

---

2 A carpenter when cutting the wood should strictly follow the ink-line; any deviation therefrom would spoil his work. The ink-line is synonymous with the law: any deviation from the law (by being too lenient or too harsh) will have disastrous consequences.

3 In a state led by an erratic ruler, where laws are not followed and norms are violated, the two major handles of reward and punishment (based as they are on making life pleasant for those who are rewarded and scaring those who are due punishment) will not work.

安危 SECURITY AND DANGER

HF 25.2 (*Xilun* 480, *Xin jiaozhu* 526)

使天下皆極智能於儀表，	If you make all in the world exert their intelligence and ability according to clear standards
盡力於權衡，	and put in all their effort according to scales and weights,[4]
以動則勝，	then they will succeed when they take action,
以靜則安。	and they will be secure when they stay inactive.
5 治世使人樂生於為是，	If, in ordering the world, you make people enjoy their life when they do what is right,
愛身於為非，	and care for themselves when they are about do what is wrong,
小人少而君子多。	then petty men will be few and noble men will be many.[5]
故社稷長立，	As a result, the altars of soil and grain will be permanently stable,
國家久安。	and the state will be enduringly secure.
10 奔車之上無仲尼[A 脂/脂 nrjid/njiʰ]，	You will not find Confucius in a deserter's carriage,
覆舟之下無伯夷[A 脂/脂 rid/ji]。	nor will you find Boyi under a capsized boat.[6]
故號令者，	Orders and ordinances
國之舟車也。	are the boats and chariots of the state.
安則智廉生，	When there is security, the intelligent and pure will emerge;

---

4 Both visible standards *yibiao* 儀表 and scales and weights *quanheng* 權衡 are objective criteria that should direct the actions of all. If these criteria are not violated at the whim of the ruler, then the political system functions perfectly.

5 Han Fei suggests that being a "noble man" or a "petty man" is the result of social forces and social factors. Furthermore, the law and the methods of political philosophy actually create such social forces and social conditions. Then, paradoxically, those who behave as noble men will be the majority and those who behave as petty men will be a minority. However, in this statement the words "noble man" and "petty man" are not used in the essentialist acceptation of Confucians. One might almost translate: "what is generally described as a noble man," and "what is generally described as a petty man."

6 Both Confucius and Boyi are invoked here as highly moral and good persons. In a well-run state they would neither try to escape (a runaway chariot refers to fleeing to another state), nor endanger themselves (recall that Boyi starved himself to death in protest against the Zhou government; chapter 14, note 24). In other words, a perfectly governed state engenders universal compliance.

15 危則爭鄙起。	when there is danger, the contentious and disdainful will arise.
故安國之法，	So the functioning of the law in a secure state
若饑而食，	is like eating when hungry
寒而衣，	or putting on clothes when cold –
不令而自然也。	it is a natural state of affairs and not the result of orders.
20 先王寄理於竹帛，	The former kings committed their principles to bamboo and silk.[7]
其道順，	Their Way followed along with the natural pattern of things.
故後世服。	and so later ages submitted to it.
今使人去饑寒，	Now, if you were to order somebody to eradicate hunger and cold,
雖賁、育不能行；	then even [Meng] Ben or [Xia] Yu would be unable to carry this out.[8]
25 廢自然，	If you reject what is natural,
雖順道而不立。	then even if you follow some 'Way', you will not succeed.
強勇之所不能行，	If you insist on what even the strong and courageous cannot do,
則上不能安。	then the superior cannot find security.
上以無厭責已盡。	If the superior insatiably demands resources that are already exhausted,
30 則下對"無有"；	their subordinates will reply, "We have nothing."
無有，	And when they have nothing,
則輕法。	they will make light of the law.
法所以為國也，	Laws are that by which a state is made,
而輕之，	and if people make light of them,
35 則功不立，	achievements will not be established,
名不成。	and your name will not be accomplished.[9]

23 〔今〕〔今〕（校注 280）.　32 〔無有〕（校注 280）.

7　This is one of the rare occasions in which Han Fei, who elsewhere (e.g., chapters 49–50) ridicules reliance on the former kings' model, does precisely that (for other positive invocations of the former kings, see, e.g., 6.3, 19.2 and 19.8). Here Han Fei anachronistically attributes to these former kings the practice of writing down their principles on bamboo and silk.

8　For these two men, see chapter 24, note 6.

9　As noted in chapter 24, note 8, the pair "achievements and the name" 功名 permeates chapters 24–29 (and is the title of chapter 28).

安危 SECURITY AND DANGER

HF 25.3 (*Xilun* 482, *Xin jiaozhu* 526)

聞古扁鵲之治其病也，	I have heard that, in ancient times, Bian Que treated diseases
以刀刺骨；	by cutting to the bone with his knife;[10]
聖人之救危國也，	when a sage saves an imperilled state,
以忠拂耳。	then, out of loyalty, he will offend the [ruler's] ear.
5 刺骨，	One cuts to the bone,
故小痛在體而長利在身；	and as a result, on a small scale, there is pain in the body, but long-term gain for the person;
拂耳，	one offends the [ruler's] ear,
故小逆在心而久福在國。	and as a result, on a small scale, opposes what is in the [ruler's] mind, but achieves long-term fortune for the state.
故甚病之人利在忍痛，	Therefore, a person who is seriously ill benefits from bearing pain;
10 猛毅之君以福拂耳。	a fierce and headstrong ruler sees good fortune in what offends the ear.
忍痛，	If one is able to bear pain,
故扁鵲盡巧；	Bian Que will make use of all his skills;
拂耳，	if one tolerates offence to one's ear,
則子胥不失。	one will not lose the likes of [Wu] Zixu.[11]
15 壽安之術也。	This is the technique leading to longevity and security.
病而不忍痛，	If, in the case of illness, you cannot bear pain,
則失扁鵲之巧；	you will not make use of Bian Que's skills;
危而不拂耳，	if, in the face of danger, you do not tolerate offence to your ears,
則失聖人之意。	you will not make use of the advice of a sage.
20 如此，	If you act like this,
長利不遠垂，	then lasting benefits will not reach far,
功名不久立。	and your achievements and fame will not be of long standing.

---

10 For the sage doctor Bian Que, see chapter 21, note 26.
11 For Wu Zixu, see chapter 3, note 5.

HF 25.4 (*Xilun* 483, *Xin jiaozhu* 529)

人主不自刻以堯而責人臣以子胥，	If a ruler does not make harsh demands on himself like Yao did, but demands that his ministers behave like Zixu –
是幸殷人之盡如比干；	this is to hope in vain for all the people of Yin to be like Bigan.[12]
盡如比干，	If they all had been like Bigan,
則上不失，	those above would not have failed,
5 下不亡。	and those below would not have been ruined.
不權其力而有田成，	When [rulers] do not weigh their power, but have the likes of Tian Cheng [as ministers],[13]
而幸其身盡如比干，	hoping in vain for everybody to be like Bigan,
故國不得一安。	then the state will not attain one day of security.
廢堯、舜而立桀、紂，	If you discard Yao and Shun and establish Jie and Zhòu,[14]
10 則人不得樂所長而憂所短。	people will not be able to rejoice in their strengths, but will worry about their shortcomings.
失所長，	If you lose sight of their strengths,
則國家無功；	then there will not be any people with achievements all in the state;
守所短，	if you keep an eye [only] on their shortcomings,
則民不樂生。	the people will not enjoy their life.
15 以無功御不樂生，	To have people without achievements control those who do not enjoy their life –
不可行於齊民。	this cannot be practiced in relation to the common people.
如此，	If you act like this,

---

12 For Bigan, see chapter 3, note 11. Both Bigan and Wu Zixu were martyred due to loyalty; their forthrightness brought about their doom.

13 On Tian Cheng (Tian Chang, the ultimate example of the usurper in *Han Feizi*), see chapter 7, note 3.

14 This is a rare instance in *Han Feizi* whereby canonical paragons (Yao and Shun) are contrasted with canonical villains (Jie and Zhòu) as models for the ruler to follow or avoid. Compare with chapter 40, in which the entire reasoning based on the ruler's qualities is discarded as meaningless.

安危 SECURITY AND DANGER

則上無以使下，	superiors will not have the means to command inferiors;
下無以事上。	inferiors will not have the means to serve superiors.

15 張抄 repeats 以無功御不樂生 (校注 281).

HF 25.5 (*Xilun* 484, *Xin jiaozhu* 530)

安危在是非，	Security and danger have to do with right and wrong,
不在於強弱。	not with strength or weakness.
存亡在虛實，	Survival or ruination depend on [military] unpreparedness versus well-preparedness,
不在於眾寡。	not on having many or few [soldiers].[15]
5 故齊，	Thus Qi
萬乘也，	was a state of ten thousand chariots,
而名實不稱，	but its name and actuality did not match;
上空虛於國，	the ruler had a hollow title in the state.
內不充滿於名實，	Within the state, he did not fulfil [the duties attached to] his title;
10 故臣得奪主。	therefore a minister was able to seize dominion.[16]
桀，	Jie
天子也，	was the Son of Heaven,
而無是非：	but did not have a sense of right and wrong;
賞於無功，	he rewarded those who had no merit,

---

15 Having a powerful army with manifold soldiers is not enough. Utilising them correctly, and distinguishing between those who can really be used and those who are "hollow" (i.e. cannot be properly employed) is the crux of survival. It is tempting to speculate that Han Fei here refers to his home state of Hán, the weakest among the rival "hero-states," and that he tries to assure the ruler that proper implementation of his recommendations would compensate for Hán's numerical inferiority with regard to soldiers.

16 This refers to the arrogation of power by the Tian family. The rulers of Qi from the Jiang 姜 clan continued to rule their state on a nominal basis from the time of Tian Chang's usurpation in 481 for a whole century before their eventual deposition in 386. This was a hollow title (or "name," *ming* 名): the real power lay with the ministerial Tian/Chen lineage.

15 使讒諛以詐偽為貴；	employed slanderers and sycophants to obtain noble positions by means of treachery;
誅於無罪，	he punished the innocent,
使傴以天性剖背。	and sliced the spines of hunchbacks because of their natural condition.
以詐偽為是，	Deceit, he considered right;
天性為非，	[people's] natural condition, he considered wrong.
20 小得勝大。	And so, the smaller [state, i.e. Shang] was able to defeat the larger one (i.e. Xia).[17]

11 （殺）〔桀〕(校注 281, following 顧廣圻). 15 〔為〕(校注 281).

HF 25.6 (*Xilun* 485, *Xin jiaozhu* 532)

明主堅內，	The clear-sighted ruler is firm inside,
故不外失，	so he does not lose to outside forces.
失之近而不亡於遠者無有。	There has never been a person who lost what is near and did not also lose what is distant.
故周之奪殷也，	Thus, when Zhou seized power from Yin,
5 拾遺於庭。	it was a matter of picking up what was lying in the courtyard.[18]
使殷不遺於朝，	If Yin had not left itself lying in its very court,
則周不敢望秋毫於境。	Zhou would not have dared to have the slightest hopes at its borders;
而況敢易位乎？	how much less would they have dared to replace [Yin]?

3 （正）〔而〕(校注 281).

---

17 Jie, the last wicked ruler of the Xia dynasty is here presented as responsible for a series of political and moral perversities, as was common in late Warring States-period texts (for parallels, see Pines 2008). This was why a small Shang polity led by Tang could succeed in overpowering the great Xia.

18 Note that "courtyard" here (*ting* 庭) and "court" in the next sentence (*chao* 朝) both refer to the ruler's court.

安危 SECURITY AND DANGER 405

HF 25.7 (*Xilun* 485, *Xin jiaozhu* 532)

明主之道忠法，	The Way of the clear-sighted ruler is to be concerned with the law,
其法忠心，	and his law is to be concerned with mind [of the people].[19]
故臨之而治，	Therefore, when he supervises them, they are well governed;
去之而思。	when he leaves them [and dies], [they] miss him.[20]
5 堯無膠漆之約於當世而道行，	Yao did not establish any fixed contracts in his age, but his Way was practised;
舜無置錐之地於後世而德結。	Shun did not bequeath to his progeny enough land to place an awl in, but his virtue was solid.[21]
能立道於往古，	Those who were able to establish the Way in the past,
而垂德於萬世者之謂明主。	and whose virtue was transmitted over myriad generations, are called clear-sighted rulers.

3（法）〔治〕(校注 281, following 陶鴻慶).   5（遺）〔道〕(校注 281).   7 往（名）古 (校注 281).

---

[19] This statement does not gel very well with the disregard for popular opinion expressed by Han Fei elsewhere (especially chapter 50.11). However, if one assumes that the "mind" of the people here does not refer to their opinions on what ought to be done, and instead their hopes concerning what ought to be achieved, then Han Fei would very obviously recommend that the ruler serve the people in this latter sense. Compare to the *Book of Lord Shang*, especially 5.9, 6.9, 8.3, *et saepe*.

[20] The precise meaning of the sentence is disputed; here it is restored on the basis of Chen Qiyou's glosses.

[21] As elsewhere in this chapter, and in contradistinction from most other chapters of *Han Feizi*, here the author praises Yao and Shun as epitomes of morality. Yao's age of primeval simplicity had no need for contracts; Shun (who abdicated to Yu), did not bequeath anything to his progeny. It is the morality of these rulers (implementing the Way and manifesting virtue) which made them paragons of good rulership for myriad generations.

CHAPTER 26

守道 Attending to the Way

HF 26.1 (*Xilun* 487, *Xin jiaozhu* 533)

聖王之立法也，	When the sage kings established laws,
其賞足以勸善，	their rewards were sufficient to encourage the good,
其威足以勝暴，	their authority was sufficient to overpower the violent,
其備足以必完法。	and their preparations were sufficient to ensure the complete enactment of the law.
5　治世之臣，	As for ministers in a well-governed world,
功多者位尊，	if their achievements are many, their position will be honoured;
力極者賞厚，	if their efforts are unstinting, their rewards will be rich;
情盡者名立。	if they do their utmost, their name will be established.
善之生如春，	The good grows as when spring comes;
10　惡之死如秋，	wickedness dies as when autumn comes.
故民勸極力而樂盡情，	Thus the people feel encouraged to make their utmost efforts and rejoiced in utter loyalty.
此之謂上下相得。	This is called "superiors and inferiors are attuned to each other."
上下相得，	If superiors and inferiors are attuned to each other,
故能使用力者自極於權衡，	then those who use their strength will exhaust it on the 'scales and weights'
15　而務至於任鄙；	striving to be like Ren Bi,[1]
戰士出死，	and soldiers will go out to die,
而願為賁、育；	hoping to be like [Meng] Ben and [Xia] Yu.[2]

1　Ren Bi (fl. 306) is another famous strongman from Qin.
2　Meaning that the soldiers would fight as bravely as Meng Ben and Xia Yu (see chapter 24, note 6).

守道 ATTENDING TO THE WAY

守道者皆懷金石之心，	Those who guard the way will all have dedication as solid as metal and stone
以死子胥之節；	and they will die preserving moral integrity, like Wu Zixu did.[3]
20 用力者為任鄙，	If those who use their strength become like Ren Bi,
戰如賁、育，	fight like [Meng] Ben and [Xia] Yu
中為金石，	and have a core of metal and stone,
則君人者高枕而守已完矣。	then the ruler can sleep on his high pillow while he guards what he has already achieved.

HF 26.2 (*Xilun* 488, *Xin jiaozhu* 534)

古之善守者，	Those who were experts at guarding [the way] in ancient times
以其所重禁其所輕，	prohibited what was regarded as light [offences] through what was regarded as heavy [punishments];
以其所難止其所易，	and they stopped what was regarded as easy with what was regarded as difficult,[4]
故君子與小人俱正，	and as a result, both the noble and the petty behaved correctly.
5 盜跖與曾、史俱廉。	and [the likes of] Robber Zhi as well as Zeng[zi] and Scribe [Yu] were all incorruptible.[5]
何以知之？	How do I know this?
夫貪盜不赴谿而掇金，	A greedy thief does not go to deep ravines to collect gold.

---

3 For Wu Zixu, see chapter 3, note 5.

4 Commentators interpret this saying in light of similar pronouncements in e.g., chapter 30.2.7–8 and ultimately in light of the ideas proposed in the *Book of Lord Shang* (e.g., 7.5, 17.3). By imposing heavy penalties on light offences, the ruler is able to prevent any offences from being made whatsoever. The "easy" thing is a minor transgression; when it meets with a "difficult" thing (that is, a heavy punishment), it will be nipped in the bud.

5 Robber Zhi epitomises the utmost depravity (see an excellent portrait of him in eponymous chapter [29] of *Zhuangzi*). Zengzi (Zeng Shen 曾參, 505–435) is Confucius' disciple and epitomises filiality. Scribe Yu 史魚 is praised in *Analects* 15.7 for being "straight like an arrow." In an orderly state, even the greatest of criminals would have no choice but to behave as incorruptibly as those two paragons of morality.

赴谿而掇金，	If he were to go to deep ravines to collect gold,
則身不全。	he would not be safe.
10 賁、育不量敵，	If [Meng] Ben and [Xia] Yu had not gauged their opponents,
則無勇名；	they would not be famous for their courage;
盜跖不計可，	if Robber Zhi had not calculated his chances of success,
則利不成。	he would not have garnered his profit.
明主之守禁也，	When a clear-sighted ruler attends to prohibitions,
15 賁、育見侵於其所不能勝，	[Meng] Ben and [Xia] Yu are stopped by what they cannot defeat,
盜跖見害於其所不能取，	and Robber Zhi is harmed by what he is unable to take.
故能禁賁、育之所不能犯，	So, if you can make prohibitions that [Meng] Ben and [Xia] Yu cannot violate
守盜跖之所不能取，	and if you guard things so that Robber Zhi cannot take them,
則暴者守愿，	then the violent will behave prudently
20 邪者反正。	and the deviant will return to correctness.
大勇愿，	When the paragons of courage behave prudently
巨盜貞，	and great thieves behave impeccably,
則天下公平，	the world will be just and peaceful,
而齊民之情正矣。	and the feelings of the ordinary people will be correct.

7 C has 溪 for 谿 (but 谿 above).   22 貞（平）(校注 287).

HF 26.3 (*Xilun* 489, *Xin jiaozhu* 536)

人主離法，	When the ruler abandons the rule of law
失人，	and loses control of the people,
則危於伯夷不妄取，	he will be imperilled even by Boyi, who never took things illegally,
而不免於田成、盜跖之禍，	and he will not avoid disasters like those of Tian Cheng and Robber Zhi.[6]

---

6 Boyi epitomises moral purism (chapter 14, note 24), whereas Tian Cheng (or Tian Chang) is, conversely, the notorious usurper (chapter 7, note 3).

守道 ATTENDING TO THE WAY

5	何也？	Why is that?
	今天下無一伯夷，	In the present world, there is not a single Boyi,
	而姦人不絕世，	but no age is free of villains.
	故立法度量。	That is why [the sage kings] established laws, standards and measures.[7]
	度量信，	When standards and measures are reliable,
10	則伯夷不失是，	Boyi will not veer from what is right
	而盜跖不得非。	and Robber Zhi will not be permitted to perpetrate what is wrong.
	法分明，	When the laws are distinct and clear,
	則賢不得奪不肖，	the worthy will not be permitted to snatch from the unworthy,
	強不得侵弱，	the powerful will not be permitted to transgress against the weak,
15	眾不得暴寡。	and the many will not get to tyrannise the few.
	託天下於堯之法，	If you entrust the world to the laws of Yao,
	則貞士不失分，	then honest gentlemen will not lose their due allotment,
	姦人不徼幸。	and the wicked will not trust their luck [to escape punishment].
	寄千金於羿之矢，	If you entrust one thousand pieces of gold to Yi's [unfailing] arrows,
20	則伯夷不得亡，	then Boyi will not lose them,
	而盜跖不敢取。	and Robber Zhi will not dare to take them.[8]
	堯明於不失姦，	Yao was clear-sighted in not failing to punish villainy,
	故天下無邪；	and so there was no wickedness in all the world;
	羿巧於不失發，	Yi was so skilful that he never missed a shot,
25	故千金不亡。	so the one thousand gold pieces were never lost.

---

[7] This passage explains how admiration for a past in which there were moral paragons is not inconsistent with Han Fei's basic convictions concerning the need for laws and standards.

[8] When property is duly safeguarded, then even possessions of a loser like Boyi will be secure, and even the insatiable Robber Zhi will not make a move: he knows that should he steal, he will be punished.

邪人不壽而盜跖止。 Deviant people did not attain longevity[9] and Robber Zhi was stopped.

如此， When affairs are conducted like this,
故圖不載宰予， pictures will neither depict Zai Yu
不舉六卿； nor extol the six ministers [of Jin];[10]
書不著子胥， books will not write about [Wu] Zixu
不明夫差。 nor clarify" [the misbehaviour of] Fuchai.[11]
孫、吳之略廢， Sunzi's and Wuzi's strategies will be abandoned
盜跖之心伏。 and Robber Zhi's heart will submit.[12]
人主甘服於玉堂之中， The ruler eats well and dresses comfortably in his Jade Hall,
而無瞋目切齒傾取之患； having no troubles of angry looks, gnashing of teeth, or of his power being overturned.
人臣垂拱於金城之內， The ministers fold their hands within the metal walls [of the capital];
而無扼捥聚脣嗟唶之禍。 there are no disasters that give rise to the wringing of hands, the pursing of lips, or sighing and soughing.

4〔耳〕〔禍〕(校注 287). 5〔可〕〔何〕也(校注 287). 24〔廢〕〔發〕(校注 287).
36〔於〕(校注 287).

---

9   They were all apprehended and executed.
10   Zai Yu (522–458) is Confucius's disciple; his appellative was Ziwo 子我; as in chapter 3.2, he is conflated here with Kan Zhi 闞止, also known as Ziwo, who opposed the coup orchestrated by Tian Chang in Qi and was driven by the Chen family into exile. In the Warring States period, the latter Zai Yu was upheld as a figure martyred for his loyalty. The six ministers are the heads of the ministerial lineages in Jin who had usurped the power in that state in mid-sixth century (chapter 11, note 13). By saying that none of these (paragons of loyalty and treachery) should be discussed, Han Fei implies that in a properly run state there is no need for ministers to possess exceptional moral qualities: both the good and the bad, Boyi and Robber Zhi, would be equally law-abiding as subjects.
11   Wu Zixu, another paragon of loyalty, was ordered by his master, King Fuchai of Wu, to commit suicide (chapter 3, note 5). This is another martyr-villain pair that would not be celebrated in an orderly run state.
12   In a truly powerful state there is no need for clever strategists, such as Sunzi (traditionally dated to ca. 500), and Wu Qi (d. 381). On the other hand, even arch-villains like Robber Zhi would be forced to lie low.

守道 ATTENDING TO THE WAY

HF 26.4 (*Xilun* 491, *Xin jiaozhu* 536)

服虎而不以柙[A 葉/狎 grap/ɣap]，	Taming a tiger but not using a cage,
禁姦而不以法[A 葉/乏 pjap/pjwep]，	restraining the wicked but not using laws,
塞偽而不以符，	blocking fraud but not using tallies:
此賁、育之所患[B 元/諫 gwranh/ɣwan]，	these would be trouble even for [Meng] Ben and [Xia] Yu,
堯舜之所難[B 元/翰 nanh/nân]也。	difficult even for Yao and Shun.
故設柙，	Hence, cages are set up,
非所以備鼠[C 魚/語 hrjagx/śjwo]也，	not to guard against rats,
所以使怯弱能服虎[C 魚/姥 hagx/xuo]也；	but to enable the meek and the weak to tame a tiger.
立法，	Laws are established,
非所以備曾、史也，	not to prepare for the likes of Zengzi and Scribe [Yu],[13]
所以使庸主能止盜跖也；	but to enable a mediocre ruler[14] to stop the likes of Robber Zhi.
為符，	Tallies are introduced,
非所以豫尾生也，	not to prepare for the likes of Wei Sheng,[15]
所以使眾人不相謾也，	but to cause the common people not to cheat each other.
不獨恃比干之死節，	Do not simply rely on Bigan's dying for his probity;
不幸亂臣之無詐也；	do not succumb to thinking wishfully that rebellious ministers are without deceit.
恃怯之所能服，	Rely on what a meek man is able to tame
握庸主之所易守。	and hold fast to what a mediocre ruler easily protects.
當今之世，	Nowadays,
為人主忠計，	to make loyal plans for the ruler

---

13 On this pair of paragons of moral rectitude, see note 5 above.
14 It is important to realise that Han Fei's theories cater to the kind of mediocre ruler who has no special ability (see more in chapter 40). Note that the compound "mediocre ruler" 庸主 is very rare in pre-imperial texts. It appears only in *Han Feizi* (twice, the second time in 36.2.2) and in the *Book of Lord Shang* (25.1).
15 Wei Sheng was a proverbially faithful man. After fixing an appointment with a woman beneath a bridge, his lover did not appear, but he refused to leave. Eventually the river flooded, and he died waiting under the bridge.

為天下結德者，	and solidify virtue for the sake of the world;
利莫長於此。	nothing is more beneficial than this.
故君人者無亡國之圖，	Thus, a ruler will not chart plans that lead to the ruin of his state,
而忠臣無失身之畫。	and a loyal minister will not think up schemes that lead to the loss of his own life.
25 明於尊位必賞，	It is clear that those who are in honoured positions are bound to be rewarded,
故能使人盡力於權衡，	and therefore they are able to cause others to do their best according to scales and weights
死節於官職。	and to sacrifice their lives in office for the sake of moral principles.
通賁、育之情，	They thoroughly understand the conditions of [Meng] Ben and [Xia] Yu
不以死易生；	and do not make light of life by risking death.
30 惑於盜跖之貪，	If they are deluded by the same greed as Robber Zhi,
不以財易身；	they will still not make light of themselves on account of property,
則守國之道畢備矣。	and so the way of safeguarding the state is perfectly complete.

11 〔使〕(校注 287).　22 於（如）此 (校注 287).

CHAPTER 27

用人 Employing People

HF 27.1 (*Xilun* 494, *Xin jiaozhu* 540)

聞古之善用人者，	I have heard that those who were good at employing people in antiquity
必循天順人而明賞罰。	necessarily lined up with Heaven, followed men, and clarified rewards and punishments.
循天，	If you line up with Heaven,
則用力寡而功立；	then, with little effort, your achievements will be established;
5 順人，	if you follow men,
則刑罰省而令行；	then punishments will be used sparingly and orders will be carried out.
明賞罰，	If you are clear about rewards and punishments,
則伯夷、盜跖不亂。	then people like Boyi and Robber Zhi will not wreak havoc.[1]
如此，	If you proceed like this,
10 則白黑分矣。	then white and black will be distinguished.
治國之臣，	Ministers in a well-governed state
效功於國以履位，	attain their position by proving their merit for the state,
見能於官以受職，	receive official appointments after their abilities in office have been displayed,
盡力於權衡以任事。	do their best as determined by 'scales and weights' and are then assigned tasks.
15 人臣皆宜其能，	All ministers have appropriate abilities;
勝其官，	they cope with their official duties
輕其任，	and find their assignments light.

---

[1] As we have seen in chapter 26.3, the ideal is to have a perfect system that can be jeopardised neither by moral purists such as Boyi, nor by arch-villains such as Robber Zhi.

而莫懷餘力於心，	However, no one does less than his best
莫負兼官之責於君。	and no one assumes the responsibilities of two offices from the ruler.
20 故內無伏怨之亂[元/換 luanh/luân]，	Thus within there is no chaos created by hidden resentment,
外無馬服之患[元/諫 gwranh/ywan]。	and abroad there will be no disasters like that of [Lord] Mafu.[2]
明君使事不相干，	The clear-sighted ruler ensures that different tasks do not interfere with each other,
故莫訟；	and, as a result, nobody engages in litigation;
使士不兼官，	He ensures that officials do not hold joint appointments
25 故技長；	and, as a result, their skills grow.
使人不同功，	He ensures that no two people have responsibility for the same achievement,
故莫爭。	and, as a result, there is no competition.
爭訟止，	When competition and litigation have been stopped,
技長立，	and the growth of skills established,
30 則強弱不觳力，	then the strong and the weak will not fight it out against each other:
冰炭不合形，	like ice or charcoal, they will not merge into one shape.
天下莫得相傷，	When no one in the world is allowed to engage in harmful activities,
治之至也。	this is the acme of good government.

25 張抄 has 枝 for 技. 27 爭（訟）(校注 295). 29 張抄 has 枝 for 技. 30 觳 is read as 角.

---

2 The Lord-Who-Subjugates-Horses (Mafu jun 馬服君) was the title given to the Zhao military commander Zhao She 趙奢, inherited by She's son, Zhao Kuo 趙括 (d. 260). Kuo was well versed in military theories, but in practice he was a disaster. During the famous Changping campaign of 262–260 he replaced the cautious Zhao commander Lian Po 廉頗 and was enticed to end a stalemate with Qin by attacking the Qin army. The results were disastros: the Zhao army was cut in two, then cut off from its supplies and starved into surrender. Triumphant, the Qin general Bai Qi 白起 (d. 257) thereupon ordered the massacre of the surrendering Zhao soldiers; over four hundred thousand were reportedly killed (chapter 1, note 20). In *Han Feizi*, the Lord-Who-Subjugates-Horses epitomises a talkative and worthless man of service (see chapter 50.5).

用人 EMPLOYING PEOPLE

HF 27.2 (*Xilun* 496, *Xin jiaozhu* 542)

釋法術而心治，	If he had discarded law and techniques of rule and governed by subjective intuitions,[3]
堯不能正一國。	Yao would not have been able to keep order in a single state;
去規矩而妄意度，	if he had discarded the compass and T-square and made arbitrary assessments,
奚仲不能成一輪。	Xi Zhong[4] would not have been able to finish a single wheel;
5 廢尺寸而差短長，	if he had dispensed with feet and inches in distinguishing lengths,
王爾不能半中。	Wang Er[5] would not have been able to find the exact middle.
使中主守法術，	However, suppose a mediocre ruler[6] keeps to law and the techniques of rule,
拙匠守規矩尺寸，	or a fumbling carpenter keeps to the compass and the T-square, and to feet and inches –
則萬不失矣。	then he would not go wrong even one time in ten thousand.
10 君人者，	If the ruler of men
能去賢巧之所不能，	is able to discard what even the worthy and crafty cannot assure,
守中拙之所萬不失，	and keeps to that by which even the mediocre and fumbling never fail,
則人力盡而功名立。	then his people's productive capacity will be used to the utmost, and his achievements and fame will be established.

---

3 The opposition between professional competence in law and techniques on the one hand and *xin* 心 "heart" (here: "subjective intuitions") on the other marks a new level of theoretical reflection. The crucial phrase *xin zhi* 心治 "government by subjective intuition" does not recur elsewhere in *Han Feizi* and is very rare in pre-imperial texts in general. In *Guanzi* the term recurs twice, but in a somewhat different context. In the chapter "Techniques of the heart B" ("Xin shu xia" 心術下), the ruler should make his "heart ordered" 心治 as a precondition for ordering the realm (*Guanzi* 37: 781). In the chapter "Inward training" ("Nei ye" 內業) ordering the heart is the precondition for attaining self-control as, possibly, a first step toward universal control (*Guanzi* 49: 938).

4 A legendary wheel-maker.

5 The legendary craftsman.

6 This resumes the idea of the mediocre ruler (here *zhong zhu* rather than *yongzhu* 庸主 as in 26.4 and 36.2.2). See more in chapter 40.

HF 27.3 (*Xilun* 497, *Xin jiaozhu* 543)

明主立可為之賞，	The clear-sighted ruler establishes obtainable rewards
設可避之罰。	and institutes avoidable punishments.
故賢者勸賞而不見子胥之禍，	Therefore the worthy are encouraged by rewards and are not exposed to the disasters that struck [Wu] Zixu.[7]
不肖者少罪而不見傴剖背，	The unworthy commit few crimes and are not exposed to such things as the slicing of the hunchback.[8]
盲者處平而不遇深谿，	The blind, if they live on level ground, will not run into deep crevices;
愚者守靜而不陷險危。	the foolish, if they keep silent, will not be trapped in dangerous situations.
如此，	If you proceed like this,
則上下之恩結矣。	there will be solid goodwill[9] between superiors and inferiors.
古之人曰：	The ancients said,
"其心難知，	"Their hearts are hard to understand,
喜怒難中也。"	their delight and anger hard to predict."
故以表示目，	Therefore, show people's eyes easily visible signs,[10]
以鼓語耳，	speak to their ears with drums,
以法教心。	and instruct their minds with laws.
君人者釋三易之數而行一難知之心，	If the ruler of men discards these three easy constants and practices but one method of the heart that is hard to understand –
如此，	if he proceeds like this,
則怒積於上而怨積於下。	anger will accumulate above and resentment will accumulate below.

---

7   For Wu Zixu, see chapter 3, note 5.
8   This implicit reference is particularly interesting because it refers back to *Han Feizi* 25.5 (line 17) and links these chapters together.
9   This reference to goodwill is rare in *Han Feizi*.
10   The notion of the *biao* 表 "visible sign" is important. The laws are meant to establish visible markers which may be used by the people for orientation. In an important sense the people will then "know where they stand" because the ruler has established these *biao* "visible signs, public signposts."

用人 EMPLOYING PEOPLE

以積怒而御積怨，	If one [attempts to] control accumulated resentment with accumulated anger,
則兩危矣。	both sides will be in danger.[11]

15 行（之）一 (校注 295).

HF 27.4 (*Xilun* 498, *Xin jiaozhu* 543)

明主之表易見，	The visible signs set up by the clear-sighted ruler are easy to see;
故約立；	therefore [his] treaties will stand.
其教易知，	His instructions are easy to understand;
故言用；	therefore his words will be employed.
5 其法易為，	His laws are easy to practise;
故令行。	therefore his orders will be carried out.
三者立而上無私心，	When these three things are established and the ruler does not have private motives,
則下得循法而治，	then those below will be able to follow the laws and be well-governed.
望表而動，	They will look at the signs when they move,
10 隨繩而斲，	they will follow the carpenter's ink-line when they cut,
因攢而縫。	they will follow the model when they sew.
如此，	If he proceeds like this,
則上無私威之毒，	then, above, there is no poison of selfish majesty,
而下無愚拙之誅。	and, below, there are no punishments of the foolish and fumbling.
15 故上居明而少怒，	Therefore those above will rest in their clear-sightedness and rarely be angry,
下盡忠而少罪。	and those below will be completely loyal and rarely commit crimes.

15（君）〔居〕(校注 295).

11　This point resembles one attributed to Shen Dao 慎到; see *Shenzi Fragments* 61–65 and the discussion in Harris 2016: 31–36.

HF 27.5 (*Xilun* 499, *Xin jiaozhu* 545)

聞之曰：	I have heard it said:
"舉事無患者，	"To be without serious worries in every undertaking
堯不得也。"	is something that even Yao did not achieve."
而世未嘗無事也。	And there is no age that has not had its undertakings.
5　君人者不輕爵祿，	A ruler who does not lightly confer ranks and stipends
不易富貴，	or who does not readily enrich and ennoble [his followers],[12]
不可與救危國。	is not one with whom one might save an imperilled state.
故明主厲廉恥，	Therefore a clear-sighted ruler encourages the pure and decent
招仁義。	and attracts men of benevolence and righteousness.
10　昔者介子推無爵祿而義隨文公，	In ancient times, Jie Zitui had no rank or stipends but, for reasons of righteousness, followed Lord Wen.
不忍口腹而仁割其肌，	He could not bear the lord's hunger, and, out of sheer goodness of heart, cut off a piece of his own flesh.[13]
故人主結其德，	Therefore, rulers have certified his virtue,
書圖著其名。	and books have propagated his name.
人主樂乎使人以公盡力，	The ruler of men delights in making men exert themselves for the common cause,
15　而苦乎以私奪威；	but loathes that they seize majesty for selfish reasons;

12　The phrasing here is puzzling. One would have thought that a good ruler would *not* distribute ranks and stipends lightly according to *Han Feizi*. However, here, apparently, Han Fei emphaisises that a ruler should not be stingy with regard to the benefits he confers upon his subjects.

13　The story of the selfless Jie Zitui, who faithfully accompanied the future Lord Wen of Jin on his wanderings but later refused to accept any reward for his service is told in *Zuozhuan* (Xi 24.1d). By the late Warring States period the story had acquired many legendary embellishments, such as Jie feeding Lord Wen with his own flesh.

用人 EMPLOYING PEOPLE 419

人臣安乎以能受職，	ministers are comfortable accepting duties according to their abilities,
而苦乎以一負二。	but loathe that single person is assigned two responsibilities.
故明主除人臣之所苦，	Therefore, the clear-sighted ruler removes what ministers detest
而立人主之所樂。	and establishes what the ruler delights in.
20 上下之利，	As for what benefits both superiors and inferiors,
莫長於此。	nothing is better than this.
不察私門之內，	If [the ruler] does not investigate what happens behind private gates,[14]
輕慮重事，	if he makes light of planning and values only concrete actions,
厚誅薄罪，	if he metes out excessive punishments for slight crimes,
25 久怨細過，	if he harbours continuing rancour over minute transgressions,
長侮偷快，	if he keeps humiliating people for taking secret pleasures,
數以德追禍，	if, again and again, he courts disaster through his generosity –
是斷手而續以玉也，	these are like cutting off a person's hand to replace it with jade,[15]
故世有易身之患。	so therefore the world has experienced the woe associated with replacing the ruler.

8 厲 is read as 勵.

HF 27.6 (*Xilun* 501, *Xin jiaozhu* 548)

| 人主立難為而罪不及， | If the ruler sets up something that is hard to realise and condemns those who does not reach their target, |

---

14 Referring to powerful ministers.
15 The image is most surprising in this context.

則私怨生；	then private resentment will arise.
人臣失所長而奉難給，	If ministers lose their fortes and are given tasks that are difficult to carry out in a satisfactory way,
則伏怨結。	then hidden resentment will take form.
5 勞苦不撫循，	When [the ruler] does not assuage those who toil bitterly,
憂悲不哀憐；	nor pity those who are distressed and aggrieved,
喜則譽小人，	if, when delighted, he praises petty men,
賢不肖俱賞；	and so the worthy and the unworthy are equally rewarded,
怒則毀君子，	if, when angry, he maligns noble men,
10 使伯夷與盜跖俱辱；	and so Boyi and Robber Zhi are equally humiliated,
故臣有叛主。	then among the ministers there will be those who rebel against the ruler.

3 （立）〔生〕(校注 295).

HF 27.7 (*Xilun* 502, *Xin jiaozhu* 548)

使燕王內憎其民而外愛魯人，	Suppose the King of Yan hated the population within [his own state] and loved the people of Lu who lived beyond it;[16]
則燕不用而魯不附。	he would not be able to govern Yan, nor would Lu become attached to him.
民見憎，	His people, being hated,
不能盡力而務功；	would not be able to exert themselves and strive to prove their merit,
5 魯見說，	and although Lu would receive his pleasure,
而不能離死命而親他主。	its people would not be able to risk their own death and become close to another king.
如此，	Under these circumstances,
則人臣為隙穴，	the ministers would hide in crevices and caves,
而人主獨立。	and the ruler would stand isolated.

---

16   Yan is located far to the north of Lu; the states did not share a border.

用人 EMPLOYING PEOPLE

10　以隙穴之臣而事獨立之主，　For a minister hiding in crevices and caves to serve a ruler who is isolated –
　　此之謂危殆。　　　　　　　this is called precarious.

3 〔民〕(校注 295).

HF 27.8 (Xilun 503, Xin jiaozhu 549)

　釋儀的而妄發，　　　　If you set aside the target and shoot wildly,
　雖中小不巧；　　　　　then although you may hit something very small, this does not show that you are skilled.
　釋法制而妄怒，　　　　If you abandon the law and show your anger in an arbitrary manner,
　雖殺戮而姦人不恐。　　then although you may carry out executions, the wicked will not be fearful.
5　罪生甲，　　　　　　If the crime arises from A
　禍歸乙，　　　　　　　but the calamity hits B,
　伏怨乃結。　　　　　　hidden resentment will be formed.
　故至治之國，　　　　　Therefore, in a perfectly governed state,
　有賞罰而無喜怒，　　　there are rewards and punishments, but no joy or anger.
10　故聖人極有刑法，　　Thus the sage puts every effort into having punishments and laws,
　而死無螫毒，　　　　　and when culprits die, there is no venomous sting.
　故姦人服。　　　　　　As a result, the wicked submit,
　發矢中的，　　　　　　loosed arrows will hit their targets,
　賞罰當符，　　　　　　rewards and punishments will fit and match,
15　故堯復生，　　　　　and, as a result, Yao will be born again,
　羿復立。　　　　　　　and Yi will arise anew.
　如此，　　　　　　　　Under these circumstances,
　則上無殷、夏之患，　　the rulers will not suffer the disasters of Yin and Xia dynasties;[17]
　下無比干之禍，　　　　their subjects will not suffer the misfortune of Bigan.

17　These dynasties declined and were overthrown, whereas the Zhou dynasty died out without being overthrown.

20 君高枕而臣樂業，	The ruler will sleep on his high pillows and the ministers will delight in their occupations.
道蔽天地，	Their Way will cover Heaven and Earth;
德極萬世矣。	their virtue will last for ten thousand generations.

HF 27.9 (*Xilun* 504, *Xin jiaozhu* 550)

夫人主不塞隙穴而勞力於赭堊，	If the ruler does not stop up crevices and holes [in his palaces], but exerts himself at having them painted red and white,
暴雨疾風必壞。	then violent thunderstorms and vicious winds are bound to destroy them.
不去眉睫之禍而慕賁、育之死，	If he does not remove the disasters before his eyes, but is full of admiration for the deaths of [Meng] Ben and [Xia] Yu,[18]
不謹蕭牆之患而固金城於遠境，	if he is not careful about the troubles within his palace, but strengthens firm walls on distant frontiers,
5 不用近賢之謀而外結萬乘之交於千里，	if he does not use the advice of worthy men close at hand, but cultivates external ties with great powers a thousand miles away,
飄風一旦起，	then, when the whirlwind arises one morning,
則賁、育不及救，	[Meng] Ben and [Xia] Yu will have no time to come to his rescue,
而外交不及至，	and his external connections will have no time to arrive on the scene.
禍莫大於此。	There is no disaster greater than this.
10 當今之世，	In our times,
為人主忠計者，	those who make loyal plans for rulers

---

18 It is not clear what was heroic about deaths of Meng Ben and Xia Yu (the former was probably executed after the weight-lifting event at the court of King Wu of Qin in 306 ended in the king's injury and premature death). Perhaps for Han Fei these proverbial strongmen were associated with heroic deaths. Admiring their heroism (and by extension dreaming of military success) would not save the ruler from a plotter from within. Cf. Shen Buhai's 申不害 (d. 337) warning, that the enemy should not storm the barred gate of the capital: the enemy is the one in the palace (translated by Creel 1974: 344).

必無使燕王說魯人，	must not let the ruler of Yan delight in the people of Lu;
無使近世慕賢於古，	he must not let the present age admire worthies of antiquity,
無思越人以救中國溺者。	he must not long for a man from Yue to save a person who is drowning in the central kingdoms.[19]
15 如此，	If he acts like this,
則上下親，	then superiors and inferiors will be close to each other;
內功立，	success will be established within the state,
外名成。	and beyond it fame will be achieved.

---

19 Yue people were renowned as skilful swimmers, but being far from the Central Plains they had no way of saving a man were he to drown in the "central kingdoms."

CHAPTER 28

功名 Achievements and Names

HF 28.1 (*Xilun* 506, *Xin jiaozhu* 551)

明君之所以立功成名者四：	There are four things by which the clear-sighted ruler can achieve results and establish a name for himself:
一曰天時，	The first is the seasons of Heaven;
二曰人心，	the second is the minds of the people;
三曰技能，	the third is skill and ability;
四曰勢位。	the fourth is positional power.
非天時，	If it is not the right season,
雖十堯不能冬生一穗；	then even ten Yao could not grow a single ear of grain in winter;
逆人心，	if something goes against the minds of the people,
雖賁、育不能盡人力。	even [Meng] Ben and [Xia] Yu could not fully utilise the people's productive capacity.[1]
故得天時，	So, when you accord with Heaven's seasons,
則不務而自生；	things grow effortlessly;
得人心，	when you accord with the minds of the people,
則不趣而自勸；	people will urge themselves on without being admonished;
因技能，	if you rely on skill and ability,
則不急而自疾；	then, without rushing, you will naturally be fast;
得勢位，	if you accord with positional power,
則不推進而名成。	then, without self-promotion, your name will be established –
若水之流，	like the flowing of water
若船之浮。	or the floating of a boat.

---

1 Once again, the invocation of Meng Ben and Xia Yu (chapter 24, note 6) as potential organisers of the people is odd.

功名 ACHIEVEMENTS AND NAMES

20　守自然之道，　　　　　　　If you keep to the Way of what is so of itself,
　　行毋窮之令，　　　　　　　then you will enact orders that will not be obstructed,
　　故曰明主。　　　　　　　　and so you will be said to be a clear-sighted ruler.

4 張抄 has 枝 for 技.　11 〔不〕(校注 299).　21 毋 is read as 無.

HF 28.2 (*Xilun* 507, *Xin jiaozhu* 552)

　　夫有材而無勢，　　　　　　Now, if you have talent but not a position of power,
　　雖賢不能制不肖。　　　　　then, although you may be worthy, you cannot control the unworthy.
　　故立尺材於高山之上，　　　So, if you place a one-foot piece of timber on top of a high mountain,
　　則臨千仞之谿，　　　　　　it will overlook a ravine that is one thousand fathoms deep.
5　材非長也，　　　　　　　　It is not that the piece of timber is long,
　　位高也。　　　　　　　　　but its position is high.

　　桀為天子，　　　　　　　　When Jie was Son-of-Heaven,
　　能制天下，　　　　　　　　he was able to control All-under-Heaven.
　　非賢也，　　　　　　　　　This was not because he was worthy:
10　勢重也；　　　　　　　　　it was because his positional power was weighty.
　　堯為匹夫，　　　　　　　　When Yao was a commoner,
　　不能正三家，　　　　　　　he could not rectify even three households.
　　非不肖也，　　　　　　　　This was not because he was unworthy:
　　位卑也。　　　　　　　　　it was because his position was lowly.[2]

15　千鈞得船則浮，　　　　　　If something the weight of a tonne attains [the support of] a ship, it will float,
　　錙銖失船則沉，　　　　　　but if something the weight of a few grammes is missing from the ship, it will sink.
　　非千鈞輕錙銖重也，　　　　It is not that a tonne is light and a few grammes are heavy:
　　有勢之與無勢也。　　　　　it is a question of being or not being in the right position.

2　Compare to Shen Dao's views cited in chapter 40.

故短之臨高也以位，	When something short can look down from someplace high up, that is because of position,[3]
20　不肖之制賢也以勢。	when the unworthy control the worthy, it is because of positional power.
人主者，	As for the ruler,
天下一力以共載之，	the world supports him with united strength;
故安；	therefore he has security.
眾同心以共立之，	the multitudes are of like mind in jointly establishing him;
25　故尊。	therefore he is honoured.
人臣守所長，	The ministers cleave to their strengths,
盡所能，	and exhaust their abilities [in his service];
故忠。	therefore they are loyal.
以尊主御忠臣，	If, as an honoured ruler, you command loyal ministers,
30　則長樂生而功名成。	you will long enjoy life[4] and your achievements and your name will be accomplished.
名實相持而成，	One's name and achievements depend on each other to be accomplished;
形影相應而立，	a shape and its shadow respond to each other to be established.
故臣主同欲而異使。	Thus, a minister and the sovereign have the same aims but different missions.
人主之患在莫之應，	The threat to the sovereign is when nobody responds to him.
35　故曰：	So it is said:
一手獨拍，	"If one hand claps alone,
雖疾無聲。	even if it claps hard, there will be no sound."
人臣之憂在不得一，	The worry for a minister is when he cannot concentrate on one thing.
故曰：	So it is said;
40　右手畫圓，	If with the right hand you draw a circle

3　The pun on "position" is the same in classical Chinese and in English.
4　For the notion of *le sheng* 樂生 "enjoy life," see *Han Feizi* 25.1 (but note that there it applies to the people as a whole, not to the ruler).

功名 ACHIEVEMENTS AND NAMES   427

左手畫方，   and with the left hand you draw a square,
不能兩成。   you cannot finish them both."

故曰：   So it is said:
至治之國[A 之/德 kwək/kwək]， "In a state that is governed perfectly,
45 君若枹[A 幽/尤 bjəgw/bjôu]， the ruler is the drumstick
臣若鼓[B 魚/姥 kwagx/kuo]，   and the minister are the drum.
技若車[B 魚/魚 kjag/kjwo]，   Skill is like the carriage;
事若馬[B 魚/馬 mragx/ma]。   tasks are like the horses."

故人有餘力易於應，   Thus, someone with surplus strength finds it easy to respond to things,
50 而技有餘巧便於事。   and if his skills have surplus aptitude, he can live up to his tasks."[5]

立功者不足於力，   If those who strive to establish achievements are insufficient in their strength,
親近者不足於信，   if those who are close [to the ruler] are insufficient in their good faith,
成名者不足於勢，   or if those who strive to accomplish a name have insufficient positional power,
近者不親，   then those who are close [to the ruler] do not show close concern
55 而遠者不結，   and those who are distant feel no ties [to him].
則名不稱實者也。   In that way, the name will not match the actuality.

聖人德若堯、舜，   The virtue of the sage may be like that of Yao and Shun;
行若伯夷，   his demeanour may be like that of Boyi;
而位不載於世，   but if his position is not supported by the people of the world,
60 則功不立，   his achievements will not be established
名不遂。   and his fame will not follow.

故古之能致功名者，   Therefore, those in antiquity who were able to attain success and a name –

---

5 This sequence of "therefore it is said"-phrases is puzzling, and it suggests that the text we have today bears something of the character of a draft or a commentary to an unknown text.

眾人助之以力，	the multitudes supported them with their strength,
近者結之以成，	those close to them attached themselves to them by their earnestness;
65 遠者譽之以名，	those who were at a distance from them praised their name,
尊者載之以勢。	those who were honoured supported them by their [positional] power.
如此，	[If you conduct matters] like this,
故太山之功長立於國家，	your achievements will be as high as Mt. Tai and you will be enduringly established in the state;
而日月之名久著於天地。	your name will be as brilliant as that of sun and moon, and will forever shine in all the world.
70 此堯之所以南面而守名，	This is how Yao faced south [as the ruler] and preserved his good name;
舜之所以北面而效功也。	this is how Shun faced north [as the minister] and delivered achievements for him.

29 主（主）御 (校注 300). 33 張抄 lacks 主. 50 〔便〕(校注 300). 54 （已）〔不〕(校注 300, following 陶鴻慶). 64 成 is read as 誠.

CHAPTER 29

大體 The Cardinal Tenets

HF 29.1 (*Xilun* 512, *Xin jiaozhu* 555)

古之全大體者：	Those in ancient times who comprehensively mastered the cardinal tenets
望天地，	gazed out across Heaven and Earth,
觀江海，	observed the rivers and the sea,
因山谷；	and cleaved to the lines of the mountains and valleys –
5 日月所照，	wherever sun and moon shine,
四時所行，	wherever the four seasons progress,
雲布風動；	wherever clouds spread and wind moves.
不以智累心，	They neither encumbered their minds with wisdom,[1]
不以私累己；	nor encumbered themselves with selfishness.[2]
10 寄治亂於法術，	They consigned matters of order and chaos to laws and techniques,
託是非於賞罰，	entrusted matters of right and wrong to rewards and punishments,
屬輕重於權衡；	and consigned questions of light and heavy to the scales and weights.
不逆天理，	They neither acted contrary to Heaven's patterns,
不傷情性；	nor harmed the nature [of the people].
15 不吹毛而求小疵[A 佳/支 dzjig/dzjĕ]，	They neither split hairs, seeking minor flaws,
不洗垢而察難知[A 佳/支 trig/tjĕ]；	nor washed away dirt to investigate what is difficult to understand.

---

1 The crucial concept of *lei* 累 "to get entangled with, be encumbered with" has a Daoist flavour. This text advocates a legalist way of unentangled and unencumbered existence. Even *zhi* 智 "cleverness, sophistry" does not have its usual force of "professional competence" here.

2 Namely, they strove neither to understand nor to possess the realm in its entirety. To be sure, this is a very "Daoist" vision, which has little to do with Han Fei's usual ideal. This fascinating line outlines something, even, of a legalist meditation technique through which the *ji* 己 "the Self; oneself" is freed from egotistic concerns.

不引繩之外[B 祭/秦 ŋwadh/ŋwâi] ，	They did not draw things in from beyond the ink-line [of the law];
不推繩之內[B 微/隊 nədh/nuâi] ；	they did not push things out from within the ink-line [of the law].
不急法之外[B 祭/秦 ŋwadh/ŋwâi] ，	They were not over-eager about things that are beyond the scope of the law;
20 不緩法之內[B 微/隊 nədh/nuâi] ；	they were not lax about things that are within the scope of the law.
守成理，	They kept to the established pattern
因自然；	and adapted to what was naturally so.³
禍福生乎道法，	People's bad or good fortune originated in the Way and the law⁴
而不出乎愛惡；	and did not result from the ruler's love or hatred.
25 榮辱之責在乎己，	Responsibility for glory and disgrace lay with people themselves
而不在乎人。	and did not depend on others.
故至安之世，	Thus, in an age with perfect peace,
法如朝露，	the law was like the morning dew:
純樸不散[C 元/翰 sanh/sân] ，	it was pure and simple and undiluted.
30 心無結怨[C 元/願 ʔwjanh/ʔjwɐn] ，	In the hearts of men, there was no resentment,
口無煩言[C 元/元 njan/ŋjen] 。	in their mouths, no irritated speech.
故車馬不疲弊於遠路[D 魚/暮 glagh/luo] ，	As a result, cart-horses were not exhausted on long roads
旌旗不亂於大澤[D 魚/陌 drak/ɖɐk] ，	battle banners were not displayed chaotically in the great marshes;
萬民不失命於寇戎[E 中/東 njəŋw/-joŋ/ńźjuŋ] ，	the myriad people did not lose their lives because of invasions or belligerency;

---

3 Note the insistence, here again as in *Han Feizi* 27.1, on the category of the *zi ran* 自然 "what is so of itself, the natural," which is linked to the *li* 理 "the pattern that things naturally make." Legal pragmatism is embedded, for Han Fei, in a Daoist-inspired cosmic naturalism.

4 The combination *dao fa* 道法 "the Way and the Law" or "the Law of the Way" is profoundly significant. There is no longer a monopoly of the positive law made by man. This has, alongside with it, the Way, the way things naturally are in and of themselves. This strongly reminds of what Randall P. Pereenboom calls foundational naturalism, "the cosmic natural order serves as the basis, the foundation, for construction of human order" (Pereenboom 1993: 27). Notably, "Dao fa" is the name of the first chapter of the so-called Yellow Thearch's Manuscripts (*Huangdi shu* 黃帝書; chapter 8, note 16). The latter epitomise the so-called Huang-Lao thought analysed by Pereenboom in his monograph.

大體 THE CARDINAL TENETS

35 雄駿不創壽於旗幢[E 撞 東/江 druŋ/-ruŋ/ɖǎŋ]；	valiant men did not impair their longevity under banners and standards.
豪傑不著名於圖書[F 魚/魚 sthjag/śjwo]，	Bravoes did not have their names recorded in books
不錄功於盤盂[F 魚/虞 gwjag/ju]，	and did not have their achievements inscribed on platters and vessels.
記年之牒空虛[F 魚/魚 hjag/xjwo]。	The wooden strips for the chronicles were empty.[5]
故曰：	So it is said:
40 利莫長於簡[G 元/產 krianx/kǎn]，	"There is no more lasting benefit than simplicity;
福莫久於安[G 元/寒 ʔan/ʔân]。	there is no more enduring fortune than peace."

27 故（致）至 (校注 304)。

HF 29.2 (*Xilun* 515, *Xin jiaozhu* 555)

使匠石以千歲之壽操鉤，	Suppose that Craftsman Shi had a lifespan of a thousand years and wielded the hook,[6]
視規矩，	observed the compass and the T-square,
舉繩墨，	and held the plumb-line and ink,
而正太山；	trying to straighten Mount Tai;
5 使賁、育帶干將而齊萬民；	suppose that [Meng] Ben and [Xia] Yu bore the Ganjiang sword, trying to bring the myriad people in line –
雖盡力於巧，	though they might fully exert themselves with their skills
極盛於壽，	and enjoy plenteous longevity,
太山不正，	Mount Tai would not be straightened,
民不能齊。	and the people would not be brought in line.
10 故曰：	So it is said:
古之牧天下者，	When the ancients shepherded [the people of] the world,
不使匠石極巧以敗太山之體，	they did not order Craftsman Shi to use all his skill in order to ruin the body of Mount Tai,

---

5 Empty year records refer to the chronicles of the type of the canonical *Springs-and-Autumns Annals*: when no events of significance (such as wars and diplomatic meetings) occurred, the season was left blank with a single record, e.g. "Summer. Fourth month" (see Chen Minzhen 2023).

6 The hook was a tool used when working with curved objects.

CHAPTER 29

⋯貝、育盡威以傷萬民之性。	and they did not ask [Meng] Ben or [Xia] Yu to use all of their authority to damage the innate nature of the people.
因道全法，	If you act in accordance with the Way to perfect the law,
15 君子樂而大姦止。	then the noble men will be delighted and great villainy will be stopped.
澹然閒靜，	You will be serene and tranquil,
因天命，	adapting to Heaven's decrees,
持大體。	holding on to the cardinal tenets –
故使人無離法之罪，	Then, you will cause people never to commit crimes by deviating from the law;
20 魚無失水之禍。	and fish will not suffer the disaster of losing their water.
如此，	When you act like this,
故天下少不可。	there is little in the world that cannot be done.

35 駿 is read as 俊.

HF 29.3 (*Xilun* 517, *Xin jiaozhu* 559)

上不天則下不遍覆[A 幽/宥 phjəgwh/phjôu]，	If the ruler is not like Heaven, he will not be able to cover everybody below.
心不地則物不必載[A 之/海 tsəgx/tsậi]。	If his mind is not like Earth, he will not invariably support things.
太山不立好惡[B 魚/暮 ʔagh/ʔuo]，	Mount Tai does not establish peculiar likes and dislikes;
故能成其高；	therefore it is able to achieve its height.
5 江海不擇小助[B 魚/御 dzrjagh/dzjwo]，	The [Yangzi] River and the sea are not choosy about small streams;
故能成其富。	therefore they can achieve their abundance.
故大人寄形於天地而萬物備[C 之/至 bjiagh/bji]，	Thus the great man will entrust his physical frame to Heaven and Earth, and the myriad things will be complete;
歷心於山海而國家富[C 之/宥 pjagh/pjôu]。	he will roam his mind among the mountains and seas, and his state will be rich.
上無忿怒之毒，	Above, there will be no poisonous rage,
10 下無伏怨之患，	below, no threats from hidden resentment.

大體 THE CARDINAL TENETS

上下交樸，	Relations between superiors and inferiors will be simple
以道為舍。	and they will use the Way as their dwelling.
故長利積，	As a result, lasting profit will be accumulated,
大功立，	and great achievements realised;
15 名成於前，	your name will be established in relation to your forebears
德垂於後，	your virtue handed down to posterity.
治之至也。	That is the acme of good government.

11 （撲）〔樸〕(校注 304).

Printed in the United States
by Baker & Taylor Publisher Services